Lecture Notes of the Institute for Computer Sciences, Social Informatics and Telecommunications Engineering 246

More information about this series at http://www.springer.com/series/8197

Yi-Bing Lin · Der-Jiunn Deng
Ilsun You · Chun-Cheng Lin (Eds.)

IoT as a Service

Third International Conference, IoTaaS 2017
Taichung, Taiwan, September 20–22, 2017
Proceedings

 Springer

Editors
Yi-Bing Lin
National Chiao Tung University
Hsinchu, Taiwan, Taiwan

Der-Jiunn Deng
Department of Computer Science
and Information
National Changhua University of Education
Changhua, Taiwan

Ilsun You
Seoul, Korea (Republic of)

Chun-Cheng Lin
Department of Industrial Engineering
and Management
National Chiao Tung University
Hsinchu, Taiwan

ISSN 1867-8211   ISSN 1867-822X (electronic)
Lecture Notes of the Institute for Computer Sciences, Social Informatics
and Telecommunications Engineering
ISBN 978-3-030-00409-5   ISBN 978-3-030-00410-1 (eBook)
https://doi.org/10.1007/978-3-030-00410-1

Library of Congress Control Number: 2018954066

This Springer imprint is published by the registered company Springer Nature Switzerland AG
The registered company address is: Gewerbestrasse 11, 6330 Cham, Switzerland

Preface

We are delighted to introduce the proceedings of the Third European Alliance for Innovation (EAI) International Conference on IoT as a Service (IoTaaS 2017). This conference brought together researchers, developers, and practitioners from around the world who are leveraging and developing technologies and applications for IoT as a service.

The technical program of IoTaaS 2017 consisted of 46 full papers that were presented at the conference. Aside from the high-quality technical paper presentations, the technical program also featured two keynote speeches and three special sessions. The two keynote speeches were given by Imrich Chlamtac from EAI/CREATE-NET/University of Trento and Tao Zhang from CISCO. The three special sessions organized were Wearable Technology and Applications (WTAA), Building Smart Machine Applications (BSMA), and Security and Privacy in the Internet of Things, Services, and People (SP-IoTSP). The WTAA special session aimed to address the challenges of maintaining the high efficiency of WTAA in terms of high recognition rate, energy consumption, computational costs, and so forth. The BSMA special session aimed to explore how to construct smart machine architecture for industry against the background of IoT and big data. The SP-IoTSP special session aimed to investigate recent research and future directions for IoTSP security and privacy.

Coordination with the steering chair, Imrich Chlamtac, and the steering committee members, Benny Mandler, Yi-Bing Lin, and Der-Jiunn Deng, was essential for the success of the conference. We sincerely appreciate their constant support and guidance. It was also a great pleasure to work with such an excellent Organizing Committee team and we thank them for their hard work in organizing and supporting the conference. We are particularly grateful to the Technical Program Committee, led by our TPC co-chairs, Prof. Der-Jiunn Deng and Prof. Ilsun You, who completed the peer-review process of technical papers and put together a high-quality technical program. We are also grateful to Conference Manager Michaela Miklusakova for her support, and all the authors who submitted their papers to the IoTaaS 2017 conference and special sessions.

We strongly believe that the IoTaaS conference provides a good forum for researchers, developers, and practitioners to discuss all aspects of science and technology that are relevant to IoT as a service. We also expect that future IoTaaS conferences will be as successful and stimulating, as indicated by the contributions presented in this volume.

August 2018

Yi-Bing Lin
Der-Jiunn Deng
Ilsun You
Chun-Cheng Lin

Conference Organization

Steering Committee Chair

Imrich Chlamtac   Create-Net, Italy and EAI, Belgium

Steering Committee Members

Athanasios V.   National Technical University of Athens, Greece
    Vasilakos
Jun Suzuki   University of Massachusetts, Boston, USA
Giancarlo Fortino   University of Calabria, Italy

Organizing Committee

General Chair

Zhelong Wang   Dalian University of Technology, China

General Co-chair

Giancarlo Fortino   University of Calabria, Italy

TPC Chairs

Qiong Wang   Technische Universität Dresden, Germany
Dongyi Chen   University of Electronic Science and Technology of China, China
Hassan Gasemzadeh   Washington State University, USA
ThanosVasilakos   Lulea University of Technology, Sweden
Min Chen   Huazhong University of Science and Technology, China
Mehmet Yuce   Monash University, Australia
Xiangchen Li   China Institute of Sport Science, China

Local Chair

Sen Qiu   Dalian University of Technology, China

Special Track Chairs

Raffaele Gravina   University of Calabria, Italy
Wenfeng Li   Wuhan University of Technology, China

Publications Chair

Hongyu Zhao   Dalian University of Technology, China

Website Chair

Jiaxin Wang   Dalian University of Technology, China

Sponsorship and Exhibits Chair

Long Liu   Dalian University of Technology, China

Conference Manager

Lenka Bilska   EAI, Belgium

Technical Program Committee

Zhiqiang Zhang	University of Leeds, UK
Fan Wu	Monash University, Australia
Xiao Fang	Dresden University of Technology, Germany
Wendong Xiao	University of Science and Technology Beijing, China
Mehrab Ramzan	Dresden University of Technology, Germany
Pengjie Zhang	University of Chinese Academy of Sciences, China
Raffaele Gravina	University of Calabria, Italy
Qiong Wang	Dresden University of Technology, Germany
Ahmed Khorshid	University of California, Irvine, USA
Fabrizio Messina	University of Calabria, Italy
Hongyu Zhao	Dalian University of Technology, China
Claudio Savaglio	University of Calabria, Italy
Pasquale Pace	University of Calabria, Italy
Omid Dehzangi	University of Michigan, USA
Ibrahim Alquaydheb	University of California, Irvine, USA
Jianjun He	Dalian Minzu University, China
Xin Liu	Dalian University of Technology, China
Sen Qiu	Dalian University of Technology, China

The Applications for IoT Sensor Bricks (Abstract of Poster and Demo)

Chun-Ming Huang, Chih-Chyau Yang, Yi-Jie Hsieh, Yi-Jun Liu,
Wei-Lin Lai, Jun-Ying Juan, Chun-Yu Chen, Shian-Wen Chen,
and Chien-Ming Wu

National Chip Impementation Center, NARLabs 7F, No. 26, Prosperity Rd 1,
Science Park, Hsin-Chu City, Taiwan
ccyang@cic.narl.org.tw

Abstract. In this demonstration, the applications of IoT sensor bricks [1] including the color sensor system, temperature/UV sensor system, SpO2 sensor system, motion sensor system and alcohol sensor system are presented. Users can stack multiple sensor bricks together to build a unique IoT sensor system according to the requirements. The corresponding APPs of smart phone for 6 sensor systems are used to interact with visitors to experience the IoT sensor bricks. A video [2] is played to introduce the features of this commercial product and its sample applications in life. The firmware development/debug environment including the debug hardware and its GNU tool chains are also explained in this demonstration. Visitors can therefore understand that the proposed IoT sensor bricks is a modular wireless sensing system which features an open architecture and reusability. It has a sharable power supply unit, a computing unit, a communication unit, an output unit, and a sensing unit. The IoT sensor bricks can be disassembled and assembled at will; it is equipped with NFC, Bluetooth communication and wireless charging. Data gathered by IoT sensor bricks can be converted to useful applications and displayed in the smart phone. The demo materials for each sensor system include the alcohol swabs for the alcohol sensor system, pantone color paper for the color sensor system etc. are utilized to facilitate the demonstration.

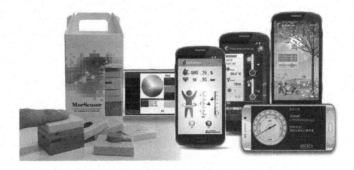

Fig. 1. The IoT sensor bricks and its smart phone applications

Keywords: Internet of Things (IoT) · Wearable · Sensor bricks
Sensor platform

References

1. Huang, C.-M., Hsieh, Y.-J., Lai, W.-L., Liu, Y.-J., Juan, C.-Y., Chen, S.-Y., Chen, C.-Y., Chue, J.-J., Yang, C.-C., Wu, C.-M.: A modular wireless sensor platform and its applications. In: IEEE International Symposium on Circuits and Systems (ISCAS), pp. 1–4 (2017)
2. Wireless Sensing Bricks Video. https://youtu.be/iTH84HEivgw

Contents

Special Session: Wearable Technology and Applications (WTAA 2017)

Special Session: Building Smart Machine Applications (BSMA 2017)

Poster and Demo

**Special Session: Security and Privacy in Internet of Things,
Services and People (SP-IOTSP 2017)**

Invited Papers

Mainland China

IoTaaS Main Track

Contention Window Size Adjustment in Unsaturated IEEE 802.11 WLANs

Chun-Hsien Sung[1(✉)] and Der-Jiunn Deng[2]

[1] School of Civil and Commercial Law, Beijing Institute of Technology,
Zhuhai, China
scotsung@gmail.com

[2] Department of Computer Science and Information Engineering,
National Changhua University of Education, Changhua, Taiwan
djdeng@cc.ncue.edu.tw

Abstract. In next generation mobile networks, more and more throughput of network is required under the dense environment. There are some researches discuss how to solve the predicament of throughput. But they usually analyze it under the saturated environment. Most of their contention window size are also not optimal to fetch the maximum throughput. This paper is the first one to fetch the fixed optimal window size under the unsaturated environment which is closer to the real network. It is based on the Distributed Coordination Function (DCF) in Medium Access Control layer of IEEE 802.11 Wireless LAN to control the contention window size for reducing the collision problem and improving the throughput. A simplified one-dimension Markov Chain with a new idle state is proposed to simulate the unsaturated model. Then the formula of transmission probability under the unsaturated model and the equation which is used to fetch the optimized contention window size are analyzed. Comparing with the related analysis model in the simulation of the throughput and the collision rate. The result shows that the proposed model under unsaturated environment is better than before.

Keywords: IEEE 802.11 · Optimal contention window · Dense environment
Collision rate

1 Introduction

The international standard IEEE 802.11 for Wireless Local Area Networks (WLANs) has been proposed [1] in 1985. This standard describes the physical layer (PHY) and medium access control sub-layer (MAC) specification for wireless connectivity which the nodes is fixed and movable in a local area. It has experienced tremendous growth with the proliferation of IEEE 802.11 devices in the last ten years. The IEEE 802.11 standard also experienced a number of amendments to improve. Recently, IEEE started a task group to investigate and deliver the technologies for the scenarios of dense networks with a large number of nodes and access point. In the previous amendments,

© ICST Institute for Computer Sciences, Social Informatics and Telecommunications Engineering 2018
Y.-B. Lin et al. (Eds.): IoTaaS 2017, LNICST 246, pp. 3–10, 2018.
https://doi.org/10.1007/978-3-030-00410-1_1

they always focus on the higher speed physical layer (PHY) transmission. They emphasized increasing the link throughput, rather than efficient use of diverse. But in the scenarios of dense networks, the interference from neighboring devices will increase and there are severe collisions from channel contention. It will give rise to network performance degradation drastically and cause the whole networks disabled. From past experience, we found that the value of theoretical maximum throughput on the physical layer could not effectively reflect on the MAC layer. Therefore, the new 802.11ax amendment not only focuses on improving providing 4x the throughput of 802.11ac, it but also hopes to improve the metrics reflect the user experience. Unlike previous amendments, it measured the average throughput per node at the MAC data service access point. So we want to ameliorate the algorithm of the MAC layer to improve performance. Improvements will be made to support dense environments such as outdoor hotspot and stadiums [2]. In IEEE 802.11 standard, the backoff parameters of its collision avoidance mechanism is very inefficient. There are many ways to solve it; one of them is by appropriately tuning the contention window size and backoff algorithm.

In the past, there have many research literatures to study how to adjust the contention window size for the maximize throughput. But most of their analysis are not based on the optimal contention window size. They cannot effectively maximizes the throughput. And the other part of the analysis literatures are under the saturated environment. In the real network, the traffic is heterogeneous traffic. It is more like an unsaturated environment. The models they proposed can't be valid in real 802.11 WLANs. Hsiao's thesis [3] is the only one who has both these two characteristics. However, it is a pity that he did not complete the simulation. In this thesis, our contribution is to propose a one-dimensional model as unsaturated traffic model and compute the optimization of contention window size. Our thesis is the first one to fetch the maximize throughput under the unsaturated environment by the optimal contention window size.

2 Difficulties for Legacy 802.11 in Dense Environments

With the popularization of the Internet, people use the Internet has become increasingly frequent. More and more number of nodes connected to the Internet at the same time; the network has become a dense environment. When the network is congested, a node operating under the IEEE 802.11. And it will cause great challenges for the algorithm. From past experience we have learned that CSMA/CA and BEB algorithm generate some problems when running on the actual network. We will describe each of these issues below.

2.1 The Collision Problem

The first one is the collision problem. To begin with, after the successful transmission, the contention window size will set back to the initial value *CWmin*. It leads to a high probability of collisions when the next frame to be sent, then repeat retransmission collision problems will constantly occur. In order to successfully transfer, the small contention window size may have to take a long time to grow. But it is not fair to the large contention window size, too. Not only because of the large window size which is generated from previously failed many times spent a lot of time, but it also waits for a long time to count to zero. It will result in the phenomenon of starvation. And the characteristic of the BEB algorithm is always favor the last successfully transmitted node. It might lead to the fairness problem intensified, which result in the degradation of system throughput. Repeated retransmission acts also caused a lot of unnecessary waste of energy. For example, in Fig. 1 [4] is a network topology.

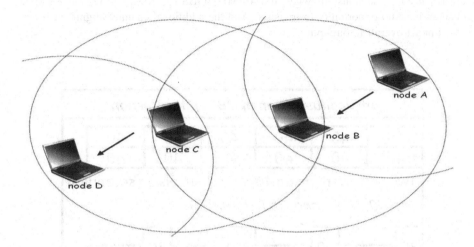

Fig. 1. The fair problem of wireless environments.

Node A wants to connect to node B and node C wants to connect to node D respectively. But node B will not receive data from node A. That is because node C will "grab" the channel by using a smaller contention window size.

2.2 The Interference Between Channels

The second one is the interference between channels. In the dense environment, we place more channels in a geographical area of network. With the distance between channels getting closer, and it causes more interference between each other. There are two types of the interference: One is the adjacent channel interference which is produced by its transmissions on adjacent or partially overlapped channels. And the other is the co-channel interference which is caused by the same frequency channel. Interference is the main reason why the capability of network cannot be fully utilized.

The interference of transmissions on adjacent or partially overlapped channels, which is called Overlapping Basic Service Set (OBSS) phenomenon. Figure 2 is a very simple illustration [5]. In the illustration, both the 80 MHz BSS and the 40 MHz OBSS have enough traffic to transmit all the time, so that they can take turns in winning the channel contention effectively. T is the nominal throughput of each, and the benchmark chosen is that of two separate non-overlapping 40 MHz channels. As can be seen, without the bandwidth adaptation, total throughput and individual throughputs of both BSS and OBSS are reduced. With bandwidth adaptation, 80 MHz throughput is increased, and total throughput is even double. If the 40 MHz OBSS overlapped with the primary 40 MHz of the 80 MHz channel, no matter with bandwidth adaptation or not, the 80 MHz transmission is completely blocked. It is cause that primary channels always need to be transmit, when the 40 MHz OBSS is transmitting, the 80 MHz channel have no opportunity to transmit. And the additional channel alignment issues also impact overall throughput.

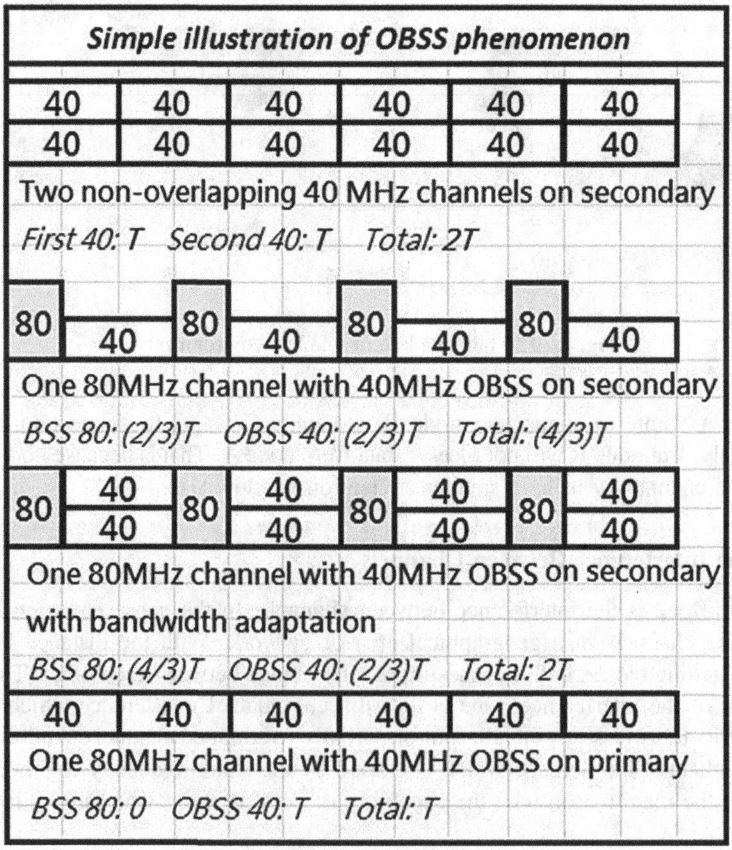

Fig. 2. Simple illustration of OBSS phenomenon.

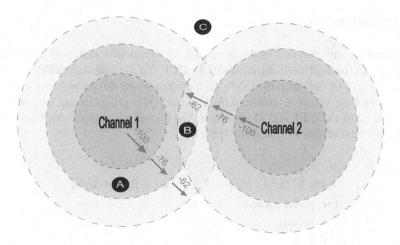

Fig. 3. The co-channel interference of wireless environments.

Considering Fig. 3 [6], it is the co-channel interference which is caused by the same frequency channel in dense environment. Node A is in the range of Channel 1 and node b is in the range of both Channel 1 and Channel 2. But the transmission of node b will not better than node a's transmission since the interference between the same frequency Channel 1 and Channel 2. There is also likely to have a dead angle. Node c is not in the range of any channel, so it will have no transmission. The throughput of network will get worse.

Now, these issues have surfaced. The increased interference from the co-channel problem and severe collisions from channel contention in dense environments give rise to network performance degradation. It always cause the whole networks disabled. When entering the next internet generation 802.11ax, WLAN devices are increasingly required to support a variety of applications such as voice, video, cloud access, and traffic offloading. And the 802.11ax amendment hope to enable supporting at least four times improvement in the average throughput per node in a dense deployment scenario, while maintaining or improving the power efficiency per node. Therefore, we must proposed an improved method to solve those problems.

In [7], the authors computed a theoretical upper bound of IEEE 802.11 distributed coordination function on achievable throughput. They pointed out that by appropriately tuning the backoff algorithm to control the contention window size, the scheme can achieve better performance and operate close to the theoretical limit. However, the proper adjustment of the contention window is often very complex calculation, especially in the dense environment. Bianchi [8] also proposed that the optimal window size is fixed under the saturated environment. Although the saturated environment is not consistent with the real network environment. But we can calculate the new algorithm to fetch the optimal window size through his methods.

3 Simulation Results

In this chapter, our proposed model compared with Bianchi's analytical model in [8] and the legacy backoff mechanism of 802.11 DCF. To validate our model, we adopt NS-2 as the tool of our simulation. NS-2 is a discrete-event driven and object oriented network simulator which is written in the C++ and OTcl programming language. The data rate is adopt the IEEE 802.11g standard. The system parameters which are used to obtain numerical results as following Table 1:

Table 1. Default attribute values used in the simulation

MAC packet payload	8192 bits
MAC header	272 bits
PHY header	128 bits
ACK frame size	112 bits + PHY header
PHY data rate	54 Mbit/s
Propagation delay	1 μs
Slot time	9 μs
SIFS duration	16 μs
DIFS duration	34 μs
Minimum CW size	32
m	5
Transmission method	OFDM
Frequency	5 GHz
Channel bandwidth	80 MHz
Spectral efficiency	21.665 bps/Hz (4 × 4, 80 MHz)
EIRP	22–29 dBm
OFDM symbol duration	4 ms (800 ns guard interval)

In Fig. 4, we show the relation between λ value, nodes number and fixed optimal contention window size. If the contention window size is fixed at the optimal contention window value, it can get the maximum throughput. We compare contention window size of our model in different λ values with Bianchi's derivation. We can see that the contention window size is linear increasing while the nodes increase no matter in our model or Bianchi's model. And in any case of identical node number, the contention window size of Bianchi's model is bigger. In our model when the λ value increase then the optimal contention window size increases. But it remains the same in Bianchi's model. That is because his model was developed in the saturated environment.

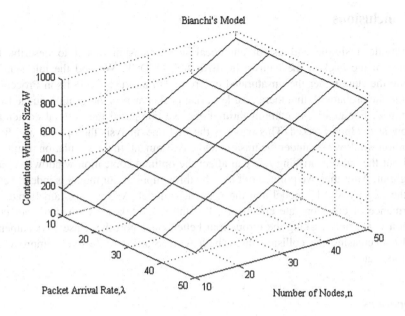

(a) Bianchi's Model

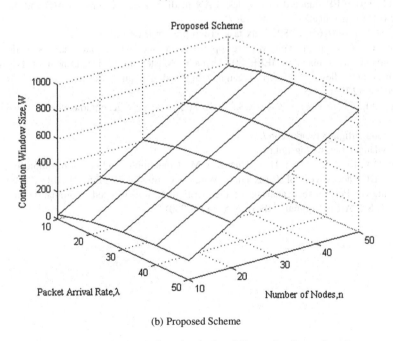

(b) Proposed Scheme

Fig. 4. Contention window size under different λ value and nodes.

4 Conclusions

We provide a simple and useful analytical one-dimension model to describe the behavior of the backoff mechanism in IEEE 802.11 DCF. We add the idle state to describe the state under the unsaturated environment, and use the Poisson Process to compute the probability that there is at least one packet arrives the waiting queue to be transmitted. For getting maximum throughput, we computed the optimal contention window size which is fixed. This paper is the first one analysis the optimal and fixed contention window size under the unsaturated environment. In the simulation result, we found out the packets arriving rate can affect the optimal contention window size and throughput. After that, we pointed out that the throughput of our model is indeed better than the Legacy 802.11 model and the Bianchi's model. And we also ameliorate the performance of collision rate effectively. For the IEEE 802.11ax standard, our contribution is not only making the throughput better to support the dense environments, but also decreasing the collision rate which will be able to effectively improve the utilization rate.

References

1. 802.11-1997-IEEE standard for wireless LAN medium access control (MAC) and physical layer (PHY) specifications. IEEE (1997)
2. IEEE 802.11-14/0165r1: P802.11ax task group press release (2014)
3. Hsiao, C.: Contention window size optimization and throughput analysis under the unsaturated environment of IEEE 802.11 DCF. Master thesis, Department of Electrical Engineering College of Electrical Engineering and Computer Science National Taiwan University (2013)
4. Deng, D.J., Chen, K.C., Cheng, R.S.: IEEE 802.11ax: next generation wireless local area networks
5. http://blog.airtightnetworks.com/
6. http://wlaniconoclast.blogspot.tw/
7. Deng, D.J., Ke, C.H., Chen, H.H., Huang, Y.M.: Contention window optimization for IEEE 802.11 DCF access control. IEEE Trans. Wireless Commun. 7(12), 5129–5135 (2008)
8. Bianchi, G.: Performance analysis of the IEEE 802.11 distributed coordination function. IEEE J. Sel. Areas Commun. 18(3), 535–547 (2000)

Interoperability in Internet of Things Infrastructure: Classification, Challenges, and Future Work

Mahda Noura[1(✉)], Mohammed Atiquzzaman[2], and Martin Gaedke[1]

[1] Technische Universität Chemnitz, Chemnitz, Germany
{mahda.noura,martin.gaedke}@informatik.tu-chemnitz.de
[2] University of Oklahoma, Norman, OK 73109, USA
atiq@ou.edu

Abstract. The Internet of Things (IoT) is an important research area, and substantial developments for a wide range of devices and IoT platforms is evident. However, one of the critical issues in IoT is that the different proprietary IoT platforms and systems are still not interoperable; unable to talk with each other. In this paper, we survey the state-of-the-art on interoperability in IoT. First, we provide a classification of techniques and schemes looking at IoT interoperability from different perspectives. For each category, we present the approaches proposed in the papers. Second, we use the interoperability classification as a baseline to compare some of the existing IoT research projects and identify gaps in the existing solutions. Our findings will help domain experts and professionals to get an overview and categorization of existing interoperability solutions in IoT and select an appropriate approach to help increase the number of interoperable IoT products.

Keywords: Fragmentation · Internet of Things · Interoperability
IoT platforms

1 Introduction

In the past decade, an abundance of IoT devices and platforms have been integrated into a wide range of applications like the market, healthcare, agriculture, utilities, energy, transportation, industrial control, and buildings, etc. Numerous studies forecast the substantial development of the IoT in the coming years. e.g., International Data Center (IDC) predicts that by 2020 the IoT solutions market will grow to $7.1 trillion [1], which will include 50 billion Internet-connected devices [2]. The European project Unify-IoT[1], lately identified that there are more than 300 IoT platforms in the current market.

Those studies are encouraging, since they suggest a tremendous impact of the IoT over the coming years. However, a new McKinsey analysis [3] points out a substantial threat to the predicted economic value: *missing interoperability*. Particularly, the

---

[1] http://unify-iot.eu.

© ICST Institute for Computer Sciences, Social Informatics and Telecommunications Engineering 2018
Y.-B. Lin et al. (Eds.): IoTaaS 2017, LNICST 246, pp. 11–18, 2018.
https://doi.org/10.1007/978-3-030-00410-1_2

authors state that 40% of the potential benefits of IoT can be obtained with the interoperability between IoT systems, i.e. two or more dissimilar systems are able to work together.

The current IoT market is fragmented due to the extreme degree of heterogeneity in terms of device protocols, controllers, network connectivity methods, application protocols, standards, data formats and so on. The absence of interoperability in IoT is due to a lack of standardisation [4, 5]. Vendors are intentionally defining different IoT platforms, proprietary protocols and interfaces which are incompatible with other solutions. Therefore, these vendors create different verticals and mostly closed ecosystems, which are sometimes called *stove pipes* or *silos*. To be precise, the components in one silo cannot talk to the components in another silo. For example, currently, before customers can access different IoT things they generally need a dedicated application for that particular thing preloaded onto the smartphone, such as the Philips Hue or the Belkin WeMo switch. This way the customer will have many devices, each with their own application, that work independently of each other. Also, there are data interoperability issues when developers want to create an innovative IoT application exploiting resources from different IoT applications and or/services (such as Oral-B or the Apple HealthKit) in heterogeneous domains (e.g., smart health, smart home, etc.). These issues ultimately lead to vendor lock-in of end-users.

Considering the importance of interoperability in IoT, first we need to understand interoperability and the existing solutions to analyze what is needed and identify the platforms that are ahead to help increase the number of interoperable IoT products. A classification of IoT interoperability is provided in Sect. 2. Then, based on the classification, a survey of the existing H2020 IoT research projects is presented in Sect. 3. Finally, the paper concludes in Sect. 4.

2   Interoperability Classification in IoT

Interoperability is a major topic in many different domains and there are several distinct definitions of this term in the literature. Between the diverse definitions for interoperability, we quote the most noteworthy one in our context. The IEEE defines interoperability as "the ability of two or more systems or components to exchange information and to use the information that has been exchanged" [6]. According to this definition, there are many scientific challenges: the ability to get the data, to exchange information, and the ability to use the information once it has been received.

Standard organizations and open source communities have been working to address interoperability issues in different parts or levels. We divide the existing interoperability solutions in the literature according to the level of interoperability that has been achieved between IoT platforms or systems: device level, networking level, syntactic level, semantic level, cross-platform level, and cross-domain interoperability. The categories are described in the following subsections.

Device Level Interoperability. Various communication technologies such as: WiFi, 3G/4G, ANT+, ZigBee have emerged since only one wireless technology cannot support the different requirements of IoT markets. However, in the absence of a de-facto communication standard(s), not all smart devices implement all these communication technologies. Device level interoperability refers to enabling the integration of such heterogeneous communication technologies and standards supported by different IoT devices. This layer should focus on accessing devices through unifying interfaces and the ability to integrate new devices into any IoT platform. For example, consider a smart home scenario where the light bulbs and thermostats use ZigBee, speakers communicate with Bluetooth, and switches communicate through WiF. Interoperability in this example enables different devices to understand and translate between these disparate communication technologies. An ideal IoT platform would offer a pool of standardized communication protocols where the device manufacturers may select the appropriate protocols (e.g. CoAP for constrained devices). In the literature device level interoperability relies either on a gateway solution (sometimes called protocol converters) that can be extended using plug-ins, to support new communication protocols or by instructing the device vendors to only use the protocols that are supported (such as Fosstrak[2]). For example, the Apple HomeKit[3], If-This-Then-That (IFTTT)[4] and Eclipse Ponte[5], Lightweight M2M[6] (LWM2M) are some of the gateway solutions in the literature.

Network Level Interoperability. Network level interoperability deals with mechanisms to exchange messages between systems through different networks (networks of networks) to provide end-to-end communication. To make systems interoperable, each system should be able to exchange messages with other systems through various types of networks. In this level, protocol interoperability is the main focus. At the standardization level, the IETF has developed a set of standards for routing including RPL, CORPL, and CARP and solutions for encapsulation including 6LowPAN, 6TiSCH, 6Lo, and Thread [7]. In addition, the cloud has been used as a medium to address interoperability at this level. This is called Fog of Things [8], where the computing, storage and networking services are placed at the edge of the network rather than centralized cloud servers. Fog of Things aims for providing value to the data before making it available on the web facilitating the interoperability of the devices at the edge and preparing the managed data for further applications to be interoperable. Another new solution to address interoperability in this level is software-based approaches such as Software Defined Networking (SDN) which hides all the control and management operations from the IoT devices by setting them inside a middleware layer [9], which alleviates the dependency from vendors.

Syntactic Level Interoperability. Syntactic level interoperability refers to interoperation of the format as well as the data structure used in any exchanged information or service between heterogeneous IoT system entities. This level of interoperability is important to enable smooth message transition between different IoT systems. Web

---

[2] https://fosstrak.github.io/.

[3] www.apple.com/ios/home.

[4] https://ifttt.com.

[5] http://www.eclipse.org/proposals/technology.ponte/.

[6] http://technical.openmobilealliance.org/Technical/technical-information/omna/lightweight-m2m-lwm2m-object-registry.

technologies such as HTTP, JSON, REST and SOAP architecture of the World Wide Web, an approach referred to as the Web of Things (WoT) is proposed to provide greater interoperability. The WoT enables developers to connect things using web technologies and tools to create new applications and mashups. The use of the web provides a one-for-all solution for providing higher degree of interoperability, since there is no need to install/develop specific software and drivers for various devices, enabling the connection of heterogeneous devices in dissimilar domains. The Web supports different content types which resolve the challenge of working with different data formats in different applications across multiple platforms. Some of the most common web-based representations of the resources are plain text, JSON, XML and EXI. XML helps achieve syntactic interoperability by encoding syntactic information into XML documents, providing platform and language independence, vendor neutrality, and extensibility, which are all crucial to interoperability. In addition, JSON is becoming popular in the IoT market, as it is lightweight, simple and offers capabilities close to the XML ones without requiring the overhead (e.g. schema) and processing requirements of XML. Also, the Sensor Web Enablement[7] (SWE) framework provide a standard set of web service interfaces towards making it easier to share sensor data. Moreover, there are many efforts for IoT/Cloud convergence [10], and several IoT cloud-enabled platforms (ThingWorx[8], OpenIoT[9], Xively[10], and ThingsSpeak[11]) are available at the syntactic level to facilitate the aggregation of data and services from heterogeneous IoT devices.

Semantic Level Interoperability. Semantic level interoperability deals with the technologies needed for enabling the meaning of information to be shared by communicating parties. To enable building new innovative, applications which make use of data from multiple existing vertical IoT silos these systems must not only be able to exchange information but also have a common understanding of the meaning of this data. This level is concerned with data and information models which will describe: the things, application functionalities, data modeling and service descriptions, in a uniform way to enable machines to read and understand the data sent and received. For example, consider two smart lightening deployments, which have been planned and implemented independently. There is a need to combine both deployments to calculate the amount of energy gains reached. This is challenging because each deployment speaks diverse languages at the data level. They have different data formats as well as different semantics, such as units of measurement, sensor types and features, mathematic constructs and so on. The technologies from the Semantic Web have been used to address interoperability in this level. Ontologies are used to define a common, machine-readable dictionary that is able to express resources, services, APIs and related parameters (such as Semantic Sensor Network, IoT-Lite, and Architectural Reference Model). Other semantic web techniques such as Resource Description Framework

---

(RDF), RDF Schema, Web Ontology Language, Linked Data and SPARQL are used for representing web resources in a uniform form and reasoning over them. In this level, there are issues such as: (1) ontology heterogeneity (e.g., ontology designed by different persons differ in the structure), terms used to describe data (e.g., t, temp and temperature are several terms to describe temperature), and the meaning of data exchanged according to the context (e.g., body temperature differs from room temperature). Semantic interoperability can be achieved through agreed-upon information models of the terms used as part of the interfaces and exchanged data. Moreover, catalog based approaches such as HyperCat[12], allows distributed data repositories to be used jointly by applications.

Cross-platform Interoperability. The Cross-Platform interoperability is the main requirement to have an interoperable IoT system. This interoperability level enables federation across different IoT platforms by integrating data from various platforms specific to one vertical domain such as smart home, smart healthcare, smart garden, etc. For example, assume that a user wants to use a single application to manage the smart lighting at home and in the office. Currently, two different applications are required; one for his home automation system, and the other for the office environment. The cross-platform interoperability level allows managing devices at both home, in the office, and other place.

Cross-domain Interoperability. Cross-Platform solutions focus on specific activities that are limited to one domain. The Cross-domain interoperability enables the federation of different platforms within heterogeneous domains to build horizontal IoT applications. This federation will not try to mandate a specific protocol at any levels of the protocol stack as the only standard across domains. In contrast, it is essential that IoT platforms can choose the desired protocols to control the end-to-end communications and data exchange (from sensors to gateways to cloud-based platforms) based on their requirement and purpose. In the literature, some IoT solution providers wrap and offer their domain-specific platforms in a 'Sensing as a Service' way [11], which provides third parties useful information with respect to a single domain. For example, a smart home platform can provide domain-specific enablers such as air temperature and the lighting conditions. These enablers can then be exploited by other IoT platforms, such as smart healthcare, to provide more innovative applications and scenarios.

3   Analysis of Current IoT Interoperability Platforms

To assess the maturity of IoT interoperability, we determine the features discussed in Sect. 2 that are supported by state-of-the-art IoT platforms. We analysed some of the recent H2020 European research projects as shown in Table 1. These projects are developing interoperability solutions at different interoperability levels. In the following, we discuss the mappings of the interoperability levels and the method and solutions provided by the projects. In addition, we discuss some shortcomings.

---

[12] www.hypercat.io.

Table 1. A summary of the IoT platforms supporting interoperability requirements. ✓ = supported; ✗ = not supported

Interoperability Level	TagIt Smart!	Big IoT	SymbIoTe	AGILE	bIoTope	BUTLER	Open-IoT	UniversAAL	FIESTA-IoT	RERUM	VICINITY	VITAL	iCore	FIWARE	Inter-IoT
Device	✗	✗	✗	✓	✗	✓	✗	✓	✗	✓	✓	✓	✓	✗	✓
Network	✗	✗	✗	✗	✗	✗	✗	✗	✗	✗	✓	✗	✓	✗	✓
Syntactic	✗	✓	✓	✗	✓	✗	✓	✓	✓	✓	✓	✓	✗	✓	✓
Semantic	✗	✓	✓	✗	✗	✓	✓	✗	✓	✗	✓	✓	✗	✓	✓
Cross-Platform	✗	✓	✓	✗	✓	✗	✗	✓	✓	✓	✗	✓	✗	✓	✓
Cross-Domain	✗	✓	✓	✗	✓	✗	✗	✓	✓	✗	✗	✗	✗	✓	✓

3.1 Interoperability Among IoT Platforms

TagItSmart![13] offers a set of tools and enabling technologies integrated into a platform with open interfaces to make mass-market products connected using smart printed QR codes, smartphone, and cloud. However, interoperability support is limited to the device level in this project. Similarly, the AGILE project focuses on the integration of heterogeneous devices by build a modular IoT gateway, which provides RESTful APIs to interact with user devices. The configuration of the gateway is performed automatically based on the hardware configuration, reducing the gateway setup time. The bIoTope[14] provides a platform that enables stakeholders to create new IoT systems and to rapidly harness available information using Systems-of-Systems (SoS) capabilities for connected smart objects by providing standardised open APIs for the interoperability between smart objects of different platforms. Two Open API standards are mentioned Open Messaging Interface and Open Data Format. Different from other projects, the SymbIoTe[15] provides a middleware which focuses on the federation of IoT platforms. Syntactic interoperability is addressed by a high-level API which acts like an adapter to provide a uniform access to resources of all platforms. Semantic interoperability is addressed by semantic mapping between the platform-specific information models, where platform-specific extension of one platform is translated into the platform-specific exaction of the other platform. Similar to SymbIoTe, the Big-IoT[16] project focuses on the federation between IoT platforms, developing a generic, unified Web API for smart object platforms focusing on syntactic and semantic interoperability enabling application developers to interact with different IoT platforms. Vital[17] provides syntactic interoperability using SOA and enables RESTful web services for communication interchange mechanism, and semantic interoperability is

---

[13] http://tagitsmart.eu.

[14] www.biotope-project.eu.

[15] http://iot-epi.eu/project/symbiote.

[16] http://big-iot.eu.

[17] http://vital-iot-eu/.

achieved by using a common-data model using Linked Data standards such as RDF (for modelling and accessing metadata and data), JSON-LD, and ontologies. Vital also aims to integrate different IoT platform, but it doesn't address cross-domain mechanisms and is limited to smart city domain. Unlike BigIoT, Vital stores the data coming from IoT systems. The VICINITY[18] platform supports semantic interoperability (building on LinkSmart/Hydra [12]) and the use of existing ontologies (e.g. from Ready4SmartCities[19], oneM2M[20]) to provide "interoperability as a service". The openIoT project focuses on an open source middleware for creating real-time IoT services on demand. However, it does not address cross-platform and cross-domain mechanisms. The Inter-IoT[21] aims to provide an interoperable and open IoT framework for the integration of heterogeneous IoT platforms with the consideration of cross-domain interoperability. Unlike the other existing projects, this project considers interoperability at all the mentioned levels. The FIESTA-IoT[22] project is considering the semantic interoperability of testbeds regardless of the application domain.

3.2   Interoperability Analysis Results

From the analysis of the approaches taken by different projects shown in Table 1, it is clear that most of the projects address two to five interoperability levels and their focus is providing interoperability solutions to connect existing IoT commercial and open source platforms. It is also clear that there are several efforts towards solving the interoperability issue within the application and data and semantic layer. This is because interoperability at the application level is still not mature since the existing solutions lack information models and have a strong relationship with the underlying communication architecture (RPC or RESTful design). In addition, many of the projects proposing semantic-based components are not interoperable with each other. For instance, the existing projects don't use the same data model to structure the data produced by smart objects or the same reasoning approach to deduce new knowledge from data produced by smart devices. Moreover, current implementations focus on specific IoT application domains neglecting cross-domain interoperability.

To allow the development of applications on top of IoT platforms, the IoT platforms should provide the developers an APIs to their functionality. Further, to enable an efficient development of cross-IoT platform applications, these APIs should be uniform across the platforms to the extent possible. Today's IoT platforms almost all provide a public REST API to access the services. The APIs are usually based on RESTful principles; however, most platforms use custom REST APIs and data models which complicates the mashing up of data across multiple platforms. From our results, using standards such as HyperCat (See footnote 12) should be adopted to address such issues.

---

[18] http://vicinity2020.eu/vicinity.

[19] http://www.ready4smartcities.eu.

[20] www.onem2m.org.

[21] www.inter-iot-projects.eu.

[22] http://fiesta-iot.eu.

4   Conclusion

In this paper, we have answered two questions: what are the different categories for an interoperable IoT ecosystem and how interoperability has been addressed in the literature. At the device level gateways and smartphone solutions are the main method to address the connectivity issues. In the networking level, IPv6 and other standard technologies such as SDN, NFV and Fog are promising. From the Syntactic and Semantic perspectives, web technologies (open APIs, RESTful web services, JSON-like dictionary, and mashups) and semantic web technologies provide a high degree of interoperability. Finally, interoperability at the higher levels (cross-platform and cross-domain) can be achieved by the collaboration and agreement between IoT platform owners on many essential issues such as exposing the resources, interfaces, services, and data models. The main results of our research are that we believe that there is not likely a common set of standards that will be universally accepted which will allow IoT devices and platforms to work together. However, by applying some of the presented techniques interoperability can be improved.

References

1. Lund, D., Morales, D.: Worldwide and regional Internet of Things (IoT) 2014–2020 forecast : a virtuous circle of proven value and demand. International Data Corporation (IDC), Technical Report (2014)
2. Evans, D.: The Internet of Things: how the next evolution of the internet is changing everything. In: CISCO White paper, vol. 1, no. 2011, pp. 1–11 (2011)
3. Manyika, J., et al.: The Internet of Things: Mapping the Value Beyond the Hype, p. 3. McKinsey Global Institute, New York City (2015)
4. Da Xu, L., He, W., Li, S.: Internet of Things in industries: a survey. IEEE Trans. Ind. Inform. **10**(4), 2233–2243 (2014)
5. Agrawal, S., Das, M.L.: Internet of Things - a paradigm shift of future internet applications. In: Nirma University International Conference on Engineering (NUiCONE), pp. 1–7 (2011)
6. Radatz, J., Geraci, A., Katki, F.: IEEE standard glossary of software engineering terminology. IEEE Std, vol. 610121990, no. 121990, p. 3 (1990)
7. Salman, T., Jain, R.: Networking protocols for Internet of Things, pp. 1–28 (2013)
8. Workshops, A., Serrano, M.: SOFT-IoT : self-organizing FOG of things (2016)
9. Jararweh, Y., Al-Ayyoub, M., Darabseh, A., Benkhelifa, E., Vouk, M., Rindos, A.: SDIoT: a software defined based internet of things framework. J. Ambient Intell. Humaniz. Comput. **6** (4), 453–461 (2015)
10. Alamri, A., Ansari, W.S., Hassan, M.M., Hossain, M.S., Alelaiwi, A., Hossain, M.A.: A survey on sensor-cloud: architecture, applications, and approaches. Int. J. Distrib. Sens. Netw. **9**(2), 917923 (2013)
11. Soldatos, J., Kefalakis, N., Serrano, M., Hauswirth, M.: Design principles for utility-driven services and cloud-based computing modelling for the Internet of Things. Int. J. Web Grid Serv. 6 **10**(2–3), 139–167 (2014)
12. Eisenhauer, M., Rosengren, P., Antolin, P.: HYDRA: a development platform for integrating wireless devices and sensors into ambient intelligence systems. In: Giusto, D., Iera, A., Morabito, G., Atzori, L. (eds.) The Internet of Things, pp. 367–373. Springer, New York (2010). https://doi.org/10.1007/978-1-4419-1674-7_36

Orientation Training System for Elders with Dementia Using Internet of Things

Lun-Ping Hung[1]([✉]), Chien-Liang Chen[2], Chien-Ting Sung[1], and Chia-Ling Ho[3]

[1] Department of Information Management,
National Taipei University of Nursing and Health Sciences, Taipei City, Taiwan
lunping@ntunhs.edu.tw
[2] Department of Computer Science and Information Engineering,
Aletheia University, Taipei City, Taiwan
[3] Department of Marketing and Logistics Management,
Taipei City University of Science and Technology, Taipei City, Taiwan

Abstract. Dementia is an irreversible disease, its prevalence increases with age, the elderly with dementia increasing with years become a nonnegligible population, the government and the public shall be prepared for this tide. The information and communication technology is improved continuously in recent years, the Internet of Things technology becomes mature increasingly, which is helpful to the life aspects of home, traffic and shopping, and it can be combined with clinical knowledge and experience for the environment of health care, promoting the senile dementia treatment field to face how to use the complete architecture of Internet of Things to provide an effective adjuvant therapy mechanism. The early dementia temporal orientation training mechanism can be built by using the concept of health care Internet of Things. The infrastructure proposed in this study combines xBeacon sensing equipment with novel hybrid operation modes, including Received Signal Strength Indication (RSSI) positioning, event analysis method and intelligent cutting algorithm, to reduce the slightly disabled patients' troubles in direction judgment and the probably derived anxiety and unease. The effective record and analysis of routine behavior pattern support the elderly to maintain the mobility in daily life independently, promoting the "home-based care for the aged" and "Aging in Place" visions and the attainment of objectives effectively.

Keywords: Orientation training system · Dementia · Internet of Things

1 Introduction

The dementia is a progressively degenerative and irreversible disease, it affects memory, thinking, behavior and sentiment. Differing from generally simple aging or hypomnesia, it is a disease of cerebral defuctionalization, a progressive cerebral degeneration syndrome. The symptoms include the failure of memory, and the cognitive function is affected, including the degeneration of linguistic ability, sense of space, judgment, computational ability, personality change and abstract thinking, and there will be behavioral and psychiatric symptoms, including disturbing behavior,

© ICST Institute for Computer Sciences, Social Informatics and Telecommunications Engineering 2018
Y.-B. Lin et al. (Eds.): IoTaaS 2017, LNICST 246, pp. 19–26, 2018.
https://doi.org/10.1007/978-3-030-00410-1_3

heteroptics, acousma and delusion. Most findings indicate that besides pharmacotherapy, the non-pharmacotherapies, such as environmental adjustment (familiar, stable and secure environment), activity arrangement, change in communication mode, cognitive training, reminiscence therapy, light, massage, music therapy, aromatherapy, pet therapy, multi-sensory stimulation therapy and art therapy, can improve the dementia patients' behavioral and psychiatric symptoms and slow down the development of course.

The morbidity of dementia increases with age. Taiwan Alzheimer's Disease Association estimates according to the estimated data of total population growth in the "Taiwan Population Projection" published by National Development Council in August 2016 and the dementia 5-year prevalence, the population of dementia was about 240 thousand in 2016, that will be more than 460 thousand in 2031, when there will be more than 2 persons suffering from dementia per 100 Taiwanese. The course is divided into mild cognitive impairment, mild (initial stage), moderate (intermediate stage) and serious (late stage). The disease degenerates at uncertain time, there are individual differences. The mild cognitive impairment (MCI) is a transition region between normal aging and the initial symptom of dementia. Clinically, about 10–15% of MCI develops into dementia annually, there will be problems in complex assignments or social environment, but the simple daily life is not affected [1]. The Cognitive Abilities Screening Instrument (CASI) is a clinical diagnosis tool extensively used in the field of dementia, for evaluating the patient's indexes of capacity for action. The cardinal symptoms of dementia are hypomnesia and cognitive impairment. The present diagnosis is still based on cognitive function degeneration. The CASI is developed from several common scales, including the questions in The Mini-Mental State Examination (MMSE), The Modified Mini-Mental Scale (3MS) Test, The Hasegawa Dementia Screening Scale (HDSS) and HDSS revision (HDS-R) [2]. The CASI remedies the defect of "cognitive psychological function test limit" in the MMSE and enhances other evaluation abilities. The score of CASI can be obtained after CASI analysis, and it can be converted into the score of MMSE for different studies' and clinical diagnoses' reference. The CASI contains the following tests of 9 dimensions: Attention (ATTEN), Mental manipulation (MENMA), Short-term memory (STM), Long-term memory (LTM), Orientation (ORIEN), Language (LANG), Drawing (DRAW), Abstract thinking and judgment (ABSTR) and Animal-name fluency (ANML). The scale characteristics have enlarged the fractional scale of short-term memory and temporal orientation which are most likely to be abnormal, so that it is easy to find and track any change in the score of the dimensions of the patient.

In this paper, a temporal orientation training mechanism conforming with clinical dementia is designed by xBeacon cut orientation assisted search technique in the concept of temporal orientation in dementia treatment, the disease development rate is reduced by giving appropriate stimulation and training, the patient's anxiety and unease resulted from disorientation can be reduced by the training process. The research objective is to enhance the safety and effectiveness of temporal orientation training, so that the patients are trained in an environment closer to the reality for greater effectiveness.

2 Literature Review

According to the references about dementia, the fields of medical treatment to technology-assisted life are covered. Many studies mentioned the necessity of patient position information, because one of the common symptoms of the patients with dementia is getting lost. It is often heard that the patients went out but forgot the way home, and had accidents, psychologically worrying their families and making the care difficult. Holthe et al. proposed a technology-assisted electronic calendar system, and proved that the electronic technology assisted with the patient's memory effectively [14]. Baruch et al. developed a home environment-based system in 2004. Related systems are installed in the living room and bedroom, a sound reminder is given when the time is up, so as to remind the patient to do what he wants to do, and the patient's anxiety and confusion are reduced successfully [15].

In terms of the studies about preventing the patient with dementia from getting lost, Ogawa et al. developed a system combining a low power consuming smart phone with PC. The patient with dementia carried the smart phone in the limited range for indoor location tracking, when the patient walked out of the range, the system sent the patient's positioning information via E-Mail to a relevant person's phone automatically, and the patient's smart phone gave warning sound to prevent the patient from being missing [16]. Ikarashi et al. designed a home-based tracking system for the patients with dementia by using GPS (Global Positioning System), PHS (Personal Handyphone System) and PC, the patient moved freely at home and his movement track was recorded to track the patient with dementia [17]. The above studies used the architecture of Internet of Things and different methods, the patient's position was detected successfully. The findings show that if the patient's position is known, the carer's burden and mental stress can be reduced, and the patient is prevented from getting lost effectively, reducing accidents. These findings show the importance of patient location positioning.

To sum up the aforesaid viewpoints, performing the Internet of Things technology and health care domain expertise can assist the patients with dementia with autonomous life and reduce the carers' burdens. As this study shall detect the patient's position intensively and instantly, the power consumption is a major consideration. The xBeacon based on Bluetooth wireless transmission is selected as front-end sensor to solve the power consumption problem, with a portable and handy mobile device, the trainer's burden can be reduced. This study uses xBeacon sensing equipment and RSSI positioning function to track the position information of the patient with mild dementia. A training mechanism about direction-sense is provided, so as to help the patient in training direction-sense more effectively, to enhance the patient's independence ability by such a design, the anxiety and unease are reduced effectively, and the dementia-induced degeneration is mitigated.

3   Research Method Procedure and Analysis

The system architecture is divided into front end sensing layer, middle end transmission layer and back end data layer and application layer. The sensing layer of this system uses xBeacon and smart phone as front-end sensing equipments for environmental induction and information gathering. The transmission layer uses Bluetooth wireless transmission, WIFI and the 3rd-Generation communication technology for data transmission. The data layer uses hybrid positioning calculation system to calculate the received information data and store them in database. The application layer provides different pictures for different users. The home-based positioning system displays different pictures according to different permissions.

3.1   Node Signal Strength Positioning Design and Application

This is signal strength localization method, the "region" of the location can be marked out rapidly. The more annunciators are laid, the more accurately the region of the location can be marked out. This study assumes that the sensors P on the patients are distributed over area M randomly, M_n is the possible region of each sensor, and the sensors are in their range of R_n. When there is not any mobile node, the possible range of each sensor is the entire M-region. In the experiment, the possible position range of sensor is reduced by the bisecting normal L_n between different mobile nodes, so as to obtain more accurate positioning result. In order to find the location of sensor, the training assistant can be regarded as a mobile node. The mobile node is the site where the reader stops. When the reader stops in environmental region, the reader collects the information of sensors in the range, and averages the sensor intensity values received in situ as the comparative data of each mobile node. The mobile node $C1$ receives the information of sensor P and $C2$ receives the information of sensor P, the stored comparative data are different as the distances are different.

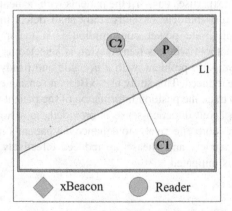

Fig. 1. Region segment of two mobile nodes (Color figure online)

As shown in Fig. 1, the sensor is placed in the area coverage, marked as English coded yellow diamond, the reader stops in two different positions randomly, marked as number coded circle. The signal strength value of Sensor **P** is received during stopping. The bisecting normal L_1 between two points divides the area **M** into M_a and M_b blocks. In terms of mobile node **C1** and mobile node **C2**, as the Sensor **P** is closer to **C2**, the strength value of **C2** is greater than that of **C1**. Therefore, the location of Sensor **P** is in the region M_a on the left of bisecting normal **L1** between mobile nodes **C1** and **C2**.

As shown in Fig. 2, If the **r(P, C)** is the signal strength value from Sensor **P** to Point **C**. When the reader stops at mobile node **C**, **d(Ci, Cj)** is the distance between points **Ci** and **Cj**. The following theorem can be concluded from the aforesaid description, if a space contains a sensor and mobile nodes **C1** and **C2**, if **r(P, Ci)** $\leq$ **r(P, C2)**, **d(P, Ci)** $\leq$ **r(P, C2)**. Therefore, by dividing mobile nodes, all the possible ranges of sensor will be convex polygon. There are **C * (C−1)/2** bisecting normals according to mobile node **C**, and the increasing mobile nodes will duplicate the number of bisecting normals and reduce the possible range of sensor effectively.

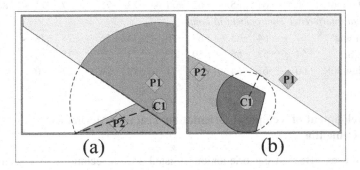

Fig. 2. Segment of sensor signal strength

3.2   Hybrid Indoor Signal Location Algorithm Intelligent Cutting Positioning Design

In this study, the accuracy of signal strength can influence the subsequent strength cutting method and positioning of mobile endpoint. In order to test the signal difference of xBeacon, different models and brands of Android intelligent mobile devices are used for experiment, it is used as reader to test whether the read RSSI values are different or not when different devices are used. This study will use three intelligent mobile devices, which are Redmi note, Samsung and ASUS, the measurement is conducted in a clear indoor environment and a home environment full of signals and compartments respectively to find the difference. As the indoor environment is complex, the electronic signals, electronic products, power supplies, indoor layouts and compartment materials will result in errors in xBeacon signal collection, not only influencing the signal strength, but also causing reflection and refraction problems, leading to signal distortion. According to Table 1, the mobile device of the same brand will have signal errors in different indoor environments. When the signal has errors, the indoor positioning accuracy will be lost.

Therefore, this study will use hybrid algorithm to design intelligent cutting positioning mode, combined with the RSSI signal value collected by xBeacon, the location is judged according to the location fingerprinting database, and the node signal strength localization method is used to mark out the patient's possible region, the location is judged by algorithm under the effect of dual positioning, so as to enhance the patient positioning precision. The convex polygon region is used for patient positioning, convenient for the carer to find the patient under the guidance of visual effect, enhancing the safety, and the patient's anxiety during disorientation can be reduced by training.

Table 1. The signal values of xBeacon in indoor

	1 m	2 m	3 m	4 m	5 m
Open space environment in indoor					
Samsung	−59 ~ −61	−65 ~ −67	−70 ~ −72	−74 ~ −75	−78 ~ −80
ASUS	−54 ~ −55	−66 ~ −68	−69 ~ −72	−77 ~ −78	−80 ~ −82
Redmi note	−60 ~ −61	−65 ~ −67	−71 ~ −73	−75 ~ −77	−78 ~ −80
Signal interference environment in home					
Samsung	−61 ~ −64	−65 ~ −68	−70 ~ −74	−76 ~ −78	−78 ~ −81
ASUS	−54 ~ −57	−66 ~ −69	−69 ~ −73	−77 ~ −78	−80 ~ −83
Redmi note	−60 ~ −61	−64 ~ −68	−71 ~ −73	−74 ~ −77	−80 ~ −82

3.3 Development of Temporal Orientation Training Mechanism for Dementia

This study uses xBeacon cut orientation assisted search technique to design a supplemental training mechanism for temporal orientation of clinical dementia, combined with a new generation BLE device, node signal strength cutting and sensor division technique to create an indoor environment training mechanism. The action track is followed by immediate addressing of the location of the patient with dementia. The training assistant leads the patient with dementia to walk on the preset path for the first time, and reminds the patient of the route to impress the patient. Afterwards, the patient walks on the preset path alone with xBeacon. The training assistant does not need to accompany the patient in the training process, but to watch the patient's movement aside. In case the patient got lost, the patient's range and right location are searched for according to the system menu guidance, and then the training is completed with assistance.

The dementia temporal orientation training mechanism is divided into 3 parts, xBeacon sensor end for transmitting information, kernel program end for information operation and processing and mobile application end for result visualization. The mobile application device with the patient receives the signal information of xBeacon sensor in the range. There are two types of sensors used in the environment. One is placed in a fixed position in the environment to assist in locating the patient. The second type is mounted on the patient for finding the patient during training. The mobile device receives the signal strength of xBeacon in the regions and related codes. These regions include bedroom, kitchen, living room, bathroom and dining room which are indoor environments for the patient with dementia.

The kernel program end is the relay software for receiving information, the database for storing information and the finder for calculating information. The relay software receives the sensor information from the mobile device via Wi-Fi. According to the uses of sensors, the data are classified and the signal strength data are converted into the database storage format, written in the database after data processing. The database stores the ID number of each xBeacon, signal strength and each patient's information. The relay software writes the received information in the database, the positioning calculation system reads the database information to judge the location. The possible position range of sensor is marked out and cut according to the sensor strength values received by different mobile nodes. When the positioning is finished, the hybrid positioning calculation system stores the result in the database, as shown in Fig. 3, the mobile application end receives the range of sensor after calculation, which is visualized on the screen of mobile device, the location of the patient with dementia is searched for on the indoor map on the screen.

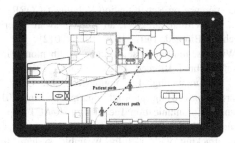

Fig. 3. The diagram of visualized system

4   Conclusion

This study develops an assistant mechanism for dementia temporal orientation training, the cooperative temporal orientation training mode for assistant and patient is created preliminarily, helping the patients with mild dementia and problems in temporal orientation maintain viability. With the support of information and communication technology, the system can record the training process and prevent the patient from getting lost. In addition, based on the architecture of Internet of Things, the patient's treatment situation can be known and tracked instantly, implementing technology assisted treatment to upgrade the medical care effect. It can even assist the doctors in deciding on clinical treatment in the future development.

References

1. Sun, Y., et al.: A nationwide survey of mild cognitive impairment and dementia, including very mild dementia, in Taiwan. PLoS ONE **9**(6), e100303 (2014)
2. Teng, E.L., et al.: The cognitive abilities screening instrument (CASI): a practical test for cross-cultural epidemiological studies of dementia. Int. Psychogeriatr. **6**(1), 44–58 (1994)., discussion 62
3. Alghamdi, S., van Schyndel, R., Khalil, I.: Accurate positioning using long range active RFID technology to assist visually impaired people. J. Netw. Comput. Appl. **41**, 135–147 (2014)
4. Yao, D., et al.: Energy efficient indoor tracking on smartphones. Future Gener. Comput. Syst. **39**, 44–54 (2014)
5. Bluetooth Special Interest Group. https://www.bluetooth.com/what-is-bluetooth-technology/discover-bluetooth
6. Varsamou, M., Antonakopoulos, T.: A bluetooth smart analyzer in iBeacon networks. In: 2014 IEEE Fourth International Conference on Consumer Electronics Berlin (ICCE-Berlin), pp. 288–292 (2014)
7. Robinson, H., MacDonald, B., Broadbent, E.: The role of healthcare robots for older people at home: a review. Int. J. Soc. Robot. **6**(4), 575–591 (2014)
8. Sabanovic, S., Bennett, C.C., Wan-Ling, C., Huber, L.: PARO robot affects diverse interaction modalities in group sensory therapy for older adults with dementia. In: 2013 IEEE International Conference on Rehabilitation Robotics (ICORR), pp. 1–6 (2013)
9. Hossain, M., Ahmed, D.: Virtual caregiver: an ambient-aware elderly monitoring system. IEEE Trans. Inf. Technol. Biomed. **16**(6), 1024–1031 (2012)
10. Junnila, S., et al.: Wireless, multipurpose in-home health monitoring platform: two case trials. IEEE Trans. Inf. Technol. Biomed. **14**(2), 447–455 (2010)
11. Fahim, M., Fatima, I., Sungyoung, L., Young-Koo, L.: Daily life activity tracking application for smart homes using android smartphone. In: 2012 14th International Conference on Advanced Communication Technology (ICACT), pp. 241–245 (2012)
12. Hardegger, M., Mazilu, S., Caraci, D., Hess, F., Roggen, D., Troster, G.: Action SLAM on a smartphone: at-home tracking with a fully wearable system. In: 2013 International Conference on Indoor Positioning and Indoor Navigation (IPIN), pp. 1–8 (2013)
13. Toplan, E., Ersoy, C.: RFID based indoor location determination for elderly tracking. In: 2012 20th Signal Processing and Communications Applications Conference (SIU), pp. 1–4 (2012)
14. Holthe, T., Walderhaug, S.: Older people with and without dementia participating in the development of an individual plan with digital calendar and message board. J. Assist. Technol. **4**(2), 15–25 (2010)
15. Baruch, J., Downs, M., Baldwin, C., Bruce, E.: A case study in the use of technology to reassure and support a person with dementia. Dementia **3**(3), 372–377 (2004)
16. Ogawa, H., Yonezawa, Y., Maki, H., Sato, H., Morton Caldwell, W.: A mobile phone-based safety support system for wandering elderly persons. In: Conference Proceeding IEEE Engineering in Medicine and Biology Society, vol. 5, pp. 3316–3317 (2004)
17. Ikarashi, A., Nonaka, S., Magara, K., Ohno, H.: The searching system for wandering demented aged person using GPS. Electr. Eng. Jpn. **2002**(122), 609–616 (2002)

Demand-Based Radio Resource Allocation for Device-to-Device Communications: A Game Approach

Chih-Cheng Tseng[✉] and Jyun-Yao Shih

National Ilan University, No. 1, Sec. 1, Shennong Rd., Yilan City 26047,
Yilan County, Taiwan (R.O.C.)
tsengcc@niu.edu.tw, sdl767fl3@hotmail.com.tw

Abstract. With the proliferation of the number of mobile devices, it is urgent to develop new technologies to cope with the rapidly growing volume of mobile data. Device-to-device (D2D) communication has been considered as one of the key technologies to solve this problem. In this paper, under the premise that D2D pairs share the uplink spectrum of cellular user (CU), a radio resource allocation scheme is proposed to allocate resource blocks (RBs) to D2D pairs while the co-channel interference threshold of CU is met. The D2D pairs whose total number of demanded RBs falls within a predefined range are organized into a coalition. Based on the total number of demanded RBs, the proposed scheme first allocates RBs to each coalition. Then, in each coalition, the Nash Bargaining Solution (NBS) is used to further allocate RBs to the belonging D2D pairs. The simulation results show that the reuse ratio of the Reusable RBs is nearly 100%. In addition, when the required number of RBs is greater than that can be allocated, the proposed scheme proportionally allocates RBs to all D2D pairs.

Keywords: D2D communication · Radio resource allocation · Coalition
Nash Bargaining Solution

1 Introduction

In response to the rapid growth of the amount of mobile data, device-to-device (D2D) communication technology has been considered as one of the possible solutions. In addition to reducing the loading of evolved NodeB (eNB) and enhancing the overall system capacity, D2D communications also greatly reduce the data transmission delay due to the short distance between two D2D devices. However, since D2D communication technology is not fully mature yet, there are still many issues that need to be further explored, such as radio resource allocation, power control, device discovery, and D2D mode selection. Among them, many of the literature addressed to the radio resource allocation problem. One of the possible solutions to this problem is to improve the spectrum efficiency. To improve the spectrum efficiency, one of the alternatives is the D2D communications share the uplink spectrum used by the Cellular Users (CUs).

© ICST Institute for Computer Sciences, Social Informatics and Telecommunications Engineering 2018
Y.-B. Lin et al. (Eds.): IoTaaS 2017, LNICST 246, pp. 27–35, 2018.
https://doi.org/10.1007/978-3-030-00410-1_4

This approach is also regarded as the inband underlay [1]. However, due to the co-channel interference problems, it is necessary to design a radio resource allocation scheme [2] to appropriately allocate resource blocks (RBs) to D2D pairs so that the interference to CUs can be maintained in an acceptable level. To this problem, most of the literatures aimed to maximize the overall system transmission rate. However, the requested transmission rate by each D2D pair is not considered. Therefore, this paper attempts to design a resource allocation scheme that takes user requirements in terms of the number of demanded RBs into consideration.

The rest of this paper is organized as follows. Section 2 briefly introduces the fundamental concepts used in this paper. Section 3 describes the proposed demand-based radio resource allocation scheme. The simulation results and discussions are in Sect. 4. Section 5 concludes this paper.

2 Preliminaries

D2D communication was first defined in 3GPP Release 12. The core concept of D2D communication is to allow two closely spaced devices to communicate directly without going through the eNB. The application scenario of D2D communication is very extensive. For example, within the small area, D2D pairs can share multimedia directly. In such a way, not only the transmission delay is reduced, the loading of eNB is offloaded as well [3]. One of the most critical issues for the D2D communication to be applicable is how D2D pairs share the radio spectrum with the existing CUs so that the overall spectrum utilization is increased. Hence, it is important to study how to allocate the radio resources to the D2D pairs under the premise of the interferences to the CUs are tolerable.

A brief literature review is given below. In [4], to achieve the fairness, maximize the entire system rate, and simplify the complexity of radio resource allocation in the OFDMA networks, a two-user bargaining algorithm was proposed based on the concept of Nash Bargaining Solution (NBS) [5] to fairly allocate the subcarriers when the number of mobile user is two. In case of the number of mobile users is more than two, the Hungarian algorithm was used to optimally select two mobile users to form a coalition [6, 7]. In such a way, the two-user bargaining algorithm can be applied to each coalition. With this approach, the number of combinations to allocate radio resources is greatly reduced. In contrast to be applied to the OFDMA system, the authors in [8] applied the concepts of coalition and NBS to the LTE system. Similar to [4], the coalitions in [8] are also formed with equal size while the coalition size can be more than two. All possible sizes of coalitions are generated. Unlike the subcarriers are allocated individually in [4], a fixed number of continuous subcarriers are organized into group to reduce the allocation complexity. Furthermore, to achieve the fairness, the same number of subcarrier groups are allocated to coalitions with the same size. After the subcarrier groups are allocated to all possible sizes of coalitions, the final coalition size is selected by only testing the sum rate achieved by the sampled coalition sizes.

Obviously, in order to deal with the multiuser scenarios, the use of the Hungarian algorithm in [4] greatly increases the computational complexity. Although the coalition size in [8] can be more than two, it is required to be fixed and equal among coalitions. Furthermore, to achieve the fairness, equal number of subcarriers are allocated to coalitions with the same size. However, by viewing the above approaches, the data rate requirements of the mobile users are not considered not only in coalition formation but also in RB allocation. In the application scenarios of D2D communications, we believe that it is important to meet the diverse requirements of the D2D pairs.

Unlike to limit the size of coalition, we proposed a coalition formation method that groups D2D pairs into coalition based on the number of demanded RBs. After the coalition formation, if needed, NBS is used to further allocate the allocated RBs to D2D pairs inside a coalition. Based on the proposed radio resource allocation scheme, the limited uplink radio resources can be utilized more effectively.

3   Demand-Based Radio Resource Allocation

As the system model depicted in Fig. 1, we assumed there are N_C CUs and N_{D2D} D2D pairs within the coverage area of an eNB. An eNB allocates the uplink RBs to CUs based on the semi-persistent scheduling mechanism. Besides, all D2D pairs are assumed to share the uplink RBs of CUs. After receiving the demanded data rate of D2D pair i, we assumed eNB converts it into the number of demanded RBs. In such a way, $N_i^{RB,req}$ is used to represent the number of RBs requested by D2D pair i and is assumed uniformly distributed over $[\alpha_{min}, \alpha_{max}]$. $\mathbf{C}_q$ is the set of D2D pairs in the qth coalition. We also assumed that eNB knows the locations of D2D pairs.

The SINR of D2D pair i in coalition q that reuses the uplink RBs of CU j is given by

$$SINR_{i,j}^q = \frac{P_i G_{i,i}}{P_j G_{j,i} + N},\tag{1}$$

where P_i is the transmission power of D2D pair i, $G_{i,i}$ is the channel gain between the receiver and the transmitter of the D2D pair i, P_j is the transmission power of CU j, $G_{j,i}$ is the channel gain between CU j and one of the two devices of D2D pair i that nearest to CU j, and N is the thermal noise.

Given D2D pair i in coalition q is allocated $N_i^{RB,allocated}$ RBs, the capacity is obtained by

$$R_{q,i} = 180 \times N_i^{RB,allocated} \times \log_2(1 + SINR_{i,j}^q). \quad \text{(Kbps)}\tag{2}$$

Next, we will explain how to form a coalition. As mentioned earlier, the number of demanded RBs of a D2D pair is considered as the criterion for forming coalition. In particular, when a coalition $\mathbf{C}_q$ (excluding the last formed coalition), the aggregated

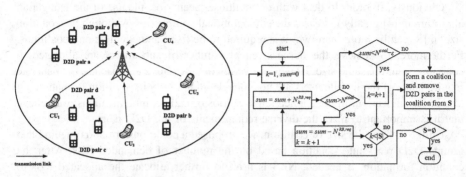

Fig. 1. System model   **Fig. 2.** Flow chart for coalition formation.

number of demanded RBs for all D2D pairs in the coalition $N_{q,total}^{RB,req} = \sum_{i \in C_q} N_i^{RB,req}$ is bounded by

$$N^{coal} - \varepsilon \leq N_{q,total}^{RB,req} \leq N^{coal}, \tag{3}$$

where N^{coal} is the maximum aggregated number of demanded RBs in a coalition and ε is a tolerance value. Both of them are system parameters. As to the last formed coalition, the total number of demanded RBs is allowed to be less than $N^{coal} - \varepsilon$. The flow chart for coalition formation is depicted in Fig. 2. In this flow chart, k is an index of D2D pair, *sum* is the up-to-date aggregated number of demanded RBs, and **S** is a set of D2D pairs in which D2D pairs are listed based on the descending order of the number of demanded RBs. For example, by employing the coalition formation flow chart in Fig. 2 to the example network as shown in Fig. 3, **S** = {**a**, **b**, **c**, **e**, **d**} and three coalitions, $\mathbf{C}_1$ = {**a**}, $\mathbf{C}_2$ = {**b**, **c**}, and $\mathbf{C}_3$ = {**e**, **d**}, are generated if $N^{coal} = 4$ and $\varepsilon = 1$.

Since D2D pairs are assumed to use the uplink RBs of CUs, it is necessary to properly allocate RBs to D2D pairs so that the interference to CUs below a tolerable threshold. To achieve this, first, if the SNR of a RB used by CU perceived at the eNB is higher than a threshold $SNR_{th}^{RB,CU}$, this RB is eligible to be shared to D2D pairs and is referred as a Reusable RB. In addition, if a RB whose SINR perceived at the receiver of a D2D pair is higher than $SINR_{th}^{RB,D2D}$, it is regarded as a Preferred RB by this D2D pair. After receiving the Preferred RBs reported from a D2D pair, the Available RBs, RBs that are available to this D2D pair, of this D2D pair are determined at the eNB by finding the intersection among Reusable RBs and Preferred RBs. Since the Preferred RBs might different among D2D pairs, the Available RBs might also different among D2D pairs.

After finding the Available RBs, they are first allocated to coalitions and, then, to the D2D pairs in a coalition. Let $\mathbf{B}_i^{RB}$ be the set of Available RBs of D2D pair i. This set will be updated whenever an Available RB is allocated. The steps to allocate

Available RBs to coalitions are illustrated in Table 1. For simplicity, we use RB in Table 1 to represent the Available RB. In addition, in any case, only consecutive Available RBs can be allocated to coalitions and D2D pairs.

Following, we will explain how to allocate Available RBs to coalitions obtained by employing the flow chart in Fig. 2 to the example network in Fig. 3. As described in Table 1, eNB allocates Available RBs to coalitions based on the order that coalition is formed. Hence, Fig. 4 shows how eNB allocates Available RBs to C_1. We assume each CU is allocated with 3 RBs. From the third row to the seventh row, a "1" indicates that the corresponding RB is an Available RB of the D2D pair; otherwise, it is a "0". Since D2D pair **a** is the only member in C_1, according to the third row of Table 1, we have $I = J = K = L = \{0, 1, 2, 3, 4, 5\}$. Since $N_{1,total}^{RB,req} = 3$ and $|K| = 6$, there are 4 RB allocation combinations, $\{0, 1, 2\}$, $\{1, 2, 3\}$, $\{2, 3, 4\}$, and $\{3, 4, 5\}$. To increase the RB utilization, the one with the smallest total popularity value is selected. The popularity value of an Available RB of a D2D pair is defined as the ratio of the number of D2D pairs that also regard this RB as an Available RB and the total number of D2D pairs in the network. For example, the popularity value of RB 3 of D2D pair **a** is $(1 + 1 + 0 + 0 + 1)/5 = 0.6$. As shown in Fig. 4, the total popularity value of $\{0, 1, 2\}$ is the smallest among others. Hence, they are allocated to C_1. Since there is only D2D pair **a** in C_1, allocating Available RBs to C_1 is equivalent to allocating Available RBs to D2D pair **a**.

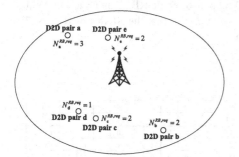

RB No.	0	1	2	3	4	5	6	7	8	9
CU No.	0	0	0	1	1	1	2	2	2	3
B_a^{RB}	1	1	1	1	1	1	0	0	0	0
B_b^{RB}	0	0	0	1	1	1	1	1	1	0
B_c^{RB}	1	1	1	0	0	0	1	1	1	0
B_d^{RB}	0	0	0	0	0	0	1	1	1	1
B_e^{RB}	0	0	0	1	1	1	0	0	0	0
I=J=K=L	1	1	1	1	1	1	0	0	0	0
Popularity a	0.4	0.4	0.4	0.6	0.6	0.6	0	0	0	0
Allocation	a	a	a	0	0	0	0	0	0	0

Fig. 3. An example network with 5 D2D pairs and the number of demanded RBs.

Fig. 4. Available RB allocation for C_1.

Next, eNB allocates Available RBs to C_2 in which $N_{2,total}^{RB,req} = 4$. However, as shown in Fig. 5 which is obtained from Fig. 4, $I = K = \{6, 7, 8\}$ and $J = L = \{0, 1, 2, 3, 4, 5, 6, 7, 8\}$. Based on Table 1, RBs in **K** will be first allocated to C_2. Then, by removing RBs in **K** from **L**, $L\backslash K = \{0, 1, 2, 3, 4, 5\}$. To meet the RB continuity requirement, RB 5 is selected and allocated to C_2. However, how to further allocate RBs 5, 6, 7, and 8 to D2D pairs **b** and **c** will be mentioned later.

Finally, eNB allocates Available RBs to C_3 in which $N_{3,total}^{RB,req} = 3$. From Fig. 6 which is also obtained from Fig. 4, we know $|K| = 0$. Hence, by employing the greedy algorithm to allocate Available RBs with the highest SINR to D2D pairs in C_3, RBs 3 and 4 are allocated to D2D pair **e** and RB 9 is allocated to D2D pair **d**.

Now, we will explain how to further allocate Available RBs to D2D pairs in C_2. The allocation of Available RBs to D2D pairs in a coalition is modelled as a Nash Bargaining game in which the players are the D2D pairs in the coalition, the goods are the Available RBs allocated to the coalition, and the payoff of an Available RB is its capacity. The NBS of a Nash Bargaining game can be obtained by the following formula:

$$\underset{R_{q,1},R_{q,2},\ldots,R_{q,|C_q|}}{\arg \max} \prod_{m=1}^{|C_q|} (R_{q,m} - R_{\min}^{q,m}), \tag{4}$$

where $|C_q|$ is the number of D2D pairs in C_q, $R_{\min}^{q,m}$ is the minimum acceptable capacity of the m-th D2D pair in C_q and is set to 0, $R_{q,m}$ is the capacity of the m-th D2D pair in C_q and is calculated based on (2). In our problem, among all possible RB allocation combinations, NBS is to find one whose resulting set of $R_{q,m}$ satisfies (4). Furthermore, in the Nash Bargaining game, the number of Available RBs assigned to the D2D pair is based on the number of RBs it demands. In case of the number of Available RBs allocated to C_q is less than the total number of demanded RBs of the D2D pairs in C_q, the number of Available RBs allocated to each D2D pair in C_q is proportional to the number of RBs it demands.

From Fig. 5, among the four allocated RBs, RB 5 can only be used by D2D pair **b**. In this case, without violating the RB continuity requirement, the NBS, i.e., the solution to (4), is to allocate RBs 5 and 6 to D2D pair **b**, while RBs 7 and 8 to D2D pair **c** as listed in the last row of Fig. 5 under the assumption that the SINRs of RBs 6, 7, and 8 perceived at D2D pairs **b** and **c** are the same.

Table 1. Steps to allocate RB to coalitions.

1: **for** each coalition C_q, $q=1, 2, \cdots$
2:   $I = \bigcap_{i \in C_q} B_i^{RB}$ and $J = \bigcup_{i \in C_q} B_i^{RB}$
3:   K is the set of RBs selected from the largest
4:   consecutive RBs in **I**.
5:   L is the set of RBs selected from the largest
6:   consecutive RBs in **J** that contains **K**.
7:   **if** $|K|=0$
8:     Allocate RBs by greedy algorithm.
9:   **else if** $|K| \geq N_{q,total}^{RB,req}$
10:     Allocate $N_{q,total}^{RB,req}$ RBs from **K**.
11:   **else**
12:     Allocate $|K|$ RBs from **K** and at most
13:     ($N_{q,total}^{RB,req} - |K|$) RBs from **L\K**.
14:   **end if**
15: **end if**
16: **end for**

RB No.	0	1	2	3	4	5	6	7	8	9
CU No.	0	0	0	1	1	1	2	2	2	3
I=K	0	0	0	0	0	0	1	1	1	0
J=L	1	1	1	1	1	1	1	1	1	0
Allocation	0	0	0	0	0	1	1	1	1	0
NBS						b	b	c	c	

Fig. 5. Available RB allocation for C_2.

RB No.	0	1	2	3	4	5	6	7	8	9
CU No.	0	0	0	1	1	1	2	2	2	3
I=K=L	0	0	0	0	0	0	0	0	0	0
J	0	0	0	1	1	1	1	1	1	1
Allocation	0	0	0	e	e	0	0	0	0	d

Fig. 6. Available RB allocation for C_3.

4   Simulation Results

In this simulation, the CUs and D2D pairs are randomly and evenly distributed within the coverage of the considered eNB under the condition that each D2D pair is at least 35 meters away from the eNB [9]. In each simulation run, the positions of D2D pairs and CUs, the number of demanded RBs of each D2D pair, and the channel condition are randomly generated. We assumed the RB allocation cycle, i.e., how long the RB allocation take place, follows the semi-persistent RB scheduling cycle which is usually between 20 ms to 600 ms. In the simulation, $\alpha_{max} = 9$, $\alpha_{min} = 1$, and $SINR_{th}^{RB,D2D} = 30$ dB. The rest of parameter values used in the simulation are listed in Table 2. In Table 2, X is a lognormal random variable with zero mean and standard deviation σ. The presented results are the average of the results collected in 1,000 simulations.

Table 2. Simulation parameters.

Parameter	Value
Cell radius	500 m
Carrier frequency	2 GHz
System bandwidth	10 MHz
Pathloss for D2D link [9]	Max($20\log(d[m]) + 38.44$, $22.7\log(d[m]) + 33.02) + X$, $d \leq 17.06$ Max($20\log(d[m]) + 38.44$, $40\log(d[m]) + 11.73) + X$, $d > 17.06$
Pathloss for cellular link [10]	$22\log(d[m]) + 34.02 + X$, $d \leq 320$ $40\log(d[m]) - 11.02 + X$, $d > 320$
Standard deviation σ	D2D: 7 dB, CU: 4 dB
Transmission power	CU: 23 dBm, D2D: 20 dBm, 23 dBm (default)
Noise spectral density	-174 dBm/Hz
N_C	10
N^{coal}	10
ε	1
dis^{max}	50 m

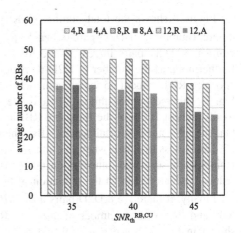

Fig. 7. The average numbers of Reusable (R) and Available (A) RBs for $SNR_{th}^{RB,CU} = 35$, $40 = 35, 40$, and 45 dB and $N_{D2D} = 4, 8$, and 12, respectively.

First, we demonstrate the relationship between $SNR_{th}^{RB,CU}$ and the average numbers of Reusable and Available RBs. In Fig. 7, the average number of Reusable and Available RBs decrease as $SNR_{th}^{RB,CU}$ increases. This is mainly because the condition for a RB to be regarded as a Reusable gets stricter as $SNR_{th}^{RB,CU}$ increases. Besides, we also find the number of D2D pairs has very limited effect on the average number of Reusable RBs. However, due to the increase of the interference as the number of D2D pairs increases, the average number of Available RBs decreases.

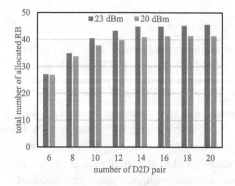
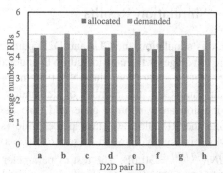

Fig. 8. The total number of allocated RB for different number of D2D pair.

Fig. 9. The average number of demanded and allocated RBs for each D2D pair.

Figure 8 shows the total number of RBs allocated to D2D pairs with respect to different numbers of D2D pairs when $SNR_{th}^{RB,CU}$ = 40 dB. From the figure, when the number of D2D pairs increases, the total number of allocated RBs also increases. Furthermore, as the number of D2D pairs equals or great than 14, the total number of allocated RBs is about 45 which approaches the number of Reusable RBs indicated in Fig. 7. This means that almost all Reusable RBs are allocated to D2D pairs. In other words, almost 100% of the Reusable RBs are reused by the D2D pairs. We also noted that the total number of allocated RBs when the transmission power of D2D pair is 20 dBm is less than that when the transmission power of D2D pair is 23 dBm. This is mainly because as the transmission power is reduced, the SINR of D2D pair is also reduced, which results in the reduction of the number of Available RBs.

Finally, if there are 8 D2D pairs and $SNR_{th}^{RB,CU}$ = 40 dB, the number of demanded RBs and the average number of allocated RBs for each of the eight D2D pairs are shown in Fig. 9. Since α_{max} = 9 and α_{min} = 1, it can be seen from Fig. 9 that the average number of demanded RBs is approximately 5. In other words, the total number of demanded RBs is about 40. But, as shown in Fig. 7, about 35.5 RBs are allocated to the 8 D2D pairs. In this case, as shown in Fig. 9, each D2D pair is proportional fairly to be allocated about 4.4 RBs.

5 Conclusions

To solve the D2D radio resource allocation under the condition of sharing CU uplink RBs, this paper takes the numbers of demanded RBs of D2D pairs into account and uses the total number of demanded RBs in a coalition as the criterion to group D2D pairs into coalitions. By taking the intersection and union of the Available RBs, Available RBs are allocated to coalitions. Furthermore, when needed, the Nash Bargaining Solution is used to further allocate RBs to D2D pairs inside a coalition. Simulation results show that the proposed RB allocation scheme not only almost 100% reuses the Reusable RBs but also allocates Available RBs to D2D pairs inside a coalition in a proportional fairness way.

Acknowledgment. This research was partially supported by the Ministry of Science and Technology of Taiwan under the grant number 104-2221-E-197-003.

References

1. Asadi, A., Wang, Q., Mancuso, V.: A survey on device-to-device communication in cellular networks. IEEE Commun. Surv. Tutor. **16**(4), 1801–1818 (2014)
2. Panaitopol, D., Mouton, C., Lecroart, B., Lair, Y., Delahaye, P.: Recent advances in 3GPP Rel-12 standardization related to D2D and public safety communications. arXiv preprint arXiv:1505.07140 (2015)
3. Feng, D., Lu, L., Yi, Y.-W., Li, G., Feng, G., Li, S.: Device-to-device communications in cellular networks. IEEE Commun. Mag. **52**(4), 49–55 (2014)
4. Han, Z., Ji, Z., Liu, K.J.R.: Fair multiuser channel allocation for OFDMA networks using Nash Bargaining Solutions and coalitions. IEEE Trans. Commun. **53**(8), 1366–1376 (2005)
5. Nash Jr., J.F.: The bargaining problem. Econometrica **18**(2), 155–162 (1950)
6. https://en.wikipedia.org/wiki/Cooperative_game
7. https://en.wikipedia.org/wiki/Coalition
8. Vatsikas, S., Armour, S., De Vos, M., Lewis, T.: A fast and fair algorithm for distributed subcarrier allocation using coalitions and the Nash Bargaining Solution. In: IEEE Vehicular Technology Conference (VTC Fall), pp. 1–5. IEEE Press, New York (2011)
9. 3GPP: 3rd Generation Partnership Project; Technical Specification Group Radio Access Network; Study on LTE Device to device Proximity Services; Radio Aspects (Release 12). TR 36.843 V12.0.0 (2014)
10. 3GPP: 3rd Generation Partnership Project; Technical Specification Group Radio Access Network; Evolved Universal Terrestrial Radio Access (E-UTRA); Further Advancements for E-UTRA Physical Layer Aspects (Release 9). TR 36.814 V9.0.0 (2010)

A Cooperative RBAC-Based IoTs Server with Trust Evaluation Mechanism

Hsing-Chung Chen[1,2(✉)]

[1] Department of Computer Science and Information Engineering,
Asia University, Taichung City, Taiwan
shin8409@ms6.hinet.net
[2] Department of Medical Research, China Medical University Hospital,
China Medical University, Taichung City, Taiwan

Abstract. With the recent advances in ubiquitous communications and the growing demand for low-power wireless technology, smart mobile device (SMD) access various Internet of Things (IoTs) resources through heterogeneous wireless networks (HWNs) at any time and place alternately. There are some new requirements for integrating IoTs servers in which each one is individually gathering its local resources in HWNs, which cooperatively supports SMD to get some flexibility or temporary contract(s) and privileges in order to access their corresponding desired service(s) in a group of collaboration IoTs servers. However, traditional access control schemes designed for a single server are not sufficient to handle such applications across multiple cooperative IoTs servers to get rich services in IoTs environments. It does not take into account both security and efficiency of IoTs servers, which securely share their resources. Therefore, the cooperative IoTs-based RBAC (Role-based Access Control) model with trust evaluation function for reducing internal security threat in the RBAC servers is proposed in this paper, where RBAC is an access control mechanism via managing the users' roles and giving their corresponding access rights. Finally, a cooperative RBAC model with both trust evaluation function and cooperation trust evaluation function is designed and presented for reducing internal security threats in collaborative IoTs servers.

Keywords: Role-based Access Control (RBAC) · Cooperative RBAC
Internet of Things · Trust evaluation

1 Introduction

Due to the development of communication technology among Internet of Things (IoTs) [1, 2] and heterogeneous wireless networks (HWNs), many emerging application services have been developed. These application services include the following features or disadvantages. First, these application services often use Location Based Services (LBS) to provide information to the smart mobile device (SMD). Although LBS services bring huge incomes for the SMD manufacturers, APP (application) software development companies and telecommunication operators, these new application services have suffered a lot of new challenges in access control. Second, some services are accessed by SMD from a remote server in HWNs. It cannot provide handover function

© ICST Institute for Computer Sciences, Social Informatics and Telecommunications Engineering 2018
Y.-B. Lin et al. (Eds.): IoTaaS 2017, LNICST 246, pp. 36–42, 2018.
https://doi.org/10.1007/978-3-030-00410-1_5

in order to get the access rights for continuous access to server. Therefore, leaving the wireless coverage area of the Base Station or AP (Access Point), the SMD which is accessing some services will be interrupted. Furthermore, the SMD logs in to the server with the privileges provided by the original registration server. It can get the privileges to similar servers through the cooperation negotiation mechanism among these servers. Thus, new access control (AC) techniques are required to meet this situations.

At present, AC has been researched for various applications, and there are different AC approaches for different environments. The general RBAC model is one of the AC technologies formally was first proposed by Ferraiolo et al. [3] in 1992. Their model defined that there is a user's assigned a role to access the resources managed by a remote server. The user's access rights should be determined by his assigned role. Each role has its associated set of some individual member(s). The role is the basis component of the RBAC model that categorizes users based on their various properties. The basic model [4–10] of the RBAC as shown in Fig. 1 [10] includes the sets of five basic data elements such as *Users* (U), *Roles* (R), *Objects* (OBJ), *Operations* (OPT) and *Permissions* (P). *Users* are considered to be human beings, machines, networks, smart devices or intelligent agents that could perform some activities. *Roles* are defined as a set of permissions to access the specific resources. *Permissions* are approvals to execute operations on one or more objects. *Operations* are the executions of a specific function that is invocated by a user. *Objects* are entities that contain or receive information, or have exhaustible system resources. Moreover, the basic model of the RBAC is introduced its concept of role activation as part of a user's session within a computer system [3–5, 10]. There are three relations in the traditional RBAC model, which are hierarchical roles relations, static separation of duty relations, and dynamic separation of duty relations. It also provides the user-to-role assignment and permission-to-role assignment functions.

The remainder of this paper is organized as follows: in Sect. 2, we first formalize the cooperative IoTs-based RBAC model. In Sect. 3, we present discussions comparisons, and security analyses. Finally, we draw our conclusions and examine future work in Sect. 4.

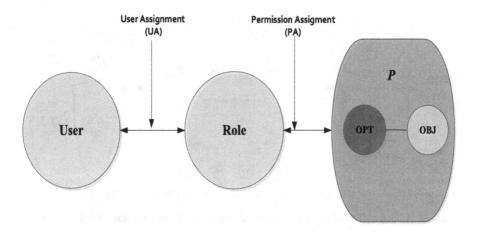

Fig. 1. Basic traditional RBAC model [10].

2   A Cooperative IoTs-Based RBAC Model

In this section, the basic definitions and cooperative IoTs-based RBAC model are formulated in Subsects. 2.1 and 2.2 below.

2.1   Basic Definitions of Cooperative IoTs-Based RBAC Model

The cooperative IoTs-based RBAC model is shown in Fig. 2. The components of the core cooperative IoTs-based RBAC model are illustrated in Fig. 2. They are denoted below. First, the set of SMDs (D, for short), and the results of both trust evaluation as well as cooperation trust evaluation will be recorded for all assignment. Second, the set of trust values T is consisting of local trust evaluation (T_L, for short) and cooperation trust evaluation (T_C, for short). Third, the set of sessions (S, for short). Fourth, the set of roles is denoted as R, where $R = R_L \cup R_V$, R_L is a local role set mapping to a local role hierarchy (LRH) and R_V is a virtual role set mapping to a virtual role hierarchy (LRH). Fifth, the set of permissions is represented as P consisting of a local role set P_L and a virtual role set P_V where and $P = P_L \cup \left(\cup_{x=1,2,...l} P_{V_x} \right) = P_L \cup P_{V_1} \cup P_{V_2} \cup \ldots \cup P_{V_l}$. Sixth, the set of the objects $O = \{O_L \cup O_V\}$ accessed by SMDs is consisting of local IoTs objects (O_L, for short) and virtual IoTs objects (O_V, for short). Moreover, the two major relations of the cooperative IoTs-based RBAC model are also explained in next subsection. First, the smart device assignment (DA) is the smart device-to-role assignment relation consisting of the smart device-to-local role assignment relation (LDA) and the smart device-to-virtual role assignment relation (VDA). Second, the permission assignment (PA) is the role-to-permission assignment consisting of the local role-to-local IoTs objects assignment relation (LPOA) and the virtual role-to-virtual IoTs objects assignment relation (VPOA).

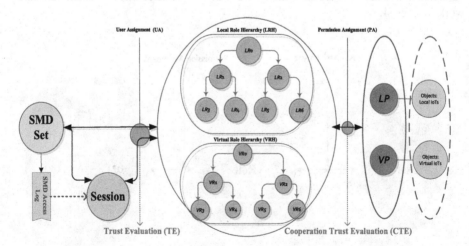

Fig. 2. A cooperative RBAC-based model designed for the architecture of IoTs server.

2.2   Cooperative IoTs-Based RBAC Model

According to the basic explains of the sets: D, O, T, S, R, and P, which are mentioned above, several functions are then given their further definitions in this subsection. The relation function of the smart device assignment DA consisting of the smart device-to-local role assignment relation (LDA) and the smart device-to-virtual role assignment relation (VDA) represents the assignment function based on the success of both SMD trust evaluation function (TE function, for short) and cooperation trust evaluation function (CTE function, for short) from a smart device set D mapping to the roles set $R = R_L \cup R_V$, R_L is a local role set and R_V is a virtual role set. The both trust evaluation functions TE function and CTE function used to associate SMDs with their corresponding trust values calculated by the cooperative trust evaluation (CTE) algorithm in [10]. The permission assignment (PA) represents the assignment of the role-to-permission assignment consisting of the local role-to-local permission (LPA) and the virtual role-to-virtual permission assignment relation (VPA). The permission-to-object assignment consisting of both the local permission-to-local IoTs object assignment relation (LPOA) and the virtual permission-to-virtual IoTs objects assignment relation (VPOA). In addition, the trusted SMD assigned to a single session s ∈ S, which is evaluated by both trust evaluation functions TE function $\gamma l\_trust\ evaluation(\bullet)$ and CTE function $vr\_cooperative\ trust\ evaluation(\bullet)$ representing SMDs associated with this single session s. The detail of the generalization definitions of the cooperative IoTs-based RBAC model are defined and shown in *Definition 1*.

Definition 1: The generalized model of the cooperative IoTs-based RBAC;

- *D, O, T, S, R, and P represent the finite sets of SMDs, the set of objects O accessed by SMDs consisting of O_L and O_V, trust values $T = T_L \odot T_C$ where $\odot$ is the sum operation function inputted by both T_L and T_C, sessions, roles $R \subseteq \{R_L \cup R_V\}$ and permissions P consisting of P_L and P_V plus $P = P_L \cup \left(\bigcup_{x=1,2,\ldots,l} P_{V_x} \right) = P_L \cup P_{V_1} \cup P_{V_2} \cup \ldots \cup P_{V_l}$, which are assigned by the cooperative IoTs-based RBAC model, respectively;*
- *$TE \subseteq D \times T \times O_L \times O_V$, the trust evaluation function that associates SMDs with their corresponding trust values calculated by the CTE algorithm in [10] by cooperative evaluating of their access local IoTs objects O_L and virtual IoTs objects O_V via the co-members in a specific session s ∈ S during the serving time period;*
- *$CTE \subseteq D \times T \times O_V$, the trust evaluation function that associates SMDs with their corresponding trust values calculated by the CTE algorithm in [10] by cooperative evaluating of their access virtual IoTs objects VO via the co-members in a specific session s during the serving time period;*
- *$DA \subseteq D \times T \times R_L \times R_V$, the SMD assignment relation function that associates SMDs with roles available upon the successful SMD's trusted evaluation;*
- *$\gamma_l\_trust\ evaluation(\gamma_l \in R_L) \rightarrow 2^D$, the mapping of a local role γ_l onto a set of trusted SMDs, where the function $\gamma_l\_trust\ evaluation(\bullet)$ is defined as $\gamma_l\_trust\ evaluation(\gamma_l) = \{d \in D | (u_x, \gamma_l) \in DA\}$;*

- $vr\_cooperative\ trust\ evaluation(v\gamma \in R_V) \rightarrow 2^D$, the mapping of a virtual role γ_v onto a set of trusted SMDs, where the function $vr\_cooperative\ trust\ evaluation(\bullet)$ is defined as $\gamma_v\_trust\ evaluation(\gamma_v) = \{d \in D | (u_x, \gamma_v) \in DA\}$;

- The permission assignment (RPA) represents the assignment of the role-to-permission assignment consisting of both local role-to-local permission (LRPA) and the virtual role-to-virtual permission assignment relation (VRPA), where $LRPA \subseteq R_L \times P_L$ represents the local permission assignment relation function that it assigns a local permission p_l to a local role γ_l, and $VRPA \subseteq R_V \times P_V$ represents the virtual permission assignment relation function in which it assigns a virtual permission p_v to a local virtual γ_v;

- The permission-to-object assignment POA consisting of both the local permission-to-local IoTs object assignment relation (LPOA) and the virtual permission-to-virtual IoTs object assignment relation (VPOA), where $LPOA \subseteq P_L \times O_L$ represents the local IoTs object assignment relation function that it assigns a local IoTs object O_l to a local permission p_l, and $VPOA \subseteq P_V \times O_V$ represents the virtual IoTs object assignment relation function in which it assigns a virtual IoTs object O_v to a virtual permission p_v;

- $r\_p\&o(\gamma \in R, (d_x, t_x) \in T) \rightarrow 2^O$, the mapping of a role $\gamma = (\gamma_l, \gamma_v) \in R \subseteq \{R_L \cup R_V\}$ onto a power set of IoTs objects 2^O based on the availability of the trust pair $(d_x, t_x) = TE(d_{x-1}, t_{x-1}) \odot CTE(d_{x-1}, t_{x-1})$, where $O \subseteq \{O_L \cup O_V\}$, $t_x \in T$ and the function $r\_p\&o(\bullet)$ is defined as $r\_p\&o(\gamma \in R, (d_x, t_x)) = \{o \in 2^O | (\gamma(d_x, t_x)), p \in P\} \in RPA \cup POA$;

- $trust\_s(d_x \in D, t_x \in T) \rightarrow 2^S$, where the function $trust\_s(\bullet)$ assigns a trusted SMD onto a set of sessions;

- $s\_r(\varsigma \in S) \rightarrow 2^R$, the mapping of each session ς to a set of roles;

- $s\_rpa\&poa\_trusted\ pair(\varsigma \in S, (d_x, t_x) \in T) \rightarrow 2^O$, a power set of IoTs objects 2^O available only a trust pair $(d_x, t_x) = TE(d_{x-1}, t_{x-1}) \odot CTE(d_{x-1}, t_{x-1})$ for a session s, such as $\bigcup_{\gamma \in s\_rpa\&poa\_trusted\ pair} r\_rpa\&poa(\gamma, (u_x, t_x))$, where $O \subseteq \{O_L \cup O_V\}$.

∎

3 Discussions and Security Analysis

In this section, the features of our cooperative IoTs-based RBAC model are discussed and their corresponding security issues are also analyzed.

1. Two specific roles which are local roles set and virtual roles set are introduced in this cooperative IoTs-based RBAC model. At first, both local roles set and virtual roles set are organized in a hierarchy privileges, individually. Each local role with high privilege could be allowed to access the permissions belonging to the local role with low privilege. In the same way, each local role with high privilege could be allowed to access the permissions belonging to the local role with low privilege. Each local role will be assigned to a local permission which is allowed to access a group of local IoTs coordinators or devices. Similarly, each virtual role will be assigned to a virtual permission which is allowed to access a group of external IoTs

coordinators or devices depending to the contract between serving IoTs-based RBAC server and cooperative IoTs-based RBAC server.

2. There are two trust evaluation functions are defined in this cooperative IoTs-based RBAC model, which are both trust evaluation functions TE function $\gamma_l\_trust\ evaluation(\bullet)$ and CTE function $vr\_cooperative\ trust\ evaluation(\bullet)$ in *Definition* 1. The reputation evaluation for each local role assignment together with the virtual role assignment during a time period or a short session s will be calculated the trust values by the cooperative trust evaluation (CTE) algorithm proposed in [10]. In this model, the strength of the security depends on the robustness of among two trust evaluation functions and the evaluation algorithm [10].

3. For each session, SMD will be assign a local role together with a virtual role. He could access the resources from local IoTs coordinators or devices managed by his serving RBAC server as well as cooperative IoTs coordinators or devices managed by the cooperative RBAC server. All access records consisting of the local records regarding to local IoTs coordinators or devices and the remote access records regarding to virtual IoTs coordinators or devices will be logged in a database. Finally, each assignment of local role and virtual role to a SMD will be logged its trust data evaluated from the serving RBAC server and cooperative RBAC server (s). In the other words, the trusted SMD assigned to a single session s ∈ S, which is evaluated by both trust evaluation functions TE function $\gamma_l\_trust\ evaluation(\bullet)$ and CTE function $vr\_cooperative\ trust\ evaluation(\bullet)$ representing SMDs associated with this single session s.

4   Conclusions

The model we proposed in this paper will provide future mobile e-commerce servers that could be developed with a high potential to exploit an internal security threat that can be developed or can be applied to a multi-server service that could reduce the internal security threat. The research results will provide a new generation of IoTs resources based on cooperative and hierarchical control, and therefore our approach has a very large application field and development space.

Acknowledgements. This work was supported in part by Asia University, Taiwan, and China Medical University Hospital, China Medical University, Taiwan, under Grant ASIA-105-CMUH-04. This work was also supported in part by the Ministry of Science and Technology (MOST), Taiwan, Republic of China, under Grant MOST 104-2221-E-468-002.

References

1. Chen, H.-C., Chang, C.-H., Leu, F.-Y.: Implement of agent with role-based hierarchy access control for secure grouping IoTs. In: The 14th IEEE Annual Consumer Communications & Networking Conference (CCNC), 8–11 January 2017, Las Vegas, USA, pp. 120–125 (2017)
2. Zhong, S., Zhang, L., Chen, H.-C., Zhao, H., Guo, L.: Study of the patterns of automatic car washing in the era of internet of things. In: The 31st IEEE International Conference on Advanced Information Networking and Applications (AINA-2017), 27–29 March 2017, Tamkang University, Taipei, Taiwan, pp. 82–86 (2017)
3. Ferraiolo, D.F., Kuhn, D.R.: Role-based access controls. In: Proceedings of the 15th National Computer Security Conference, 13–16 October 1992, pp. 554–563 (1992)
4. Odelu, V., Das, A.K., Goswami, A.: Scheme for a user hierarchy based on a hybrid algorithm. Smart Comput. Rev. 3(1), 42–54 (2013)
5. Sandhu, R.S., Coyne, E.J., Feinstein, H.L., Youman, C.E.: Role-based access control models. Computer 29, 38–47 (1996)
6. Balamurugan, B., Krishna, P.V.: Enhanced role-based access control for cloud security. Artif. Intell. Evol. Algorithms Eng. Syst. 324, 837–852 (2015)
7. Akl, S.G., Taylor, P.D.: Cryptographic solution to a problem of access control in a hierarchy. ACM Trans. Comput. Syst. 1(3), 239–248 (1983)
8. Ghodosi, H., Pieprzyk, J., Chames, C., Naini, R.S.: Algorithm for hierarchical croups. In: Proceedings of 1'st Security and Privacy Conference, pp. 275–285 (1996)
9. Cao, J., Yao, Z.A.: An improved access control scheme for hierarchical groups. In: Proceedings of the 19th International Conference on Advanced Information Networking and Applications, pp. 719–723 (2005)
10. Chen, H.-C., Hui-Kai, S.: A cooperative trust bit-map routing protocol using the ga algorithm for reducing the damages from the InTs in WANETs. J. Internet Serv. Inf. Secur. (JISIS) 4(4), 52–70 (2014)
11. Chen, H.-C.: TCABRP: a trust-based cooperation authentication bit-map routing protocol against insider security threats in wireless ad hoc networks. IEEE Syst. J. 99, 1–11 (2015). https://doi.org/10.1109/JSYST.2015.2437285
12. Chen, H.-C.: A trusted user-to-role and role-to-key access control scheme. Soft Comput. 1–13 (2015). https://doi.org/10.1007/s00500-015-1715-4

Home Healthcare Matching Service System Using IoT

Tzong-Shyan Lin, Pei-Yu Liu, and Chun-Cheng Lin[(⊠)]

Department of Industrial Engineering and Management,
National Chiao Tung University, Hsinchu 300, Taiwan
{shawn.iem98g, category83531, cclin321}@nctu.edu.tw

Abstract. Home healthcare services enable patients to live in an environment and amongst people they are familiar with while receiving the healthcare they need. However, to provide such an arrangement, readings from healthcare devices need to be read and analyzed on a regular basis to determine healthcare services needed by patients. Then the services that are needed are matched with a limited number of healthcare professionals capable of providing the services needed. In this paper, we present a system we developed to that is capable of meeting the above requirements, but in a manner that enables patients to feel they are in charge of their healthcare while meeting licensing requirements, legal requirements, and travel schedule restrictions of professional healthcare personnel.

Keywords: Home healthcare · Personnel matching

1 Introduction

Home healthcare involves licensed healthcare professionals providing medical treatment or rehabilitation care to patients in their homes [4]. Such arrangements enable patients to live a quality life, in an environment in which they are familiar and comfortable with [2], and amongst friends and family members. It also reduces the burden of on overcrowded healthcare facilities. However, when patients are residing in their homes as opposed to healthcare facilities, healthcare professionals cannot personally monitor the health status of patients as closely as those residing in healthcare facilities normally do. The emergence of IoT technologies enables us to overcome this gap.

IoT enabled healthcare devices is a new category of devices that can transfer readings directly into information systems via communication devices without direct involvement of health professionals. This key factor makes home health care economically viable, the eliminating the need for frequent periodic visits by healthcare professionals to homes of patients just to record the readings of healthcare devices.

Many offsite systems are already available to receive and process the data received from healthcare devices. However, these systems are typically operation at one of the two following extremes. At one extreme, systems provide graphical analysis of the health data received and may suggest patients to seek healthcare if the results of the

© ICST Institute for Computer Sciences, Social Informatics and Telecommunications Engineering 2018
Y.-B. Lin et al. (Eds.): IoTaaS 2017, LNICST 246, pp. 43–49, 2018.
https://doi.org/10.1007/978-3-030-00410-1_6

readings indicate such need. However, patients need to seek proper healthcare services on their own without detailed guidance. At the other extreme, the devices transfers the health data to healthcare institutions directly, if necessary healthcare personnel will contact patients and provide them with instructions on actions that are to follow. The problem with the first extreme is that these systems leave patients on their own to seek proper healthcare services based on the analysis of healthcare data. This may be challenging for many home care patients, especially those suffering from reduced mental capacity. The latter extreme completely bypasses the patient and gives healthcare providers control of the process. Many systems also lack the ability to aggregate the health readings from multiple devices and provide a comprehensive analysis.

To overcome these limitations, we developed a cloud based home healthcare service that directs patients to receive healthcare services from proper medical personnel licensed to perform the service while letting patients remain in control of the healthcare process.

2 Cloud-Based Home Healthcare Service

In this section we describe the cloud based home healthcare service that we developed. We will provide a general description of its operation, and then technical details of each phrase in the operation. Finally, we will provide a detailed use case to further illustrate the operation of the system.

2.1 General Description of Operations

To participate in the cloud based home healthcare service (the cloud), each patient will need to download an app onto his or her smart mobile phone to act as a window of communication with the patient (Fig. 1). Each patient will have supported IoT healthcare devices that connect to the app on the smart mobile phone via Bluetooth Low Energy (BLE). The smart mobile phone should have at least a 3G or higher mobile connection to ensure normal operations. The mobile app relays the data received to the cloud based healthcare service. In addition, the mobile app receives information from the cloud that requires the attention of the patient. Such information include alerts of malfunctioning devices, health situations that warrant attention, and responses to requests for home healthcare services. The patent can also use the mobile app the submit request for home healthcare services.

A patent participating in the cloud based home care service will need to pair each of his or her IoT enabled healthcare devices, such as wearable diabetic glucose patches, heartrate sensors, and pacemaker monitors via the Bluetooth Low Energy (BLE) to the mobile app. The cloud will receive period data readings from these pair devices and issue alerts to the mobile app if updated data readings discontinues for a certain amount of time. The mobile app will then notify the patient of such irregularity. The cloud will also provide updated concise health reports to the patient via the mobile app. If the results of a health report warrant the need for attention from healthcare professionals, the mobile app will notify the patient of the type of healthcare service recommended and offer assistance in scheduling a visit from a healthcare professional with the appropriate license to address the health issue. If the patient accepts the recommendation, the patient will need to enter times he or she is available to receive home healthcare service. The mobile app will relay the request along with the time availability back to the cloud. After receiving the request, the cloud will then attempt to schedule a healthcare professional to visit the patient at the time requested. The cloud will take into consideration factors such as the work hour preferences, licensed specializations of healthcare professionals, travel routes from previous scheduled visit, language requirements of patients, and legal restrictions when scheduling the new visit. The mobile app will notify the patient as to whether his or her request for healthcare service is successful. If the scheduling request is successful, a notification will be sent to the patient to notify him or her that the appointment with the healthcare professional. In cases where the scheduling request have failed, a notification is sent to the patient indicating the failure to schedule an appointment with the healthcare professional.

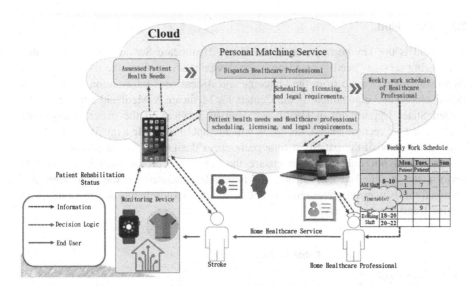

Fig. 1. Operational overview of home healthcare matching service

The matching of health needs of patents and healthcare professionals is achieved by applying the Analytic Hierarchy Process (AHP) [6] and Taguchi Loss Function [5] to select personnel capable of meeting the licensing requirements. Then we apply Genetic Algorithm (GA) [1] to the shortlisted personnel to generate a list of qualified healthcare professionals that are available to perform the necessary services while meeting the legal requirements that determine the maximum hours for each day and the arrangement of workdays. Then the Variable Neighborhood Search (VNS) [3] is applied to analyze the travel routes of qualified healthcare professionals to ensure that the healthcare professional selected to perform the service is capable of traveling to the home of the patient in need from their previous assignment within the time preferences of the patient. In addition, it also ensures the healthcare professional is capable of traveling [7] to the next scheduled assignment on time (that was previously determined and scheduled).

2.2 Mobile App

The mobile app runs on an Android 6.0 based mobile phone. Notification services on the mobile phone are used by the mobile app to alert patients their attention to the app is needed. The mobile phone supports Bluetooth 4.0 so that the Bluetooth Low Energy (BLE) protocol is used to communicate with the IoT healthcare devices. Communication with the cloud is conducted via mobile networks. To ensure smooth performance, a 3G or 4G mobile data connection on the patent's mobile phone is needed to ensure smooth communications with the cloud.

2.3 The Cloud

The cloud is the key component of the Home Healthcare Service. It is responsible discovering service "needs" based on heath device readings from the mobile app and then using logic derived from the Outcome and Assessment Information Set (OASIS) [8] developed and maintained by the Centers for Medicare & Medicaid Services of the United States Department of Health and Human Services. If the patient accepts the "needs" that are recommended, the cloud will attempt to schedule a qualified healthcare professional to visit the patient at time preferences designated by the patient.

The cloud not only needs to ensure the healthcare professional is licensed to perform the qualified tasks, but also the timetable generated for the healthcare professional meets licensing requirements and legal labor requirements as shown below in Tables 1 and 2 respectively.

Table 1. Licensing requirements

#	Licensed tasks
1	General health and wound treatment
2	Insertion and removal of urinary catheter, tracheostomy, and nasogastric tube
3	Operation of urinary catheter, tracheostomy, and nasogastric tube
4	Bladder and intestine irrigation. Bladder training. Collection of urine and stool specimen
5	Rehabilitation care. Sanitary education. Nutrition care
6	Personal care for severely handicapped persons. (Such as dressing, bathing, etc.)
7	Lite housekeeping and meal delivery service

Table 2. Legal Requirements

#	Description of legal requirement
1	Minimum work hours (per month)
2	No more than 8 working hours per day
3	Consists of 2 or more consecutive workdays
4	Consists of 6 or less consecutive workdays

The matching of health needs of patents and healthcare professionals is achieved by first applying the Analytic Hierarchy Process (AHP) to the healthcare requirements and as patient preferences to determine the weight of variables used to select personnel capable of meeting the licensing requirements and satisfying patient preferences. If these requirements and patient preferences include quantitative variables, we apply the Taguchi Loss Function to analyze the quantitative variables. A list of personnel with an acceptable matching score meets licensing requirements. Figure 2 displays a graphic presentation of this process.

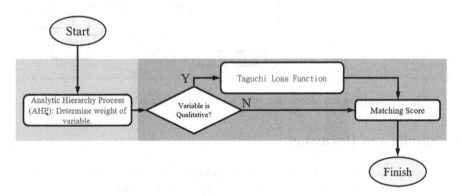

Fig. 2. Process to generate the matching score

Then we apply Genetic Algorithm (GA) (see Fig. 3) to the shortlisted personnel to generate a list of qualified healthcare professionals that are available to perform the necessary services while meeting the legal requirements that determine the maximum hours for each day and the arrangement of workdays.

Next, the Variable Neighborhood Search (VNS) is applied to analyze the travel routes of qualified healthcare professionals to ensure that the healthcare professional selected to perform the service is capable of traveling to the home of the patient in need from their previous assignment within the time preferences of the patient. In addition, it also ensures the healthcare professional is capable of traveling to the next scheduled assignment on time (that was previously determined and scheduled).

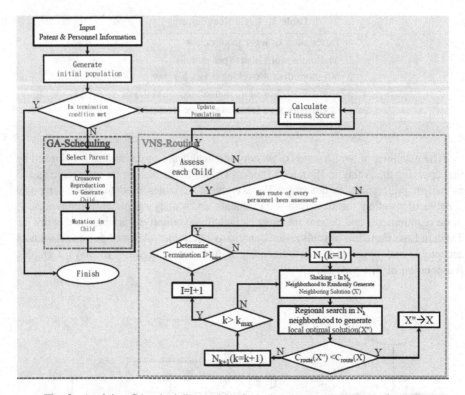

Fig. 3. Applying GA-scheduling and VNS routing to generate personnel match

3   Results and Discussion

In this paper, we demonstrate our service as deployed meets the labor regulations that apply to healthcare personnel. Furthermore, it also schedules healthcare personnel to service locations that can be traveled to in the time allocated. This is critical for actual deployment.

One area in which our service can be improved is the selection of least-cost option when multiple personnel meets all the requirements. Healthcare personnel are usually licensed to perform multiple tasks, however, some are licensed in more categories than others. When assigning personnel to a patient, it would be useful assign the personnel with the least additional licensed categories whenever possible, so that personnel with more additional licensed categories can be saved for future home patient requests, thus reducing the probability not being able to satisfy homecare patent requests in the upcoming days.

4   Conclusion

The Home Healthcare Matching Service demonstrates the feasibility of utilizing IoT healthcare devices in the home to monitor and provide homecare service suggestions that enable patients to be in control. It also successfully addresses another difficult question, which is delivering the actual service to the home of patents. Not only are there logistical limitations, mainly traveling to the homes as scheduled, but also licensing regulations that limit the tasks that each personnel can perform as well as labor regulations on the workhours and days personnel are able to work. These overcoming logistics limitations and complying with regulations is critical deploying such service to home healthcare patients.

References

1. Algethami, H., Pinheiro, R.L., Landa-Silva, D.: A genetic algorithm for a workforce scheduling and routing problem. In: 2016 IEEE Congress on Evolutionary Computation (CEC). IEEE (2016)
2. Darkins, R.A., et al.: Care Coordination/Home Telehealth: the systematic implementation of health informatics, home telehealth, and disease management to support the care of veteran patients with chronic conditions. Telemed. e-Health **14**(10), 1118–1126 (2008)
3. Dhahri, A., Zidi, K., Ghedira, K.: A variable neighborhood search for the vehicle routing problem with time windows and preventive maintenance activities. Electron. Notes Discrete Math. **47**, 229–236 (2015)
4. Gokalp, H., Clarke, M.: Monitoring activities of daily living of the elderly and the potential for its use in telecare and telehealth: a review. Telemed. e-Health **19**(12), 910–923 (2013)
5. Liao, C.-N., Kao, H.-P.: Supplier selection model using Taguchi loss function, analytical hierarchy process and multi-choice goal programming. Comput. Ind. Eng. **58**(4), 571–577 (2010)
6. Saaty, T.L.: The Analytical Hierarchy Process, Planning, Priority. Resource Allocation. RWS Publications, Pittsburgh (1980)
7. Yalçındağ, S., Matta, A., Şahin, E., Shanthikumar, J.G.: The patient assignment problem in home health care: using a data-driven method to estimate the travel times of care givers. Flex. Serv. Manuf. J. **28**(1–2), 304–335 (2016)
8. Outcome and Assessment Information Set (OASIS)—Centers for medicare and medicaid services. https://www.cms.gov/oasis

Medical Internet of Things and Legal Issues Regarding Cybersecurity

Chien-Cheng Chou[1,2(✉)]

[1] Center for General Education, Taipei University of Marine Technology,
No. 150, Sec. 3, BinHai Rd., Danshui Town, New Taipei 25172, Taiwan
gary12081l@gmail.com
[2] Chinese Society of Health Law and Policy, New Taipei, Taiwan

Abstract. The Internet of Things (IOT) raises legal and regulatory challenges, mainly in the area of privacy and security. To the Medical application, IOT controlling/liability are more important to the Cybersecurity. This article will refer certain legal issues regarding privacy and security matters to MIOT, and provide certain updated standards, regulations and protective measures.

Keywords: Telemedicine · MIOT · IOT · Cybersecurity · Privacy

1 Introduction

IOT poses extreme legal and regulatory challenges to the sensitive personal information matters, according to the general legal norms, the sensitive personal information includes medical, psychological, sexual, social, financial, and legal data. The afore-mentioned information also concerns to a universal substance of human rights, i.e. privacy and its security. Nevertheless, although law and technology have long been proposed whether a solution to either ethical, commercial, or political equation is possible, the practice of IOT concerned to Big Data and the Cloud technics, the combination of these three applications is still under-explored in the legal field.

Accordingly, IOT is a combination network of physical devices and many items, mainly refers a network connectivity that enables data collections and exchanges among electronics, software and sensors. MIOT is aforementioned applications to medical matters, which converges medication, medicine and certain physical devices; such applications will transform healthcare into not only less costs and inefficiencies method but also more live savings. Such objects are in accordance with the current healthcare policy majorly concentrated on cost control, increased access and eventual universality, and the quality standards maintenance and enhancement. In other words, healthcare policy tries to reach a triangle of access versus cost versus quality, which leads certain achievements: (1) the care experience improvements, (2) the health populations improvements, and (3) the cost reductions [3]. These achievements are affordable via a pre-patient treatment term, which tends to keep the wellness of people before they become ailing. The strategies are provisions of ones' own care engagement, coordinated care designation, and real-time diagnosing, that keeps people healthy and out of the hospital [1].

© ICST Institute for Computer Sciences, Social Informatics and Telecommunications Engineering 2018
Y.-B. Lin et al. (Eds.): IoTaaS 2017, LNICST 246, pp. 50–53, 2018.
https://doi.org/10.1007/978-3-030-00410-1_7

2 The Challenges Fall into Two Main Categories: Fiscal/Policy and Technology

Since IOT applications refer a network connectivity that enables data collections and exchanges among electronics, software and sensors, MIOT is an adoption of Electronic Health Records (EHRs) in the IOT applications. The adoption seems simple, but had reformed a tradition ink-and-paper medical records managing system. In recent decades, certain the medical records managing system might be digitized because of the events of computer technology, but the managements were mainly kept in a closed system. Data exchanges were established merely upon medical institutions for the purposes of diagnosis and therapy to individual patient [6].

MIOT new data exchange mechanism for EHRs will enable researchers and healthcare providers to share information and reach a macro observation from the EHRs cloud or big data. Since MIOT provided a revolutionary treatment method, certain fiscal, policy and technology issues emerged. In particular, privacy and security will be a major concern in both policy and technology matters.

A huge technical barrier is the state of EHRs data. Although the collection of information is named cloud or data, the collection is actually composed by numbers of silos. Every exchanging individual records between silos and collecting data from different sources also refer to probability of data leakage. However, personal information of medical records and medical treatment is highly sensitive, and is covered by many regulations regarding collecting and usage. To the matters of MIOT, FDA provided a draft guidance, which introduced a variety of privacy-related measures to IOT and wearable technology.

3 Legal Issues to MIOT

In 2015, the US FDA (Food and Drug Administration) issued and updated the guidance document to inform associated manufacturers, distributors, and other entities about the possible MIOT applications to the regulatory authorities [4]. In other words, the document provided an expansion applicability of mobile apps that would be concluded into FDA's jurisdiction.

The U.S. Department of Health and Human Services (HHS) issued the HIPAA Privacy Rule to enforce HIPAA requirement. The Privacy Rule addresses the use and disclosure of the health information for individuals by covered entities subject to the Rule. It also creates a standard for individual privacy rights to control and understand how their health information is used. To the matters of privacy and security, certain MIOT devices are addressed to comply the HIPAA (Health Insurance Portability and Accountability Act) requirements.

"Connectors: applications that connect smartphones and tablets to FDA- regulated devices, thus amplifying the devices' functionalities."
"Replicators: applications that turn a smartphone or tablet itself into a medical device by replicating the functionality of an FDA-regulated device."

"Automators and customizers: apps that use questionnaires, algorithms, formulas, medical calculators, or other software parameters to aid clinical decisions."

"Informers and educators: medical reference texts and educational apps that primarily aim to inform and educate."

"Administrators: apps that automate office functions, like identifying appropriate insurance billing codes or scheduling patient appointments."

"Loggers and trackers: apps that allow users to log, record, and make decisions about their general health and wellness [7]."

The HIPAA compliance included four main requirements.

Administrative Safeguards: ...to ensure the proper employee management, training and oversight for staff that come into contact or manage protected health information.

Technical Safeguards: ...technical measures manage providers, including encryption and decryption systems, audit controls, emergency access procedures.

Physical Safeguards: ...physical measures around the security of the data, including data redundancy and failure requirements.

The HIPAA is a series of privacy regulations that requires health care providers and organizations to develop and follow procedures that ensure the confidentiality and security of protected health information (PHI). The HIPPA regulations also applies to the associated business entities. Therefore, the way PHI transferring, receiving, handling, or sharing are covered. The forms of PHI include paper, oral, and electronic, etc.

Therefore, under the requirement of both MITO guidance and HIPPA, manufacturers of mobile medical apps are subject to a network of privacy standards and are required to follow associated controls established by the regulations.

4 Conclusions

MIOT applications are seen as new realms, and are expected with remarkable benefits to the markets. On the other hand, privacy and security-related challenges are also considerable to the MIOT practices. Profound benefits will be brought by new technologies, but the preemptive policy interventions will also limit new innovation opportunities. To the lawmakers point of view: "It's always better to legislate in anticipation of problems being created, but sometimes it actually takes the event to have occurred, which triggers the political outrage that then makes it possible to legislate.[1]"

To the challenges raised by MIOT developments, the authorities should not turn a blind eye, because these technologies involve to consumers' lives and more careful consideration and constructive solutions to the social warfare. The major task will be a balance striking between approach to privacy and security concerns and economic and social innovation.

---

[1] By Sen. Ed Markey in the US Congress, Darren Samuelsohn, What Washington really knows about the Internet of Things (06/29/2015) http://www.politico.com/agenda/story/2015/06/internet-of-things-caucus-legislation-regulation-000086.

References

1. Affordable Care Act Patient Protection and Affordable Care Act § 2712(a), Pub. L. No. 111–148, 124 Stat. 119 (2010)
2. Bauer, H., Patel, M., Veira, J.: The Internet of Things: Sizing Up the Opportunity [Internet] McKinsey & Company, New York; c2016 [cited at 2016 Jul 1]. http://www.mckinsey.com/industries/high-tech/our-insights/the-internet-of-things-sizing-up-the-opportunity
3. Berwick, D.M., Nolan, T.W., Whittington, J.: The Triple Aim: Care, Health, and Cost, 27 HEALTH AFF. 759, 759 (2008). http://content.healthaffairs.org/content/27/3/759.full.pdf
4. FDA, Mobile Medical Applications, Guidance for Industry and Food and Drug Administration Staff. https://www.fda.gov/MedicalDevices/DigitalHealth/MobileMedicalApplications/ucm255978.htm
5. Flores, M., Glusman, G., Brogaard, K., Price, N.D., Hood, L.: P4 medicine: how systems medicine will transform the healthcare sector and society. Per Med. **10**(6), 565–576 (2013). [PMC free article] [PubMed]
6. Kruse, C.S., Kothman, K., Anerobi, K., Abanaka, L.: Adoption factors of the electronic health record: a systematic review. JMIR Med. Inform. **4**(2), e19 (2016). [PMC free article] [PubMed]
7. Cortez, N.: The Mobile Health Revolution? 47 U.C. Davis L. Rev. 1181, April 2014
8. Scheen, A.J.: Precision medicine: the future in diabetes care? Diabetes Res. Clin. Pract. **117**, 12–21 (2016). [PubMed]
9. van Leeuwen, N., Swen, J.J., Guchelaar, H.J., 't Hart, L.M.: The role of pharmacogenetics in drug disposition and response of oral glucose-lowering drugs. Clin. Pharmacokinet. **52**(10), 833–854 (2013). [PubMed]
10. Zanella, A., Bui, N., Castellani, A., Vangelista, L., Zorzi, M.: Internet of things for smart cities. IEEE Internet Things J. **1**(1), 22–32 (2014)

Fuzzy-Based Protocol for Secure Remote Diagnosis of IoT Devices in 5G Networks

Vishal Sharma[1], Jiyoon Kim[1], Soonhyun Kwon[1], Ilsun You[1(✉)],
and Hsing-Chung Chen[2]

[1] Department of Information Security Engineering, Soonchunhyang University,
Asan-si 31538, Republic of Korea
vishal_sharma2012@hotmail.com, 74jykim@gmail.com,tnsgus08@gmail.com,
ilsunu@gmail.com
[2] Asia University, Taichung, Taiwan
cdma2000@asia.edu.tw

Abstract. Internet of things (IoT) aims at connecting a large number of devices for supporting "Connectivity to All" in the 5G networks. With connections between the majority of computing devices, capturing a single entity can expose the perimeter of the entire network. Remote diagnosis of the IoT devices can help in identification of such loopholes. However, if an intruder is already present in the network, it can falsify the diagnostic procedures and can cause serious threats to the network. Thus, an efficient strategy is required which can provide remote diagnosis along with the secure validation of IoT devices. In this paper, fuzzy logic is used to resolve the safety decisions and remote diagnosis of IoT devices in 5G networks. The proposed solution uses a two-pass methodology to generate inference rules at the central as well as the local inference engine. The proposed approach evaluates the network in two phases. The first phase emphasizes on the remote diagnosis and the second phase emphasizes on the remote validation. On the basis of these phases, a remote assessment protocol is also proposed which helps in remote validations with lower overheads and ease of deployment.

Keywords: IoT · Fuzzy · Security · Remote-diagnosis · 5G

1 Introduction

The modern era has changed every entity into a computing object making a way for connecting a billion of devices as predicted for 2020 [1,2]. With the aim of "Connectivity to All", Internet of Things (IoT) has emerged victorious in defining new rules and standards for the exchange of services between the network entities. IoT is seen as a next big market for computing as it provides control over every day's activity [3,4]. IoT supports connectivity of our daily usage objects and entities via a common network. This allows easy access to information as well as control over the connected devices. The management of

© ICST Institute for Computer Sciences, Social Informatics and Telecommunications Engineering 2018
Y.-B. Lin et al. (Eds.): IoTaaS 2017, LNICST 246, pp. 54–63, 2018.
https://doi.org/10.1007/978-3-030-00410-1_8

network has been facilitated by IoT. IoT has enabled to access data without any excessive burden on a single computing entity. It also reduces the time and cost involved in the evaluation of acquired data. Supply chain maintenance, information gathering, remote monitoring are some of the key advantages of IoT networks [5–7].

Despite a large number of advantages of IoT networks, there are certain challenges and issues associated with their actual operations and deployments. The middleware which connects different IoT devices needs to be compatible with every entity in the network. A non-compatible middleware may cause re-planning of the entire network. Further, the incompatible units in IoT directly influence the cost of operation as well as the deployment complexities. Another major issue is the mode of communication and standards to be used for all the types of information flows. The standard may vary, but the underlying hardware should be operable without any change in the type of media and information. Privacy of data and security are the other requirements of services over IoT networks. Overcoming these issues allows the development of a highly robust, fault-tolerant and stable network without much complexity as well as cost [8,9].

IoT devices are used to make different applications and information seeking solutions. However, one crucial issue which is generally not considered is the evaluation of the IoT devices. Every IoT device in a network requires periodic updates in operations and firmware [10]. The introduction of the new security measures is often required in these types of network. All these procedures are subject to the level of information about the IoT device. The information regarding the functionalities of every device can be obtained using remote diagnosis. Remote evaluation of IoT nodes helps in identification of the state of operations as well as the working conditions. However, remote diagnosis procedures are always under the threat of attackers as a control over a single IoT device may open the perimeter of the entire network. Misleading information regarding the state of IoT device makes the network vulnerable to various types of attack. Thus, remote diagnosis needs to be secure and validated to protect the network from any attacker.

Remote diagnosis can be secured by using the security protocols for IoT devices. Some of the key security solutions which can be extended for securing the remote diagnosis of IoT networks include lightweight security protocols by Lee et al. [11] and Raza et al. [12], two-way authentication by Kothmayr et al. [13]. Remote monitoring solutions which are usually used for medical purposes can be altered to check the functionality of IoT devices [14]. Deployment of various intrusion detection systems can also be considered for securing the remote diagnosis of IoT devices. Although all such solutions can be efficient, these will surely increase the overheads because of excessive computational burden.

Modern day IoT devices are small and have limited resources; also these are operated over the same channel which is used for other communication activities. Thus, the solution for remote diagnosis needs to adopt the similar policies and should not cause excessive overheads while analyzing the IoT devices. Thus, aiming at such requirement, a fuzzy-based secure assessment protocol is proposed in this paper. The proposed protocol utilizes the two-pass aspect-oriented fuzzy inference system, one for the remote diagnosis and the other for remote validation. The success of the proposed approach lies in its low-complex and less overhead solution for analyzing any IoT devices considering its properties irrespective of the type of connectivity between them.

2   Problem Definition

Connections between large numbers of computing devices are highly sensitive, time bound and vulnerable to various types of threats. To make the network function all the time without fail, it is necessary to diagnose its devices for any threat and fault. However, the identification procedures and diagnosis strategies need to be secure to prevent any intruder from falsifying the exact state of IoT devices. Wrong information about the devices may cause the analyzing node to see a correct network even in the presence of a faults or threats. This problem can be worst in the presence of a large number of devices as it becomes extensively slower to identify every potential threat on the IoT device. There is a requirement of efficient solutions which are low-complex and can be used to securely diagnose every device in the network without fail as well as with lower computational overheads.

3   Network Model

The proposed approach utilizes the core components of the standard 5G network which comprises a core node, controlling switches, multiple hubs, terminals, and Access Points (APs). The standard 5G-IoT network emphasizes on providing services to IoT devices either by a direct connection between the near APs or via a Home Gateway (HGW). The network further comprises Mobile Nodes (MNs) that opt for diagnosing the particular IoT device remotely. The proposed approach does not alter the actual architecture of the 5G networks, rather it uses a fuzzy support system on all the crucial nodes as shown in Fig. 1. The fuzzy inference engines are deployed on all the hubs that conduct fuzzy-based layoffs with both the MN and the IoT devices via APs or HGW. A local fuzzy inference engine can also be deployed on the HGW. However, this is an optional validation procedure which may enhance the security but may also cause much latency. A heavy functionality-based fuzzy inference evaluator is also deployed on the core node of the 5G network. This is also termed as the validation server. This server comes in operation only when the validation of the fuzzy rules is to be conducted for any MN or the IoT device.

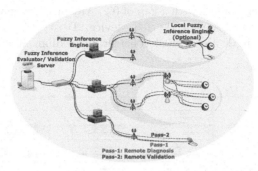

Fig. 1. An illustration of the fuzzy-based 5G architecture considered in the proposed solution.

4 Proposed Approach

The proposed approach uses two-pass fuzzy inference system as shown in the network model. The proposed approach relies on the decision taken by the fuzzy inference engine operable at each hub and validates the decisions periodically by using the IoT-context over the validation server. The fuzzy inference system over each hub operates over three main parameters, namely, trust score, content pattern, and connection strength. All these parameters are calculated for every instance of an IoT device and the output from the fuzzy inference system helps in confirming the safety level of an IoT device. The details of these parameters are as follows:

- Trust Score: It is calculated as the ratio of the total connections made by an IoT device to a legitimate entity in the network to the total legitimate connections available in the network. This parameter helps in identification of the current role and relation of each IoT device with every connectable entity in the network. A higher value means a node is known to multiple legitimate entities and is safe to operate.
- Content Pattern: It is calculated as the ratio of the total incoming requests from an IoT device to the permissible incoming requests. This helps to check if the device is falsifying the traffic or not. A lower value refers to the safe state and a higher value means a possible threat.
- Connection Strength: It is evaluated in the context of the reliability of an IoT device and is defined as the ratio of the total responses made by an IoT device in lieu of the total requests made by the server. A higher value refers to safe operations and a lower value identifies a potential threat.

The fuzzy inference rules operable at each hub for every IoT device are shown in Fig. 2. The figure shows a threat state with a safety value extremely lower at 0.2 for a higher content pattern value and lower trust score and connection strength. The output (Safety) is defined for threat, vulnerability, possible threat, borderline, and safe states. Each of these outputs is set on low, medium and high ranging between 0 and 1 with a gap of 0.2. Any property generating output above 0.6 is treated as safe for the IoT device. Trust score, content pattern and connection strength are defined considering medium at 0.5, 0.5 and 0.6, respectively.

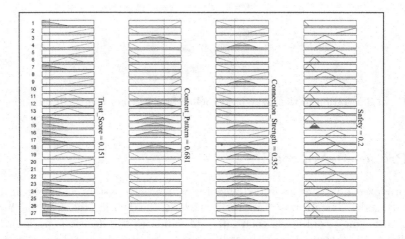

Fig. 2. An illustration of the fuzzy rules for threat decision.

4.1 Remote Diagnosis and Validation

In the proposed solution, the intermediate hub equipped with fuzzy inference servers allows checking the safety level of each device. This helps MN to believe in the report sent by an IoT device or not. The remote diagnosis process operates in parallel operation. The first operation is when an MN demands the information from a device about its working status. The second operation is when the hub identifies the IoT device from where the information is sought and computes its safety level. Once acquired, the hub shares the information with the MN to conclude the diagnosis operations. Also, the hub sends the information directly to the core server in the case of extremely low safety level for an IoT device. This initiates the remote validation procedures in the entire network. The evaluator is invoked when a hub encounters any IoT device with extremely low safety level as per the initial evaluations of the fuzzy system. The invoked evaluator determines the level of threat and alerts the corresponding entities about the status of harmful IoT device. The validation procedure is accompanied by the diagnosis steps, and thus, uses a separate pass for evaluation. The steps for remote validation after diagnosis are:

– The proposed approach uses a content to content matching procedure to identify potential threats. The key parameters used by the validation procedure
  include device-ID, type of device, energy consumption, usage, connections

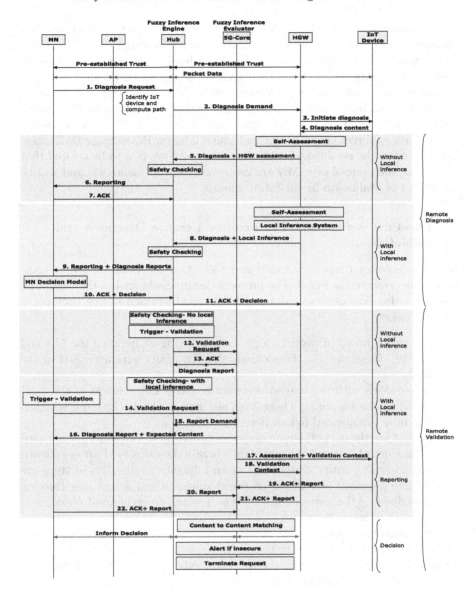

Fig. 3. Two-pass assessment protocol for remote diagnosis and validation.

supported, data rate, firmware, and registration number. Considering these parameters, the core of network maintains a corpus of this information which contains the details of every legal entity and updates it in coordination with the hub. The hub sends the periodic updates to the core for the details of IoT devices. Also, once an IoT validation request is received by the validation server, it also fetches the similar contents to verify its correctness.

- The validation server takes into account the information from both the MN as well as the IoT devices. The validation server analyzes the frequency of variations in the content and checks for threat level to other devices. Once the content matching is performed, the validation server generates alert messages to every hub which informs the corresponding MN. This helps MN in taking a decision for on-site evaluations. For further confirmations, a local inference engine can be used on the gateways as shown in Fig. 2. The local inference engine allows direct decisions without much latency. However, in such cases, trust needs to be established with the gateways. Also, it is to be noticed that the trust and control over MN are not considered in this article and will be a subject of evaluation in our future reports.

4.2   Two-Pass Assessment Protocol for Remote Diagnosis and Validation

The procedures for remote diagnosis and validation are performed as a security routine presented in Fig. 3. The protocol clearly distinguishes the validation phase from the diagnosis procedures. The detailed working of the protocol is explained below:

- The proposed protocol assumes a pre-established trust between the MN and the HGW. This trust can be secured once the entity gets activated in the network.
- Steps 1–4 deals with the diagnosis demands and is independent of the diagnosis and validation phase. These steps are used to obtain the required information from a requested IoT device.
- Steps 5–11 are the part of remote diagnosis procedures. The steps 5–7 are used in the absence of local inference system whereas the steps 8–11 are used when a local governing entity is deployed as an inference engine. These steps are the remote diagnosis pass of the proposed approach and do not uses the core as prescribed in the network model. The reports are generated on-demand irrespective of the validation.
- Next, the protocol operates for its second pass which is termed as the remote validation. Steps 12–16 are the governing rules for validation procedures and steps 17–22 are used to obtain the necessary validation context and diagnosis reports for taking final decisions.

5   Performance Case Study

In order to understand the operational activities of the proposed approach, a performance case study is conducted to analyze its operations in terms of the deployment and overheads. The details of the performance case study are presented below:

- **Deployment:** The proposed approach can be deployed as a stand-alone solution as well as a server-inhabitant solution along with the other facilities of the network such as route selection, load balancing, resource allocation, etc. The proposed approach depends on the installation of fuzzy inference systems on the key entities of the network. This installation is software assisted and algorithmic thus requires normal computational resources and no excessive network nodes. In a network, where cost and latency are not an issue, and security is a primary aspect, separate servers can be used to deploy the inference systems. However, such deployment provides deep security but at the cost of excessive computations.

- **Overheads:** The success of any approach depends on the overheads caused by it during the regular network operations. The proposed approach with its two pass facility is capable of managing the IoT networks efficiently without leveraging excess computational burden on its entities. The overheads of the proposed approach are evaluated in terms of cost of operations and response time.

  - **Cost of operations:** It identifies the run-time complexities and the number of computations required by both the diagnoses and the validation passes. The complexity of the fuzzy inference system for the remote diagnosis depends on the number of combination and the number of inputs considered for generating the safety outputs. The proposed approach utilizes three variables as an input each with three possible states, thus, the fuzzy part of the proposed approach is operable in constant time, which does not yield much complexity. The number of times an entity requests the reports from the other entities depends on the timestamp and the intermediate nodes for both diagnosis and validation procedures. Thus, the run-time complexities are the function of the number of hops and the timestamp. Small periodic updates will increase the cost of operation as well as the number of computations associated with each pass. Since the proposed approach utilizes only single-pass validation, the cost of operation is extremely low and depends only on the number of entities involved in operations.

  - **Response time:** It is the time taken by the proposed approach for deciding the safety of a particular IoT device. Without the involvement of core, the response time will depend on the time consumed in generating the fuzzy rules, inference decision, and the message exchanges. Since the fuzzy rules are defined during the initial setup of the network, the overall response time for diagnosis depends only on the inference decision and the message exchange time. However, the diagnosis time is much affected if the approach accounts for local validation along with the central validation in its second phase. In the case of local validation, the response time increases with a scale of the number of such units installed in the network. In general operations, the proposed approach is highly suitable for scenarios with pre-registered context with the core server that maintains the device-corpus for validation.

6   Conclusion

In this paper, a scenario of remote diagnosis of IoT devices along with its validation in 5G networks was considered. The proposed approach allowed identification of the safety levels of any IoT device as per the requirement of a mobile node. The proposed solution used two-pass aspect-oriented fuzzy logic to generate inference rules at the central as well as a local inference engine. These fuzzy rules helped in identification of the safety levels of an IoT device. The proposed approach evaluated the network in two phases. The first phase emphasized on the remote diagnosis and the second phase emphasized on the remote validation. On the basis of these phases, a remote assessment protocol was also proposed which helped in remote diagnosis and validation with lower overheads and ease deployment. The details of actual implementation and evaluations in the real-time with variant attacker environments will be presented in the future reports.

References

1. MacGillivray, C., Turner, V.: Worldwide internet of things forecast, 2015–2020, May 2015. http://www.idc.com/getdoc.jsp
2. Sharma, V., You, I., Kumar, R.: ISMA: intelligent sensing model for anomalies detection in cross platform osns with a case study on IOT. IEEE Access **5**, 3284–3301 (2017)
3. Sharma, V., Lim, J.D., Kim, J.N., You, I.: SACA: self-aware communication architecture for IOT using mobile fog servers. Mob. Inf. Syst. **2017**, 1–17 (2017)
4. Kumar, R., Sharma, V., Kaur, R.: UAVs assisted content-based sensor search in the Internet of Things. Electron. Lett. (2017). https://doi.org/10.1049/el.2016.3487
5. Skarlat, O., Schulte, S., Borkowski, M., Leitner, P.: Resource provisioning for IOT services in the Fog. In: 2016 IEEE 9th International Conference on Service-Oriented Computing and Applications (SOCA), pp. 32–39. IEEE (2016)
6. Aram, S., Shirvani, R.A., Pasero, E.G., Chouikha, M.F.: Implantable medical devices; networking security survey. J. Internet Serv. Inf. Secur. (JISIS) **6**, 40–60 (2016)
7. Jiang, X., Ge, X., Yu, J., Kong, F., Cheng, X., Hao, R.: An efficient symmetric searchable encryption scheme for cloud storage. J. Internet Serv. Inf. Secur. (JISIS) **7**, 1–18 (2017)
8. Sbeyti, H., Malli, M., Al-Tahat, K., Fadlallah, A., Youssef, M.: Scalable extensible middleware framework for context-aware mobile applications (SCAMMP). J. Wirel. Mob. Netw. Ubiquitous Comput. Depend. Appl. (JoWUA) **7**, 77–98 (2016)
9. Baiardi, F., Tonelli, F., Isoni, L.: Application vulnerabilities in risk assessment and management. J. Wirel. Mob. Netw. Ubiquitous Comput. Depend. Appl. (JoWUA) **7**, 41–59 (2016)
10. Hernández-Ramos, J.L., Jara, A.J., Marin, L., Skarmeta, A.F.: Distributed capability-based access control for the Internet of Things. J. Internet Serv. Inf. Secur. (JISIS) **3**(3/4), 1–16 (2013)
11. Lee, J.-Y., Lin, W.-C., Huang, Y.-H.: A lightweight authentication protocol for internet of things. In: 2014 International Symposium on Next-Generation Electronics (ISNE), pp. 1–2. IEEE (2014)

12. Raza, S., Shafagh, H., Hewage, K., Hummen, R., Voigt, T.: Lithe: lightweight secure coap for the Internet of Things. IEEE Sens. J. **13**(10), 3711–3720 (2013)
13. Kothmayr, T., Schmitt, C., Hu, W., Brünig, M., Carle, G.: DTLS based security and two-way authentication for the Internet of Things. Ad Hoc Netw. **11**(8), 2710–2723 (2013)
14. Jara, A.J., Zamora-Izquierdo, M.A., Skarmeta, A.F.: Interconnection framework for mhealth and remote monitoring based on the Internet of Things. IEEE J. Sel. Areas Commun. **31**(9), 47–65 (2013)

An Overview of 802.21a-2012 and Its Incorporation into IoT-Fog Networks Using Osmotic Framework

Vishal Sharma[1], Jiyoon Kim[1], Soonhyun Kwon[1], Ilsun You[1(✉)], and Fang-Yie Leu[2]

[1] Department of Information Security Engineering, Soonchunhyang University, Asan-si 31538, Republic of Korea
vishal_sharma2012@hotmail.com, 74jykim@gmail.com, tnsgus08@gmail.com, ilsunu@gmail.com
[2] Computer Science Department, ThungHai University, Taichung City 407, Taiwan
leufy@thu.edu.tw

Abstract. The increase in the number of devices has caused a major issue for the service providers to support the users irrespective of the type of services demanded by them. With the advent of fog computing, a near user evaluation site is available that can lower the burden on the core network by providing cloud-like services to the users. However, handling multiple IoT devices near-site requires fast and media independent handovers. This paper incorporates $802.21a\text{-}2012^{TM}$ into the fog network by overcoming the trust requirement and pre-registration policies of this standard using osmotic computing. The proposed framework uses an Osmotic Absorption Key (OAK) to control the handoffs between the fog layers. The proposed solution is highly flexible and inexpensive in terms of implementation cost for handling handoffs of dynamic IoT devices in Fog networks.

Keywords: Fog computing · Osmotic computing · MIH · Handovers

1 Introduction

Connecting billions of devices is not an easy task because of the difference in the make and configuration of each device. Internet of Things (IoT) aims at bridging the gap between the devices allowing them to help our everyday operations. With the number of devices increasing exponentially, it becomes important to reduce the gap between the center of operations and the requesting equipment. Fog computing, as stated by CISCO, is a unique solution for reducing the gap between the requesting device and the service providers by facilitating near-user computing [1].

The concept of fog computing has enhanced the implementation and maintenance of IoT devices. Fog computing is a self-sufficient mini-cloud near the user

© ICST Institute for Computer Sciences, Social Informatics and Telecommunications Engineering 2018
Y.-B. Lin et al. (Eds.): IoTaaS 2017, LNICST 246, pp. 64–72, 2018.
https://doi.org/10.1007/978-3-030-00410-1_9

with similar facilities as that of public/private cloud for computational offloading [2]. Fogging although reduces the level of data which is shifted towards the main hub or the public cloud, yet has some complexities associated with its fully-functional deployments because of complex cloud infrastructure [3–7]. With a large number of users transmitting over the fog layers, it is evident that the number of handoffs will be very high, which needs to be tackled efficiently without leveraging excessive computational burden on the fog servers [8,9]. Further, this problem becomes severe due to the difference in the type of IoT devices, which demands handoffs between the different fog setups.

Handoffs between different media can be tackled by the use of Media Independent Handoffs (MIH) IEEE 802.21 [10]. This standard allows easy transitions between the devices operating with different media across the Point of Attachments (PoA). However, 802.21 MIH cannot assure the security during handoffs, which is extended in its lateral version under the name IEEE 802.21a [11]. Although 802.21a is efficient in providing secure MIH, yet is suffers from a disadvantage of requiring one legal network entity to support pre-established trust for every Mobile Node (MN). Also, the execution time for the handovers is high in extremely dynamic networks. In this paper, osmotic computing is considered as a solution which operates with the push key operations of the 802.21a to support unbundled media access proactive authentication. Three different handover scenarios are presented between the MN and the mobile PoA. The proposed osmotic framework provides key absorption strategy and uses an Osmotic Absorption Key (OAK) to control the handoffs between the fog layers.

2   Background to MIH Standards

This section presents an overview of 802.21 MIH and a detailed functionality of 802.21a-2012^{TM}.

2.1   802.21 MIH

Focusing on the need for seamless and media independent handovers, IEEE 802.21 standard was proposed by the internet work group. The work group for 802.21 readily resolved the issues which existed in IEEE 802.11 and 802.16 to support handoffs at high transmission rates with lower latency. 802.21 is based on the context of an MN and all other components are obtained on the basis of their relationship with the corresponding MN [12,13]. 802.21 uses a variety of service triggers to perform handoffs which include, link-up, link-down, rollback, and a handover complete, etc. All these events are triggered using MIH_SAP command. The command services are the controlling units which define the handoff policies to support MIH. Three different services are defined in MIH, namely, Information Services (MIIS), Event Services (MIES) and Command Services (MICS). The other details on the standard MIH framework can be obtained from Refs. [10,12] and [13].

2.2   802.21a-2012^{TM}

Despite being efficient, the 802.21 is unable to provide any security mechanisms during handovers. Also, it does not consider the authentication mechanism between the MNs, PoA, and Point of Service (PoS). A variant of this standard was proposed to support the security over 802.21 with an extended name of 802.21a-2012^{TM} [11,14,15]. The new variant is capable of providing enhanced security during handoffs by defining new functions for MIH and new MIH messages. IEEE 802.21a standard focuses on providing service access security and proactive authentication in two different passes. The first pass regulates the service authentication and the second pass controls the proactive authentication and key management. With an addition of new services, this standard is capable of reducing the latency issues of earlier standards. An illustration of service authentication and proactive authentication for this standard is presented in Fig. 1(a). The PoAs are the media independent entities which are operable using different communication standards but served by a common PoS. Once an MN moves across the network, the PoS provides the handover support by overcoming the media-dependent issues allowing both services as well as proactive authentication to the requesting MN. However, there exists a gap in this standard as the source PoS is unaware of the target PoA (tPoA), which may allow loopback attacks on the network.

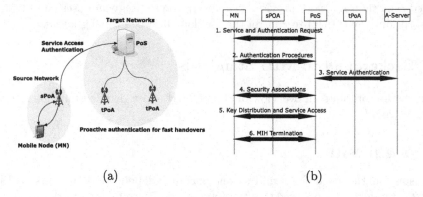

(a)   (b)

Fig. 1. (a) Service assessment and proactive authentication for 802.21a-2012^{TM}. (b) EAP-based service protection in 802.21a-2012^{TM} [11,14].

802.21a-Service Authentication. The service security in MIH is provided either by using Transport Layer Security-based MIH or by Extensible Authentication Protocol (EAP)-based MIH. The choice of two depends on the application scenario and registration policies of MN. However, as stated in the initial draft of 802.21a, EAP-based authentication is considered for general authentication as most of the current scenarios operate on a pre-established trust over the MN.

– TLS-based Service Protection: This approach allows protected transport layer sessions for securing the MIH service messages. The security is driven by a

Master Session Key (MSK) by using a three field packet data unit. MSK is the key role player between the MN and the PoS whereas PoA has the least significant role in supporting the MN message authentication.

- EAP-based Service Protection: This approach is suitable for the scenarios where the authentication server maintains the trust of an MN with the underlying infrastructure. EAP-service authentication can be used by considering any of the existing mechanisms for service protection. In the standard 802.21a, basic EAP is used to protect the MIH services as shown in Fig. 1(b). The first step generates the service request and indicates the PoS for authentication. The second step controls the authentication phase between the MN and the PoS. The third step controls the authentication between the authentication server and the PoS. The fourth step handles the security associations. The fifth step handles the access phase for acquiring the requested services and finally, the sixth step terminates the MIH procedures [14].

802.21a-Proactive Authentication. The proactive authentication for the MIH-802.21a is provided either as an unbundled media access proactive authentication or as a bundled media access proactive authentication.

- Unbundled proactive authentication: This authentication procedure utilizes the media specific authentication by forming a tunnel between the communicating entities. The unbundled authentication can be significant in the scenarios that have a large number of MNs which are not pre-registered with the authentication server or the specific trust management entity of the network. However, the utility of unbundled proactive authentication in such scenarios requires further extension in the 802.21a standard as the requesting MN needs to be authenticated over a secure channel between the source PoS and the tPoA. Currently, such support is not provided by this standard [11,14,15].
- Bundled proactive authentication: This authentication procedure is suitable for the scenarios with a pre-established trust for every MN. Thus, considering this property, the bundled proactive authentication utilizes the EAP-based service protection in combination with the key generation operations to support proactive authentication in MIH framework. The success of security depends on the types of application and key operations used for generating the security keys. In general cases, bundled operations use Media Specific Root Key and Media Specific Pairwise Master Key along with pull or push operations [11,14].

802.21a-Key Management. Key management in 802.21a is provided by three different approaches, namely, push key, reactive pull key and optimized proactive pull key distributions. The choice of approach depends on the application scenario and type of connectivity between the PoA and the PoS. Push key and reactive pull key are used for EAP-based scenarios with reactive pull key providing a faster authentication. Optimized proactive pull key is used in the scenarios where no proactive trust exists between the entities involved in the handovers.

3   Problem Statement and Our Contribution

With the advent of security over MIH standards (802.21a), it becomes relatively easier to provide handover solutions to the mobile fog users. However, despite the capabilities of 802.21a-2012^{TM}, there are certain key issues that restrict its use for extremely mobile IoT devices that are operational under fog computing environments. The first issue is the non-correspondence between the tPoA and the PoS as 802.21a-2012^{TM} does not provide any support for the previously connected PoS and the tPoA. However, the initial draft of 802.21a-2012^{TM} aims at using EAP-based solution by considering the pre-established trust for MN as provided by the service providers for service access authentication. Although, this is an effective strategy yet does not stand well in the case of mobile PoA. The second issue is the placement of the authentication server in fog computing environments. Further, the requirement of the pre-registration of MN, as well as the mobile PoA between the PoS, is an open problem for using 802.21a-2012^{TM} in IoT-Fog environments.

The proposed approach integrates the fog computing with the virtual osmotic computing paradigm. This helps in resolving the issues related to the requirement of pre-registration of MN that otherwise prohibits the use of unbundled media access authentication of 802.21a-2012^{TM}. The proposed approach provides a framework which not only incorporates the 802.21a-2012^{TM} for supporting dynamic IoT devices in fog computing, but also reduces the overall handover time. The proposed osmotic framework is capable of handling mobile PoA and also manages the keys during the entire session which are used to relate the source PoS with the tPoA.

4   Osmotic Framework for Dynamic IoT-Fog Networks

Osmotic computing has been introduced as a new area of research for integrating the edge cloud systems [9]. Two core applications of osmotic computing are the management of services and the balancing of computational loads [2,8]. This computing is derived from the chemical osmosis process which uses a semipermeable membrane to allow the movement of solvent for balancing the concentration of the solution on its both sides. The semipermeable membrane acts as a decision support system for the movement of solvent. In this paper, osmotic computing is extended for providing 802.21a-2012^{TM}-assisted handovers in fog networks. The proposed approach is developed as an osmotic framework which is capable of resolving the problems with the unbundled media access handovers in 802.21a-2012^{TM} by virtually supporting the trust between the PoS and the PoA. The proposed approach considers three different scenarios each comprising a mobile PoA as a key entity in supporting handovers for highly dynamic MNs as shown in Fig. 2.

- The first handover scenario arises when an MN moves across the PoAs within the same PoS. Both the source PoA (sPoA) and tPoA are operated by the same PoS. Such scenario can be handled directly by using the 802.21a standard transition approach.

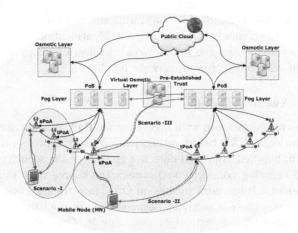

Fig. 2. An illustration of the network setup considered for analyzing 802.21a-2012 MIH using osmotic framework.

– The second handover scenario arises when an MN moves across the PoAs which are served by different PoS. In traditional 802.21a, such scenarios are suggested to use the ERP-based MIH proactive authentication. However, this solution requires pre-registration of MN, thus, cannot be directly applied to the second scenario.
– The third handover scenario arises between the mobile PoA and the PoS. The PoAs are considered to be moving at a high speed in a network between the PoSs.

IEEE 802.21a does not support the handover in the second and the third scenario and is resolved with the help of the proposed osmotic framework.

4.1 Key Management

The virtual osmotic layers help in managing the keys which are to be used for authenticating the mobile PoA across the PoS. For the first scenario, the standard push key solution of 802.21a can be applied. The virtual osmotic layer of each fog layer provides the keys for authentication, and all the push key operations are handled by the osmotic layer. The first scenario is exactly the one considered in the standard implementation of 802.21a. For second and third scenarios, the osmotic layer has way more role than mere an authentication server. It operates as the new entity and the source PoS and target PoS are cooperated by a pre-established trust which is maintained by tunneling one osmotic layer to the other osmotic layer. These operations are secured by absorption policies of the osmotic computing. The proposed approach uses an OAK to validate each osmotic layer as well as the PoS. OAK facilitates the use of unbundled proactive authentication by overcoming the communication issue between the source PoS and the tPoA which is not handled in the traditional 802.21a. The osmotic layer pushes the OAK into the network which helps in identification of the controlling PoS. This allows control over the IoT devices which are moving at a very high speed and do not offer much time to execute handovers.

4.2 Mobility-Aware Handoffs

For service access authentication with highly mobile PoA, it is not suitable to use the standard solution as EAP-based authentication requires pre-establishment of trust. Also, the unbundled approach does not guarantee the security since there is no facility for securing connectivity between the source PoS and the tPoA. The proposed osmotic framework pushes an OAK into the network via osmotic layer which facilitates the connectivity between the every entity in the network and the trust is maintained instead of assuming it. Once the MN reaches a terminal PoA, the PoS makes a key request to the osmotic authentication server, which relies on pushing the OAK in the network. It also shares an identical key with the tunneled osmotic layers. Once an MN communicates with the tPoA, it shares the new key which is generated using the previous OAK. This new key is transferred to an osmotic server of the target PoS which validates the new key by generating its source key and matching it with the one shared by the source osmotic layer. This procedure involves management of multiple keys by each osmotic authentication server as it may be tunneled to multiple layers at the same instance.

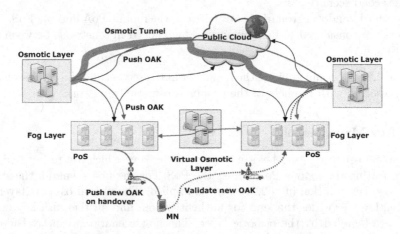

Fig. 3. An illustration of osmotic tunneling for OAK push operations.

5   Performance Case Study

The proposed approach overcomes the trust establishment issues with the 802.21a and allows an osmotic facility to incorporate it for handovers in dynamic

IoT-Fog networks. The mobile PoA can be authenticated between the source PoS and the target PoS by an OAK which is used to tunnel source and target osmotic layers. This allows the sharing of context as well as key information over the secured channel as shown in Fig. 3. The performance of the proposed osmotic framework is studied for two aspects, namely, cost and flexibility. The details of which are as follows:

- Cost: The cost of operation in the proposed approach varies with the scenario. The first scenario with IoT devices operates with the same cost as that of 802.21a standard and does not vary despite the target application. However, for the other two scenarios, the osmotic layer plays an important role by periodically pushing an OAK whenever a handover is initiated. The cost of operation for handovers of PoA and MN depends on the time consumed in maintaining a tunnel between the source and the target osmotic layer and the time taken in generation and validation of OAK. The unbundled authentication is strengthened by the proposed solution by providing secure communication between the source PoS and tPoA, however, it may cause some latency if the device overlaps with the multiple handover contexts at the same time. In the normal case, this communication depends only on the time taken by the PoA in absorbing the OAK from the tunneling source.
- Flexibility: The proposed approach is extremely flexible in implementation. In the proposed solution, the osmotic framework is considered which operates over a virtual layer that is created by using the servers from the fog layer. However, the proposed approach can be easily extended by deploying an independent osmotic network as suggested by the initial definition of osmotic computing. The virtual osmotic layer is considered to reduce the time in generation and acquisition of OAKs.

6   Conclusion and Future Directions

This paper presents an overview of security solutions for media independent handovers by considering 802.21a-2012^{TM} standard. An osmotic framework is presented which provides a strategy for incorporating 802.21a-2012^{TM} into the dynamic IoT-Fog networks. Three different handover scenarios are presented considering the MN and mobile PoA. The proposed osmotic framework provides key absorption strategy which operates similar to the push key but uses an Osmotic Absorption Key (OAK) to control the handoffs between the fog layers. The proposed solution is highly flexible and capable of handling extremely dynamic nodes by providing a handoff security even between the source PoS and tPoA. Further investigations and detailed implementation of the osmotic-assisted handovers in IoT-Fog networks using 802.21a-2012 will be presented in the future reports.

Acknowledgement. The work is supported by the Basic Science Research Program through the National Research Foundation of Korea (NRF) funded by the Ministry of Education (2016R1D1A1B03935619) as well as the Basic Science Research Program through the National Research Foundation of Korea (NRF) funded by the Ministry of Science, ICT and Future Planning (2014R1A1A1005915).

References

1. Bonomi, F., Milito, R., Zhu, J., Addepalli, S.: Fog computing and its role in the Internet of Things. In: Proceedings of the First Edition of the MCC Workshop on Mobile Cloud Computing, pp. 13–16. ACM (2012)
2. Sharma, V., Srinivasan, K., Jayakody, D.N.K., Rana, O., Kumar, R.: Managing service-heterogeneity using osmotic computing, arXiv preprint arXiv:1704.04213 (2017)
3. Yi, S., Li, C., Li, Q.: A survey of fog computing: concepts, applications and issues. In: Proceedings of the 2015 Workshop on Mobile Big Data, pp. 37–42. ACM (2015)
4. Sbeyti, H., Malli, M., Al-Tahat, K., Fadlallah, A., Youssef, M.: Scalable extensible middleware framework for context-aware mobile applications (SCAMMP). Wirel. Mob. Netw. Ubiquitous Comput. Depend. Appl. (JoWUA) 7, 77–98 (2016)
5. Baiardi, F., Tonelli, F., Isoni, L.: Application vulnerabilities in risk assessment and management. J. Wirel. Mob. Netw. Ubiquitous Comput. Depend. Appl. (JoWUA) 7, 41–59 (2016)
6. He, Q., Dong, Q., Zhao, B., Wang, Y., Qiang, B.: P2p traffic optimization based on congestion distance and DHT. J. Internet Serv. Inf. Secur. (JISIS) 6, 53–69 (2016)
7. Jiang, X., Ge, X., Yu, J., Kong, F., Cheng, X., Hao, R.: An efficient symmetric searchable encryption scheme for cloud storage. J. Internet Serv. Inf. Secur. (JISIS) 7, 1–18 (2017)
8. Sharma, V., You, I., Kumar, R., Kim, P.: Computational offloading for efficient trust management in pervasive online social networks using osmotic computing. IEEE Access PP(99), 1 (2017)
9. Villari, M., Fazio, M., Dustdar, S., Rana, O., Ranjan, R.: Osmotic computing: a new paradigm for edge/cloud integration. IEEE Cloud Comput. 3, 76–83 (2016)
10. De La Oliva, A., Banchs, A., Soto, I., Melia, T., Vidal, A.: An overview of IEEE 802.21: media-independent handover services. IEEE Wirel. Commun. 15(4), 96–103 (2008)
11. Marin-Lopez, R., Bernal-Hidalgo, F., Das, S., Chen, L., Ohba, Y.: A new standard for securing media independent handover: IEEE 802.21a. IEEE Wirel. Commun. 20(6), 82–90 (2013)
12. de la Oliva, A., Melia, T., Vidal, A., Bernardos, C.J., Soto, I., Banchs, A.: IEEE 802.21 enabled mobile terminals for optimized WLAN/3G handovers: a case study. ACM SIGMOBILE Mob. Comput. Commun. Rev. 11(2), 29–40 (2007)
13. Lim, W.-S., Kim, D.-W., Suh, Y.-J., Won, J.-J.: Implementation and performance study of IEEE 802.21 in integrated IEEE 802.11/802.16 e networks. Comput. Commun. 32(1), 134–143 (2009)
14. 802.21a-2012 - IEEE standard for local and metropolitan area networks: media independent handover services - amendment for security extensions to media independent handover services and protocol. IEEE 802.21a, May 2012
15. Park, H., Lee, H.H., Lee, S.-H.: IEEE 802 standardization on heterogeneous network interworking. In: 2014 16th International Conference on Advanced Communication Technology (ICACT), pp. 1140–1145. IEEE (2014)

A Distributed Power Control Scheme for the Mitigation of Co-Tier Downlink Interference for Femtocell in the Future 5G Networks

Kuo-Chang Ting[1], WenYen Lin[2], and Chia-Pin Wang[3(✉)]

[1] Department of Business Administration and Department of Information Engineering, Minghsin University of Science and Technology, No. 1, Xinxing Rd., Xinfeng, Hsinchu 30401, Taiwan
ting@must.edu.tw
[2] Department of Information Management,
National Taichung University of Science and Technology, No. 129, Sec. 3, Sanmin Rd, North Dist., Taichung City 404, Taiwan
qqnice@gmail.com
[3] Department of Electrical Engineering, National Taiwan Normal University, 162, Heping East Road Section 1, Taipei, Taiwan
chiapin@ntnu.edu.tw

Abstract. LTE Femtocell network categorized as small cell technology will play an important role in the future 5G networks owing to the fact that it cannot only expand the coverage of wireless communication systems but it can also increase frequency reuse. As the times of Internet of thing" (IOT) is coming, the data volume will be explosive tremendously in the future. Hence the need to deploy femtocell is stringent. However, the growing deployments of femtocell base stations (FBSs) have brought a serious issue of inter-FBS interferences (also referred to as co-tier interference) due to their easy and convenient installation. In this article, we propose a systematic approach to reduce FBS co-tier downlink interference under the scenario that FBSs are densely deployed in an environment. Power control for FBS is performed when the number of warning messages issued from Femtocell User Equipment (FUE) is greater than a threshold for a typical distributed power control scheme. However, it will reduce the *SINR* of its served FUEs; therefore reducing the total capacity. In our proposed LAGPC scheme, A FBS performs power control only when the number of FUEs connected to other FBSs interfered by itself is greater than that of its served FUEs. Our proposed scheme has been validated through simulations that it could effectively reduce co-tier downlink interference in shared-spectrum femtocell environments, thereby boosting system performance by 40% on average.

Keywords: Femtocell · Co-tier downlink interference · Alarm signal
FBS-excessive interference source · Power control · IOT

1   Introduction

On the roadmap to the fifth generation (5G) wireless network, the goals are set to attain 1000 times higher mobile data volume per unit area, 10–100 times higher number of connecting devices and user data rate, 10 times longer battery life and 5 times reduced latency [1–3]. In order to attain the goals set above, femtocells play an important role in the next generation of 5G wireless network and IOT times. This is due to the fact that femtocell cannot only increase the frequency reuse but also that it can save power and increase SINR because of the short distance connection characteristic. Furthermore, femtocell network can expand the coverage, off-load the burden of the Macrocell Base Station (MBS), and enhance the total capacity by means of the back-haul connection with ultra-wide bandwidth. Furthermore, the sensor in IOT system generally is low power so the transmit distance in the last mile of network layer is very short as usual. As a result, the small cell technology such as femtocell will become significantly important and popular in the future. However, the growing deployment of FBSs is destined to bring a serious issue of inter-FBS interference (also referred to as co-tier interference) due to their easy and convenient installation. This problem is especially serious when the FBSs are densely deployed in an urban area. Every household deploys its own femtocell to increase the transmission rate but it might also incur serious co-tier interference at the same time due to residence proximity. In fact, cross-tier interference arising from the FBSs and MBSs also becomes a critical issue due to the deployment of femtocells. To cope with the co-tier or cross-tier interference, various power control schemes to migrate the penalty have been proposed [4, 6, 7]. Game theory such as Stackelberg game [8, 9] has been applied in power control and resource allocation negotiation between the FBS and MBS through the pricing mechanism so that leader and followers can achieve balance in terms of throughput, outage probability, spectrum efficiency and so on. The Fractional Frequency Reuse (FFR) scheme proposed in [10] is used to tackle the co-channel interference problem in OFDMA network. Simulation result shows that FFR method can increase SINR value in all scenarios considered. In scenario 1 with random distance, where the distances between MBS and FBS, between FBS and FUE, and between MBS and FUE are 572.503, 33.8378, and 541.288 meters, respectively. The SINR value increases from 57.8716 dB to 182.291 dB by 124.4194 dB. In scenario 2, where the distances between MBS and FBS, between FBS and FUE, and between MBS and MUE are 604, 37.5366, and 641.291 meters, respectively. The SINR value can increase from 78.5277 dB to 183.222 dB by 104.6943 dB in this scenario. Results in [5] also show that the quality can be improved and the interference can be mitigated for both Macrocell and FUE by applying the FFR scheme. However, this scheme suffers from the uneven distribution of FBSs and the frequency reuse is also restricted. In order to solve the former problem for the densely deployed femtocell networks, the enhanced Inter-Cell Interference Coordination (eICIC) has been extensively studied and adopted as a standard for LTE-A and surely will also be a standard for the future 5G networks. The Small Cell Group Muting (SCGM) scheme proposed in [13] is based on the eICIC technology and is used to mitigate the interference among neighboring small cells. The key motivation of this scheme is that one subframe of LTE-A is composed of 14 OFDM symbols for each resource block (RB) [14]. Some OFDM symbols are muted for some FBSs and others are not so that the interference can be mitigated or even be avoided. Simulation results show that the scheme can boost the average throughput by 7–15%. In this article, we propose a systematic approach to reduce co-tier downlink interference for FBSs under the scenario that FBSs are densely deployed. Our proposed Loading Aware Green Power Control (LAGPC) scheme is used to suppress the co-tier interference among FBSs. The key idea of this scheme is that if once a FUE is within the coverage of other FBSs, it will send a waning message to these FBSs. If the number of warning messages received by any FBS is greater than the number of its served FUEs, this FBS will decrease its power level by one dB gradually until the number of warning messages is no longer than the number of its served FUEs. If the number of its served FUE is very small for a FBS, even to zero, this FBS surely should reduce to its power level until no warning messages issued from the FUEs connected to other FBSs appear. The scheme is distributed and very easy to implement. The algorithm code developed for this scheme can be integrated into the control firmware of FBSs.

In the next parts of this article, system model of our proposed scheme will be presented, and addressed in Sect. 2. Simulation results and discussions will be addressed in Sect. 3. Conclusions and the future works are given in Sect. 4.

2 System Model

The access methods of FBSs can be divided into three types, Open Subscriber Group (OSG), Closed Subscriber Group (CSG), and Hybrid Subscriber Group (HSG). In OSG, all FUEs can connect to all FBSs so that the MBSs can release the service loading from the requests of UEs. On the other hand, the FUEs must login in the FBS by their registration accounts in CSG. HSG is with the mixture characteristics of OSG and CSG. In this article, we assume the access method is OSG. About the spectrum allocations can be divided into two types split spectrum reuse and shared spectrum reuse. In the split spectrum reuse, the spectrum is portioned into two parts. One part is used by MBSs and the other part is used by FBSs. On the contrary, all spectrum or bandwidth is shared by FBSs and MBSs in shared spectrum reuse. In this article, we assume the partition scheme is shared spectrum reuse. We also assume that there are totally M FBSs and N FUEs located in the considered environment. We focus on the co-tier interference and the interference among the FBSs and MBSs is assumed to be very small so that it can be ignored. Our scheme assumes that once a FUE senses interference, it will broadcast a warning message to all FBSs within its range. If the number of warning messages received by a FBS is greater than a given threshold, it should be aware of the fact that it is causing interference to an excessive number of FUEs and will identify itself as an FBS-Excessive Interference (FBS-EI) source. Under the circumstance, it should reduce its power level to mitigate the interference toward other FUEs through a distributed FBS-EI detection algorithm. This scheme is distributed and easy to implement. On the contrary, Femtocell Management System (FMS)-based schemes such as those in [11] and [12] use a centralized control by a managing server. This server must collect a large amount of data in order to determine the source of interference through a special algorithm. Hence, these centralized approaches might be rather complicated and impractical to implement. In order to simplify the process of looking for the interference sources, our scheme is based on the observation that if the coverage of an FBS overlaps with that of neighboring FBSs, the FBS will likely interfere with the FUEs served by the neighboring FBSs. The interfered FUEs will send out warning messages. The message issued from the same FUE within a short period will be treated as the same so the number of warning message will not change in this scenario. The number of warning messages received by an FBS can be used as an indicator of the severity of interference. The procedures of finding a FBS-EI source mentioned above is illustrated in Fig. 1.

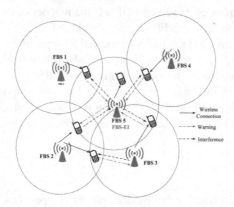

Fig. 1. Illustration of the procedures for identifying an FBS-EI source.

Figure 1 shows that the service area of FBS-5 overlaps with those of FBS-1, FBS-2, FBS-3, and FBS-4. Therefore, FBS-5 will receive a lot of warning messages from the FUEs served by neighboring FBSs and FBS-5 will be aware that it is an FBS-EI source if the number of the warning messages received from other FUEs is greater than the threshold. As a result, FBS-5 will reduce its power level to mitigate the interference toward the FUEs served by other FBSs. It is noted that the coverage area of an FBS depends on the radio sensitivity of FUEs; the radio sensitivity is assumed to −56 dBm in this article. Without loss of generality, the radio sensitivity is assumed to the signal strength corresponding to the 20-meter radius coverage with the transmit power of 23 dBm for each FBS. Of course, the radius can be extended to 25 m or farther. In fact, it can be treated as an environment parameter. The coverage of each FBS is based on receiver sensitivity, −56 dBm in this article, so due to some blockages, whether the shape of the coverage area in Fig. 1 is a circle or not might not be a problem. It is noted that the number of FUEs served by FBS 5 is only 1 as in Fig. 1, but the number of warning messages from other FUEs of other FBSs such as FBS 1, 2, 3, 4 is as high as 4. Hence FBS 5 will be aware that it is a FBS-EI, then the power control is performed by FBS 5 and the coverage of Fig. 1 will be reshaped into Fig. 2. On the contrary, the FBS 3 in Fig. 1 does not hold this condition, so it will not regard itself as a FBS-EI, so no power control is needed as in Fig. 2.

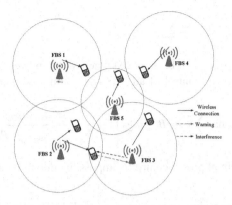

Fig. 2. Illustration of FBS interference on FUEs after the power reduction of FBS 5.

In order to attain the goals set above, we propose a Loading Aware Green Power Control (LAGPC) algorithm for this scheme to proceed with this mechanism. In this scheme, three assumptions are made:

(1) Every FUE is assumed to connect to the nearest FBS.
(2) Every FUE in the coverage of other FBSs can detect the interference from these FBSs.
(3) Every FBS will receive the FUEs' waring messages if they are in the coverage of these FUEs.

If we denote the power of all FBSs as matrix $\mathbf{P} = [p_1, p_2,..., p_M]$ and the channel states among all FBSs and FUEs as $\mathbf{H} = [h_{ij}]$, a $M \times N$ matrix, the interference power state $\mathbf{I} = \mathbf{P} \otimes \mathbf{H} = [I_k]$. Note that the element (I_k) operated with $\otimes$ can be defined by

$$I_k = \sum_{i=1, j=FBS(k), i \neq j}^{M} P_i h_{ik}. \tag{1}$$

It is noted that h_{ik} denotes the channel state for FBS i to FUE k, it can be given by

$$h_{ik} = 10^{-3.7}(D_{ik})^{-3} \tag{2}$$

based on 3GPP TR25.952 25. *FBS* (k) denotes the ID of FBS which FUE k connected to. The Received Signal Strength (RSS) sensed by all FUEs, $\mathbf{R} = \mathbf{P} \otimes \mathbf{H} = [R_k]$ and the element of R, $[R_k]$ can be given by

$$R_k = P_{FBS(k)} h_{FBS(k)k}. \tag{3}$$

The total capacity C can be given by

$$C = \sum_{i=1}^{N} B \times log_2(1 + \frac{R_k}{I_k + \eta}). \tag{4}$$

The maximal capacity C_{Max} can be achieved when all the powers of FBS are properly controlled. If we let power control of all FBSs be optimal, we can get C_{Max} by

$$C_{Max} = \underset{P}{arg\ max} \sum_{k=1}^{N} B \times log_2 \left[1 + \frac{P_{FBS(k)}h_{FBS(k)k}}{\sum_{i=1, j=FBS(k), i \neq j}^{M} P_i h_{ik} + \eta}\right]. \tag{5}$$

Unfortunately, the optimal power control is impossible due to the reasons listed in the followings:

(1) The complexity of optimal power control for all FBSs is NP-hard if a brute-force calculation is applied because the possible number of power level to be taken is exponentially large with the order of the number of FBSs. If the number of FBSs is 100 assumed in this article, the possible combinations can be up to PL^{100} if PL is the possible number of power levels.
(2) An individual distributed FBS cannot know all channel states of all UEs to FBSs, that is, the matrix **H** listed before is NP-hard to be known.

In fact, all the FUEs are mostly interfered by their neighboring FBSs located in the close proximity. The interferences from other distant FBSs should not be taken into consideration because these interferences from distant FBSs might also be hard to be sensed. A FBS can tune its power level according to the number of FBS-EI waring messages it received. If this FBS reduces its power level, all the FUEs issuing FBS-EI messages can boost their data rate due to the interference reduction. In addition, if the number of FUEs served by this FBS-EI is very small even to zero; this power reduction for this FBS-EI has little or no impact on the total capacity of this FBS. On the contrary, if the number of FUEs served by this FBS-EI is very large, the power reduction could reduce the inferences toward other FUEs connected to other FBSs at cost of reducing the total capacity of the FBS-EI cell itself as well. In our proposed scheme, if the number of FUEs interfered by this FBS-EI is s, the ID of the FBS-EI is i, and the power of this FBS-EI, P reduces to P' ($P > P'$), the interferences revived from this FBS-EI for an individual FUE k will reduce from $P_i h_{ik}$ to $P'_i h_{ik}$. In the meanwhile, the total capacity of these m FUEs will increase from

$$C_S = \sum_{i=1}^{s} B \times log_2(1 + \frac{R_k}{P_i h_{ik} + \eta}) \tag{6}$$

to

$$C'_S = \sum_{i=1}^{s} B \times log_2(1 + \frac{R_k}{P'_i h_{ik} + \eta}) \tag{7}$$

if set S in (6) and (7) consists of the s FUEs. The total capacity of the FBS-EI will reduce from

$$C_T = \sum_{k=1}^{n} log_2(1 + \frac{P_i h_{ik}}{I_k + \eta}) \qquad (8)$$

to

$$C_T' = \sum_{k=1}^{n} log_2(1 + \frac{P_i' h_{ik}}{I_k' + \eta}) \qquad (9)$$

if set T consists of the n FUEs connected to the FBS-EI where I_k denoted as unknown interferences received from other FBSs for any individual FUE in this set T. If we set the SINR increase benefit in percentage be C_{inc} and the SINR loss in percentage be C_{dec} from this power reduction as $(C_S' - C_S)$ and $(C_T - C_T')$, respectively, the FBS-EI should perform power reductions is based on the criterion that C_{inc} is greater than C_{desc} in terms of total capacity. C_{inc} and C_{desc} can be estimated and reduced from (6), (7), (8), (9), (10) and (11) if the thermal noise is very small compared to the interferences. In fact, the number of FUEs not connected to the FBS-EI and surround about this FBS is not limited to m. Therefore, the number of FUEs beneficial from the power reduction is not limited to m; thus C_{inc}, C_{desc} can be given by (10) and (11), respectively.

$$C_{inc} \approx \sum_{k=1}^{s} log_2(\frac{P_i}{P_i'}) = log_2(\frac{P_i}{P_i'})^s \qquad (10)$$

$$C_{desc} \approx \sum_{k=1}^{n} log_2(\frac{P_i}{P_i'}) = log_2(\frac{P_i}{P_i'})^n \qquad (11)$$

It is noted that set S can be given by

$$S = \{k | P_i h_{ik} > R_{min}\} \qquad (12)$$

and

$$s = |S|. \qquad (13)$$

It is noted that if n is zero, that is, there is no FUE connected to the FBS-EI, C_{desc} is destined to be 1, in other word, no SINR is lost no matter how low the P_i' is. If both s and n are greater than 0, the capacity gain denoted by $G = B \times (C_{inc} - C_{dest})$ can be given by (14) reduced from (10) and (11) where B is the bandwidth occupied by the system.

$$G = B \times (C_{inc} - C_{desc}) = B \times log_2(\frac{P_i}{P_i'})^{\frac{n}{s}}. \qquad (14)$$

Equation (14) shows that if n is greater than s, G is positive. On the contrary, if n is less than s, G is negative. The larger of n/s and power reduction ratio, the larger the gain is. If no power reduction is performed by the FBS-EI, that is the power reduction ratio is 1, G is zero based on (14). Therefore, the outcome is no gain and no loss in this scenario. In fact, s is determined by R_{min} and P_i. If P_i reduces, s decreases. Then, s is a function of the power P_i and R_{min}.

This model motivates us to propose the LAGPC algorithm described in Fig. 3 and the variables shown in Fig. 3 are explained in Table 1.

3   Simulation Results and Discussion

The simulation parameters are listed in Table 2. In this study, suppose there are totally 100 FBSs and 300 as well as 400 FUEs randomly distributed over a 200×200 m^2 area. There are 3 and 4 FUEs served by one FBS on average for the 300 and 400 FUEs, respectively. Any FUE will connect to a FBS which is the closest to it and it can get the best channel gain from this FBS connection. A total of 10 runs of simulations are performed to investigate the behavior of IAPC and LAGPC.

Table 1.   Notations used in LAGPC scheme

P_j	The transmission power level of the FBS-j in dBm
P_{npc}	The transmission power level of FBS with no power control (NPC) in dBm
RS_{i,j_k}	The receiving signal strength of FUE k of FBS-i (or FUE$_{i\_k}$) from FBS-j in dBm
I_{j,i_k}	The interference received by the FUE$_{i\_k}$ from FBS-j in dBm
k	The ID of FUE served by FBS
η	Thermal noise
R_{min}	The minimal Received Signal Strength (RSS) for each FBS to receive any message theoretically
ψ	The minimal strength of the received signal from FBS-EI for FUE to send warning messages
RSS_{j,j_k}	The RSS for FUE$_{j\_k}$ received from FBS-j
L_{i,i_k}	The path loss from FBS-i to FUE$_{i\_k}$ in dB
C_{i_k}	The capacity of the kth FUE of FBS-i
$\lvert$FBS-$i\rvert$	The number of FUEs served by FBS-i
$LMAX_i$	The largest path loss among all FUEs served by FBS-i
n_i	The number of warning messages received by FBS i from FUE$_{i,j\_k}$ and $j = FBS(k)$, $i \neq j$ so far for each run
m_i	The number of FUEs served by FBS-i
D_{i,i_k}	Distance of FBS i to the FUE k

Input: M FBSs, N FUEs, $\sum_{i}^{M} |\text{FBS-}i| = N$

Input: $i = 1$ to M, $k = 1$ to $|\text{FBS-}i|$.

Output: The new power distribution of femtocell.
Begin a Run
       For $1=0$ to M //initialize NWM to zero $\{ NWM_i = 0\}$
For $i=1$ to M {
  $k \leftarrow 1$
  $LMAX_i = L_{i,i\_k} = P_{npc} - RSS_{i,i\_k}$
    For $k=2$ to $|\text{FBS-}i|$
    $L_{i,i\_k} = P_{npc} - RSS_{i,i\_k}$
    If $L_{i,i\_k} > LMAX_i$ then$\{ LMAX_i = L_{i,i\_k}\}$
    If (FUE$_{i\_k}$ senses interference from FBS$>=j$) then
        Send a warning message to FBS-j ($i \neq j$)
}
For $i=1$ to M {
  //The following algorithm is implemented by individual FBS
  If FBS-i receives interference from FUE then
    $n_i \leftarrow n_i + 1$
  If $n_i > m_i$ then {
    $P_{min} \leftarrow R_{min} + LMAX_i$
    If ($P_i > P_{min}$)
        $P_i \leftarrow P_i - 1$
  }
}

Fig. 3. Our proposed IAPC scheme

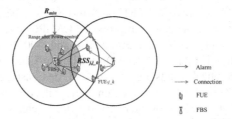

Fig. 4. Illustration of the power control of FBS-EI

Table 2. Simulation parameter values

Parameter	Value
Map range	200 m × 200 m
Number of FBSs (M)	100
Number of FUEs (N)	300, 400
FBS radius of coverage	20 m
FBS transmit power (max)	23 dBm
Bandwidth	10 MHz
Frequency	2 GHz
Minimal sensitivity to receive (R_{min})	−56 dBm
T value	1, 2, 3, 4

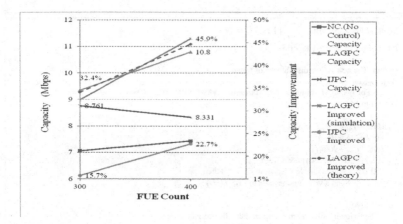

Fig. 5. Capacity and capacity improvement for IJPC and LAGPC.

In our previous proposed scheme, IAPC [15], the value T denotes the threshold number of warning messages received by one FBS to reduce its power level. If T is equal to 1, it implies that an FBS receiving any warning message will treat itself as a FBS-EI source and will reduce its transmission power immediately. In order to evaluate the performance of our proposed LAGPC and compare it with that of the previous proposed scheme, IJPC, the throughput improvement is shown in Fig. 5.

Figure 5 shows that the improvements of average capacity for IJPC are only 15.7% and 22.7% for the 100 FBSs with 300 FUEs and 400 FUEs to be served, respectively. On the contrary, the improvements for our proposed LAGPC scheme can be as high as 32.4% and 45.9% for the FBSs with 300 FUEs and 400 FUEs. The theoretical improvement based on (14) is shown in the Dotted line of Fig. 5. Figure 5 shows that the simulation and theoretical results are very close. It demonstrates the preciseness of our model. For the IJPC, if the T is set to be one only, all FBSs are inclined to reduce their power level so that the SINR of their served FUEs decreases on average. On the contrary, the SINR of FUEs does not reduce frequently if the value T is over 2 because the criterion to reduce power level is stricter compared to that of T being one. We show the effect of the value of T on the SINR of all FUEs for these ten run simulations in Fig. 6. Hence, our scheme could reduce the total power consumption by about 50%; it could also be a green communication scheme based on our LAGPC algorithm. The capacity comparison of IJPC with that of No Power Control (NPC) scheme is illustrated in Fig. 5. Figure 5 shows that the average capacity can increase from 4.8 Mbps to 5.8 Mbps for each FUE. Therefore, the total capacity can increase by 20.8% on the average. The impact of T value on the throughput improvement for IJPC can be shown in Fig. 7.

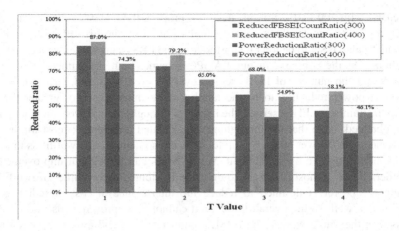

Fig. 6. The reduced FBS-EI count and reduced power reduction ratio with various T values for our previous proposed IJPC scheme.

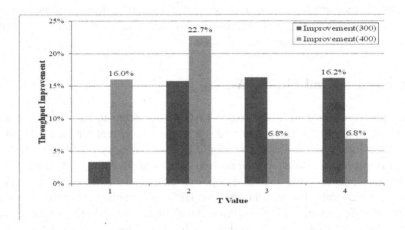

Fig. 7. The T value impact on the throughput improvement of IJPC.

Figure 7 shows that if the number of FUEs is 300 served by 100 FBSs, the throughput improvement with T value 1 for IJPC is only 3%. It illustrates that if we set the definition of FBS-EI as only one warning message received, most of the FBSs are inclined to reduce their power level and their throughput also reduces as well; therefore the total throughput improvement is also limited. On the contrary, if we set T value over or equal to 2 as the criterion to be FBS-EI for any FBS, the throughput improvement can be about 16.0%. However, if the number of FUEs increases to 400 served by 100 FBSs, the scenario of T value set to 1 can have throughput improvement as high as 16%. It accounts for the fact that the interference for the scenario with 400 FUEs is much higher that of the scenario with 300 FUEs intuitively. Hence, power reduction is much critical to the interference reduction as well as total capacity. It is interesting that the maximal throughput improvement occurs when the T value is 2 for the scenario with 400 FUEs. It motivates us to propose the LAGPC scheme. The IJPC scheme does not consider the number of FUEs served by the FBS-EI itself, so if the threshold T value is set to be too high or too low, the FBSs cannot achieve the maximal throughput. On the contrary, in our LAGPC scheme, both the number of warning messages and the number of FUEs served by FBS are considered, so if we set the criterion of power reduction to be the number of warning messages greater than or equal to the number of FUEs served, the maximal throughput improvement, about 46% can be obtained. Note that the throughput is calculated on average; most throughput improvement can be over 50% even up to 70%, but sometimes it is worthless to apply this scheme to improve the throughput. We owe this bad throughput improvement to the border effects. If most FUEs are so unlucky distributed at the border of two FBSs, reducing the power is destined to reduce the interference at cost of reducing the throughput as well, so the overall throughput cannot be improved. This issue will be discussed in the future works. The FBSEI count reduction and power reduction ratio with 300 FUEs and 400 FUEs by applying IJPC scheme are shown in Fig. 6. Figure 6 illustrates the FBSEI count ratio and power reduction ratio can be as high as 87.0% and 74.3% with T value = 1. This large scale power reduction is at cost of lower higher throughput improvement. It is also certainly that as T value increases, the reduction ratio decreases, but the best throughput improvement is 22.7% when the optimal T value is 2 as shown in Fig. 7.

4 Conclusion and Future Works

In this article, we propose a distributed LAGPC algorithm to reduce the downlink interference under the co-channel shared spectrum environment for the femtocell and the future 5G networks so that the average SINR and capacity can increase by about 44% on average. On the contrary, our previous proposed algorithm, IJPC is only 22.7% with T value 2, the best case of IJPC. The power reduction ratio of LAGPC can be up to around 70% slightly lower than that of IJPC at benefit of double throughput improvement on average. This algorithm is distributed and easy to implement as stated before. The centralized control system such as Femtocell Management System (FMS) might have better performance. However, it is really very hard for FMS to control and collect the distributed data for each FBS. It seems not practical at all.

Despite that the average capacity improvement can be up to 44%, we find that the improvement is not so stable. In some scenario, the distribution of many FUEs lies on the boarder of two FBSs so that the FUEs cannot get good SINR connection from the FBSs' service under this co-channel environment. There are many schemes supposed to solve this problem. Enhanced Inter-Cell Interference Coordination (eICIC) is one of the schemes, proposed to suppress this interference by changing the shared-channel to partition-channel allocation through the communications between the two FBSs so that the FUEs on the border of the two FBSs would not interfere with each other. On the other hand, a FUE is not aware of the location of its FBS connected to. If a cross-layer scheme can be applied to our proposed LAGPC by guiding the FUE approaching toward its connected FBS, the connected SINR can be improved and the interference is expected to be mitigated tremendously. We list these as our future works.

Acknowledgment. This research was supported by MOST of Taiwan under contract numbers 104-2221-E-197-007, 105-2221-E-159-001 and 104-2221-E-197-009.

References

1. Luo, F.L., Zhang, C.: 5G standard development: technology and roadmap. In: Signal Processing for 5G: Algorithms and Implementations, 1st edn. Wiley-IEEE Press (2016). https://doi.org/10.1002/9781119116493.ch23
2. Dat, P.T., Kanno, A., Yamamoto, N., Kawanishi, T.: 5G transport networks: the need for new technologies and standards. IEEE Commun. Mag. **54**(9), 18–26 (2016)
3. Agiwal, M., Roy, A., Saxena, N.: Next generation 5G wireless networks: a comprehensive survey. IEEE Commun. Surv. Tutor. **18**(3), 1617–1655 (third quarter 2016)
4. Jo, H.S., Mun, C., Moon, J., Yook, J.-G.: Interference mitigation using uplink power control for two-tier femtocell networks. IEEE Trans. Wirel. Commun. **8**(10), 4906–4910 (2009)
5. Wang, H., Zhu, C., Ding, Z.: Femtocell power control for interference management based on macrolayer feedback. IEEE Trans. Veh. Technol. **65**(7), 5222–5236 (2016)
6. Chandrasekhar, V., Andrews, J., Shen, Z., Muharemovic, T., Gatherer, A.: Power control in two-tier femtocell networks. IEEE Trans. Wirel. Commun. **8**(8), 4316–4328 (2009)
7. Zhang, L., Yang, L., Yang, T.: Cognitive interference management for LTE-A femtocells with distributed carrier selection. In: IEEE 72nd VTC 2010-Fall, pp. 1–5 (2010)
8. Tseng, C.C., Peng, C.S., Lo, S.H., Wang, H.C., Kuo, F.C., Ting, K.C.: Co-tier uplink power control in femtocell networks by Stackelberg game with pricing. In: Global Wireless Summit, Aalborg, Denmark, 11–14 May 2014
9. Liang, Y.S., Chung, W.H., Ni, G.K., Chen, I.Y., Zhang, H., Kuo, S.Y.: Resource allocation with interference avoidance in OFDMA femtocell network. IEEE Trans. Veh. Technol. **61**(5), 2243–2255 (2012)
10. Giovany, T.I., Usman, U.K., Prasetya, B.: Simulation and analysis of interference avoidance using fractional frequency reuse (FFR) method in LTE femtocell. In: ICOICT, pp. 192–197 (2013)
11. Bouras, C., Kavourgias, G., Kokkinos, V., Papazois, A.: Interference management in LTE femtocell systems using an adaptive frequency reuse scheme (2012)
12. Zhang, Y.P., Feng, S., Zhang, P., Xia, L., Wu, Y.C., Ren, X.: Inter-cell interference management in LTE-A small-cell networks. In: IEEE 77th VTC-Spring, pp. 1–6 (2013)
13. Arulselvan, N., Chhawchharia, M., Sen, M.: Time-domain and frequency-domain muting schemes for interference co-ordination in LTE heterogeneous networks. In: IEEE International Conference on Advanced Networks and Telecommunications Systems, pp. 1–6 (2013)
14. 3rd Generation Partnership Project; Technical Specification Group Radio Access Network; TDD Base Station Classification (Release 2000). ftp://www.3gpp.org/tsg_ran/TSG_RAN/TSGR_12/Docs/PDFs/RP-010457.pdf
15. Wang, H.-C., Kuo, F.-C., Tseng, C.-C., Wang, B.-W., Ting, K.-C.: Improving LTE femtocell base station network performance by distributed power control. Univers. J. Electr. Electron. Eng. **4**(5), 113–119 (2016)

Analyzing Traffic Characteristics and Performance for LTE Uplink Resource Allocation

Fang-Chang Kuo[(✉)]

National Ilan University, Yilan City, Taiwan
kfc@niu.edu.tw

Abstract. Many resource allocation schemes have been proposed based on different criteria such as system throughput, fairness, transmission power, user priority and others. According to the 3GPP specifications, however, as long as a GBR bearer is admitted, the eNB has to ensure the Guaranteed Bit Rate (GBR) of the bearer before it is disconnected or dropped. However, the 3GPP hasn't defined how to measure GBR. In previous papers, we present how to use Exponentially Weighted Moving Average (EWMA) algorithm to define the measurement of data rates, so as to facilitate resource allocation works. In this paper, we discuss the characteristics of traffic patterns under the constraint of EWMA, as well as the impact on the performance of eNB that serving such traffics. According the simulation results, we also suggest that the more bursty traffic patterns should be charged with higher rates.

Keywords: Uplink scheduling · Resource allocation · EWMA

1 Introduction

Dynamic Resource Allocation (DRA) in an LTE system concerns the process for an eNB (Evolved Node B) to allocate radio resource blocks (RBs) to user equipment (UE), such that the UE can transmit data to eNB. Many DRA schemes for have been proposed. Initially, some DRA schemes, such as Recursive Maximum Expansion (RME), emphasize on maximizing the system throughput of an eNB [1, 2]. Then, some researchers raised that fairness is also a very important criterion, and proposed some schemes, such as frequency domain Round Robin (RR) [3] and Proportional Fair (PF) [4, 5]. However, one of the important tasks of eNB is to admit or reject the establishment requests for new radio bearers, at the same time it also needs to ensure high radio resource utilization and to ensure proper QoS for the in-progress sessions [6]. As a result, some schemes emphasizing bearer QoS were proposed [7–9].

The throughput of a Guaranteed Bit Rate (GBR) bearer is expressed in terms of the GBR, which is declared when the UE requests to establish the bearer. GBR is the bit rate that can be expected when there is data pending for transmission [10]. However, 3GPP hasn't clearly defined how to measure GBR. As a result, it is hard to verify whether the QoS, in term of GBR, is guaranteed. Besides, it is quite general that a UE generates traffic with silences of different durations. As a result, it is also hard for a UE to declare the data rate and also hard for the eNB to allocate RBs for the UE.

© ICST Institute for Computer Sciences, Social Informatics and Telecommunications Engineering 2018
Y.-B. Lin et al. (Eds.): IoTaaS 2017, LNICST 246, pp. 86–93, 2018.
https://doi.org/10.1007/978-3-030-00410-1_11

In order to facilitate DRA work, we employed Exponentially Weighted Moving Average (EWMA) [11] to define the GBR of a bearer, and designed a DRA scheme, named AAG (Allocate As Granted). We showed that AAG has outstanding performance in terms of UE satisfaction, packet delay, and system throughput, then we also extended it to new versions AAG-2 and AAG-LCG [12, 13]. The new versions aim at guaranteeing the QoS of all GBR bearers, while efficiently distributing RBs to non-GBR bearers, so as to improve resource utilization.

In the next section we describe our previous works about how EWMA is employed by AAG scheduling scheme to facilitate resource allocation work. The characteristics of EWMA are analyzed in Sect. 3, and the corresponding simulation is depicted in Sect. 4. We then make conclusion and describe future works in Sect. 5.

2 Previous Works

In order to analysis the characteristics of EWMA, here we first briefly describe its principle and how it is employed by AAG to obtain outstanding performance.

Let $R_{m,GBR}^{grant}$ be the GBR that is granted by the eNB for the m-th UE (UE_m). We may convert $R_{m,GBR}^{grant}$ to another form $B_{m,GBR}^{grant}$ which stands for "the number of bits that is permitted to be transmitted per TTI (Transmission Time Interval)." For UE_m, let $B_m(n)$ denotes the number of bits transmitted at the n-th TTI. Define $\bar{B}_m(n)$ as the average number of bits per TTI that has transmitted after the n-th TTI. Then, based on the definition of EWMA, we obtain

$$\bar{B}_m(n) = (1 - \alpha)\bar{B}_m(n - 1) + \alpha B_m(n), \tag{1}$$

where $\alpha \in (0,1)$ is the weighting factor. The $\bar{B}_m(n)$ should not be less than $B_{m,GBR}^{grant}$ if eNB wishes to provide UE_m with average data rate that is no less than $R_{m,GBR}^{grant}$. As a result, the eNB should plan to allocate some RBs to transmit the following number of bits

$$B_m^{plan}(n) = \min\left\{ \max\left[\frac{B_{m,GBR}^{grant} - (1 - \alpha)\bar{B}_m(n - 1)}{\alpha}, 0 \right], L_m(n - 1) \right\}, \tag{2}$$

where the new term $L_m(n - 1)$ is the total queue length of the UE_m. This term is obtained through the Buffer Status Report (BSR) sent by UE_m to indicate how many bits are waiting for transmission. With this term, eNB can prevent wasting RBs if there is not so many bits pending in the buffer.

In order to ensure the throughput of every UE, AAG allocates RBs to UEs according to the descending order of the priority values defined as follows

$$P_m(n) = \frac{B_{m,GBR}^{grant} - \bar{B}_m(n - 1)}{B_{m,GBR}^{grant}}. \tag{3}$$

This term is also an indication of how a UE is satisfied with the current average data rate as compared with the declared one.

3   Characteristic Analysis of EWMA

As mentioned above, there could be lots of silences for the duration of a session. Based on EWMA, the number of bits that a UE authorized to transmit GBR traffic has been expressed in (2) and the corresponding priority metric is expressed in (3). Let's count out the term $L_m(n - 1)$ representing the pending number of bits, and concentrate on discussing the characteristics of EWMA. As a result, the longer duration the UE keeps silent, the more bits it can transmit with higher priority metric. To the extreme condition, if the UE_m keeps silent for a very long period (duration), the term $\bar{B}_m(n - 1)$ would approach zero. As a result, based on (2), the number of bits that the UE authorized to transmit as a burst would approach

$$\frac{B_{m,GBR}^{grant}}{\alpha}. \tag{4}$$

We define this value as the Maximum Burst Size (MBS) corresponding to a bearer specified with the set of parameters $(B_{m,GBR}^{grant}, \alpha)$. For example, when α is 0.01 the MBS is 100 times of $B_{m,GBR}^{grant}$. By the way, the corresponding priority metric for sending such a burst would approach to one, which is the maximum value. However, if the silent duration is not long enough, the UE is only allowed to transmit a smaller burst size, which can be derived as follows.

Starting from the n-th TTI, assume UE_m keeps silent for τ TTIs, then

$$\bar{B}_m(n + \tau) = (1 - a)^\tau \cdot \bar{B}_m(n) \tag{5}$$

Based on (2), we have

$$B_{in}^{plan}(n + \tau) = \frac{B_{m,GBR}^{grant} - (1 - \alpha)^\tau \cdot \bar{B}_m(n)}{\alpha}. \tag{6}$$

If $\bar{B}_m(n) = B_{m,GBR}^{grant}$ before it get into silent mode, we may express the burst size that the UE can transmit after a silence of τ TTIs as following

$$MBS[1 - (1 - \alpha)^\tau], \tag{7}$$

where the maximum burst size, MBS, is defined in (4).

Based on (7), we illustrate burst size as a function of silence duration and parameter α in Fig. 1, where the burst size is expressed as a value that is normalized by the corresponding MBS expressed in (4). Take a UE with α being 0.01 as an example, if it keeps silent for 0.1 or 0.01 s, it has the credit to respectively transmit a burst which is 0.63 or 0.09 times of the MBS. As we can see, when a UE goes into silence, it begins to accumulate credit for transmitting more bits. At the same time, however, it begins to

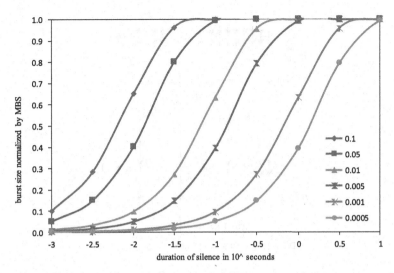

Fig. 1. Burst sizes as a function of silence duration and parameter α

lose some of its transmission credit. Let's consider another scenario where the UE_m keeps transmitting for τ TTIs at a data rate $B_{m,GBR}^{grant}$, rather than keeps silent. Then the number of bits that it transmits is $B_{m,GBR}^{grant} \cdot \tau$, which is larger than the legal burst size expressed in (7).

In the position of a UE which has nothing to transmit for a while, it would like to accumulate the transmission credit and then transmit a bigger burst at a later moment. As we can see, the EWMA can help preserve the transmission credit to a certain degree during the silence period. However, from the aspect of an eNB, if lots of UEs transmit bursts at a moment, the eNB is prone to be overloaded at this moment, and some of the packets will suffer from longer delay and even overdue. That means for some of the UEs, their GBRs aren't guaranteed within limited delay. This is what an eNB needs to avoid. Fortunately, by employing EWMA, the legal burst size is bounded by (7). If a UE generates a bigger burst, only the QoS of the legal part should be ensured. The eNB is irresponsible to immediately allocate RBs for the illegal part because it also needs to ensure the QoS of other UEs. As a result, we may regard EWMA as a suitable algorithm to compromise the expectation of both UEs and eNBs.

4   Performance Evaluation

In order to observe the impact of traffic parameters on the performance of eNB, we simulate the environment where some UEs declare the same GBR and generate bursty traffic patterns, while the eNB dynamically allocates RBs based on the AAG scheme presented in [12].

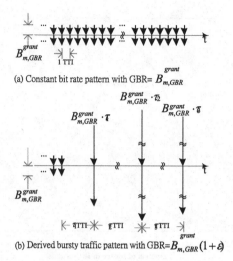

(a) Constant bit rate pattern with GBR= $B_{m,GBR}^{grant}$

(b) Derived bursty traffic pattern with GBR=$B_{m,GBR}^{grant}(1+\varepsilon)$

Fig. 2. Derived bursty traffic pattern that complied with a specific traffic parameters.

4.1   Method for Generating User Traffic Patterns

We need to emulate some bursty traffic patterns generated by UEs. There could be numerous traffic patterns complying to a specific parameter set ($B_{m,GBR}^{grant}, \alpha_m$). A constant bit rate (CBR) pattern shown in Fig. 2(a) is a special one. We may use such a CBR pattern to derive bursty patterns as shown in Fig. 2(b). The characteristic of such a bursty pattern is that after a silence of deration i TTIs, a burst with proportional number of bits $B_{m,GBR}^{grant} \cdot \tau_i$ is generated. Such a burst is regarded as a packet in this paper. A longer silence duration is followed by a larger burst size. However, as we have explained in Sect. 3, although keeping silent can accumulate transmission credit, some of that is lost at the same time. As a result, it is not allowed for a UE to send out so many bits at a TTI, unless the granted GBR is enlarged. Thus, we enlarge the granted GBR by an extra ratio ε. That is to say, we enlarge the granted GBR to $B_{m,GBR}^{grant}(1+\varepsilon)$. Then based on (7) we can calculate τ_{max} (ε, α), the maximum value of τ, by the following equation

$$\alpha\tau \le [1 - (1 - \alpha)^\tau](1+\varepsilon). \tag{8}$$

Given α and ε, then τ_{max} (ε, α) is the maximum silence duration that the following burst, which is a packet with $B_{m,GBR}^{grant} \cdot \tau_i$ bits, is legal (authorized) to be sent out immediately. For example, if $\varepsilon = 0.15$, the τ_{max} equals 29 and 15 for α being 0.01 and 0.02, respectively. For the sake of diversity when emulating the generated traffic patterns, the chosen silence durations τ_i are uniformly distributed between 80% and 100% of τ_{max}.

4.2   Simulation Environment and Results

The simulation parameters employed are listed in Table 1. Here we consider a simplified environment where each UE generates only one traffic pattern. And we choose α being 0.01 and 0.02 for the traffic patterns used in scenario 1 and 2, respectively. However, the long term averages of these patterns are the same because they have the same $(1 + \varepsilon)B_{m,GBR}^{grant}$. In average, the patterns with smaller α would result in longer silence durations and larger burst sizes. We regard such patterns as more bursty in this paper.

Table 1. Simulation parameters

Parameters	Values (scenario 1/2)
$B_{m,GBR}^{grant}$	1.5 Mbps
Extra ratio ε for generating input patterns	0.15
EWMA weight α for UEs and the eNB	0.01/0.02
τ_{max}	29/15
Extra ratio ε for allocating RBs at eNB	0.1, 0.15
No. of UEs (assume only one bearer per UE)	10–40

As for the eNB, different values of extra ratio ε are employed to observe the impact of load on packet delay. The packet delay of a packet is defined as the duration measured from its arrival at the UE buffer until the transmission is completed.

Figure 3 shows the 90 percentile packet delay corresponding to the number of UEs served by the eNB before being overloaded. The delay increases with the increase of load because of the increased possibility that more burst packets are generated simultaneously. The delay decreases with the increase of the extra ratio at the eNB because higher mean rate is allowed.

Note that in order to have the same 90 percentile delay, less number of UEs can be accommodated for smaller value of smaller α, which means more bursty traffic pattern. For example, with ε being 0.15, the delay for 15 UEs with α being 0.01 is almost the same as that for 30 UEs with ε being 0.02. That means the more bursty patterns should be declared with smaller values of α, while they would induce higher impact on the eNB. The result is that less UEs can be accommodated if the same delay is expected. From the billing point of view, the more bursty traffic patterns should be charged with higher rates if the same QoS is expected.

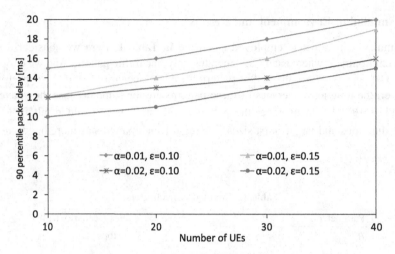

Fig. 3. 90 percentile packet delay vs. system load

5   Conclusion and Discussion

In this paper, we present how to use EWMA algorithm to define the measurement of GBR of a bearer and show how it facilitates uplink resource allocation. We discuss the characteristics of traffic patterns under the constraint of EWMA and explain that EWMA is a suitable algorithm to accommodate the expectation of both UEs and eNBs. Simulation results also suggest that the more bursty traffic patterns, which need to be declared by smaller EWMA weighting factors, should be charged with higher rates because they induce higher impact on the eNB.

It is for further study about how to select parameter values for different kinds of practical traffic. It would also be worthy to analyze the performance when an eNB accommodates UEs with traffics of different parameter values.

Acknowledgements. This paper is supported by Ministry of Science and Technology of Taiwan under grant No. 104-2221-E-197-016. The author would like to thank Jia-Hao Xu and Zhen-Hao Huang for helping the simulation work.

References

1. Ruiz de Temino, L., Berardinelli, G., Frattasi, S., Mogensen, P.: Channel- aware scheduling algorithms for SC-FDMA in LTE uplink. In: IEEE 19th International Symposium on Personal, Indoor and Mobile Radio Communications, PIMRC (2008)
2. Liu, F., She, X., Chen, L., Otsuka, H.: Improved Recursive Maximum Expansion Scheduling Algorithms for Uplink Single Carrier FDMA System. In: IEEE 71st Vehicular Technology Conference (VTC 2010-Spring), pp. 1–5 (2010)
3. Iosif, O., Banica, I.: LTE uplink analysis using two packet scheduling models. In: 19th Telecommunications Forum (TELFOR), pp. 394–397 (2011)

4. Lee, S.-B., Pefkianakis, I., Meyerson, A., Xu, S., Lu, S.: Proportional fair frequency-domain packet scheduling for 3GPP LTE uplink. In: IEEE INFOCOM, pp. 2611–2615 (2009)
5. Calabrese, F.D., et al.: Search-tree based uplink channel aware packet scheduling for UTRAN LTE. In: IEEE Vehicular Technology Conference, VTC Spring 2008, pp. 1949–1953
6. 3GPP, TS 36.300 v. 12.4.0 (2015)
7. Hatoum, R., Hatoum, A., Ghaith, A., Pujolle, G.: Qos-based joint resource allocation with link adaptation for SC-FDMA uplink in heterogeneous networks. Presented at the 12th ACM International Symposium on Mobility Management and Wireless Access (2014)
8. Safa, H., El-Hajj, W., Tohme, K.: A QoS-aware uplink scheduling paradigm for LTE networks. In: IEEE 27th International Conference on Advanced Information Networking and Applications, AINA, pp. 1097–1104 (2013)
9. Marwat, S.N.K., Zaki, Y., Goerg, C., Weerawardane, T., Timm-Giel, A.: Design and performance analysis of bandwidth and QoS aware LTE uplink scheduler in heterogeneous traffic environment. In: 8th International Wireless Communications and Mobile Computing Conference (IWCMC), pp. 499–504 (2012)
10. 3GPP, TS 23.401 v. 13.2.0. General Packet Radio Service (GPRS) Enhancements for Evolved Universal Terrestrial Radio Access Network (E-UTRAN) Access (2015)
11. Exponentially weighted moving average (EWMA). https://en.wikipedia.org/wiki/Moving_average
12. Kuo, F.-C., Ting, K.-C., Wang, H.-C., Tseng, C.-C., Chen, M.-W.: Differentiating and scheduling LTE uplink traffic based on exponentially weighted moving average of data rate. Mob. Netw. Appl. (2016). https://doi.org/10.1007/s11036-016-0693-9. (First Online: 15 February 2016)
13. Kuo, F.-C., Ting, K.-C., Wang, H.-C., Tseng, C.-C.: On demand resource allocation for LTE uplink transmission based on logical channel groups. Mob. Netw. Appl. (2017)

Reusing Resource Blocks by Efficient Grouping for D2D in LTE Networks

Fang-Chang Kuo[1], Kuo-Chang Ting[2], Chih-Cheng Tseng[1(✉)], and Jia-Hao Xu[1]

[1] National Ilan University, Yilan City, Taiwan
`tsengcc@niu.edu.tw`
[2] Departments of Business Administration and Information Engineering, Minghsin University of Science and Technology, Hsinchu, Taiwan

Abstract. D2D (Device to Device) communication is one of the key technologies that 3GPP intends to develop for 5G communication systems. It can not only reduce the burden of eNB, but also increase the capacity of the cellular network. It is also very useful when disasters happen, while the mobile communication systems are not available. Due to limited resource blocks (RB), researchers suggest that D2D pairs which can mutually tolerate the induced interference are grouped into a clique. Then the pairs in the same clique are assigned with the same RBs, so as to reuse RBs and increase the system capacity. The previous method evaluates SINR by using the locations of the devices and free space path loss formulae. In this way, however, the possible obstacles between a pair of devices are not considered. To deal with this problem, in this paper, we propose an approach where the SINR is evaluated by a practical way that employs the Reference Signals Received Power (RSRP) reported by the devices. Our approach can also prevent cliques from being formed improperly, so as to ensure its positive effect.

Keywords: D2D · Reuse RB · RSRP

1 Introduction

1.1 Motivation

With the rapid progress in the networks, the mobile network information also grows rapidly, leading to the introduction of D2D technology in the future LTE systems. D2D technology can reduce the burden of the base station, it can also increase the overall system capacity [1].

Resource allocation is an important issue for D2D technologies. In order to increase the system capacity, we need to improve the efficiency of spectrum utilization with limited radio resources. One of the methods is to group D2D pairs that can tolerate the interference from each other into the same clique. Then, assign the pairs in the same clique with the same RBs, so as to reuse the RBs. There are some problems with the method presented in the literature. As a result, we propose a highly feasible approach to reuse RBs.

© ICST Institute for Computer Sciences, Social Informatics and Telecommunications Engineering 2018
Y.-B. Lin et al. (Eds.): IoTaaS 2017, LNICST 246, pp. 94–100, 2018.
https://doi.org/10.1007/978-3-030-00410-1_12

1.2 D2D Communications

In this paper, the environment under consideration is unicast D2D communication. The first phase for unicast D2D communication is Proximity Discovery. In order to prevent interference, a DUE (D2D User Equipment) transmits discovery signal for the partner to receive [2–4]. 3GPP specifies two types of the operation [2].

- Type 1 (UE-selected) is a procedure where resources for discovery signal transmission are selected from a pool of resources allocated by the eNB on a non UE specific basis.
- Type 2 (eNB scheduled) is a procedure where resources for discovery signal transmission are allocated by the eNB on UE specific basis.

In our proposed approach, which will be presented in Sect. 2, the Type 2 is employed at this phase.

After the proximity relationship is established between two devices, these two devices are named as a pair. Then the eNB needs to allocate some continuous uplink RBs for the pair to transmit direct data and direct control information. 3GPP also defines two modes for this function [2].

- Mode 1: eNB or relay node schedules the exact resources for a DUE to use.
- Mode 2: a DUE on its own selects resources from resource pools.

The mode 1 will be employed in our proposed approach.

1.3 Resource Reuse Schemes and Related Problems

One of the ways to increase the capacity of an eNB is to improve the efficiency of employed spectrum. Because the sensitivity of a UE is much lower than that of an eNB, a UE is less likely to be interfered by the other UE. Some researchers suggested that the D2D pairs that can tolerate the interference from each other are included into the same clique. Then the pairs in the same clique are assigned with the same RBs for transmission, so as to reuse the RBs [5]. Based on the clique forming concept of [5], author of [6] proposed to allow a cellular UE to share RBs with a clique of pairs. For convenience, we name the clique forming scheme used in [5] as LCF, which is the acronym of "Location based Clique Forming" scheme.

However, there are three problems with the LCF scheme. In this paper, we present an approach to prevent these problems. At first, we briefly describe the LCF scheme and mention the challenges faced.

1.4 LCF Clique Forming Scheme

There are basically two steps for the LCF to form cliques.

Step 1: Determining whether two pairs are harmonic to each other

The first step in forming a clique is to determine whether two pairs can tolerate the interference from each other. By referring to Fig. 1, in this paper, we define that two pairs are harmonic to each other if any of the four devices can tolerate the interference

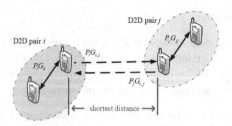

Fig. 1. Illustration for calculating SINR

coming from any device of the other pair when the devices use the same RBs. For LCF scheme, pair i and pair j are harmonic to each other if

$$SINR_{i,j} = \min\left(10\log\left(\frac{P_iG_{ii}}{P_jG_{i,j}+N}\right), 10\log\left(\frac{P_jG_{jj}}{P_iG_{i,j}+N}\right)\right) \geq -6.7 \text{ dB}, \qquad (1)$$

where P_i is the transmit power of D2D pair i, G_{ii} is the channel gain in D2D pair i, and $G_{i,j}$ is the free space channel gain between D2D pair i and pair j with the shortest distance between the devices of the two pairs. N is the thermal noise. All of the channel gain mentioned in LCF scheme consider only the free space path loss, which is calculated according to the following formula

$$\begin{cases} Max(20\log(d)+38.4, 22.7\log(d)+33.02), d \leq 17.06 \text{ m} \\ Max(20\log(d)+38.4, 40\log(d)+11.73), d \leq 17.06 \text{ m} \end{cases} \qquad (2)$$

Here the threshold -6.7 dB for $SINR_{i,j}$ is the minimum SINR for decoding the lowest efficiency QPSK signal. This value corresponds to the condition that CQI = 1 in Table 1 [7].

Table 1. Mapping between CQI and modulation coding schemes (MCS)

CQI	modulation	SINR range (dB)	Code rate	Spectral efficiency
1	QPSK	−6.7<SINR≤−4.7	0.076	0.152
2	QPSK	−4.7<SINR≤−2.3	0.12	0.234
3	QPSK	−2.3<SINR≤0.2	0.19	0.377
4	QPSK	0.2<SINR≤2.4	0.30	0.601
5	QPSK	2.4<SINR≤4.3	0.44	0.870
6	QPSK	4.3<SINR≤5.9	0.59	1.175
7	16-QAM	5.9<SINR≤8.1	0.37	1.476
8	16-QAM	8.1<SINR≤10.3	0.48	1.914
9	16-QAM	10.3<SINR≤11.7	0.60	2.406
10	64-QAM	11.7<SINR≤14.1	0.45	2.730
11	64-QAM	14.1<SINR≤16.3	0.55	3.322
12	64-QAM	16.3<SINR≤18.7	0.65	3.902
13	64-QAM	18.7<SINR≤21.0	0.75	4.523
14	64-QAM	21.0<SINR≤22.7	0.85	5.115
15	64-QAM	SINR>22.7	0.93	5.554

Step 2: clique forming

The second step is to form cliques. In order to obtain high reuse rate of RBs, LCF scheme tries to make cliques as large as possible and then tries letting cliques to reuse the RBs assigned for cellular UEs. Here we only focus on the process to form cliques. Based on graph algorithm, every pair is regarded as a node. If two pairs are harmonic with each other, the two nodes, which represents the two pairs, are connected by an edge. By employing Bron-Kerbosch Algorithm, the maximum clique and some small cliques are obtained.

1.5   Problems with LCF Clique Forming Scheme

A. Problem 1

When applying (1) and (2) to check whether two pairs are harmonic, LCF scheme uses the coordinates of the two pairs to calculate SINR based on free space path loss formulas. However, if there is any obstacle between the two devices of a pair, this scheme would over-estimate the SINR in (1).

B. Problem 2

LCF scheme depends only on Bron-Kerbosch Algorithm to form cliques. That means a pair can be included into an existing clique as long as it is individually harmonic with every pair in the clique. However, when the number of pairs in a clique increases, the interference to every pair increases accordingly, and then some of the pairs may not meet the minimum SINR requirement for D2D communication.

C. Problem 3

When more and more pairs are included in a clique, the number of required RBs for some pairs could probably increase dramatically, and it may be unworthy for the clique members to reuse the same RBs.

In this paper, therefore, we propose an approach to overcome the three problems mentioned above.

We describe the proposed approach in Sect. 2. The simulation results are presented in Sect. 3. Finally, we address the conclusion and future works in Sect. 4.

2   Proposed Approach

The steps of our approach are the same as those of LCF, but the processes in the steps are different.

Step 1: Determine whether two pairs are harmonic – based on measured RSRP

During the phase of Type 2 Proximity Discovery, a discovery signal is transmitted on the RBs allocated by the eNB. We assume that the RSRP (Reference Signal Received Power) is obtained and reported to the eNB. Then, the P_iG_i and P_jG_j in (1) are obtained directly. This method can prevent the problem 1 with LCF scheme. Since a cellular UE will return the RSRP to the eNB, it is a feasible assumption that a device of a D2D pair reports RSRP of the received discovery signal.

Step 2: Clique forming - consider all the interferences in the whole clique

The problem 2 mentioned above shows that if there are too many pairs in a clique and they make high interferences as a result, some of the pairs cannot communicate. The problem 3 even points out that it may be unworthy for the members of a clique to reuse the same RBs. In order to solve problem 2, we check the SINR of each pair of all possible cliques. If a clique includes a pair with SINR less than −6.7 dB, this clique is removed. As for the problem 3, we propose to raise the minimum SINR requirement for the definition of being harmonic and being a member of a clique. Then the definition for pair i and j to be harmonic is modified as follows

$$SINR_{i,j} = \min\left(10\log(\frac{P_i G_{ii}}{P_j G_{i,j} + N}), 10\log(\frac{P_j G_{jj}}{P_i G_{i,j} + N})\right) \geq SINR_{\min,k}, \qquad (3)$$

where the $SINR_{\min,k}$ is the minimum SINR requirement corresponding to CQI = k in Table 1. Besides, the minimum SINR requirement for a pair being in a clique is also set as $SINR_{\min,k}$. For example, if $k = 8$, $SINR_{\min,8} = 8.1$ dB. As for the LCF scheme, the requirement corresponds to $k = 1$, while it doesn't check SINR requirement for a pair to be in a clique.

With higher k, the number of pairs in a clique would decrease in average. However, once a pair is included in a clique, the required number of RBs would be less because of higher SINR.

3   Simulation Results

The simulation environment includes only one eNB and the D2D pairs are uniformly distributed with minimum distance 35 m apart from the eNB. The parameters are listed in Table 2. Both the minimum SINR requirement for being harmonic and being a member of a clique are set the same as $SINR_{\min,k}$, $k = 1$–15. The simulation result is presented in Fig. 2. If the eNB allocates RBs for every pair without reusing by ways of clique forming, the number of required RBs is 139. However, if the minimum SINR requirement for being harmonic and forming clique is $SINR_{\min,1} = -6.7$ dB, the required number of RBs is still as high as 133, which corresponds to only 4% reduction. That means with low SINR threshold, there may be lots of pairs included in cliques, the interferences inside a clique would be high, and each pair may need more RBs. Finally, clique forming cannot effectively reduce the RB demand.

On the contrary, for more stringent SINR thresholds, for example $k = 10$, the cliques may include less pairs. However, the required numbers of RBs are not more because of higher SINR values. As the result, the total RB demand is reduced to only 40% of that without clique forming.

Table 2. Simulation parameters

Parameter	Value
Cell radius	500 m
Carrier frequency	2 GHz
System bandwidth (uplink)	20 MHz
Shadowing standard deviation	7 dB
Antenna gain	0 dBi
Transmission power	23 dBm
Noise spectral density	-174 dBm/Hz
Minimum distance between D2D user and eNB	35 m
Number of D2D pairs	20
Requested data rate for each D2D pair	3 Mbps
Minimum SINR requirement for clique forming, SINRmin,k,	$k = 1 \sim 15$

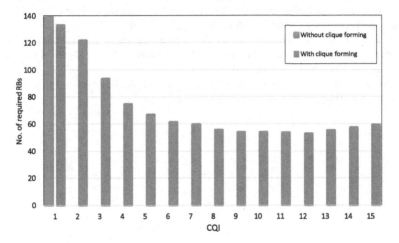

Fig. 2. Number of required RB versus SINR thresholds indicated by CQI

4 Conclusion and Future Works

In order to solve the three problems with the LCF clique forming scheme, we propose a new approach based feasible assumption. With regard to reusing RBs, we evaluate the efficiency based on different SINR thresholds that determines whether two pairs are mutually harmonic and whether a pair can be in a clique. Simulation results reveal that the lowest threshold, which just meets the minimal requirement for decoding, is not suitable because more RBs are needed with low SINR. On the contrary, higher SINR thresholds may result in better performance.

The future works is to consider more parameters and try to save more number of RBs by the clique forming method. It is also important to find a rule to choose a suitable SINR threshold, so as to get better performance.

Acknowledgements. This paper is supported by Ministry of Science and Technology of Taiwan under grant No. 104-2221-E-197-016. The author would like to thank Wei-Hsuan Tsai for helping the simulation work.

References

1. Feng, D., Lu, L., Yuan-Wu, Y., Li, G.Y., Li, S., Feng, G.: Device-to-device communications in cellular networks. IEEE Commun. Mag. **52**(4), 49–55 (2014)
2. 3GPP, TR 36.843 V12.0.1, Study on LTE device to device proximity services; radio aspects (2014)
3. Tang, H., Ding, Z., Levy, B.C.: Enabling D2D communications through neighbor discovery in LTE cellular networks. IEEE Trans. Sig. Process. **62**(19), 5157–5170 (2014)
4. Bagheri, H., Sartori, P., Desai, V., Classon, B., Al-Shalash, M., Soong, A.: Device-to- device proximity discovery for LTE systems. In: 2015 IEEE International Conference on Communication Workshop (ICCW), pp. 591–595. IEEE (2015)
5. Vatsikas, S., Armour, S., De Vos, M., Lewis, T.: A fast and fair algorithm for distributed subcarrier allocation using coalitions and the Nash bargaining solution. In: 2011 IEEE Vehicular Technology Conference (VTC Fall), pp. 1–5. IEEE (2011)
6. Shih, J.-Y.: Resource Allocation for D2D Communications Using Two-Stage Coalition Formation and Nash Bargaining Solution in LTE Networks. Master, Electrical Engineering, National Ilan University, Taiwan (2016)
7. Ghosh, A., Ratasuk, R.: Essentials of LTE and LTE-A. Cambridge University Press, Cambridge (2011)

An IoT Platform for Smart Plant Care

Whai-En Chen[1(✉)], Ming-Yih Chang[2], Kuan-Lin Chou[1],
and Jin-Qiu Shi[2]

[1] Department of Computer Science and Information Engineering,
National Ilan University, No. 1, Sec. 1, Shennong Rd.,
Yilan City 260, Yilan County, Taiwan
wechen@niu.edu.tw
[2] Department of Biomechatronic Engineering, National Ilan University,
No. 1, Sec. 1, Shennong Rd., Yilan City 260, Yilan County, Taiwan

Abstract. The Internet of Things (IoT) technology is changing the agriculture to smart farming which enables farmers to face new challenges in agriculture. This paper develops an IoT platform for smart plant care where the sensors detect the environment parameters and report them to the server. The server invokes the fan and LED by calculating the parameters. In addition, the parameters are stored into the SD card when the connection to the server is failure. Once the emergency event occurs, the platform notifies the users by dialing the phone number instead of polling the system. This way saves the unnecessary messages exchange and power consumption.

Keywords: Arduino · Agriculture · IoT · Growth chamber · Smart farming

1 The Plant Care System

In this paper, we utilize a plant care system as an example to demonstrate a plant growth chamber. The plant care system is designed for hydroponic vegetables such as lettuce.

The plant care system consists of a cylinder [Fig. 1(a)], several electronic components and several sensors [Fig. 1(b), (d)], a Wi-Fi module and a micro-controller [Fig. 1(c)].

In the plant care system, we utilize ATmega328 (Arduino UNO board) as the micro-controller. The micro-controller connects to the sensors, the electronic components and the Wi-Fi module. The micro-controller receives the environment information (e.g., temperature and humidity) through the sensors, checks whether the value is within the threshold and sends the environment information to the server through the Wi-Fi module. For example, if the value is over the threshold (e.g., temperature is more than 25 °C), the micro-controller will activate the thermos electric cooling chip (i.e., the electronic component) to lower the temperature.

Growth cylinder [Fig. 1(a)] divided into two layers (upper and lower). The upper layer places the plant such as lettuce and devices, including a load cell [Fig. 1(d)], humidity and temperature sensors [Fig. 2(a)], five 3-watt white LED lights [Fig. 2(b)], a 150-watt thermoelectric cooling chip [Fig. 2(c)], an infrared sensor [Fig. 2(d)], a CO_2

© ICST Institute for Computer Sciences, Social Informatics and Telecommunications Engineering 2018
Y.-B. Lin et al. (Eds.): IoTaaS 2017, LNICST 246, pp. 101–107, 2018.
https://doi.org/10.1007/978-3-030-00410-1_13

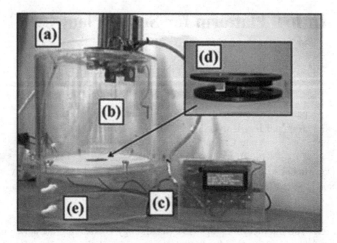

Fig. 1. Plant care system diagram

sensor [Fig. 2(e)] and a light sensor [Fig. 2(f)]. The lower layer sets drain hole [Fig. 1 (e)] used to easy to adjust the nutrient solution.

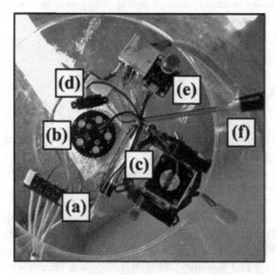

Fig. 2. Electronic components and sensors diagram

The humidity and temperature sensor [Fig. 2(a)] measures the relative humidity and temperature value. Take lettuce for example, the suitable relative humidity and temperature ranges are 70%–80% and 20 °C–25 °C. Based on the relative humidity value, the micro-controller adjusts the relative humidity through the thermoelectric cooling chip. When the temperature decreases lower than the dew point, the moisture condenses and the relative humidity is decreased.

The light intensity affects the growth of the plant. If the light intensity is not enough, the plant's growth will be slow. For example, the range 150–250 μmol/m^2/s is suitable for lettuce's growth. In plant care system, we use five 3-watt white LED lights [Fig. 2(b)] as the light source for plant illumination. The photoperiod are set to light/dark 16/8 h.

The temperature affects the growth of the plant, and thus the temperature should be controlled in a range that is suitable for the plant's growth. For example, the range 20–25 °C is the suitable temperature for lettuce's growth. In the plant care system, we use 150-watt thermoelectric cooling chip [Fig. 2(c)] to control the temperature.

The infrared sensor [Fig. 2(d)] measures height from growth cylinder's top to the plant's leaf crown. The plant height is the growth cylinder's height (22.5 cm) minus the measuring result.

CO_2 is also an important factor in plant growth. We use the CO_2 sensor [Fig. 2(e)] to monitor CO_2 concentration. Generally, we maintain the CO_2 concentration in the range 1100–1300 ppm. The CO_2 solenoid valve connects with a CO_2 cylinder. Through switching the CO_2 solenoid valve, we can adjust CO_2 concentration in growth cylinder.

The load cell (Fig. 1(d)) is used to measure the plant's weight.

The sensors monitor environment condition and transfer the result to the micro-controller. Then, the data will be transferred to the server. The server receives the data and executes the related procedures. One is used to store the data into the database, and the other is used to check the data is unusual or not. If the data is abnormal, the server will send the notification message to the user's handset. The users can check the data by the phone.

Figure 3 illustrates the data transmission architecture. The micro-controller connects to the server through an 802.11 Wi-Fi module. The module can be changed to Zigbee, Bluetooth or LoRa for different environments. The micro-controller invokes an HTTP (Hyper Text Transfer Protocol) library to generate the HTTP GET or POST requests to the server. The HTTP request contains the parameter names and values reported by the sensors. The user equipment (f) connects to the server through 3G (i.e., UMTS) or 4G. The server is developed by using apache, PHP and My SQL software. In addition, a phone is connected to the server through COM port (i.e., USB) and used to make a phone call to notify the system administrators.

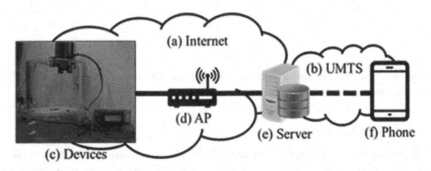

Fig. 3. Data transmission architecture

2 Solutions for Connection Failure and Emergency Notification

The server in the IoT platform stores the parameters reported from the micro-controller, calculates the optimized solutions and notifies the micro-controller taking actions. However, the wireless connection may not be always stable. This paper considers this situation and provides the solution for the connection failure. In addition, the emergency event (e.g., temperature is too high) may occur and the administrator should be notified. In this paper, we propose a PUSH mechanism instead of polling the server. The solutions are elaborated as follows.

2.1 Connection Failure Solution

Consider the wireless connection may be failure, we add an SD module to the micro-controller. Before sending the data to the server, the micro-controller checks whether the connection is successful. If yes, the micro-controller uploads the parameter names and values to the server through the HTTP requests. In addition, the micro-controller checks if there is any buffered data stored in the SD card. If the file exists, the micro-controller reads the parameters and uploads the parameters to the server. The example codes are shown as follows.

```
If(client.connect(SITE_URL, 80))//Check the connection
{
  if(LSD.exists(picName))//Check if the file exists
  {
    LFile dataFile = LSD.Open("dataSD.txt", FILE_READ);
    if(dataFile) //Open File Successful
    {
      dataFile.seek(0); //Move to Starting Point
      len = dataFile.size();
      dataFile.read(bufFile, len); //Read Seneor Data
      dataFile.close();
      befFile[len] = '\0';
    } else
    {
      //report error
    }
  }
}
```

On the contrary, if the connection is failure, the micro-controller stored the parameters into a file in the SD card.

2.2 Emergency Notification

In traditional solution, the handset periodically sends the request to the server to check whether there is an emergency event. Since the emergency event does not occur frequently, most of the query messages are unnecessary that consume the wireless bandwidth and the battery power of the handset.

Figure 4 illustrates the emergency notification flow that is proposed by this paper. When the emergency event is detected and reported by the micro-controller [1], the server utilizes the **adb** command to invoke the android phone to make a phone call to the administrator's handset [2]. Upon receipt of the call, the application on the handset checks the caller identifier. If the caller identifier comes from the server, the application terminates the call and notifies the user by the sounds, vibration and light [3].

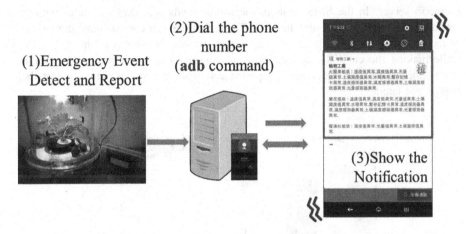

Fig. 4. Emergency notification flow

The script file (i.e., a batch file on Windows) is shown as follows. The script makes a call, waits **20** s, and terminates the call. Note that the call can be terminated by the called party. If the call is not terminated, the sever should terminate the call. Otherwise, the call enters the voicemail system. In this example, the script waits **20** s.

```
@echo on
adb shell am start -a android.intent.action.call -d
tel:%phonenumber
TIMEOUT 20
adb shell input key event 6
echo finish
```

On the android handset, the application utilizes **PhoneReceiver** to receive the incoming phone call information (i.e., the caller identifier).

3   Performance Evaluation

In this system, we would like to understand the performance of the proposed notification method. We compare the proposed method with the SMS (Short Message Service) which is also a PUSH service.

Figure 5 demonstrates the test environment which includes a server and two android handsets. The server is connected to one handset through the COM port (USB cable), and the handset is used to send the SMS message or make a phone call. The server and the handsets synchronize their clocks through the same NTP (Network Time Protocol) server. In the SMS method, the server sends the SMS messages with the sending timestamp to the called handset. The called handset can calculate the latency. In the proposed method, the server stores the sending timestamp in the notification while making the call. The application sends the request to retrieve the notification (with timestamp) after receiving the phone call from the server. The handset then obtains the latency.

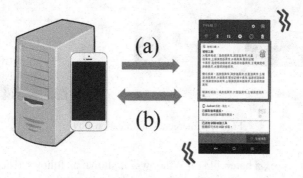

Fig. 5. Performance test environment

The comparison of the SMS and the proposed method are listed in Table 1. We observe that the latency of the SMS and that of the proposed method are very similar. However, the SMS is one-way communication from the server to the client. The proposed method a bi-directional communication. Using the proposed method, the server can record the timestamps that the notification arrives the handset and the user.

Table 1. The comparison of the SMS and proposed notification methods.

Notification method	SMS	Proposed method
Average latency	5.23 s	5.62 s
Variance	0.1501	0.2376
Communication	One-way (server → client)	Bi-direction

4 Conclusion

The Internet of Things (IoT) technology is changing the modern agriculture to smart farming which enables farmers to face new challenges in agriculture. This paper develop an IoT platform for smart plant care where the sensors detect the environment parameters and report them to the server. The server invokes the fan and LED by calculating the parameters. Specifically, we utilize a plant care system as an example to demonstrate the growth chamber. The plant care system is designed for hydroponic vegetables such as lettuce.

Besides the development of the sensor platform, we also consider the wireless connection failure. In this case, the parameters are stored into the SD card. Once the connection is recovery, the buffered data are retransmitted to the server. In this way, the data are not lost due to wireless link failure. We design the local control system instead of the cloud server to handle the environment control during the wireless failure. This part is not discussed in this paper.

When the emergency event occurs, the proposed IoT platform notifies the system administrators by dialing the phone number. This way saves the unnecessary messages exchange and power consumption. Through the experiments, the notification is almost the same fast (about 5 s) as the SMS and the proposed method provides bi-directional communications.

To sum up, the proposed IoT platform can provide reliable data records and effective emergency notification system which can be applied to the smart framing applications.

Acknowledgements. The work is supported by MOST projects 105-2218-E-197 -001 and 105-2218-E-007 -029.

References

1. Bing, F.: Research on the agriculture intelligent system based on IOT. In: 2012 International Conference on Image Analysis and Signal Processing, pp. 1–4 (2012)
2. Kapoor, A., Bhat, S.I., Shidnal, S., Mehra, A.: Implementation of IoT (Internet of Things) and image processing in smart agriculture. In: 2016 International Conference on Computation System and Information Technology for Sustainable Solutions (CSITSS), pp. 21–26 (2016)
3. Nakutis, V., et al.: Remote agriculture automation using wireless link and IoT gateway infrastructure. In: 2015 26th International Workshop on Database and Expert Systems Applications (DEXA), pp. 99–103 (2015)
4. Shenoy, J., Pingle, Y.: IOT in agriculture. In: 2016 3rd International Conference on Computing for Sustainable Global Development (INDIACom), pp. 1456–1458 (2016)
5. Foster, I., Kesselman, C.: The study and application of the IOT technology in agriculture. In: 2010 3rd International Conference on Computer Science and Information Technology, pp. 462–465 (2010)

Dandelion Mirror: An Interactive Visual Design Using IoTtalk

Chung-Yun Hsiao[1(✉)], Chih-Chieh Huang[2], Yi-Bing Lin[1],
and Yun-Wei Lin[1]

[1] Department of Computer Science, National Chiao Tung University,
Hsinchu 30010, Taiwan, R.O.C.
phoebe.cyhsiao@gmail.com, jyneda@gmail.com,
liny@cs.nctu.edu.tw
[2] Center of General Education and College of Arts,
National Tsing Hua University, Hsinchu 30013, Taiwan, R.O.C.
scottie.c.c.huang@gmail.com

Abstract. IoTtalk is a platform for IoT device interaction, which has been used to develop many IoT applications such as home automation. This paper uses Dandelion Mirror artwork as an example to show how interactive visual design can be conveniently implemented in IoTtalk. The Dandelion Mirror artwork conducts cyber physical interaction, which animates a dandelion in a mirror when a person smiles at that mirror. The dandelion grows larger as the person smiles bigger. The flower also vibrates following the heartbeat rate of the person. In our approach, the camera detecting the face expression and the heartbeat rate is considered as an input IoT device, and the mirror display for dandelion animation is considered as an output IoT device. In IoTtalk, the features of the dandelion animation are considered as the actuators that can be independently controlled. IoTtalk nicely connects these IoT devices, where various features can be created for interactive visual design with little or without any programming effort.

Keywords: IoTtalk · Interactive visual design · IoT platform
Cyber physical interaction

1 Introduction

Through cyclical and collaborative processes between people and technology, interactive design emphasizes a user-oriented field of study on meaningful communication of media [1–3]. An interactive design typically involves real-time interaction between human and machines. Several studies have focused on interaction between human behavior and visual objects, i.e., interactive visual design. Examples for such interactive visual design include Wii and Kinect game system, human-computer interaction, and so on.

This paper implements an interactive visual design called Dandelion Mirror. In this design, the smile expression and the heartbeat rate (HBR) of a person in front of the mirror affect the size and the shape of a dandelion animation displayed in the mirror.

© ICST Institute for Computer Sciences, Social Informatics and Telecommunications Engineering 2018
Y.-B. Lin et al. (Eds.): IoTaaS 2017, LNICST 246, pp. 108–116, 2018.
https://doi.org/10.1007/978-3-030-00410-1_14

Dandelion Mirror conducts cyber physical integration, where smile and HBR are detected in the physical domain and the dandelion animation is illustrated in the cyber domain.

We use the Internet of Things (IoT) approach to implement Dandelion Mirror. In an IoT system, the IoT devices interact with each other through a network server following protocols such as AllJoyn, OM2M, OpenMTC [4] or any proprietary protocols. An example is a smart home appliance application where a remote controller (an input IoT device) controls home appliances such as a fan or a light (output IoT devices or actuators) through the IoT server/gateway. A program called network application is executed at the server to implement the desired interactions between the input and the output devices. This paper utilizes IoTtalk, an IoT platform [4, 5] that supports quick development of network application software. We use IoTtalk to implement Dandelion Mirror. Through this implementation, we will demonstrate that IoTtalk nicely connects the IoT devices, and through flexible connections, different features can be created for interactive visual design with little or without any programming effort. The paper is organized as follows. Section 2 introduces IoTtalk. Section 3 shows the implementation of the dandelion animation. Section 4 shows the implementation of the IoT device connections. Section 5 concludes our work with future research directions.

2   IoTtalk Concept and Usage

In IoTtalk, every IoT device is characterized by its functionalities or "device features". A device feature (DF) is a specific input or output "capability" of the IoT device. Consider a mobile phone as an IoT device. The input device features (IDFs) are sensors or controls that can be the microphone, the Gyro sensor, the GPS, the camera, and so on. The output device features (ODFs) are actuators such as the display screen, the speaker, and so on. An IoT device is connected to the IoTtalk server in the Internet through wireline or wireless technologies. The network application that defines the interaction between the IoT devices is developed and executed at the IoTtalk server. When the values of the IDFs are updated, an IoT device informs the network application to take some actions, and the network application sends the result to the ODF of the same or another IoT device to affect that output device. With this view, the IoT devices interact with each other through their device features.

The implementation of Dandelion Mirror in IoTtalk includes an input device called Intel-Cam and an output device called Dandelion. The hardware of Intel-Cam is an Intel RealSense Camera (model F200 or SR300), which can detect human facial expressions and the pulse rate. The detection functions are provided by Intel RealSense SDK [6]. In our approach, the connections of the input and the output devices can be easily established through the IoTtalk GUI. In this GUI, an input device is represented by an icon placed at the left of the window, which consists of smaller icons that represent IDFs, and an output device is represented by an icon placed at the right-hand side of the window, which includes ODF icons. For example, the icon in Fig. 1(a) represents the input device Intel-Cam. To implement the Dandelion Mirror application in IoTtalk, Intel-Cam detects the smile expression, and output the result through the *Smile* IDF (Fig. 1(c)). Intel-Cam also detects the heartbeats, and outputs the measure through the *HBR* IDF (Fig. 1(b)). In Fig. 1(d), the Dandelion output device is a visual Java program installed in a Mirror display [7], which has two ODFs *Size* (Fig. 1(e)) and *Vibration* (Fig. 1(f)). By connecting the *HBR* IDF to the *Vibration* ODF (Fig. 1(1)), Dandelion will animate vibration based on the frequency of the measured heartbeat rate. By connecting the *Smile* IDF to the *Size* ODF (Fig. 1(2)), when the camera detects the smile expression, the flower grows bigger.

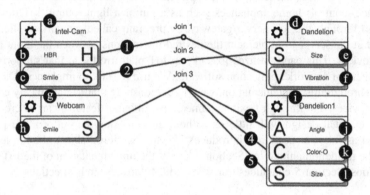

Fig. 1. The basic layout of Dandelion Mirror in IoTtalk GUI.

With IoTtalk, we can easily replace the input or the output devices of Dandelion Mirror with different implementations. For example, we can replace Intel-Cam by an ordinary webcam (Fig. 1(g)) connected to a computer or is built in a laptop that executes facial expressions provided by the OpenCV Haar feature-based cascade classifier [8]. The Webcam device can be considered as a simplified version of Intel-Cam with one IDF *Smile* (Fig. 1(h)). We also implement another output device Dandelion1 (Fig. 1(i)) with three ODFs *Angle* (Fig. 1(j)), *Color* (Fig. 1(k)) and *Size* (Fig. 1 (l)), which can change the shape. The *Smile* IDF of Webcam is connected to the *Angle*, the *Color* and the *Size* ODFs to affect Dandelion1 (Fig. 1(3), (4) and (5)). Animations of Dandelion and Dandelion1 are implemented by the same Java program but with different parameter setups. Therefore, their appearances can be very different.

Through IoTtalk GUI, both Intel-Cam and Webcam are flexibly connected to either Dandelion or Dandelion1. Initially, the colors of both flowers are white. We may connect the *HBR* IDF of Intel-Cam to the *Vibration* ODF of Dandelion (Fig. 2(1)) and the *Angle* ODF of Dandelion1 (Fig. 2(2)). In this way, the heartbeats detected by Intel-Cam will control Dandelion's vibration and Dandelion1's angle. Both *Smile* IDFs of Intel-Cam and Webcam are linked to Join2 and then connected to the *Size* ODF of Dandelion (Fig. 2(3)). If the smile detected by Intel-Cam is bigger than that by Webcam, Join2 sends the value 1 (large flower) to the *Size* ODF of Dandelion. Otherwise the value 0 (no flower) is sent to Dandelion. Join3 links both *Smile* IDFs to the *Size* ODF of Dandelion1 (Fig. 2(4)). If the smile detected by Intel-Cam is bigger than that by Webcam, Join3 sends the value 0 to the *Size* ODF of Dandelion1. Otherwise the value 1 is sent to Dandelion1. With connections Join2 and Join3, big Dandelion appears and Dandelion1 disappears if the smile detected by Intel-Cam is bigger than that by Webcam. On the other hand, if the smile detected by Webcam is bigger, then Dandelion1 appears and Dandelion disappears. Therefore, two persons can play a competition game with Dandelion Mirror. Join4 links both *Smile* IDFs to the *Color* ODF of Dandelion1 (Fig. 2(5)) so that if the smile detected by Webcam is bigger than that by Intel-Cam, the color of Dandelion1 turns yellow. Otherwise, Dandelion1 is white. To achieve the effects of Join2, Join3 and Join4, we need to program functions at these connections. We will elaborate on the details in Sect. 4.

We may also control the color of Dandelion1 by a color sensor as shown in Join5 (Fig. 2(6)). In this connection, the input device is a MorSensor [4] plugged in a color sensor.

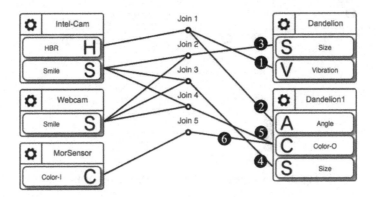

Fig. 2. An advanced layout of Dandelion in IoTtalk GUI.

3   The Dandelion Output Device

This section describes the output device Dandelion1 (Fig. 1(i)) with three ODFs *Size*, *Angle* and *Color*. In IoTtalk, the software for an output device consists of two parts. The actuator application implements the dandelion animation software. The device application (DA) provides the driver for wired or wireless communication to the IoTtalk server. The DA receives the data sent from the IoTtalk server and forwards them to the actuator application through the ODFs. These ODFs are specified in the Device Feature Window (Fig. 3). This window is provided by IoTtalk to manage the device features [4]. The Device Feature Window for the *Size* ODF (Fig. 3(1)) has one parameter (Fig. 3(2)) that represents the maximum level of the Dandelion to be grown. This parameter ranges from 0 to 10 (Fig. 3(3) and (4)). Figure 4 shows the Dandelion with *Size* = 8. The *Angle* ODF represents the growth direction of the Dandelion, which ranges from 0 to 120° (Fig. 3(5) and (6)). Figure 4 illustrates the dandelion with the *Angles* of 37° and 90°, respectively. The *Color* ODF represents the color of the Dandelion in the RGB format. That is, this ODF has three parameters, each of them ranges from 0 to 255 (Fig. 3(7), (8) and (9)).

The DA for the IoTtalk devices can be found in [5]. We use Java to implement the actuator application for the Dandelion animation that continuously draws graphical patterns to mimc the morphology of a dandelion. There are two types of parameters. The parameters for the display layout include the width (Fig. 4(1)), the height (Fig. 4 (2)), and the background color (Fig. 4(3)). As shown in Fig. 5, the parameters for the dandelion animation include the stalks s_0, s_1, s_2, s_3, the included angle between s_2 and the horizontal line (*Angle*) and the included angle between s_2 and s_3 (Angle1). These parameters are summarized in Table 1.

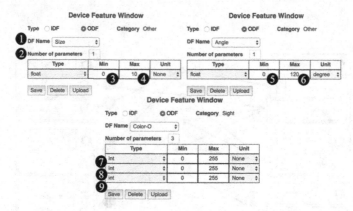

Fig. 3. Device feature window for Dandelion ODFs.

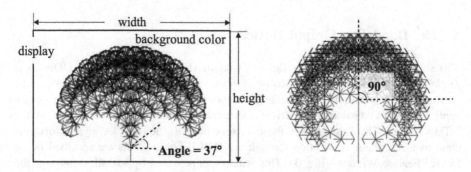

Fig. 4. Dandelion1 grows with different angle values (size = 8).

Dandelion is a fractal art implemented by a binary tree data structure in which each node has two children, the left child node and the right child node. Dandelion grows from the root node (level-0) denoted as $n_{R,0}$, which connects to stalk s_0 (see Fig. 5) with a default length of 384 pixels as defined in Table 1. For level $l \geq 1$, a level-l node is denoted as $n_{D,l}$ where $D = R$ if it is the right child node of its parent node, and $D = L$ if it is the left child node. Figure 5 shows the graphical patterns between the root node

$n_{R,0}$ and its children $n_{R,1}$ and $n_{L,1}$, respectively. The pattern consists of one stalk s_1, two stalks s_2 and two stalks s_3, which is a line with arrows at both ends. The length of stalk s_1 varies with level l expressed as

$$s_1(l) = s_1(0)(1 + 0.05l). \tag{1}$$

where $s_1(0)$ is the length of s_1 at level-0 with a default value 30 pixels as defined in Table 1. The other two stalks s_2 and s_3 have the default values of 17 pixels and 24 pixels, respectively. Angle1 has the default value 120°.

Table 1. The parameters of Dandelion.

	Parameter	Data type	Variable name	Default value
ODFs	Size	int	Size	0
	Angle	float	Angle	0.0
	Color	int	color_r	0
		int	color_g	0
		int	color_b	0
Display layout	Width	int	width	1024 pixels
	Height	int	height	768 pixels
	Background color	int	bg_color_r	255
		int	bg_color_g	255
		int	bg_color_b	255
Dandelion animation	Stalk s_0	int	s0	384 pixels
	Stalk s_1 at level-0	int	s1	30 pixels
	Stalk s_2	int	s2	17 pixels
	Stalk s_3	int	s3	24 pixels
	Angle1	float	a1	120°

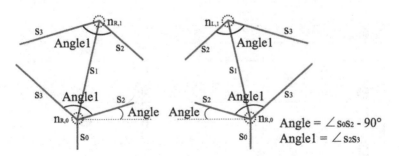

Fig. 5. Graphical patterns of Dandelion at level-0.

4 The Join Functions

IoTtalk allows one to select or implement functions at a Join point. The inputs of the function are the IDFs connected to the join point, and the output is sent to the ODFs connected to the join point. The user can select or implement very simple Join functions to create interesting I/O interactions. In Fig. 2, the function implemented at Join 2 has two inputs, i.e., the *Smile* IDFs of Intel-Cam and Webcam, and the result is sent to the *Size* ODF of Dandelion. By clicking the Join2 circle in the GUI, a window is popped up for the user to write a new function or select a predefined function [4]. The window consists of one or more IDF tables (Fig. 6(1)), one Join Function table (Fig. 6 (2)) and one or more ODF tables (Fig. 6(3)). For Join2, we select the predefined "larger than" function in the Join Function table (Fig. 6(4)), which is implemented in Python as

```
def run(a, b):
    if a > b: return 1
    else: return 0
```

where the input "a" is sent from Intel-Cam and the input "b" is sent from Webcam. Before the value 0 or 1 is sent to the *Size* ODF of Dandelion, it can be manipulated by another function in the ODF table. We select the "times10" function in the Size ODF table (Fig. 6), which is implemented as

```
def run(*args):
    return 10 * args[0]
```

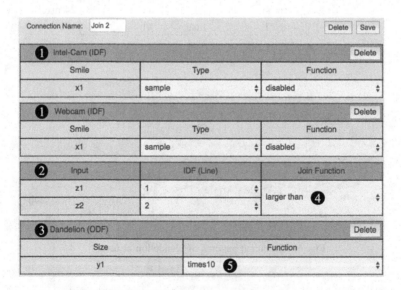

Fig. 6. The functions selected at Join2.

Therefore, if the smile detected by Intel-Cam is bigger than that by Webcam, the execution of these functions retunes the value 10. Otherwise, the value 0 is returned. The function implemented at Join3 is the same as that for Join2 except that the "larger than" function in the Join Function table is replaced by the "smaller than" function, and the final result reverses that of Join2.

5 Discussion and Conclusions

This paper designed and implemented the Dandelion Mirror artwork using IoTtalk. IoTtalk provides simple yet powerful connection mechanism for IoT device interaction, which can effectively and flexibly implement various features for cyber and physical interaction. There are two major components of this visual interactive artwork, a camera and a mirror that displays a dandelion animation. In IoTtalk, the camera is considered as a physical IoT input device, and the dandelion animation is a cyber IoT output device. We showed that with the concept of IDF and ODF, Dandelion Mirror can be conveniently implemented in IoTtalk. Through the ODFs, all features of the dandelion animation (angles, stalks, colors, size, vibration and so on) become the actuators that can be independently controlled in IoTtalk. Also, through IDFs, all detection mechanisms (for facial expression, color, heartbeat rate and so on) become the sensors that can be used to affect all actuators.

In the original design of this artwork, a dandelion in the mirror grows larger as a person in front of the mirror smiles bigger. With IoTtalk, we can easily modify Dandelion Mirror to create many novel and surprising ideas. For example, two sets of Dandelion Mirror can extend single person-dandelion interaction to multiple person-dandelion interactions. We showed how to modify the original Dandelion Mirror to a two-person competition game such that only the dandelion of the person with bigger smile will be displayed in his/her mirror. The IDF/ODF connections can also be easily modified to create multiple-person collaboration game on Dandelion Mirror.

Furthermore, many sensors and actuators have been connected to IoTtalk, and these IoT devices can be used to extend the interactive visual design. For example, the color sensor of MorSensor can affect the color of the dandelion animation. To conclude, we have demonstrated that IoTtalk nicely connects the IoT devices, and through flexible configurations, various features can be created for interactive visual design with little or without any programming effort.

Acknowledgements. The first version of Dandelion1 is implemented by Qing Liu.

References

1. Crawford, C.: The Art of Interactive Design. William Pollock, San Francisco (2003)
2. Kolko, J.: Thoughts on Interaction Design. Morgan Kaufmann, San Francisco (2011)
3. Saffer, D.: Designing for Interaction. New Riders, Berkeley (2010)
4. Lin, Y.B., et al.: EasyConnect: a management system for IoT devices and its applications for interactive design and art. IEEE Internet Things J. 2(6), 551–561 (2015)

5. Lin, Y.B., Lin, Y.W., Huang, C.M., Chih, C.Y., Lin, P.: IoTtalk: a management platform for reconfigurable sensor devices. IEEE Internet of Things J. (2017). https://doi.org/10.1109/jiot.2017.2682100
6. Intel RealSense SDK Developer Reference. https://software.intel.com/intel-realsense-sdk/
7. Huang, S.C.: MSOrgm (motivational sensitive organism). Leonardo **42**(4), 374–375 (2009)
8. Open Source Computer Vision. http://opencv.org

Metaheuristic-Based Scheme for Spectrum Resource Schedule Over 5G IoT Network

Yao-Chung Chang[1(✉)], Shih-Yun Huang[2], and Han-Chieh Chao[2]

[1] Department of Computer Science and Information Engineering,
National Taitung University, Taitung, Taiwan, R.O.C.
ycc@nttu.edu.tw
[2] Department of Electrical Engineering, National Dong Hwa University,
Hualien, Taiwan, R.O.C.
deantt67@gmail.com, hcchao@gmail.com

Abstract. Numerous international organizations agreed that future 5G must be an Ultra Dense Network (UDN) which includes machine to machine (M2M), device to device (D2D) and so on. Thus, how to increase the usage utility of spectrum and management of spectrum resources are the important research issues for 5G mobile communication. Following the requirement of 5G development organizations, this study adopts centralized cloud radio access network (C-RAN) architecture to design a novel mechanism for scheduling of all the M2M requests. The proposed metaheuristic-based scheduling mechanism guarantees that the final solution will not fall into the local optimum. Simulation results show that the proposed scheduling mechanism improves the spectrum resource utilization over 5G IoT network.

Keywords: 5G network · IoT · C-RAN · Metaheuristic scheduling mechanism

1 Introduction

Recently the new smart device technique is improved every day and the market demand bigger than a few years ago. The mobile communication network needs to support the high quality of service for devices; the 5G mobile communication network will be the solution. The 5G mobile network provides more high data rate, low latency, and the multi-input and multi-output (MIMO) technology. Communications for Internet of thing (IoT) and device to device (D2D) in the Ultra Dense Network (UDN) for 5G mobile network is also named the heterogeneity network [2]. The 5G mobile networks focus on the higher transmission speed. Besides, it supplies to improve the better quality of service. Hence, how to manage the network resource effective to enhance the network performance is a very important issue in the 5G mobile network. This study proposed an efficient spectrum resource scheduling scheme by using simulated annealing (SA) algorithm. The application needs more spectrum resource or high QoS, the value of weight will be larger. Second, the algorithm based on a given weight value will random schedule and calculate the number of the idle time slot. This study combines the meta-heuristic algorithm - SA algorithm to get the optimal solution.

© ICST Institute for Computer Sciences, Social Informatics and Telecommunications Engineering 2018
Y.-B. Lin et al. (Eds.): IoTaaS 2017, LNICST 246, pp. 117–125, 2018.
https://doi.org/10.1007/978-3-030-00410-1_15

This paper is structured as follows: Sect. 2 denotes the network resource management and scheduling mechanism of the 5G mobile network. Section 3 presents the problem definition. The description of the proposed method and detail algorithm are described in Sect. 4. The simulation results are demonstrated in Sect. 5. Finally; Sect. 6 marks conclusions of this work.

2 Related Works

The standards of 5G development and research have become ubiquitous in recent years, more and more studies focus on how to improve the QoS and increase the utility of resource allocation. The Virtual Network Embedding (VNE) is a key point that can manage the network resource efficient and improve the network performance [4]. Authors in this paper compared the three network management policies: Full SharingFull Split and Russian Dolls. By comparing three mechanisms that researchers can know the advantages and defects of how to select the management method. On the other hand, the authors analyze the network scenarios which resource mechanisms will be better. However, this study does not focus on the spectrum resource issues. In [5] mentioned the importance of spectrum resource allocation and management in the radio access network. To solve this problem, the method proposed here uses more task scheduling mechanisms to address this issue.

In [6–9], these studies described the proposed task scheduling mechanisms. In [6] authors proposed to use a task scheduling at distributed system architecture in C-RAN. One of the most important goals is to design the scheduling that throughput can be maximum. Authors will set the threshold for every BBU. Next, the BBU will start to do the task scheduling if the user s power gain of the channel is bigger than the threshold of BBU. Moreover, in another study with the issue of cloud computing resource allocation [7], authors proposed the task scheduling which is different traditional bandwidth methods. Most of those traditional methods considerate the hardware resource including CPU capacity, memory, etc. Also, they calculate the processing time of task and cost of communication. Given this, we know the spectrum resource is an issue that needs to focus. However, some smart devices do not fit in the same location, like the smart phone and vehicle device. If the device is mobile, we must care the situation for the whole network [8]. The main idea is using the friendship algorithm to solve this problem under the centralized network architecture. Finally, the authors using the Genetic Algorithm (GA) one of the meta-heuristic algorithms to solve the load balancing in the cloud computing and that can avoid the solution is the local optimal.

3 Problem Definition

In this section, we will use the independent linear program (ILP) to define the problem want to solve. This study should follow the 5G mobile communication network architecture to increase the credibility. Figure 1 is our network environment and architecture. Consider the IoT will be many devices in one area, at this time, we can define this number of devices is like the swamp. However, each small cell just can support the service for a fixed number of IoT devices and have the limited coverage range. In part of the base station, in C-RAN the radio remote heads were separated, and the base band unit (BBU) pool is responsible for computing and storage data. The BBU pool is not in base station but nearby it. When small cell collected the data from IoT devices, it will transmit the collected data to the base station through the method of wireless (fronthaul). The base station will do the scheduling to management the spectrum resource. Finally, the base station is using backhaul to connect the core network to finish the transmission.

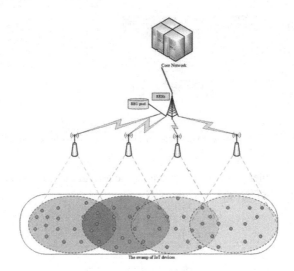

Fig. 1. The IoT with 5G mobile communication environment

At this part, we will focus on the defined our problem with using equation. For clearly to present the equation, here we will assume and define the important symbols that problem can be known easily. First, we assume there have some IoT devices N; the N is a set that presents $N = 1,,n,,N$. In this study, we assume there has the different type service of IoT devices even there are in same coverage range with small cell. Above this assumption, here we use the set $M = 1,,m,,M$ to present the types of task in our network environment, and the T_n^m is the nth devices processing the task of type m. Next, consider the problem is how to manage the spectrum resource to improve the performance. We define the resource block of task, the m_r defines the demand resource block of T_n^m. On the other hand, we also use β to present the remainder resource blocks in the channel. Figure 2 shows the state of data transmission form IoT to the base station. As our assumption, the each small cell maybe services two type of tasks or more. The different type task requires different time to send the data to small a cell. At this situation the small cell can schedule the every task easily. But if all small cell uplink there task scheduling to base station, the collision will occur at the same time slot. To avoid this situation, the base station need to do change the original schedule, but there has some task is real time data that cannot wait for long time. So how to schedule the task to reduce the waiting time is the main issue in this paper.

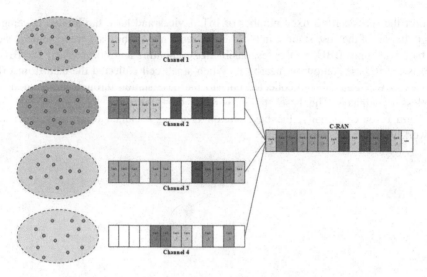

Fig. 2. The state of data transmission from IoT to base station

To define our problem, we need to consider the arrival rate for each task, the arrival rate we present the $p(T_n^m)$, the

$$p(T_n^m) = \frac{1}{\sigma\sqrt{2\pi}} e^{\frac{-(\beta-\mu)^2)}{2\sigma^2}}, \tag{1}$$

$$E(T_n^m) = p(T_n^m) * \gamma_m, \tag{2}$$

we use σ to present the standard deviation of β. μ defined the average of m_r. The γ_m is the weight of mth task type, and the $E(T_n^m)$ is expectation value. We know the arrival rate of the task, we also need to evaluate the service time when the job in the channel.

$$s_m^n = e^{\frac{m}{1+m}}, \tag{3}$$

the s_m^n defined the service time in our study. Above this equations, the waiting time of device n with type m task in the channel at this schedule can calculate,

$$w_m^n = \frac{1}{E(T_n^m) - s_m^n}. \tag{4}$$

Therefore, for improved the spectrum resource management and enhances the performance, the main goal is to find the optimal scheduling methods which have the minimum waiting time for this schedule. The Eq. (4) shows the total waiting time of task in the channel,

$$W = \sum_{n=1}^{N} w_m^n. \tag{5}$$

At the least of this section, Table 1 shows the ILP model in this study.

Table 1. ILP model

Minimize $\sum_{n=1}^{N} w_m^n$

s.t.

$$\sum_{m=1}^{M} \gamma_m = 1$$
$$p(T_n^m) \in [0, 1]$$

---

4 SA Based Weight of Task Scheduling (SWTS)

At the previous section, this paper defined the problem to solve. The most important issues are how to schedule the spectrum, and manage resource efficiently, and minimize the waiting time of the task in the system. At first, when IoT devices transmit the data to a small cell, there have different type tasks and different timing. The small cell will schedule these tasks with the first in first out (FIFO) method. Next, if all the small cells send the data to the base station; the collision will happen. To avoid this situation, we defined the weight for whole task types. Moreover, the transmission information contains fixed form data and real-time data. This paper defines the task type of real-time information with a high weight. In our proposed method, if the task has high weight, the scheduling order should be handled with high priority compared with the low weight task.

The situation of the same weight at the same time maybe happen if we use the weight of task. For this study, we will use the simulation annealing (SA) algorithm to help us find the solution. If using the weight to decide the how to do scheduling the solution have to chance is local optimal not global. The SA algorithm is one of the metaheuristic algorithms; it will randomly change the one or more task type for original scheduling and calculate the solution. If this solution is better than original solution, it will substitute the initial solution and become a new optimal solution. The SA algorithm will process this active still find the optimal global solution. However, for finding the solution can be fast, the SA algorithm has a threshold can help find the optimal solution speed. If the template small than the threshold, it can replace the solution too. The template T changes at every iteration. Here we use the $W_{optimal}$ to present the optimal solution, and ψ is defined the value of the threshold. Algorithm 1 is proposed mechanism in this paper.

Algorithm 1 SA - based on Weight of Task Scheduling (SWTS) Algorithm

---
Input: N, M, γ

Output: $W_{optimal}$ Parameter: T, ψ, δ

 1: Randomly the weight for task type;

 2: Initial the network environment;

 3: Doing the scheduling with weight value;

 4: Calculate the waiting time W and this is solution is optimal solution $W_{optimal}$;

 5: Randomly changes the task type and calculate the solution W;

 6: **If** $W < W_{optimal}$ || $T < \psi$

 7: $W_{optimal} = W$;

 8: **else if**

 9: **return**

10: **End**

11: $T = T * \alpha$;

---

5 Simulation Results

5.1 Simulation Setting

In this section shows the SWTS simulation results. The simulation tool is MATLAB R2012a, and our compare method is a greedy algorithm. Here the greedy algorithm method stands for the scheduling will satisfy the high weight of tasks at the channel first of view. On the other hand, Fig. 1 is the simulation network architecture, and Table 2 is relevant parameters in our simulation. We assume the IoT devices just send the one task in the one-time slot and the resource blocks of the channel just satisfy the complete tasks needed. The simulation parameter here we set some IoT devices (N) is 100–500, and there have 5 types of task (M). Moreover, each type of task has corresponded weight and demand number of resource blocks. In this paper, the weights and demand number of resource blocks generation is random. Table 2 is the relevant parameters in this article.

Table 2. Important parameters with simulation

Parameters	Values
Number of IoT devices	100–500
Number of task types	5
Iteration	500
Temperature	900
α	0.9

5.2 Results

At this part, we will show the simulation results. First, we compare the waiting time with the proposed method-SWTS algorithm and greedy algorithm in Fig. 3. Our method is better than the method of using greedy. This is because the greedy algorithm just considers the weight of task. Because the high priority (weight) tasks might be spending more time to transmission and processing the task, the low priority tasks need more time to wait the maximum weight tasks finish the transmission. In other words, the greedy method is not fair which the tasks have a low weight. However, at our method, the SA algorithm can randomly change the tasks at original scheduling. The tasks which have the low weight might be transmission sooner than great weight tasks; it can reduce the waiting time very efficiently.

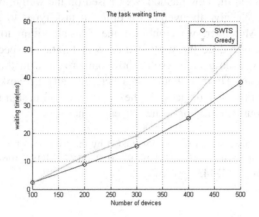

Fig. 3. The waiting time with SWTS and greedy algorithm

Finally, we consider the computing time in our method. Due to the SA algorithm is one kind of metaheuristic algorithm, it needs too much time to do the optimal scheduling. Also, it is unrealistic in 5G C-RAN communication network. In this paper, the number of change bits will add some IoT devices.

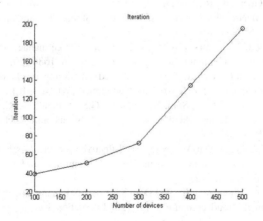

Fig. 4. The number of iterations with IoT devices

Figure 4 shows our experimental result. We can see the number of convergence does not increase very soon. Moreover, it represents our proposed method is suitable for task scheduling.

6   Conclusion

How to manage the spectrum resource is a major issue with IoT application in 5G C-RAN. The IoT might have the more different missions in this ultra dense network. In this study, we proposed the new method SA - based on the weight of task scheduling (SWTS) algorithm. We give the weight for different task types to help us to do the scheduling firstly. Moreover, we combined the SA- algorithm to get the optimal scheduling let we can reduce the waiting time with limitation spectrum resource to improve the QoS. The simulation results show our proposed method is much better than greedy algorithm. The 5G should be a heterogeneity network; this study only considers the network of IoT devices. At the future, we will design the method it can effect to do the resource allocation in heterogeneity network.

Acknowledgments. This research was partly funded by the Ministry of Science and Technology, R.O.C. under grants MOST 105-2221-E-197 -010 -MY2, MOST 106-2511-S-259 -001 -MY3 and MOST 105-2221-E-143 -001 -MY2.

References

1. Gupta, A., Jha, R.K.: A survey of 5G network: architecture and emerging technologies. IEEE Access **3**, 1206–1236 (2015)
2. Peng, M., Li, Y., Jiang, J., Li, J., Wang, C.: Heterogeneous cloud radio access networks: a new perspective for enhancing spectral and energy efficiencies. IEEE Wirel. Commun. **21** (6), 126–135 (2014)
3. Hung, S.-C., Hsu, H., Lien, S.-Y., Chen, K.-C.: Architecture harmonization between cloud radio access networks and fog networks. IEEE Access **3**, 3019–3034 (2015)
4. Trivisonno, R., Guerzoni, R., Vaishnavi, I., Frimpong, A.: Network resource management and QoS in SDN-enabled 5G systems. In: Global Communications Conference (GLOBECOM). IEEE Press (2015)
5. Olwal, T.O., Djouani, K., Kurien, A.M.: A survey of resource management toward 5G radio access networks. IEEE Commun. Surv. Tutor. **18**(3), 1656–1686 (2016)
6. Soliman, H.M., Leon-Garcia, A.: Fully distributed scheduling in cloud-RAN systems. In: Wireless Communications and Networking Conference (WCNC). IEEE Press (2016)
7. Razaque, A., Vennapusa, N.R., Soni, N., Janapati, G.S., Vangala, K.R.: Task scheduling in cloud computing. In: Long Island Systems, Applications and Technology Conference (LISAT). IEEE Press (2016)
8. Wu, L., Du, X., Zhang, H., Yu, W., Wang, C.: Effective task scheduling in proximate mobile device based communication systems. In: IEEE International Conference on Communications (ICC). IEEE Press (2015)
9. Wang, T., Liu, Z., Chen, Y., Xu, Y., Dai, X.: Load balancing task scheduling based on genetic algorithm in cloud computing. In: 12th International Conference on Dependable. IEEE Press (2014)

10. Cho, H.-H., Lai, C.-F., Shih, T.K., Chao, H.-C.: Integration of SDR and SDN for 5G. IEEE Access **3**, 1196–1204 (2014)
11. Tseng, F.-H., Chou, L.-D., Chao, H.-C., Wang, J.: Ultra-dense small cell planning using cognitive radio network toward 5G. IEEE Wirel. Commun. **22**(6), 76–83 (2015)
12. Chen, Y.-W., Liao, P.-Y., Huang, B.-T.: A chip-based distributed spectrum adjustment for fair access in cognitive radio network. J. Internet Technol. **17**(1), 11–18 (2016)

A Fuel-Efficient Route Plan App Based on Game Theory

Chi-Lun Lo[1,2], Chi-Hua Chen[3(✉)], Jin-Li Hu[4], Kuen-Rong Lo[1],
and Hsun-Jung Cho[2]

[1] Telecommunication Laboratories, Chunghwa Telecom Co., Ltd.,
Taoyuan 326, Taiwan
{cllo,lo}@cht.com.tw
[2] Department of Transportation and Logistics Management,
National Chiao Tung University, Hsinchu 300, Taiwan, ROC
hjcho001@gmail.com
[3] College of Mathematics and Computer Science, Fuzhou University,
Fuzhou 350116, Fujian, China
chihua0826@qq.com
[4] Institute of Business and Management, National Chiao Tung University,
Hsinchu 300, Taiwan, ROC
jinlihu@mail.nctu.edu.tw

Abstract. This study adopts a fuel consumption estimation method to measure the consumed fuel quantity of each vehicle speed interval (i.e., a cost function) in accordance with individual behaviors. Furthermore, a mobile app is designed to consider the best responses of other route plan apps (e.g., the shortest route plan app and the fast route plan app) and plan the most fuel-efficient route according to the consumed fuel quantity. The numerical analysis results show that the proposed fuel-efficient route plan app can effectively support fuel-saving for logistics industries.

Keywords: Fuel efficiency · Route plan · Game theory

1 Introduction

In recent years, the prices of diesel fuel and unleaded fuel have been increased to lead to higher cost of transportation for logistics industries [1]. For instance, the fuel cost of logistics industries was increased up to 35.8 billion dollars in Taiwan in 2015 [2]. Therefore, saving fuel consumption of fleet vehicles is an important challenge for logistics.

For fleet management, commercial vehicle operation systems (CVOSs) have been designed and implemented to collect the movement records of vehicles. These movement records can be periodically reported and used to track the location and speed of vehicle. Furthermore, the fuel invoices including the fuel quantity information after refueling can be uploaded into CVOS by driver. A fuel consumption estimation method based on a generic algorithm is hence proposed to analyze the movement records and the fuel quantity information for measuring the relationship the driver's behaviors and fuel consumption [3].

© ICST Institute for Computer Sciences, Social Informatics and Telecommunications Engineering 2018
Y.-B. Lin et al. (Eds.): IoTaaS 2017, LNICST 246, pp. 126–135, 2018.
https://doi.org/10.1007/978-3-030-00410-1_16

Although the fuel consumption can be estimated to detect fuel-wasting based on driver's behavior, some fuel-saving strategies (e.g., fuel-efficient route plans) should be developed and performed for reducing fuel cost. Therefore, this study adopts the proposed fuel consumption estimation method to measure the consumed fuel quantity of each vehicle speed interval (i.e., a cost function) in accordance with each individual's optimal behavior. Moreover, a mobile app is designed to consider the best responses of other route plan apps (e.g., the shortest route plan app and the fast route plan app) and plan the most fuel-efficient route based on the game theory.

The remainder of the paper is organized as follows. Section 2 remarks the detail processes of a fuel consumption estimation method. The design of proposed fuel-efficient route plan app and the game model of route plan apps are presented in Sect. 3. Section 4 gives a numerical analysis to evaluate the performance of the propose route plan app. Finally, Sect. 5 concludes this paper and discusses future work.

2   Fuel Consumption Estimation Method

A fuel consumption estimation method based on a generic algorithm was proposed and evaluated to analyze the consumed fuel quantity of each vehicle speed interval [3] for individual driver. The method can generate a fuel consumption estimation function $g(u_i)$ in according with the vehicle speed u_i in Route i to estimate the fuel quantity in each 30 s. The details of process are illustrated as follows (shown in Fig. 1).

1. The movement records (e.g., vehicle speed) and the fuel invoices (e.g., fuel quantity) are retrieved and analyzed.
2. A fitness function model and the score of each DNA (deoxyribonucleic acid) sequence are defined as Eqs. (1) and (2) to estimate the values of consumed fuel quantities $\{q_1, q_2, .., q_{14}\}$. For instance, Driver 1 drove a car which was equipped with OBU 1 during 2016; c_1 records idle speed (i.e., the value of u_i is zero) reported by OBU 1 during 2016; c_2 records the speed between 0 km/h and 10 km/h reported by OBU 1 during 2015; consequently, c_{14} records the speed higher than 120 km/h reported by OBU 1 during 2016. Furthermore, the summation of fuel quantities of OBU 1 during January 2016 is Q litres.

$$\sum_{k=1}^{14} c_k \times q_k = Q \tag{1}$$

$$s = \left| \sum_{k=1}^{14} c_k \times q_k - Q \right| \tag{2}$$

3. The sets of initial DNA sequences (i.e., the sets of consumed fuel quantities) can be randomly generated, and the score of each DNA sequence can be measured by using Eq. (2).

4. The process of the convergence check can be performed according to the maximum number of iterations, and an adaptable DNA sequence is outputted as the estimated results of the fuel consumption.
5. The processes of gene crossover and gene mutation can be performed to generate child's DNA sequences.
6. The processes of gene reproduction can be performed to support that the generated child's DNA sequences are substituted for original maternal DNA sequences for evolution. The score of each DNA sequence is calculated, and the generic algorithm is performed again.

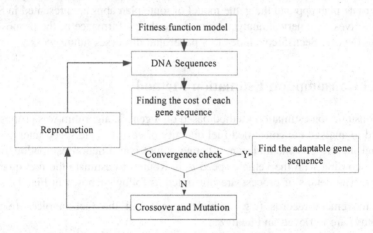

Fig. 1. The process of fuel consumption estimation method based on a generic algorithm

A fuel consumption estimation function $g(u_i)$ can be obtained by the fuel consumption estimation method. The vehicle speed u_i can be adopted into the function $g(u_i)$ to query the consumed fuel quantity c_i for individual driver. A case study of fuel consumption estimation function $g(u_i)$ is showed in Table 1.

3 Fuel-Efficient Route Plan App

For the design of fuel-efficient route plan app, the real-time traffic condition and the consumed fuel quantity of individual driving behavior are considered. However, the traffic condition may be influenced by other route plan apps (e.g., the shortest route plan app and the fast route plan app). Therefore, this study expresses the route plan as a game model to analyze the best responses of competitors to determine the fuel- efficient route plan. In this section, players in this game model are presented in Subsect. 3.1, and the scenarios and candidate strategies of route plan are defined in Subsect. 3.2. Finally, Subsect. 3.3 shows the best response of each player.

Table 1. A case study of fuel consumption estimation function

Vehicle speed interval (unit: km/hr)	Consumed fuel quantity in each 30 s (unit: litre)	Consumed fuel quantity in each hour (unit: litre)
$u_i = 0$	0.007	0.840
$0 < u_i \leq 10$	0.020	2.400
$10 < u_i \leq 20$	0.033	3.960
$20 < u_i \leq 30$	0.055	6.600
$30 < u_i \leq 40$	0.013	1.560
$40 < u_i \leq 50$	0.038	4.560
$50 < u_i \leq 60$	0.069	8.280
$60 < u_i \leq 70$	0.150	18.000
$70 < u_i \leq 80$	0.142	17.040
$80 < u_{ii} \leq 90$	0.080	9.600
$90 < u_{ii} \leq 100$	0.048	5.760
$100 < u_i \leq 110$	0.077	9.240
$110 < u_i \leq 120$	0.284	34.080
$120 < u_i$	0.492	59.040

3.1   Players

Three players who design and provide a route plan app join this game. The preferred strategy of each player is described as follows.

1. Player 1 selects the shortest route plan based on the lowest geo-distance. Player 1 plays as a traditional navigation system which does not consider the traffic condition to determine a route plan.
2. Player 2 selects the fastest route plan based on the lowest travel time. Player 2 plays as an Internet-based navigation system which does consider the traffic condition to determine a route plan.
3. Player 3 selects the fuel-efficient route plan app based on the traffic condition and fuel consumption estimation. Player 3 is proposed to plan the fuel-saving route in accordance with the traffic condition and individual behaviors.

3.2   Scenarios and Candidate Strategies

In this game, two routes (i.e., Route 1 and Route 2) from Node 1 to Node 2 are selected as candidate strategies for players (as Fig. 2 shows). There are Q vehicles distributed in these two routes, and k_i vehicles are driven in Route i. The length of Route i is defined as d_i km, and the average speed of Route i is defined as u_i km/h. The travel time t_i can be measured in accordance with d_i/u_i h. Each player can develop the route plan according to their own preferred strategies. Table 2 summarizes notations in this game-theoretic model.

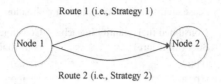

Route 1 (i.e., Strategy 1)

Route 2 (i.e., Strategy 2)

Fig. 2. Candidate strategies in the game model

Table 2. Notations

Parameter	Description
Q	The number of total vehicle from node 1 to node 2 (unit: car)
d_i	The length of route i (unit: km)
u_i	The average speed of route i (unit: km/h)
k_i	The number of vehicles in route i (unit: car)
s_i	The safe distance between each two vehicles in route i (unit: m)
t_i	The travel time of route i (unit: h)
l	The length of vehicle (unit: m)
p_j	The market share of player j (unit: %)
$g(u_i)$	The consumed fuel quantity of vehicle speed u_i in each 30 s (unit: litre)
c_i	The consumed fuel quantity of vehicle speed u_i in each 30 s (unit: litre)

3.2.1   Assumptions
The assumptions and limitations are given as follows for measuring the best response of each player.

- Player 1's strategy is not influenced by traffic condition.
- Player 2's strategy can be influenced by traffic condition, so Player 2's strategy is developed based on the best response of Player 1.
- Player 3's strategy is developed based on the best response of Players 1 and 2. The game tree is showed in Fig. 3.
- The market share of Player 3 (i.e., p_3) is about zero.
- The values of Q, p_1, p_2, d_1, and d_2 are predefined, and d_1 is longer than d_2.
- Each vehicle can be driven with the aspirational vehicle speed with the adaptable safe distance in the recommended route.
- The adaptable safe distance between each two vehicles in Route i is assumed as $u_i/2$ m [4].

3.2.2   Aspirational Vehicle Speed and Travel Time
For the calculation of aspirational vehicle speed and travel time, the required space length of each vehicle is estimated in accordance with the vehicle length and the adaptable safe distance (shown in Eq. (3)). Therefore, the number of vehicle in Route i can be determined by Eq. (4) according to the required space length of each vehicle.

After the transposition of Eq. (4), the aspirational vehicle speed can be calculated as $\frac{2000d_i}{k_i} - 2l$ by Eq. (5). Furthermore, the length of Route i can be considered to estimate the aspirational travel time by Eq. (6).

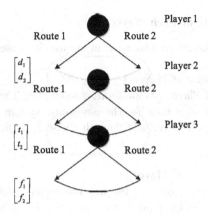

Fig. 3. Game tree for route plans

$$s_i + l = \frac{u_i}{2} + l \tag{3}$$

$$k_i = \frac{1000 \times d_i}{s_i + l} = \frac{1000 \times d_i}{\frac{u_i}{2} + l} \tag{4}$$

$$u_i = \frac{2000 \times d_i - 2 \times l \times k_i}{k_i} = \frac{2000d_i}{k_i} - 2l \tag{5}$$

$$t_i = \frac{d_i}{u_i} = \frac{d_i}{\frac{2000d_i}{k_i} - 2l} \tag{6}$$

3.2.3   The Cost Function of Each Player

The cost functions of strategies for players in this game are remarked as follows.

- The cost of Player 1's Strategy 1 is d_1 in accordance with the length of Route 1.
- The cost of Player 1's Strategy 2 is d_2 in accordance with the length of Route 2.
- The cost of Player 2's Strategy 1 is t_1 in accordance with the travel time of Route 1.
- The cost of Player 2's Strategy 2 is t_2 in accordance with the travel time of Route 2.
- The cost of Player 3's Strategy 1 is f_1 which is defined as Eq. (7).
- The cost of Player 3's Strategy 2 is f_2 which is defined as Eq. (8).

$$f_1 = t_1 \times g(u_1) = t_1 \times c_1 \tag{7}$$

$$f_2 = t_2 \times g(u_2) = t_2 \times c_2 \tag{8}$$

3.3 The Best Response of Each Player

The best responses of players are discussed in the follow subsections.

3.3.1 The Best Response of Player 1

The preferred strategy of Player 1 is the shortest route plan. Therefore, Strategy 2 will be selected when d_1 is longer than d_2. The navigation system built by Player 1 will recommend users to drive their vehicle through Route 2, so $p_1 \times Q$ vehicles will be driven in Route 2.

3.3.2 The Best Response of Player 2

The preferred strategy of Player 2 is the fast route plan. Player 2 develops a mix strategy in accordance with the ratio of r for Strategy 1 and the ratio of $(1 - r)$ for Strategy 2. In the recommendation of Player 2's app, $p_2 \times Q \times r$ vehicles will be driven in Route 1, and $p_2 \times Q \times (1 - r)$ vehicles will be driven in Route 2. Therefore, the objective function of Player 2 can be expressed as Eq. (9), and the total cost of Player 2 is defined as π in Eq. (9). The adaptable value of r can be estimated by Eq. (10) for the best response of Player 2. The proofs of Eq. (10) are presented in Appendixes A and B.

$$\min \pi = t_1 + t_2$$

$$\Rightarrow \min \left(\frac{d_1}{\frac{2000 d_1}{p_2 \times Q \times r} - 2l} + \frac{d_2}{\frac{2000 d_2}{p_2 \times Q \times (1-r) + (1-p_2) \times Q} - 2l} \right) \tag{9}$$

$$\frac{\partial \pi}{\partial r} = \frac{500 p_2 l Q^2 [d_1(p_2 r - 1) + d_2 p_2 r] \{d_1 [2000 d_2 + lQ(p_2 r - 1)]\} - d_2 p_2 lQr}{(p_2 lQr - 1000 d_1)^2 [1000 d_2 + lQ(p_2 r - 1)]^2} = 0$$

$$\Rightarrow r = \begin{cases} \frac{d_1}{p_2(d_1 + d_2)} \\ \frac{d_1(-2000 d_2 + lQ)}{lQ p_2(d_1 - d_2)} \rightarrow \text{negative} \end{cases} \tag{10}$$

3.3.3 The Best Response of Player 3

The preferred strategy of Player 3 is the most fuel-efficient route plan. The aspirational vehicle speed and travel time can be estimated in accordance with the adaptable value of r in Eq. (10) based on the best responses of Player 1 and Player 2. Player 3 can adopt the estimated vehicle speeds (i.e., u_1 and u_2) and travel time (i.e., t_1 and t_2) into Eqs. (7) and (8) to calculate the costs of Strategy 1 and Strategy 2 for the development of the route plan.

4 Numerical Analysis

In this section, a case study of numerical analysis was given to evaluate the performance of the proposed fuel-efficient route plan based on game theory. For the purpose of demonstration, this study adopted some parameters as follows to present the game in Sect. 3: $Q = 3,000$ cars, $d_1 = 15$ km, $d_2 = 12$ km, $l = 5$ m, $p_1 = 0.4$, and $p_2 = 0.6$. The best response of Player 1 was to recommend 1,200 users to drive their vehicles though Route 2. The value of r was determined as 0.79 by Eq. (10) for the best response of Player 2. For the users of Player 2's app, 1,422 vehicles were recommended to be driven through Route 1, and 378 vehicles were recommended to be driven through Route 2. The vehicle speeds of Route 1 and Route 2 were 11.10 km/h and 5.21 km/h; the travel times of Route 1 and Route 2 were 1.35 h and 2.30 h, respectively. For the best response of Player 3, Table 1 was adopted as the fuel consumption function $g(u_i)$, and the consumed fuel quantities of Strategy 1 and Strategy 2 were 5.346 L and 5.520 L which were calculated by Eqs. (11) and (12).

$$f_1 = t_1 \times g(u_1) = t_1 \times c_1 = 1.35 \times 3.960 = 5.346 \tag{11}$$

$$f_2 = t_2 \times g(u_2) = t_2 \times c_2 = 2.30 \times 2.400 = 5.520 \tag{12}$$

5 Conclusions and Future Work

This study adopts a fuel consumption estimation method to measure the consumed fuel quantity of each vehicle speed interval (i.e., a cost function) in accordance with each individual's optimal behavior. Furthermore, a mobile app is designed to consider the best responses of other route plan apps (e.g., the shortest route plan app and the fast route plan app) and plan a fuel-efficient route according to the consumed fuel quantity. The numerical analysis results showed that the proposed fuel-efficient route plan app can support fuel-saving for logistics industries.

In the future, the complex road network including several routes (i.e., multiple strategies) can be considered and selected by players. Furthermore, the market share of Player 3 can be increased to influence Player 2's strategy.

Appendix A: Partial Differential Equation Proof

The partial differential equation proof of Eq. (10) is expressed as Eq. A(1).

$$\frac{\partial \pi}{\partial r} = \frac{\partial}{\partial r}\left(\frac{d_1}{\frac{2000d_1}{p_2 \times Q \times r} - 2l} + \frac{d_2}{\frac{2000d_2}{p_2 \times Q \times (1-r) + (1-p_2) \times Q} - 2l}\right)$$

$$= \frac{\partial}{\partial r}\left(\frac{d_1}{\frac{2000d_1}{p_2 Q r} - 2l}\right) + \frac{\partial}{\partial r}\left(\frac{d_2}{\frac{2000d_2}{p_2 Q(1-r) + (1-p_2)Q} - 2l}\right)$$

$$= d_1 \frac{\partial}{\partial r}\left(\frac{1}{\frac{2000d_1}{p_2 Q r} - 2l}\right) + d_2 \frac{\partial}{\partial r}\left(\frac{1}{\frac{2000d_2}{p_2 Q(1-r) + (1-p_2)Q} - 2l}\right)$$

$$= \left[-\frac{d_1}{\left(\frac{2000d_1}{p_2 Q r} - 2l\right)^2}\frac{\partial}{\partial r}\left(\frac{2000d_1}{p_2 Q r} - 2l\right)\right] +$$

$$\left[-\frac{d_2}{\left(\frac{2000d_2}{p_2 Q(1-r) + (1-p_2)Q} - 2l\right)^2}\frac{\partial}{\partial r}\left(\frac{2000d_2}{p_2 Q(1-r) + (1-p_2)Q} - 2l\right)\right]$$

$$= \left[-\frac{2000d_1^2}{p_2 Q\left(\frac{2000d_1}{p_2 Q r} - 2l\right)^2}\frac{\partial}{\partial r}\left(\frac{1}{r}\right)\right] + \left[-\frac{2000d_2^2}{\left(\frac{2000d_2}{p_2 Q(1-r) + (1-p_2)Q} - 2l\right)^2}\frac{\partial}{\partial r}\left(\frac{1}{p_2 Q(1-r) + (1-p_2)Q}\right)\right]$$

$$= \left[\frac{2000d_1^2}{p_2 Q r^2\left(\frac{2000d_1}{p_2 Q r} - 2l\right)^2}\right] + \left[\frac{2000d_2^2\left(\frac{\partial}{\partial r}(p_2 Q(1-r)) + \frac{\partial}{\partial r}((1-p_2)Q)\right)}{(p_2 Q(1-r) + (1-p_2)Q)^2\left(\frac{2000d_2}{p_2 Q(1-r) + (1-p_2)Q} - 2l\right)^2}\right]$$

$$= \left[\frac{2000d_1^2}{p_2 Q r^2\left(\frac{2000d_1}{p_2 Q r} - 2l\right)^2}\right] + \left[\frac{2000p_2 Q d_2^2\frac{\partial}{\partial r}(1-r)}{(p_2 Q(1-r) + (1-p_2)Q)^2\left(\frac{2000d_2}{p_2 Q(1-r) + (1-p_2)Q} - 2l\right)^2}\right]$$

$$= \left[\frac{2000d_1^2}{p_2 Q r^2\left(\frac{2000d_1}{p_2 Q r} - 2l\right)^2}\right] - \left[\frac{2000p_2 Q d_2^2}{(p_2 Q(1-r) + (1-p_2)Q)^2\left(\frac{2000d_2}{p_2 Q(1-r) + (1-p_2)Q} - 2l\right)^2}\right]$$

$$= \frac{500p_2 l Q^2[d_1(p_2 r - 1) + d_2 p_2 r]\{d_1[2000d_2 + lQ(p_2 r - 1)] - d_2 p_2 l Q r\}}{(p_2 l Q r - 1000d_1)^2[1000d_2 + lQ(p_2 r - 1)]^2}$$

$$(A(1))$$

Appendix B: The Proof of Minimum Cost for Player 2

The proof of minimum cost for Player 2 is expressed as Eq. A(2).

$$\frac{\partial \pi}{\partial r} = \frac{500 p_2 l Q^2 [d_1(p_2 r - 1) + d_2 p_2 q]\{d_1[2000 d_2 + lQ(p_2 r - 1)] - d_2 p_2 l Q r\}}{(p_2 l Q r - 1000 d_1)^2 [1000 d_2 + l Q(p_2 r - 1)]^2} = 0$$

$$\Rightarrow \begin{cases} [d_1(p_2 r - 1) + d_2 p_2 r] = 0 \\ d_1[2000 d_2 + lQ(p_2 r - 1)] - d_2 p_2 l Q r = 0 \end{cases}$$

$$\Rightarrow \begin{cases} d_1 p_2 r - d_1 + d_2 p_2 r = 0 \\ 2000 d_1 d_2 + d_1 l Q p_2 r - d_1 l Q - d_2 p_2 l Q r = 0 \end{cases}$$

$$\Rightarrow \begin{cases} d_1 p_2 r + d_2 p_2 r = d_1 \\ d_1 l Q p_2 r - d_2 p_2 l Q r = -2000 d_1 d_2 + d_1 l Q \end{cases}$$

$$\Rightarrow \begin{cases} (d_1 + d_2) r = \frac{d_1}{p_2} \\ r l Q p_2 (d_1 - d_2) = d_1(-2000 d_2 + l Q) \end{cases}$$

$$\Rightarrow \begin{cases} r = \frac{d_1}{p_2(d_1 + d_2)} \\ r = \frac{d_1(-2000 d_2 + l Q)}{l Q p_2(d_1 - d_2)} \end{cases}$$

$$\Rightarrow r \in \left\{ \frac{d_1}{p_2(d_1 + d_2)}, \frac{d_1(-2000 d_2 + l Q)}{l Q p_2(d_1 - d_2)} \right\}$$

$$(A(2))$$

References

1. Petroleum Price Information Management and Analysis System: Bureau of Energy, Ministry of Economic Affairs, Taiwan (2017). https://www2.moeaboe.gov.tw/oil102/oil1022010/english.htm. Accessed 2 July 2017
2. Chan, S.Y.: The basic information of truck freight transportation. Taiwan Institute of Economic Research (2016). https://goo.gl/7zZ9ZY. Accessed 2 July 2017
3. Lo, C.L., Chen, C.H., Kuan, T.S., Lo, K.R., Cho, H.J.: Fuel consumption estimation system and method with lower cost. Symmetry 9(7), 1–15 (2017). Article ID 105
4. Bertolazzi, E., Biral, F., Lio, M.D., Saroldi, A., Tango, F.: Supporting drivers in keeping safe speed and safe distance: the SASPENCE subproject within the European framework programme 6 integrating project PReVENT. IEEE Trans. Intell. Transp. Syst. 11(3), 525–538 (2010)

Personalized Mobile Learning System via Smart Glasses

Yi-Ting Tsai[1], Shih-Jou Yu[2], Xin-Yen Chen[1],
Oscal Tzyh-Chiang Chen[1(✉)], Jerry Chih-Yuan Sun[2],
and Ching-Chun Huang[1]

[1] Department of Electrical Engineering, National Chung Cheng University,
Chiayi, Taiwan
oscal@ee.ccu.edu.tw
[2] Institute of Education, National Chiao Tung University, Hsinchu, Taiwan

Abstract. This work proposes a personalized mobile learning system using smart glasses which include outward and inward facing cameras. By using the outward facing camera, the proposed system recognizes the QR code, and then discovers the front view of a wearer. Additionally, our system employs an inward facing camera to capture eye images, find out the centers of irises, and then derive visual focal points. According to the exhibit of high interest, the audiovisual clips associated with the baseball background knowledge and stories were designed for learners visiting the baseball museum. The experimental results reveal that the proposed system can achieve a view angel deviation below 3.20°, and identify the 13.5 cm × 13.5 cm QR code at a distance of 2.3 m and a view angle of 40°. Therefore, the personalized mobile learning system proposed herein effectively provides learners with attention tracking, interest cultivation, and immersive engagement.

Keywords: Mobile learning · Smart glasses · Eye tracking
Pattern recognition · Visual focal point · QR code

1 Introduction

With the progress of science and technology, learning is not confined to the classroom. Wearing a portable device in outdoor learning has become a new trend. However, how wearable devices attract learners' attention and evoke their interest needs to be well addressed. There are many outdoor learning situations, like zoo tour, museum visit and so on, in which most of the guidance ways adopt voice navigation instead of narrators. Since most people prefer a visual or audiovisual way to catch knowledge, our work employs smart glasses to provide the audiovisual guide based on wearer's visual focal points, and thus to enhance the learning effect.

In outdoor learning, because the theme cannot take into account all learners' preferences, some of the learners may miss their subjects of interest in the learning process. At present, many outdoor learning venues, such as museums and art museums, have a number of buttons or QR codes for audio or audiovisual clips, requiring visitors to take the initiative to push the button or scan the QR code for further illustrations of the exhibit. The QR code identification generally goes through the pattern detection, decoding, and information extraction steps to catch the code message. Currently, there are many online resources that can provide QR code decoding [4, 5]. However, it may be inconvenient for visitors to find out the button or QR code, resulting in missing further information acquirement. If smart glasses with an outward facing camera can help on automatically detecting the QR codes, a visitor can receive further information easily and interact with the exhibits in a more efficient way.

Usually, a learner takes long time to look at things that are of interest, so that eye tracking is the most direct and effective way to determine whether it is a matter of interest. Pande *et al.* employed the visual tracking technique to perceive eye movements of students who were stimulated by symbolic and graphic patterns in order to understand their learning processes [1]. Yang *et al.* tracked eye movements of viewers to know their learning statuses during slide presentations where the slides included the pictures and text [2]. By introducing media from internet in the conventional teaching, Zhou *et al.* gathered eye movement information of a leaner, analyzed it to understand the learning situation, and then figured out an approach to improve the learning efficiency of this mixed teaching scenario [3]. Therefore, learning points of interest from visual focal points of most people can be referred to design effective teaching materials. In particular, when you put on smart glasses with inward facing cameras, like Tobbi smart glasses with four cameras on the frame to fulfill eye tracking, the visual focal point can be estimated to interpret the eye movement behavior for understanding interactions and situations of learning.

In order to achieve the abovementioned functions, this study proposes a personalized mobile learning system using smart glasses which have outward and inward facing cameras. Accompanied with a tablet or a smart phone to support auxiliary signal analysis, identification, and learning assessment, the proposed smart glasses can provide a wearer with multidimensional learning. The outward facing camera detects the QR code which is decoded, and then linked to the corresponding information. The inward facing camera in the proposed smart glasses captures eye images which are processed to obtain the central points of irises for eye tracking. Additionally, the central points are projected outwardly to discover visual fixation and gaze time, to deduce the points of interest. From a professional education perspective, the questionnaires and experiments were designed, and conducted by 30 subjects to attain the exhibit areas of interest from the majority. According to the areas of interest, further interaction materials such as images, texts, and films were adequately implemented to evoke learners' interests. With QR code recognition and eye tracking, the proposed system can take the initiative to present the learning materials to a visitor according to his or her visual focal point, and thus effectively enhances the learning effect.

2 Personalized Mobile Learning System

In this work, the experimental scenario is museum visit where visitors wear the proposed smart glasses with tablets or smart phones. The personalized mobile learning system is developed to provide intimate interactions according to visitor's interests from his or her visual focal points. Accordingly, the front view of a visitor at a specific position needs to be well known. Based on the front scene, the visual focal point may reveal the exhibit of interest. Meanwhile, the corresponding messages are provided to the visitor for enhancing the understanding of the exhibit. To realize this demand, the proposed smart glasses include an outward facing camera for QR code detection, an inward facing camera for eye tracking, and a display screen for information conveyance. The commercial smart glasses, SiME, from ChipSiP Technology Corp. are utilized and modified where the original outward facing camera is replaced by an inward facing camera, and the outward facing camera module from C920r USB webcam, Logitech, is mounted on the front frame of smart glasses, as shown in Fig. 1. Particularly, the 3D housing enclosing the outward facing camera module was implemented as well.

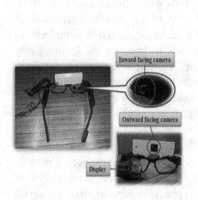

Fig. 1. Proposed smart glasses.   **Fig. 2.** Operational flow of the proposed system.

The proposed system includes three parts: (1) determination of front views from the QR code detection, (2) determination of visual focal points from eye tracking, and (3) teaching material designs from the professional survey associated with exhibits of interest. The QR code detection is to find out the front view of a subject wearing smart glasses with an outward facing camera. Before eye tracking using an inward facing camera, the 9-point calibration is performed to catch the eye movement characteristics, and to amend the wearing differentiation from each subject. The iris region of a wearer's eye is identified, and then used to determine its central point which is projected to the fixation point of the front scene. The proposed system takes the initiative to capture front scenes, and eye images for QR code detection, and eye tracking, respectively. When a subject watches the exhibit of which QR code is found, his or her visual focal point is derived at the same time. Once the visual focal point remains unchanged for 300 ms [6], the corresponding teaching material is displayed on the screen for the friendly interaction with the subject to improve learning outcomes. The operational flow of the proposed system is depicted in Fig. 2.

2.1 Determination of Front Views

The front view of a learner is consistent with the outward facing camera. In this work, the QR code pattern is used due to its clear and strict structure, and attached to the spot close to the exhibit, as displayed in Fig. 3. The proposed system actively and continuously detects the QR code pattern of the captured images from the outward facing camera. The QR code goes through binarization and morphology for pre-processing, convolution for positioning, and neural network for pattern recognition [7]. Once this code is successfully decoded, the front view of a subject at a specific position is identified based on the previously established database.

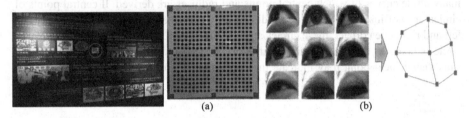

(a)   (b)

Fig. 3. Exhibit with a QR code.   **Fig. 4.** Calibration points associated with iris positions. (a) Calibration pattern. (b) Topology graph of eye movements (Color figure online)

2.2 Determination of Visual Focal Points

In order to precisely calculate the fixation point of eyes, the screen with 9 red spots and 400 small black spots distributed at a square of 50 cm × 50 cm is designed, and partitioned into four quadrants for calibration, as shown in Fig. 4(a). In this screen, each quadrant has 100 black spots where the neighboring ones have a distance of 2 cm. Figure 4(b) depicts the topological graph of eye movements of a subject who stands 1.5 m from the screen, and watches these nine red spots. This graph is not a square because the moving distance of an iris is not uniform at each side. Additionally, an inward facing camera which is not located at the central point of an eye has a shooting angle deviation. Nevertheless, the relative positions of nine red spots are correct, so that each group of 100 black spots can infer the corresponding quadrant. After calibration, four areas of left top, left bottom, right top and right bottom corresponding to iris positions are derived to accurately determine visual focal points of each subject.

It is a straightforward way to fulfill eye tracking using a camera which captures eye images. These eye images are analyzed to obtain an eye movement track. This study modifies, and simplifies the methods proposed by Zhao et al. [8] and Cuong et al. [9] with consideration of computation power of the proposed smart glasses. Figure 5 displays the computation flow of the proposed eye tracking method for determining the visual focal point. The inward facing camera of the proposed smart glasses takes an eye color image which is converted to a gray-level image based on the luminance. This gray-level image can be partitioned into two parts: bright one for skin and sclera, and dark one for pupil, iris and eyelashes. Accordingly, the gray-level histogram is built, and characterized by two Gaussian mixture models which can determine an adequate threshold. This threshold binarizes the gray-level image to yield a binary image which goes through the Gaussian blur and morphological operations for image smoothing and noise reduction, respectively. After the abovementioned processes, a complete eye contour in the binary image can be attained. The X-axis coordinates of dark points in the binary image are searched to find out leftmost and rightmost ones which have neighboring pixels with the interleaved black and white. These leftmost and rightmost dark points are viewed as eye corners. A circle is drawn based on the diameter from left to right eye corners. The maximum square inside this circle is the Region Of Interest (ROI). At the same time, the Hough transform is performed in the binary image to get many circle curves of which central points and radiuses are derived. If central points of circles are not inside the ROI, and radiuses are larger than a half of distance between left and right eye corners, these circles are not considered. Afterwards, the relative large circle is taken as the iris of which central point is used to project a visual focal point. This visual focal point may indicate the portion or whole of the exhibit of interest.

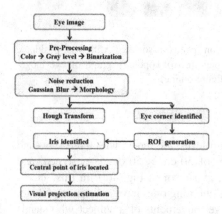

Fig. 5. Proposed eye tracking method.

Fig. 6 Photo of an exhibition area with 54 portions.

2.3 Teaching Material Design from Areas of Interest

In this study, the baseball museum of National Chung Cheng University is the experimental field. Initially, the visual focal points of learners were analyzed by means of the questionnaire to catch the hotspots from the majority. Based on the eye-mind assumptions [10], the eye gaze direction reveals the area of cognitive and attentive processes. Accordingly, the hotspot is what the learner is interested in, and pays more attention to. First, the photos associated with 16 exhibition areas were taken in the questionnaire where each photo is partitioned into many small portions. Second, 30 subjects visited the museum, stood in front of each exhibition area, selected top 20 portions of interest, and marked them on the corresponding photo in the questionnaire. Finally, after compiling the results from 30 subjects, the three portions with the highest scores in each exhibition area are determined for us to design the relevant teaching materials. Figure 6 shows the photo of an exhibition area, which is partitioned into 54 portions.

In order to design the materials that most people are interested in, this study categorizes the exhibition into four main themes: history, people, ball sets and sport care, through the field tour of the museum exhibition, and interviews with senior tour guides and experts. Additionally, learners filled in the demand questionnaire of which data were analyzed to understand the learners' suggestions and interactive preferences associated with learning topics. The results show that history and character themes need to add the video and picture supplement, ball theme is to increase the 3D graphic models and the corresponding films, and sport care theme demands the advices from experts and doctors. Based on the above results, this study has accomplished various teaching materials according to different topics of four themes. Therefore, it is hoped that learners can resonate with these teaching materials to obtain effective learning.

3 Experimental Results

In this work, the baseball museum of National Chung Cheng University is the experimental field in which subjects wore the proposed smart glasses and carried tablets for museum visits. Before going to see the exhibits, each subject followed the guideline, and watched a nine-point calibration screen to amend wearing deviations, and to align the eye position with the eye focal point. The outward facing camera of the proposed smart glasses is actively and continuously to detect the QR code based on which the front scene of a subject is effectively discovered. When the gaze time is larger than 300 ms [6], the teaching material related to the exhibit is played at the screen of the proposed smart glasses. In the following, we explore the accuracy of visual focal points, QR code detection rate, and learning effect using the proposed smart glasses.

When performing the calibration, the participant stood at a distance of 1.5 m from the 50 cm × 50 cm calibration screen. All subjects watched nine red spots one by one, and then correlated these red spots with their eye positions. Table 1 lists the eye angle deviations from 10 participants where the average eye angle deviation is 3.20°. This average value exhibits that the proposed eye tracking method for determining visual focal points is very promising.

Table 1. Eye angle deviations from 10 subjects.

Subject_1	3.45
Subject_2	2.79
Subject_3	3.69
Subject_4	3.23
Subject_5	2.96
Subject_6	2.68
Subject_7	3.56
Subject_8	3.07
Subject_9	3.66
Subject_10	2.94
Average	3.203

Table 2. Acceptable view angles and distances of two QR code patterns.

Pattern	View angles (deg)	Distances (cm)
10 cm * 10 cm	0	170
	30	140
	45	100
13.5 cm * 13.5 cm	0	280
	30	250
	40	230

To order to effectively perceive the QR code pattern at a reasonable view angle and a fair distance, two versions of QR code patterns are designed, and explored. Figure 7 shows the topologies of these two patterns with sizes of 10 cm × 10 cm, and 13.5 cm × 13.5 cm. Table 2 lists the acceptable view angles and distances of these two patterns which are correctly decoded. The experimental results illustrate that the 13.5 cm × 13.5 cm pattern has an additional rectangular shape at the right bottom, resulting in outstanding performance.

(a)   (b)

Fig. 7. Two QR code patterns (a) 10 cm × 10 cm pattern. (b) 13.5 cm × 13.5 cm pattern.

In addition to narrators, the audiovisual playback screens and handheld audio devices helping on tour guiding can effectively reduce manpower. Such screens and devices have been widely adopted in the majority of museums. However, there exist some shortcomings at fixed-position audiovisual playback screens, and handheld audio devices. This is because the time of each visitor arriving at a specific exhibition area is not consistent. The fixed-position audiovisual playback cannot match the progress of each visitor, easily resulting in learning incompletely or inattentively. Additionally, the open play may make voices of adjacent booths interfere with each other. Although a handheld audio device can provide audio playback to each visitor individually to avoid inconsistent arrival time, the visitor may feel uncomfortable owing to the headset covering the entire ear or wearing in the ear canal. Particularly, the visitor may not response to an emergency immediately owing the headset isolating external sounds to some extent. However, learning messages are addressed only by voice, which may not meet the demands of various learning enthusiasts. Therefore, this work employs smart glasses as a tour guide in a museum to increase the immersive engagement, to enrich the learning content, and to achieve personalized learning. Museum curators and educators can compile and analyze visual focal points and positions of visitors from the proposed smart glasses to attain the exhibits of interest, visit tracks, and learning situations. Based on the exhibits of high interest, we created the corresponding teaching materials to guide learners to watch these exhibits, and to increase the awareness of key knowledge. Notably, the proposed mobile learning system can effectively grasp visual focus points of a learner, proactively recommend learning materials, and assess the learning outcomes. As compared to the conventional handheld audio devices, the proposed smart glasses can superiorly convey the concept of the exhibit, attract user's attention, and thus enhance learning effect.

4   Conclusion

In this work, the personalized mobile learning system using smart glasses has been successfully developed. The proposed smart glasses have an outward facing camera for front scene determination, an inward facing camera for visual focal point determination, and a display screen for information conveyance. The front scene of a subject is perceived by detecting the QR code which is attached to a spot close to the exhibit. The visual focal point of a subject is determined by the proposed eye tracking method that identifies the central point of the iris, projecting outwardly to find the hotspot. Before eye tracking, the nine-point calibration is fulfilled to amend subject deviations. The baseball museum of National Chung Cheng University is the experimental field. Initially, the visual focal points of subjects were analyzed by means of the questionnaire to catch the hotspots from the majority. Afterwards, the teaching materials associated with the exhibit of high interest were designed. The experimental results reveal that the proposed system can have a view angle deviation smaller than 3.20°, and recognize the 13.5 cm × 13.5 cm QR code at a distance of 2.3 m with a view angle up to 40°. Compared to the handheld audio devices, the proposed smart glasses show outstanding performance on conveying the knowledge of the exhibit, and increasing user's immersion.

Acknowledgments. This work was partially supported by Ministry of Science and Technology, Taiwan, under the contract numbers of MOST 105-3011-E-194-001 and MOST 104-3011-E-194-002.

References

1. Pande, P., Chandrasekharan, S.: Eye-tracking in STEM education research: limitations, experiences and possible extensions. In: IEEE Sixth International Conference on Technology for Education (T4E), pp. 116–119. IEEE Press, New York (2014)
2. Yang, F.Y., Chang, C.Y., Chien, W.R., Chien, Y.T., Tseng, Y.H.: Tracking learners' visual attention during a multimedia presentation in a real classroom. Comput. Educ. **62**, 208–220 (2013)
3. Zhou, X., Piao, G., Jin, Q., Huang, R.: Organizing learning stream data by eye-tracking in a blended learning environment integrated with social media. In: IEEE International Symposium on IT in Medicine and Education (ITME), vol. 2, pp. 335–339. IEEE Press, New York (2011)
4. Huang, Y.P., Chang, Y.T., Sandnes F.E.: QR code data type encoding for ubiquitous information transfer across different platforms. In: IEEE Workshops on Ubiquitous, Autonomic and Trusted Computing, UIC-ATC 2009, pp. 292–297. IEEE Press, New York (2009)
5. Tribak, H., Moughyt, S., Zaz, Y., Schaefer G.: Remote QR code recognition based on HOG and SVM classifiers. In: IEEE International Conference on Informatics and Computing, pp. 137–141. IEEE Press, New York (2016)
6. Rayner, K.: Eye movements and attention in reading, scene perception, and visual search. Q. J. Exp. Psychol. **62**(8), 1457–1506 (2009)

7. Chou, T.H., Ho, C.S., Kuo Y.F.: QR code detection using convolutional neural networks. In: International Conference on Advanced Robotics and Intelligent Systems (ARIS), pp. 1–5 (2015)
8. Zhao, N., Lu, Y.: Human eye feature extraction based on segmented binarization. In: IEEE International Conference on Biomedical Engineering and Informatics, vol. 1, pp. 304–307. IEEE Press, New York (2011)
9. Cuong, N.H., Hoang, H.T.: Eye-gaze detection with a single webcam based on geometry features extraction. In: 11th International Conference on Control, Automation, Robotics and Vision, pp. 2507–2512 (2010)
10. Just, M.A., Carpenter, P.A.: A theory of reading: from eye fixations to comprehension. Psychol. Rev. **87**(4), 329–354 (1980)

Retransmission-Based Access Class Barring for Machine Type Communications

Jian-Wei Ciou, Shin-Ming Cheng$^{(\boxtimes)}$, and Yin-Hong Hsu

National Taiwan University of Science and Technology, Taipei, Taiwan
{m10215072,smcheng,m10515090}@mail.ntust.edu.tw

Abstract. Supporting trillions of devices is the critical challenge in machine type communication (MTC) communications, which results in severe congestions in random access channels of infrastructure-based cellular systems. 3GPP thus developed the access class barring (ACB) to control the expected number of simultaneous access requests in a preamble as one. The assignment of classes with specific access parameters for MTC devices becomes an critical issue in ACB since it affects the performance from the perspectives of successful access probability and access delay significantly. This paper proposes a novel classification scheme where we group MTC devices according to their number of transmission trials while without introducing extra overheads. A heuristic algorithm is proposed, where the devices with more number of retransmission failures will have more chance to access the preamble. By adaptively changing the ACB factor, the proposed heuristic algorithm can reduce the access delay effectively while maintaining high access success probability. The simulation results show the improvement of the proposed scheme from the existing ACB schemes.

Keywords: Access class barring (ACB)
Machine type communication (MTC) · RAN overloading
Retransmission

1 Introduction

Infrastructure-based Machine to machine (M2M) communications, also known as machine type communication (MTC) in 3GPP terminology, is an emerging concept that allow MTC devices to communicate with each other via the assistance of base station (known as evolved NodeB; eNB in 3GPP terminology) without or with minimal human interaction [1]. By leveraging the short-distance transmissions, MTC enables faster and more reliable communications than traditional human initiated communications [2], and is regarded as an attractive solutions for future Internet of Things (IoT) applications. With the concern of numerous number of MTC devices, how to efficiently manage massive access from MTC

© ICST Institute for Computer Sciences, Social Informatics and Telecommunications Engineering 2018
Y.-B. Lin et al. (Eds.): IoTaaS 2017, LNICST 246, pp. 145–154, 2018.
https://doi.org/10.1007/978-3-030-00410-1_18

devices to prevent radio access network (RAN) overloading and subsequent congestion is the most critical challenge [3–6]. The congestion due to significant number of simultaneous access incurs heavy delay, the waste of resources, and low access success rate.

Recently, many schemes are proposed to alleviate the RAN overloading problem, such as specific backoff [7], slotted access [8], pull-based [9], dynamic PRACH resource allocation [10], and access class barring (ACB) [11,12] schemes. Among them, ACB scheme receives a lot of attentions since the access of MTC devices are separated by using different classes in a more flexible and efficient way [13]. In particular, eNB broadcasts all MTC devices an ACB factor (i.e., access probability) p and the backoff time corresponding to different access classes. With such information, MTC device will draw a value q, where $0 \leq q \leq 1$, and if $q \leq p$, the MTC device is allowed to perform random access procedure. On the other hand, if the MTC device is barred, it can only make a new attempt after the backoff timer is expired. When RAN overloading or congestion happens, the access probability p can be set extremely small by eNB in order to avoid frequent random access attempts. However, it causes serious delay, and such tradeoff should be carefully considered when applying ACB.

In order to increase access success probability as much as possible while maintaining an acceptable access delay, ACB should be designed to be more "adaptive" to the environment. However, the original ACB scheme is hard to achieve that due to reason that the access probability p is fixed. In other words, eNB cannot adjust the ACB factor according to the current RAN loading level in a realtime fashion. This paper therefore proposes a heuristic algorithm where eNB regards the number of MTC devices who perform the preamble transmissions as the current loading level and adjust p accordingly. In particular, we consider the number of preamble retransmissions send by MTC devices who successfully perform random access. The devices with more number of retransmission trials (i.e., failures) will have more chance to access the preamble so that the fairness among MTC devices is achieved. We conduct simulation experiments, and the results show that the proposed retransmission-based ACB scheme can reduce the access delay effectively and while maintaining high access success probability comparing with the existing ACB schemes.

The rest of this work is organized as follows. The related work and background is described in Sect. 2. In Sect. 3, we present the system model. Section 4 describes the idea that how we let each MTC device know which groups it belongs in every random access occasion. Section 4.1 describes the method that eNB dynamically resets the barring factor. In Sect. 5, simulation results are presented to compare our proposed scheme with the traditional scheme. The work is concluded in Sect. 6.

2   Background and Related Work

After knowing the parameter of random access, each MTC device will randomly choose a preamble from the preamble pool, and the MTC device will increase the number of preamble transmissions by one and wait for RAR (i.e., Msg 2). Upon receiving the Msg 2 in the RAR window, the MTC device processes UL grant and Timing Alignment and prepare for sending the connection request (Msg 3). If the MTC device fails to receive Msg 2 in the RAR window due to the reason that eNB fails to detect the preamble from the device, it checks whether its number of preamble transmission is smaller or equal to the maximum number of preamble transmission. If it is, the MTC device retries to perform preamble transmission after waiting a uniform backoff time. If not, the MTC device is informed of random access procedure failure and it is not allowed to perform the procedure. Moreover, if the MTC device fails to receive contention resolution after sending connection request due to the collision of Msg 3, it performs the same behavior of failing to receive RAR. We assume that once an UE successfully transmits the preamble chosen only by itself to eNB, and it will finish the RA procedure.

When massive devices try to access the network simultaneously, it will cause RACH congestion because of the limited preamble in a PRACH slot and those devices who choose the same preamble will lead to collision in Msg 3. The congestion problem may rise intolerable delay and low access success probability so it has been considered as an essential issue in MTC.

It was shown that [14] proposed QoS guaranteed prioritized random access scheme with a dynamic access barring scheme. Different virtual resource has been allocated for different classes in order to reduce the collision probability. It was shown that [13] introduced the QoS-Aware Self-Adaptive RAN Overload Control (QoS-Dracon) mechanism to reduce the RAN overload problem, taking into account users' QoS requirements. The QoS-Dracon scheme prioritizes delay-sensitive devices over delay-tolerant ones when performing Random Access procedure. It proposed a simple function based on the number of preamble transmissions of delay-sensitive devices to estimate the RAN load.

It was shown that [15] developed a Markov-Chain based traffic-load estimation scheme according to the preamble collision status. With the estimation scheme, the eNB can adjust p (ACB factor or Access probability) adaptively based on the overload situation. There are different simulation results compared with traditional ACB mechanism when setting different parameters used to update p. The results suggested the effectiveness of the traffic-aware ACB on the control of p to balance the loads.

It was shown that [16,17] proposed a mechanism to update ACB factor adaptively. The work in [16] evaluate a congestion coefficient based on successful devices and contending device within each time region. And the ACB factor can be derived dynamically by the congestion coefficient. The work in [17] proposed an algorithm, which by using available information such as number of available preambles and number of successful preamble transmissions to dynamically update ACB factor.

3   System Model

Consider that when an extreme scenario (e.g., power outage, earthquake) happens, MTC devices will try to reestablish synchronization with eNB in a short time period. In order to simulate the extreme scenario in which a large amount of MTC devices access network in a highly synchronized manner, we adopt traffic model 2 (Beta distribution) mentioned in [4] as arrival distribution and set the PRACH configuration to 6, which means RACH will occur every 5 ms within 180 kHz. In our system model, we consider that there are total N_{sys} MTC devices and then we define a time slot as an RACH slot so that the arrival period will be 2000 time slots indexed by an nonnegative integer j ($j = 0, 1, 2, \ldots, 2000$) by reason of the 10 s distribution period according to traffic model 2.

$$p(t) = \frac{t^{\alpha-1}(T-t)^{\beta-1}}{T^{\alpha+\beta-1}Beta(\alpha, \beta)},   \tag{1}$$

where $Beta(\alpha, \beta)$ is the Beta function and $\alpha = 3, \beta = 4$.

With the knowledge of above, Eq. (1) is the probability that each MTC device will perform preamble transmissions at t^{th} RACH slot during T limited distribution of access attempts. As a result, the number of MTC devices N^j that perform preamble transmissions at the jth RACH slot is shown in the following equation

$$N^j = N_{sys} \int_{t_{j-1}}^{t_j} p(t)dt,   j = 1, 2, \ldots, 2000,   \tag{2}$$

where t_j is the jth RACH slot.

Two performance metrics are considered as follows.

– successful access probability: the probability of the successful completion of the random access procedure under the constraint of maximum number of retransmissions.
– access delay: given a successful completion of MTC transmission, the number of RACH slots spend in an access procedure i.e., from the beginning of random access attempt to the completion of the random access procedure.

4   Retransmission Based ACB Scheme

In ACB, eNB typically broadcasts information about random access before MTC devices perform the random access procedure. In the proposed scheme, we leverage this broadcasting message to enforce the grouping process of MTC devices. In particular, we include "the range of preamble" in the message so that MTC devices could identify their own group by checking the allocated preamble currently. As shown in Fig. 1, if the number of preamble transmissions is within the range of 1 to 5, the MTC devices will be classified into group 1.

Obviously, eNB cannot get the precise number of MTC devices who tried to perform preamble transmission since the failed trials cannot reach the eNB and

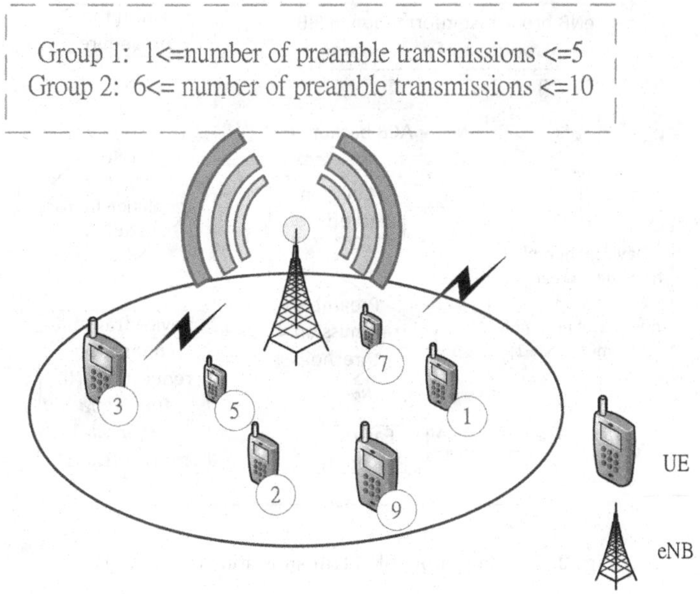

Fig. 1. Group model of proposed method

thus cannot provide any useful information. In this case, we can only estimation N' according to the existing information (e.g., the number of success preambles and the number of collision preambles). The main idea of retransmission-based ACB is that we leverage the MTC device who successfully performs preamble transmissions since they can provide additional information to the eNB. In particular, the MTC device includes "the number of preamble (re)transmissions it has ever tried" in Msg 3. With the retransmission information, the eNB is able to calculate $G_{\alpha,\beta}^m$, which is the number of MTC devices who belong to m^{th} group and who perform αth to βth preamble transmissions in an RACH slot. We can make use of $G_{\alpha,\beta}^m$ to observe RAN loading and further change the ACB factor p to cope with different loading condition. That is, our scheme could adaptively adjust the ACB factor p. The detailed message flow of the proposed scheme is illustrated in Fig. 2.

4.1 Problem Formulation

In order to get N', we consider $P_{s,i|N}$, which is the probability that an UE successfully performs its ith transmissions given N users attempting to perform preamble transmissions, and the access success probability can be derived as

$$P_{s,i|N} = p_{d,i} \left(\frac{R-1}{R} \right)^{N-1},$$

(3)

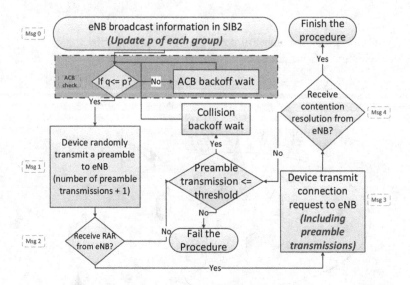

Fig. 2. Message flow of retransmission-based ACB

where $p_{d,i} = 1 - \left(\frac{1}{e}\right)^i$ is the preamble detection probability applied to model the effect of path loss and power ramping. Moreover, Eq. (3) means that an UE succeeds in the ith preamble transmission if all the other $N-1$ UEs select the other $R-1$ preambles, and the non-collided preamble is detected by the eNB.

Let N_s be the number of UEs who successfully perform preamble transmissions. As a result, we consider $E(N_s|N)$ as the expected number of UEs who successfully perform preamble transmission given N users attempting to perform preamble transmissions, and the $E(N_s|N)$ is given by

$$E(N_s|N) = \sum_{i=1}^{\theta} N_i P_{s,i|N} = \sum_{i=1}^{\theta} N_i p_{d,i} \left(\frac{R-1}{R}\right)^{N-1}$$
$$= \frac{\sum_{i=1}^{\theta} N_i p_{d,i}}{N} N \left(\frac{R-1}{R}\right)^{N-1} = \bar{p}_d N \left(\frac{R-1}{R}\right)^{N-1}, \qquad (4)$$

where θ is the maximum number of preamble transmissions and $\bar{p}_d$ is the expected preamble detection probability (e.g., $\bar{p}_d = \frac{\sum_{i=1}^{\theta} N_i^j p_{d,i}}{\sum_{i=1}^{\theta} N_i^j}$, where $\sum_{i=1}^{\theta} N_i^j = N^j$). This equation is also mentioned in [18]. We can get the expectation of UEs who successfully perform preamble transmissions given $\bar{p}_d = 1$ (ideal condition) according to the variation of N.

4.2   ACB Factor Update

Each group, whose threshold (number of preamble transmissions) is larger than other groups, has higher priority and index. Therefore, we assign each group to a different weight, and the groups with higher priority are assigned to a larger weight. The weight of group m, w_m, can be considered as the proportion of the allocation of RACH resources, so it should be defined as $\sum_{m=1} w_m = 1$. We divide MTC devices into two groups, and the weight of group 2 is higher than group 1 (e.g., $w_2 > w_1$) due to we hope the groups whose number of preamble transmissions close to maximum preamble transmissions; So that group 2 can own more RACH resources to promote the access success probability.

Algorithm 1. ACB Factor Update in Retransmission-Based ACB

Input: R, number of success preambles and collision preambles, design parameters
    w_m
1: set *time slot* = 0; $p_m = 1$, for all m
2: **while do** $N_s + N_f < N$
3:    *time slot* = *time slot* + 1;
4:    **if** (activate preamble $\geq$ 50 percent) **then**
5:       check the table and then set max(N')
6:    **else**
7:       check the table and then set min(N')
8:       $W = \{w_1, w_2, .., w_m\}$, sort W to an descending order
9:       set $w' = m^{th}$ weight in set W
10:      $p_m = \frac{w'R}{N'}$;
11:   **end if**
12: **end while**

We aim at distributing MTC devices over several RACH slots when congestion happens. The maximal $E(N_s|N)$ is achieved by setting N equal to R or $R - 1$. In other words, we hope that there are only $N \approx R$ MTC devices who attempt to perform preamble transmission in an RACH slot, so it can be derived as

$$\sum_{m=1}^{n} N'p_m = \sum_{m=1}^{n} w_m R = R, \qquad (5)$$

where the p_m is the ACB factor of group m and the R_m is the number of MTC devices who belong to group m and pass the ACB scheme. Thus, the p_m which is the ACB factor of group m is able to be obtained from Eq. (5) shown in the following.

$$p_m = \frac{W_m R}{N'} \qquad (6)$$

Our proposed algorithm is given in Algorithm 1. First, we set the default value, slot to 0 and p_m to 1 for each group (line 1). The loop (lines 2–12) run until all device finishes the RA procedure. In each time slot (line 3), we check if the activated preamble is more than the half of available preamble, if it is, we will set the N' to the bigger one (line 5). Otherwise, the N' will be set to the smaller one and the weight list will be sort in descending order and set to each group, then the factor of each group p_m will be calculated (lines 7–10).

Our algorithm to adjust ACB parameter p is shown in Algorithms 1 and 2. In these two algorithms, we take the preamble utility into account because it can reflect the number of MTC devices who attempt to perform preamble transmissions indirectly. When there are two possible N', it is determined by the preamble utility. If the preamble utility is low, we set the smaller one of the N'. Otherwise, if the preamble utility is high, we choose the larger N' to be the estimation of N.

5   Simulation Results

This subsection conducts extensively simulation experiments under the Matlab platform. We consider 20000 to 30000 MTC devices, where arrival period of those MTC devices is 10 s. The number of preambles is 54, PRACH Configuration Index is 6, sand the maximum allowable transmissions is 10. Two groups are assigned in the simulation and ACB backoff time is 320 ms while ACB factors for both group are 1. In this case, all the access requests pass the limitation of access probabiltiy of ACB scheme, which implies a huge number of MTC devices will perform random access procedure. In such an extreme case, we can evaluate the performance of adaptiveness in the proposed retransmission-based scheme. The ratio of resource (i.e., preamble) allocated for group 1 and group 2 is 3 : 7. Please note that those parameter setups follow the suggestions from [4]. We consider the typical ACB schemes with factors 0.2, 0.3, and 0.4.

Effects of the number of devices on successful access probability. Figure 3 shows effects of number of devices on successful access probability. It is observed that when the number of devices increases, the successful access probability decreases. It is due to the simple reason that a larger number of devices access the media, a higher probability that collisions will happen. Moreover, as the ACB factor becomes larger, the successful access probability becomes smaller. It is due to the reason that the ACB factor is higher, the devices have more change to access, and the successful access probability becomes smaller. The proposed retransmission-based scheme with ACB factor 1 shall have a significant low successful access probability. However, due to the feature of adaptiveness, the proposed scheme has excellent performance result which is similar to that of ACB scheme with factor 0.2.

Effects of the number of devices on access delay. Figure 4 shows effects of number of devices on access delay. Obviously, as the number of devices who request to access becomes larger, the number of collision becomes higher, and the access delay becomes longer. Moreover, as the ACB factor becomes lower, the occurrence probability of collision becomes higher, and the access delay becomes longer. Surprisingly, the proposed scheme could have a similar performance to the typical ACB scheme with factor 0.4. From the two figures, we can observe a result that the proposed retransmission-based ACB scheme could can reduce the access delay effectively while maintaining high access success probability.

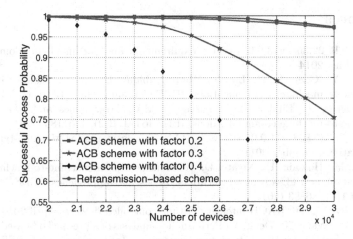

Fig. 3. Effects of congestion controls on access success probability

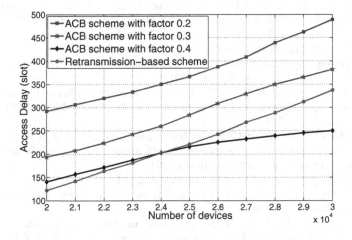

Fig. 4. Effects of congestion controls on access success delay

6   Conclusion

To resolve the challenge of RAN overloading in LTE due to the numerous access requests from MTC devices, this paper proposed a retransmission-based ACB scheme where the current loading level of RAN is leveraged to adjust the ACB factor. In this case, the MTC devices reach to the preamble access are controlled and phenomenon of RAN overloading is alleviated. In particular, we leverage the number of preamble retransmissions send by MTC devices who successfully perform random access to estimate the loading of RAN. From the simulation results, we can observe a surprising result that the proposed retransmission-based ACB scheme could can reduce the access delay effectively while maintaining high access success probability comparing with the typical ACB scheme.

References

1. 3GPP TR 22.368 v13.0.0: Service requirements for Machine-Type Communications, June 2014
2. Lien, S.-Y., Chen, K.-C., Lin, Y.: Toward ubiquitous massive accesses in 3GPP machine-to-machine communications. IEEE Commun. Mag. **49**(4), 66–74 (2011)
3. Rajandekar, A., Sikdar, B.: A survey of MAC layer issues and protocols for machine-to-machine communications. IEEE IoT J. **2**(2), 175–186 (2015)
4. 3GPP TR 37.868 v11.0.0: Study on RAN Improvements for Machine-type Communications, October 2011
5. Hasan, M., Hossain, E., Niyato, D.: Random access for machine-to-machine communication in LTE-advanced networks: issues and approaches. IEEE Commun. Mag. **51**(6), 86–93 (2013)
6. 3GPP R2-102296: RACH intensity of time controlled devices, April 2010
7. Jiang, W., Wang, X., Deng, T.: Performance analysis of a pre-backoff based random access scheme for machine-type communications. In: Proceedings of IEEE IGBSG 2011, pp. 1–4, April 2011
8. Sheu, S.-T., Chiu, C.-H., Cheng, Y.-C., Kuo, K.-H.: Self-adaptive persistent contention scheme for scheduling based machine type communications in LTE system. In: Proceedings of IEEE iCOST 2012, pp. 77–82, July 2012
9. Wei, C.-H., Cheng, R.-G., Al-Taee, F.M.: Dynamic radio resource allocation for group paging supporting smart meter communications. In: Proceedings of IEEE SmartGridComm 2012, pp. 659–663 (2012)
10. Shin, S.-Y., Triwicaksono, D.: Radio resource control scheme for machine-to-machine communication in LTE infrastructure. In: Proceedings of IEEE ICTC 2012, pp. 1–6, October 2012
11. 3GPP RAN2 70bis, R2-103742: RACH overload solutions, July 2010
12. 3GPP TR 22.011 v13.1.0: Technical Specification Group Services and System Aspects; Service accessibility, September 2014
13. de Andrade, T.P., Astudillo, C.A., da Fonseca, N.L.: Random Access Mechanism for RAN Overload Control in LTE/LTE-A Networks. In: Proceedings of IEEE ICC 2015, pp. 7607–7612, June 2015
14. Cheng, J.-P., Lee, C.-H., Lin, T.-M.: Prioritized random access with dynamic access barring for MTC in 3GPP LTE-A networks. In: Proceedings of IEEE GLOBECOM 2011 workshops, pp. 368–372, December 2011
15. He, H.-L., Du, Q.-H., Song, H.-B., Li, W.-Y., Wang, Y.-C., Ren, P.-Y.: Traffic-aware ACB scheme for massive access in machine-to-machine networks. In: Proceedings of IEEE ICC 2015, pp. 2226–2231, June 2015
16. Moon, J., Lim, Y.: Adaptive access class barring for machine-type communications in LTE-A. In: Proceedings of IEEE ICUFN 2016, pp. 398–402, August 2016
17. Duan, S., Shah-Mansouri, V., Wang, Z., Wong, V.W.S.: D-ACB: adaptive congestion control algorithm for bursty M2M traffic in LTE networks. IEEE Trans. Veh. Technol. **65**(12), 9847–9861 (2016)
18. Lin, G.-Y., Chang, S.-R., Wei, H.-Y.: Estimation and adaptation for bursty LTE random access. IEEE Trans. Veh. Technol. **65**(4), 2560–2577 (2016)

A Study on Online Corrosion Risk Perception Technology for Process Industry Safety IoTs Based on Demands of Assets Integrity Management

Liang Xiong[1], Guanglei Lv[2], Guangpei Cong[3(✉)], Fengqi He[4],
Shi He[5], and Yunjiang Sun[2]

[1] China University of Geosciences, Wuhan, China
[2] CNOOC Safety Environmental Protection Engineering Technology Research
Institute, Beijing, China
[3] Guangdong University of Petrochemical Technology, Maoming, China
125414712@qq.com
[4] Nuclear Power Institute of China, Beijing, China
[5] Nuclear Industry Management Cadre Institute, Beijing, China

Abstract. Combining developing demand on process industry safety management, an safety risk perception system for the process industry safety IoTs was proposed to a corrosion loop in a process unit. A low-dose tangential wall thickness measurement sensor based on gamma ray was adopted by this system. In addition, basic principle for realizing boundary layer recognition of the sensor was presented together with a precision measurement algorithm. In addition to merits such as without destroying insulation constructions and high-precision wall thickness measurement, the sensor of this system could be installed or dismantled online with a low cost, etc. With the system, the safety condition of a corrosion loop can be directly real-time soft measured quantitatively which is the foundation to establish the process industry safety IoTs.

Keywords: Process industry · Automatic monitoring system
Gamma ray sensor

1 Introduction

According to statistics, billions of losses in dollar are caused by corrosions under the heat insulation layer in the petroleum chemical industry [7]. Furthermore, severe corrosions are also able to lead to equipment failures and non-plan shutdown in manufacturing plants and the leakage of dangerous and harmful factors may also give rise to life casualties [8]. In most cases, such pipelines under high risks are equipped with external tube structures such as a heat insulation layer. Therefore, in a production state, it is extremely difficult to directly employ inspection techniques to perform safety management.

Research of Bruce and Lv et al. [9, 10] indicate that the serious corrosion probability for devices or pipelines under the heat insulation layer currently applied goes up

© ICST Institute for Computer Sciences, Social Informatics and Telecommunications Engineering 2018
Y.-B. Lin et al. (Eds.): IoTaaS 2017, LNICST 246, pp. 155–169, 2018.
https://doi.org/10.1007/978-3-030-00410-1_19

with the time. According to Geary, Kane and Norsworthy [11–13], as water is a critical factor incurring corrosion under insulation, corrosion phenomena become especially prominent in marine environment where the concentration of chloridion contained in corrosive media is even greater. Therefore, corrosion management for pipelines incorporating any heat insulation layer becomes particularly important. For this purpose, a simulation experiment set is invented for coating corrosion under insulation in Sinopec Safety Engineering Institute in Qingdao [14], so that simulation experiments can be carried out directly at different heat insulation layers and coatings. Besides, coating corrosions under a circumstance of alternating changes in diverse temperatures and humidity can be simulated. Studies performed by Jiang et al [15]. show that major factors that play an essential role in 20# steel corrosion under insulation include corrosive concentration, and oxygen content and temperature of the environment. Among them, temperature is the most influential factor. Comparing with alternated cooling and heating as well as isoperibol, corrosion degree under a dry-wet alternate environment is more severe.

In contrast to experiment rule researches, the domestic and overseas studies on precaution mainly focus on design, selection and preparation, etc. of thermal insulation materials [16, 17], as well as analysis and detections on those with insulation defects [18, 19], etc. Primarily, the detection on pipelines with a heat insulation layer is performed by means of pulsed eddy current testing [20, 21] which results in a large error and fails to meet practical demands on site. Regarding the study on online monitoring for pipeline corrosion under insulation, rather rough high-risk pipeline location surveys are carried out and it is less likely for online monitoring to be executed. As far as medium/down-stream enterprises in petroleum and petrochemical field are concerned, piping systems with temperature more than 60°C that occupy a proportion of about over 80% in the total number must be coated with insulation constructions. In addition, external and internal corrosions exist under the heat insulation layer simultaneously and the relevant etch state is usually changeable. Obviously, it is rather difficult for corrosion rule studies and offline detections at the earlier stage to meet safety management requirements. Considering this, an online security risk monitoring system is proposed combining RBI technology [22] and integrity management demands in this paper. Regarding the monitoring sensor that serves as an important basis for the system acting as the IoTs, a high-precision quantitative monitoring technology is put forward based on the gamma ray tangential measurement technology.

2   Frame of the Online Corrosion Risk Perception Technology for Process Industry Safety IoTs

Integrity management refers to risk/cost-benefit optimization management on the premise of risk identification during which devices and pipelines of diverse corrosion forms should be classified into several corrosion loops. Then, specific to different corrosion loops, corrosion leakage risk management is conducted. Despite that corrosion loop is a relatively small management object, risks are distributed unevenly in the interior of such a loop. The corresponding risks are mainly gathered in a few of

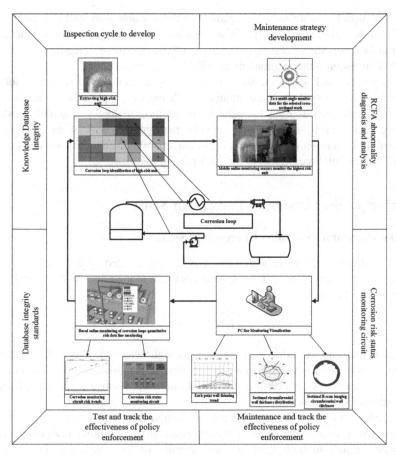

Fig. 1. Frame of online corrosion risk perception system for process industry safety IoTs

devices and pipe units. Therefore, by monitoring the most dangerous units in the loop, the goal of monitoring corrosion leakage risks in the entire loop can be realized. In line with such a principle, a corrosion risk perception system takes shape, as shown in Fig. 1. According to risk identification results of the system, movable wall monitoring sensors are arranged in the most dangerous pipelines located at the corrosion loop, so as to carry out multi-angle measurement for wall thicknesses. Industrial computer in such a monitoring system takes the responsibility to process multi-angle data, analyze circumferential distributions of wall thickness, and ultimately form circumferential B scan image (similar to CT slice photos [23, 24]; in fact, based on the CT technology, tested section slice photos are acquired by adopting ray dose information, Radon transform and Fourier slice theorem [25]). Moreover, locations of measuring points remain unchanged thanks to online monitoring of the sensor. Hence, corrosion trend analysis for various measuring points can be more accurate and reliable. Feedbacks of information obtained through industrial computer analysis are given in the risk analysis module. Through automatic analysis, risk distributions in the corrosion loop are figured out by this module. As a result, arrangement of the movable wall thickness monitoring sensor can be adjusted regularly, so as to make the corrosion status of the entire corrosion loop become increasingly "transparent". Furthermore, integrity management of such a corrosion loop becomes more reliable and precise.

However, for such a system, one of the most key technologies is such a sensor able to execute movable wall thickness monitoring. It must be applicable to various operating conditions such as high temperature in addition to low disassembly cost and convenient movement. As a result, integrity management cost of an enterprise is prevented from increasing. To sum up, high data reliability, sufficient precision and low cost are fundamental requirements for such monitoring sensors.

3   Principle and Design of Perception Sensor

3.1   Fundamental Principle of Perception Sensor

γ ray is electromagnetic wave with a low wavelength, emitted by decay of radioactive isotopes. Its attenuation during transmission conforms to the Lambert-Beer law [26], as shown in Eq. (1).

$$I = I_0 e^{-\mu_m \rho t} \tag{1}$$

where, I is intensity after the ray penetrates through detection objects; I_0 is intensity before the ray penetrates through detection objects; μ_m is mass-absorption coefficient of absorbing substance vs. γ ray; ρ is density of (absorbing) substance; t is thickness of the substance penetrated through.

According to Eq. (1), the ray with a large enough dose is able to penetrate through substances with a large thickness in theory; residual strength after ray penetration is principally related to both thickness and density of the substance. Theoretically, multiple substances exist simultaneously. As long as certain density differences lie between substances, substances through which the ray penetrates can be determined by technical approaches, such as heat incubation and metallic conduit, etc. Thus, theoretically, γ ray can be adopted to identify interior scaling under insulation of metallic conduits and pipelines, together with figuring out the thickness of both pipes and scale layers, provided that no damages are caused to the heat insulation layer.

In addition, absorption coefficient μ_m of the ray also affects residual strength after ray penetration; moreover, instead of a constant, μ_m is related to compositions of the measured substance, which may exert an enormous influence on wall thickness measurement precision and measured substance measurement. Even, it is likely for it to lead to misjudgment. As a consequence, an appropriate approach should be found to deal with such a problem. According to research findings, when the energy of γ ray exceeds 200 keV, μ_m becomes independent of the compositions of the measured substance. Therefore, under normal circumstances, radiation sources with ray energy ranging from 500 keV to 2500 keV are employed. It can be seemed that, in the case that radiation sources are invariant, the residual strength after ray penetration is only associated with density and thickness of the measured substance. On this basis, measurement requirements of monitoring sensors can be satisfied.

When the ray energy is large enough, μ_m of each substance is considered to be a constant, so that the residual energy of ray is under the impact of substance density and thickness. Therefore, receipt signals of a monitoring sensor can be calculated in line with the Eq. (2) below.

$$I = I_0 e^{-\sum_{i=1}^{n} \mu_i \rho_i t_i} \tag{2}$$

where, i refers to the categories of substances that the ray goes through. In the case that ray dose I_0 is invariant, density and thickness of the substance penetrated through in the process of ray transmission are variable, accompanied by prompt changes in I, the ray dose received by a ray sensor probe. In theory, when the ray passes a boundary layer, ray dose can be suddenly changed as far as heat insulation layer and metallic conduit ontology are concerned. If such sudden changes can be prominently identified, locations of all boundary layers can be precisely worked out. Obviously, in order to realize high-precision boundary identification, tangential irradiation is an ideal mode for the ray. The relevant reasons can be explained according to Eq. (3) below.

$$T = 2t\sqrt{\frac{D_0}{t} - 1} \tag{3}$$

Where, T is tangential thickness of the measured substance; t is its normal thickness; and, D_0 is the curvature radius of the measured substance boundary layer. In conformity with Eq. (3), it is clear that in the case of $D_0 > 1.25t$, T is larger than t. At this time, tangential ray dose attenuation is also greater than that in a normal direction. In addition, signal mutation of ray dose becomes even more prominent and it is more likely for them to be identified. In other words, boundary layer identification sensitivity and precision of tangential irradiation are higher than that of the normal in theory.

Meanwhile, if a stepping motor is adopted on the normal direction of a boundary layer, the distance (substance thickness or pipeline wall thickness) between two layers can be obtained based on the following Eq. (4).

$$t = pN \tag{4}$$

Where, p refers to the step width of the stepping motor, and N to the number of steps that the stepping motor moves between intervals of two transient signals.

Furthermore, comparing with the method of taking photos, the realization of light sensitive imaging does not rely on a rather high ray hose as far as this approach is concerned. Even a slight dose is able to satisfy identification demands of signal images. Therefore, radiation sources with very low radioactivity can be adopted without affecting the measurement precision. On this basis, security of such a technology is significantly improved, especially in narrow space such as an offshore platform.

3.2   Precision Control and Radiation Dose Selection

In line with the principle of sensor, its precision is under the control of two factors. One is the transmission accuracy of stepping motor; and, the other is the identification precision of photosensitive probe.

Considering the control of a stepping motor on one hand, it is not difficult to realize a precision control of 0.2 mm and below according to the current technical conditions. We can say that as long as stepping step width and transmission ratio are both defined, it is relatively very easy to achieve such a precision.

On the other hand, regarding the counting (measurement of residual radioactive activity) of photosensitive probe, the accuracy of sensor should also be affected. Especially when the activity of radioactive sources is very low, such an impact can be ignored. However, as it is frequently moved and used online for a long term during application, great activity of radioactive sources may incur safety issues. Therefore, a sensor is required to reduce such activity to the greatest extent provided that the corresponding precision has been met.

As required, measurement precision of a sensor is the wall thickness ± 0.1 mm. Relying on the Shannin theory, as presented in Eq. (5), the maximum metering error of the whole measurement system should be controlled at ± 0.05 mm. As the system measurement precision is influenced by the precision of mechanism motion and positioning as well as the precision of ray measurement, the theoretical measurement precision of the ray must be less than ± 0.05 mm with an aim to reach the expected system measurement precision.

$$w_t \leq \frac{w_0}{2} \qquad (5)$$

Where, w_0 stands for the expected measurable minimum precision or scale, and w_t for the measurement precision or scale that should be up to at the time of actual measurement.

From a viewpoint of measurement principle, when the system carries out primary measurement by regarding ± 0.05 mm as the scale, if the residual radioactive activity changes incurred by it are less than the metering error of this activity, as given in Eq. (6), the system fails to identify that whether such changes are caused by the primary measurement or the counting error of ray measurement. Consequently, measurement precision of such a scale cannot be guaranteed.

$$\Delta I_{0.05} \leq \Delta I_e \qquad (6)$$

Where, $\Delta I_{0.05}$ is ray measurement (activity) variation given rise to by a substance thickness of 0.05 mm; and, ΔI_ε is that caused by probe counting error.

On this basis, only when the metering error of residual radioactive activity is less than the residual radioactive activity changes brought about by a measurement based on the minimum measurement scale, the measurement precision of system can be guaranteed. In line with the Shannin theory, the metering error of residual radioactive activity must satisfy Eq. (7) below.

$$\Delta I_e \leq \frac{\Delta I_{0.05}}{2} \tag{7}$$

In the case that the metering error of residual radioactive activity is caused by the counting error, its computing method can be expressed in Eq. (8).

$$\Delta I_e = \frac{N}{\sqrt{n_N}} \tag{8}$$

Where, N is the radioactive activity value of ray, in Bq; and, n_N which is equivalent to $N \times 1$ is its cumulative count value and 1 refers to the irradiation time in second.

At the time of tangential measurement, the attenuation rule of ray obtained in line with Eq. (1) is expressed in Eq. (9).

$$I = I_0 e^{-\mu T} \tag{9}$$

Where, unit of measurement for I and I_0 is Ci; while μ stands for the attenuation coefficient of measured substance, in mm^{-1}, e for the Napierian base (e = 2.7183).

Dependent on Eqs. (3), (8) and (9), the actual wall thickness metering error given rise to by the radioactive activity metering error of ray is denoted by the following Eq. (10).

$$\Delta t_e = t_r - \frac{D_0 - \sqrt{D_0^2 - \left(\frac{\ln \frac{I \pm \sqrt{\frac{3.7 \times 10^{10} I}{I}}}{I_0}}{\mu}\right)^2}}{2} \tag{10}$$

Where, t_r is the real value of the actual wall thickness with a unit of mm; Δt_e (unit: mm) is the actual wall thickness deviation caused by radioactive activity metering error.

If Eq. (7) is converted into a criterion for the actual wall thickness, it turns into Eq. (11) shown below.

$$|\Delta t_e| \leq 0.025 \, \text{mm} \tag{11}$$

Equations (10) and (11) constitute a radioactive source activity determination criterion of the sensor measurement precision.

4   Performance Test of Monitoring Sensor

The sensor testing machine manufactured according to the operating principle above is illustrated in Fig. 2. This prototype employs a mechanical transmission mechanism.

Fig. 2. Sensor testing machine

4.1 Precision Examination Experiment of Bare Pipe and Coated Pipe

Dependent on standard measurement conditions given in Table 1, Eqs. (10) and (11) are both utilized to make the measurement duration for each point 2 s in line with the relevant application conditions. Then, when the activity of radioactive sources is 20 mCi, the corresponding parameters are presented in Table 1. Concerning the theoretical metering errors of diverse steel pipelines ($\mu = 0.05775$), they are shown in Table 2.

Table 1. Measurement conditions satisfied by design

Piping diameter (mm)	Maximum actual wall thickness (mm)
950	12.7
700	7.94
600	10
500	5.45
450	23.83
400	4.78
350	4.78
300	4.57
250	4.19
200	3.76
150	3.4
100	8.56

Table 2. Error calculation results of actual wall thickness

Piping diameter (mm)	Maximum actual wall thickness (mm)	Positive deviation based actual wall thickness (mm)	Negative deviation based actual wall thickness (mm)	Negative error of actual wall thickness (mm)	Positive error of actual wall thickness (mm)
950	12.7	12.6713	12.7292	−0.0287	0.0292
700	7.94	7.9365	7.94355	−0.0035	0.0035
600	10	9.9950	10.0051	−0.0050	0.0050
500	5.45	5.4490	5.4510	−0.0010	0.0010
450	23.83	23.7922	23.8682	−0.0378	0.0382
400	4.78	4.7794	4.7806	−0.0006	0.0006
350	4.78	4.7794	4.7806	−0.0006	0.0006
300	4.57	4.5695	4.5705	−0.0005	0.0005
250	4.19	4.1896	4.1904	−0.0004	0.0004
200	6	5.9994	6.0006	−0.0006	0.0006
150	5.00	4.9996	5.0005	−0.0004	0.0004
100	8.56	8.5592	8.5608	−0.0008	0.0008

For the experimental motor, the precision error of each step is about 0.01 mm; concerning the gear transmission set, the mean of precision errors ranges from 0.04 mm to 0.05 mm [27]. If computing results obtained in line with Table 2 are taken, the maximum negative and positive errors of actual wall thickness are −0.038 mm and 0.038 mm respectively. In addition, the maximum cumulative measurement error is 0.098, the sum of errors described above. In the case that tests are carried out specific to the most common pipes with a diameter of 150 mm and a measured wall thickness of 5 mm, as given in Fig. 3, the relevant measured value and measured error are 5.12 mm and 0.12 mm accordingly. Based on Table 2, it is clear that the theoretical computing error should be 0.0604 mm calculated according to the precision estimation method put forward in this paper. For such a high estimation precision, it is caused by insufficient error estimation for the transmission of experimental facilities. The maximum positive error is 0.038 mm. Besides, it can be seen from Table 2 that, in most cases, measurement errors of bare pipes are predominant by the mechanical transmission mechanism. Even under a circumstance of low-dose radioactive sources, the counting error of the ray can almost be ignored. However, with the increase in pipe diameter and wall thickness, the counting error also becomes larger. When testing for large caliber pipelines is carried out, such an error has the same order of magnitude as that of mechanical transmission. In this condition, it cannot be neglected.

Regarding the coated pipe under insulation, as shown in Fig. 4, on one hand, the actual thickness and measured thickness of its external insulation layer are 45 mm and 43.86 mm respectively. On the other hand, as far as its metallic conduit is concerned, the corresponding actual wall thickness and measured wall thickness are 6 mm and 6.24 mm. The relevant error is larger than that when it is still a bare pipe, because the coated pipe is subjected to influences of a heat insulation layer and the increase in measured pipe diameter.

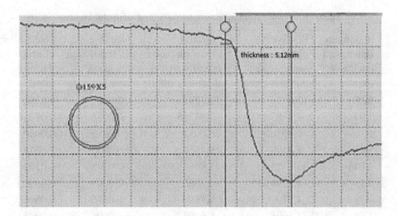

Fig. 3. Measurement result of a bare pipe with diameter 150 mm and wall thickness 5 mm

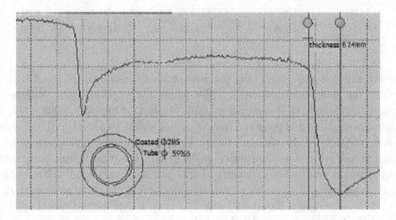

Fig. 4. Measurement result of a coated pipe with diameter 50 mm and wall thickness 6 mm

4.2 Identification and Quantitative Experiments for Boundary Layers in Various Working Conditions

In consistency with the actual monitoring situations, monitored working conditions can be divided to bare pipe, bare pipe + coated pipe, bare pipe + coated pipe + interior scaling, bare pipe + coated pipe + inner media, and bare pipe + coated pipe + interior scaling + inner media. In Figs. 3 and 4, boundary layer identifications for the bare pipe and the bare pipe + the coated pipe have been tested. Below, the testing will be primarily carried out in allusion to the other three conditions which are more complicated.

For the purpose of enhancing testing efficiency, such a monitoring sensor takes advantage of a step-by-step measurement algorithm. In the case that the pipeline is coated with multiple coating layers externally, the entire scanning process is classified into coarse scanning and fine scanning. The former serves as the first step, with an aim to determine the locations of boundary layers for both the coated pipe and the inner steel pipe; and, the latter is the second step designed to precisely define pipeline wall thickness and the thickness of the interior scaling layer.

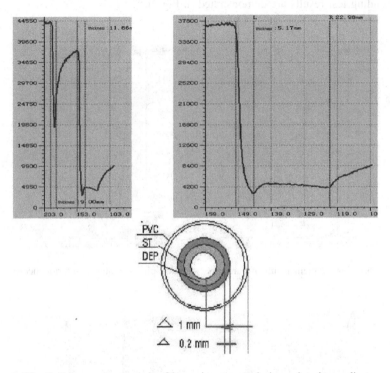

Fig. 5. Measurement result of bare pipe + coated pipe + interior scaling

As for the measurement result of bare pipe + coated pipe + interior scaling, it is given in Fig. 5. During which, $CaSO_4$ colloid is utilized to simulate the actual scaling layer. From Fig. 5, it can be seen that boundaries among PVC, heat insulation layer, metallic conduit and scaling layer can be clearly identified. In detail, that between PVC and heat insulation layer, or, metallic conduit and scaling layer, or, scaling layer and atmosphere, has a V-shaped inflection point; in comparison, a reverse V-shaped inflection point occurs to the boundary layer of heat insulation layer and metallic conduit. In terms of the thickness measurement, measured thickness of the pipe is 5.17 mm. In fact, the actual wall thickness of the pipe is 5 mm. In addition, the measured thickness of the interior scaling substances is 17.81 mm, instead of 20 mm which is their practical thickness. By contrast to the bare pipe, error of the metallic conduit goes up, while the measurement error of scaling layer lies within an acceptable range.

In addition to conveying gas, some pipes also play a role of transporting liquids. Apparently, the density of the latter is higher than the former. In line with Eq. (1), its ray absorption rate is also significantly higher than gases. Therefore, under a circumstance that a pipeline contains liquids inside, V-shaped inflection point between metal and liquid should be tested to determine whether it is as ideal as what has been shown in Fig. 5. During experiment, water whose density is greater than common substances in general pipelines is adopted to test its impacts in extreme cases. The corresponding test results are demonstrated in Fig. 6.

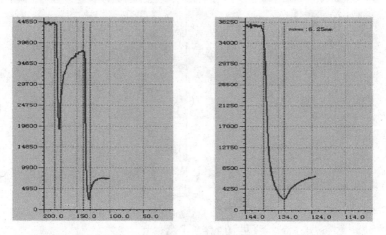

Fig. 6. Measurement result of bare pipe + coated pipe + water as interior medium

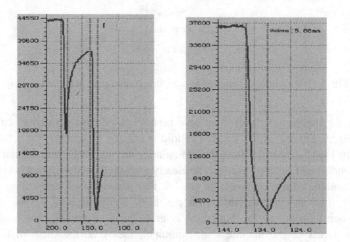

Fig. 7. Measurement result of bare pipe + coated pipe

Based on Fig. 6, due to the existence of a considerable gap between densities of metallic conduit and water, V-shaped curve for its boundary layer becomes even more obvious. However, if compared with the inflection point for metal and gas shown in Fig. 7, it appears much less weak, indicating that when densities for substances on both sides of the boundary layer are close to each other, more effective sharpening algorithm is required to identify the inflection point of signal curves. In addition, relative to results presented in Fig. 4, measurement thickness of the pipe is 6.25 mm provided that liquid medium exists inside it, as shown in Fig. 6. The corresponding wall thickness measurement error that has a little impact can nearly be ignored if compared with the testing results obtained in a gaseous environment.

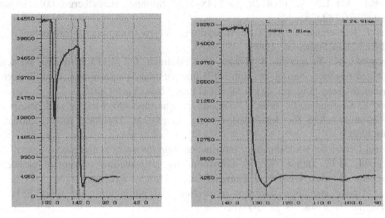

Fig. 8. Measurement result of bare pipe + coated pipe + scaling + water as interior medium

From Fig. 8, owing to the existence of liquid, it becomes more difficult to determine the boundary layer between scaling layer and interior media; moreover, the V-shaped inflection point also seems to be gentle. What needs to be noted is that they can be still identified in processes of coarse and fine scanning.

5   Conclusions

(1) The online corrosion monitoring technology designed in this paper is applicable to all monitored working conditions currently encountered. At the time of measuring boundary layers among substances, V-shaped curves can be utilized to perform accurate identification. As under a significant influence of densities for substances on each side of the detected boundary layer, the closer such densities are to each other, the gentler such V-shaped curves will be. In this case, better sharpening algorithms are needed to identify them.

(2) This monitoring technology has a rather high thickness measurement precision 0.1 mm higher than ultrasonic thickness measurement. At a later period, if a more precise electrical transmission system is employed, the corresponding precision will be substantially improved, so that diverse demands during process industry integrity management can be satisfied.

References

1. Smith, T.F., Waterman, M.S.: Identification of common molecular subsequences. J. Mol. Biol. **147**, 195–197 (1981)
2. May, P., Ehrlich, H.-C., Steinke, T.: ZIB structure prediction pipeline: composing a complex biological workflow through web services. In: Nagel, W.E., Walter, W.V., Lehner, W. (eds.) Euro-Par 2006. LNCS, vol. 4128, pp. 1148–1158. Springer, Heidelberg (2006). https://doi.org/10.1007/11823285_121
3. Foster, I., Kesselman, C.: The Grid: Blueprint for a New Computing Infrastructure. Morgan Kaufmann, San Francisco (1999)
4. Czajkowski, K., Fitzgerald, S., Foster, I., Kesselman, C.: Grid information services for distributed resource sharing. In: 10th IEEE International Symposium on High Performance Distributed Computing, pp. 181–184. IEEE Press, New York (2001)
5. Foster, I., Kesselman, C., Nick, J., Tuecke, S.: The physiology of the grid: an open grid services architecture for distributed systems integration. Technical report, Global Grid Forum (2002)
6. National Center for Biotechnology Information. http://www.ncbi.nlm.nih.gov
7. Fitzgerald, B.J., Stefan, W.: A corrosion under insulation prevention strategy for petrochemical industry piping. J. Corros. Manag. **57**, 15–19 (2004)
8. Li, J.: Under insulation corrosion protection and aluminum cold spray technology. J. Shanghai Paint. **46**, 19–22 (2008)
9. Susan, C., Faisal, K., John, S.: Analysis of pitting corrosion on steel under insulation in marine environments. J. Loss Prev. Process Ind. **26**, 1466–1483 (2013)
10. Bruce, R.: Preventing corrosion under insulation in chemical manufacturing facilities. J. JPCL **5**, 40 (1998)
11. Lv, X.-L., Tang, J.-Q., Gong, J.-M., et al.: Under insulation corrosion protection. J. Corros. Sci. Prot. Technol. **26**, 167–172 (2014)
12. Geary, W.: Analysis of a corrosion under insulation failure in a carbon steel refinery hydrocarbon line. J. Case Stud. Eng. Fail. Anal. **1**, 249–256 (2013)
13. Kane, R.D., Ashbaugh, W.G., Mcgowan, N., et al.: New industry standards, test procedures, and surface treatments combat corrosion under insulation. In: Corrosion Source-2000 Online Symposium, Washington, p. 403 (2000)
14. Norsworthy, R., Dunn, P.J.: Corrosion under thermal insulation. J. Mater. Perform. **41**, 38 (2002)
15. Qiu, Z.-G., Liu, X.-H., Qi, J., et al.: Under insulation corrosion coating simulation equipment. Technical report, Corrosion Forum (2015)
16. Jiang, Y.-J., Gong, J.-M.: Under insulation corrosion behavior of 20 steel under different simulated conditions. J. Mater. Mech. Eng. **35**, 66–70 (2011)
17. Li, J., Lin, R.-F., Chang, Y.-P.: Material selection and design of foam insulation jacket corrosion. J. Corros. Prot. **29**, 80–83 (2008)
18. Folke, B., Tomas, E.: Properties of thermal insulation materials during extreme environment changes. J Constr. Build. Mater. **23**, 2189–2195 (2009)
19. Xin, W., Ding, K.-Q., Huang, D.-L., et al.: Pulsed eddy current testing technology simulation with the insulation pipeline corrosion defects. J. Nondestruct. Test. **31**, 509–512 (2009)
20. Ren, Z.: The new technology to detect corrosion under insulation pipeline. J. Foreign Oil Field Eng. **18**, 53–54 (2002)
21. Wu, X., Li, F.-Q., Shi, K., et al.: Pulsed eddy current thickness measurement technology. J. Nondestruct. Test. **7**, 528–530 (2009)

22. Zhao, L., Chen, D.-F., Lu, Y., et al.: Application of pulsed eddy current in the metal thickness detection. J. Meas. Control Technol. **12**, 22–24 (2007)
23. Stephane, B., Anne, K.: Dynamic X-ray computed tomography. J. Proc. IEEE **91**, 1574–1588 (2003)
24. Zhao, J.-H., Qu, Z.: Industrial CT tomographic image sequence to achieve a two-dimensional re-Zhong. J. Computer development **13**, 20–22 (2003)
25. Zhang, S.-L.: Algebraic Reconstruction Method Research and Application of industrial CT image. Northwestern Polytechnical University, Xi'an (2004)
26. Wei, W.-S.: Ray fault diagnosis. J. Petrochem. **32**, 700–702 (2003)
27. Munro, R.G., Palmer, D.: Gear transmission error outside the normal path of contact due to corner and top contact. J. Mech. Eng. Sci. **213**, 389–400 (1999)

A Machine Learning Based PM2.5 Forecasting Framework Using Internet of Environmental Things

Sachit Mahajan[1,2,3](✉), Hao-Min Liu[2], Ling-Jyh Chen[2], and Tzu-Chieh Tsai[3]

[1] Social Networks and Human Centered Computing Program,
Taiwan International Graduate Program, Academia Sinica, Taipei, Taiwan
sachitmahajan@iis.sinica.edu.tw
[2] Institute of Information Science, Academia Sinica, Taipei, Taiwan
[3] Department of Computer Science, National Chengchi University, Taipei, Taiwan

Abstract. Information and communication technologies have been widely used to achieve the objective of smart city development. A smart air quality sensing and forecasting system is an important part of a smart city. In this paper, we present an approach to accurately forecast hourly fine particulate matter (PM2.5). An Internet of Things (IoT) framework comprising of Airbox Devices for PM2.5 monitoring has been used to acquire the data. Our main focus is to achieve high forecasting accuracy with reduced computation time. We use a hybrid model to do the forecast and a grid based system to cluster the monitoring stations based on the geographical distance. The experimentation and evaluation is done using Airbox Devices data from 119 stations in Taichung area of Taiwan. We are able to demonstrate that a proper clustering based on geographical distance can reduce the forecasting error rate and also the computation time.

Keywords: Internet of Things (IoT) · Air quality · Smart cities

1 Introduction

Whenever we talk about a smart city, it always revolves around leveraging the advancement in the field of Information and Communication Technology (ICT). Lately, Internet of Things (IoT) has revolutionized the smart city initiative and IoT devices have become the technological backbone of smart cities [1]. IoT has revolutionized the technology evolution and can be seen as an evolution of Internet into an omnipresent network of smart interconnected objects that not only sense the information but also interact with the outside physical world [2].

In the recent years, problems related to deteriorating air quality have been a topic of concern all over the world. Rapid industrial growth and urbanization has been an important factor behind the degrading air quality. When we talk about smart cities, not only we need continuous air quality monitoring but also

© ICST Institute for Computer Sciences, Social Informatics and Telecommunications Engineering 2018
Y.-B. Lin et al. (Eds.): IoTaaS 2017, LNICST 246, pp. 170–176, 2018.
https://doi.org/10.1007/978-3-030-00410-1_20

a system which accurately forecasts future air quality. There are various kind of pollutants based on human and environmental factors that get diffused in the air. One of the most important among all the pollutants is fine particulate matter whose size is 2.5 μm or less also known as PM2.5. These particles can cause serious damage to human health and can lead to respiratory problems [3]. In the past, some research has been done on forecasting air quality based on using mathematical models and air quality modelling softwares. But these methods still have some drawbacks that can be addressed. Our approach is different from the conventional approaches. We use a data centric and grid based approach which uses real-time data from Airbox Project [4] to perform the experiments and evaluation. The contribution of the paper is three-fold:

(1) We propose a neural network based Hybrid model for hourly PM2.5 prediction.
(2) We use real-time Airbox data to perform the hourly PM2.5 prediction.
(3) We evaluate our model by clustering stations into grids based on the geographical distance. We perform the evaluation using data from 119 stations in Taichung area of Taiwan and try to understand the relationship between forecast accuracy and computation time.

The rest of the paper is organized as follows. Section 2 includes some related works. That is followed by Sect. 3 which includes the methodology followed for this work. It gives the details about the data, the hybrid model and the clustering approach. Section 4 includes the results and the evaluation part based on the experiments. In Sect. 5, we conclude the paper and give some ideas about future work.

2 Related Work

There has been some previous research works which focused on air quality forecasting. In one of the related works [5], the authors performed PM2.5 prediction for the next 48 h. They used a data based approach which involved using a linear regression and neural network based prediction model. In [6], the authors proposed a Deep Hybrid Model for weather forecasting. Though it didn't forecast PM2.5 but it predicts temperature, dew point and wind. In one of the other works [7], the authors used a combination of remote sensing and meteorological data with the ground based PM2.5 observations. Some of the researchers have implemented machine learning techniques on big data to perform the computation [8]. However, there are some drawbacks as most of these techniques rely on feeding some features into the model. The features are for one particular location and the model is implemented on all the stations. It is easy to understand that different regions have different PM2.5 levels based on different sources of emission. So accurately performing forecasting using a generic models for all the stations is not really feasible. To tackle this issue, we introduce the concept of clustering the monitoring stations into grids based on the geographical distance between the stations.

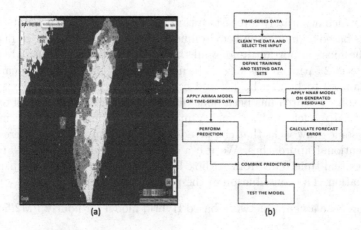

Fig. 1. (a)Visualization platform provided by g0v community (b) Hybrid Model flowchart

3   Methodology

In this part we will first explain about the Airbox Data used for the experiment. This section will also describe the Hybrid model used for performing the prediction and the clustering approach.

3.1   Airbox Data

The data is obtained from Airbox Project which involves deployment of IoT systems all over Taiwan. The Airbox device installation was carried out on a large scale initially in Taiwan. Initially it was initiated in Taipei City and on March 22, 2016, 150 devices were deployed around the city. The project has been widely acknowledged by people and has spread over other areas of Taiwan as well. 230 devices have been installed in Taichung area; 242 devices have been deployed in Kaohsiung area; 220 devices have been deployed in Tainan and 298 devices have been deployed in New Taipei City area of Taiwan. As of now, there are more than 1500 devices deployed in Taiwan and 24 cities all around the world. For this study, the data was collected for Airbox Devices deployed in Taichung area of Taiwan. To visualize the Airbox data, there have been some visualization systems developed. One of them is geographic information (GIS) based visualization system that combines the location with the measured data. Figure 1(a) shows the snapshot of visualization platform. The measurement data for this work was collected for the time period between January, 18 2017 and February 17, 2017.

3.2   Hybrid Model

We can divide a time-series into linear and non-linear components. The flowchart for Hybrid Model is depicted in Fig. 1(b). The Hybrid model is made by utilizing the Autoregressive Integrated Moving Average (ARIMA) model [9] and Neural Network Autoregressive (NNAR) model [10]. ARIMA model is good but it doesn't capture the non-linear components. An ARIMA (p, d, q) model has parameters p, d and q which are all integers. They must be greater than or equal to zero. The parameters respectively point to the order of the autoregressive (AR), integrated (I) and moving average (MA) components of the model. So we need a technique that can capture the non-linear components too. To solve that issue we can use Artificial Neural Networks (ANN). In NNAR [10] model, the input comprises of lagged time-series and the output is predicted time-series value. Authors in [11] described the implementation of a hybrid model. It can be represented as

$$Z_t = X_t + Y_t \tag{1}$$

In the above equation, X_t represents the linear components and Y_t represents the non linear components. In the initial step these two components have to be estimated from the data. Next step is the application of ARIMA model. ARIMA takes care of the linear components and the non- linear residuals are generated. We assume that R_t be the residuals generated at time t from the linear model. It can be represented as

$$R_t = Z_t - P_t \tag{2}$$

In the above equation, P_t is the forecast value for time t. The residuals are modelled using neural networks. If we assume that there are n input nodes, then the neural network model for residuals can be represented as

$$R_t = f(R_{t-1}, R_{t-2}, ..., R_{t-n}) + E \tag{3}$$

Neural network defines the non-linear function f and E is the randomly generated error. In the end, forecast from the neural network is generated and Eq. (3) is used to get the final output. For our hybrid model, we used an ARIMA (3, 1, 1) model where 3, 1, 1 are the values of p, d and q respectively. For neural network, we used an NNAR (9, 5) model which used 9 lagged inputs with 5 nodes in the hidden layer.

3.3 Clustering Approach

In order to reduce the computation time of the prediction on all stations, we apply clustering approach before implementing the prediction. First of all, we divided all the stations into different clusters according to their geographic locations. Then, we apply the prediction model on the average value of time series data in each cluster. According to the distribution of stations in Taichung, we have done the experiments to divide all stations into one-by-one to four-by-four clusters. One-by-one case denotes that we predict the whole region with only the average value of time series data in that region, shown in Fig. 2(a). In two-by-two case, we divided stations into four clusters according to the median value of their latitude and longitude, as it is shown in Fig. 2(b). In three-by-three case, we divided stations into nine clusters according to the 33th quantile value and 67th quantile value of their latitude and longitude, as it is shown in Fig. 2(c). And similarly it is done for four-by-four case as shown in Fig. 2(d).

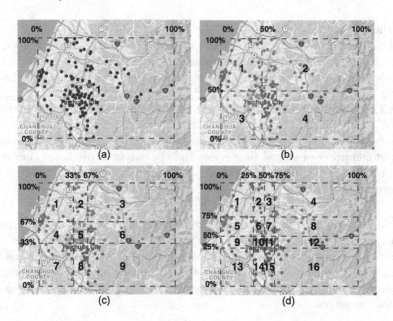

Fig. 2. (a) Without Clustering Method (b) 2×2 Clustering Method (c) 3×3 Clustering Method (d) 4×4 Clustering Method

Table 1. Average Mean error and RMSE of Grid 1×1 to Grid 4×4.

Grid	1×1	2×2	3×3	4×4
Ave. mean error	11.42	7.21	6.24	4.90
Ave. RMSE	13.95	8.93	8.06	6.17

4   Results and Evaluation

The experiments and evaluation were done using the real-time Airbox data. The Hybrid Model was trained using the six days hourly historical data. And the next one day hourly data was used for testing the model.

To analyse the results, we calculated the Root Mean Square Error (RMSE) and mean values. The results of average mean value and average RMSE value of Grid 1×1 to Grid 4×4 are shown in Table 1. The average of mean value and RMSE value is the weighted average, influenced by the number of stations in each cluster. The results show that both mean error and RMSE decrease with an increase in the number of grids. The mean error of Grid 4×4 can be reduced to less than $5\,\mu g/m^3$. This is very significant result as our aim is to perform forecast with prediction error as low as possible.

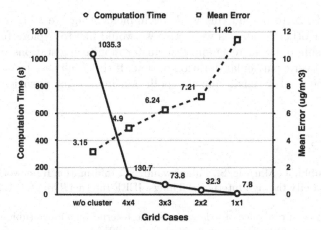

Fig. 3. Comparison of computation time and mean error among four designed cases

4.1 Evaluation

In order to evaluate our approach, we made a comparison between the computation time and mean error variation among four designed cases (4×4 grid, 3×3 grid, 2×2 grid, 1×1 grid). Before applying the grid based clustering approach, we applied the model individually on 119 stations without clustering. Although the mean error was less but still the computation time was huge. So to evaluate the system, we included the case without any cluster in the comparison result as shown in Fig. 3. The total computation time without applying clustering method went up to 1035.3 s, which is a lot when we talk about real-time computing. In the case with Grid 4×4 clustering, the computation time was reduced to 130.7 s, which is around 87% reduction from the design without clustering, while there was an increase of $1.74 \,\mu g/m^3$ mean error as the trade off. This is an acceptable trade off considering the computation time it saves.

5 Conclusion and Future Work

In this paper, we proposed a framework that uses IoT technology and machine learning techniques to forecast PM2.5 concentration. We performed the prediction using the Hybrid model which utilizes an ARIMA model and an NNAR model. Our main aim was to reduce the computation time and at the same time make sure that we get an acceptable forecast accuracy. We followed a grid based method to efficiently group 119 monitoring stations in Taichung area of Taiwan. Grids consisted of monitoring stations clustered together according to the geographic distance. To evaluate, we tested the system for grids of different sizes and showed how the computation time can be reduced with an acceptable forecasting error.

We would like to extend this work by implementing the PM2.5 prediction framework for other regions as well. Also we would like to explore further possibilities of using different techniques to cluster monitoring stations which show similar trend over a particular duration of time. If the results are favorable, these studies can be used by environmental pollution monitoring agencies for policy making.

References

1. Jin, J., Gubbi, J., Marusic, S., Palaniswami, M.: Information framework for creating a smart city through Internet of Things. IEEE Internet Things J. **1**(2), 112–121 (2014)
2. Delic, K.A.: On resilience of IoT systems: the Internet of Things (ubiquity symposium). Ubiquity **2016**(February), article no. 1 (2016)
3. Xing, Y.-F.: The impact of PM2.5 on the human respiratory system. J. Thorac. Dis. **8**(1), E69–E74 (2016)
4. PM2.5 Open Data Portal. http://pm25.lass-net.org/en/
5. Zheng, Y., et al.: Forecasting fine-grained air quality based on big data. In: Proceedings of the 21th ACM SIGKDD International Conference on Knowledge Discovery and Data Mining (KDD 2015), pp. 2267–2276. ACM, New York (2015)
6. Grover, A., Kapoor, A., Horvitz, E.: A deep hybrid model for weather forecasting. In: Proceedings of the 21th ACM SIGKDD International Conference on Knowledge Discovery and Data Mining (KDD 2015), pp. 379–386. ACM, New York (2015)
7. Lary, D.J., Lary, T., Sattler, B.: Using machine learning to estimate global PM2.5 for environmental health studies. Environ. Health Insights. **12;9**(Suppl. 1), 41–52 (2015)
8. Zheng, Y., Capra, L., Wolfson, O., Yang, H.: Urban computing: concepts, methodologies, and applications. ACM Trans. Intell. Syst. Technol. (TIST) - Spec. Sect. Urban Comput. **5**(3), 55 (2014). Article 38
9. Christodoulos, C., Michalakelis, C., Varoutas, D.: Forecasting with limited data: combining ARIMA and diffusion models. Technol. Forecast. Soc. Change **77**(4), 558–565 (2010)
10. Hyndman, R.J., Athanasopoulos, G.: Forecasting: Principles and Practice. OTexts (2013)
11. Zhang, G.P.: Time series forecasting using a hybrid ARIMA and neural network model. Neurocomputing **50**, 159–175 (2003)

Improved Single Packet Traceback Scheme with Bloom Filters

Jia-Ning Luo[1(✉)] and Ming-Hour Yang[2]

[1] Department of Information and Telecommunications Engineering,
Ming Chuan University, Taoyuan, Taiwan
deer@mail.mcu.edu.tw
[2] Department of Information and Computer Engineering,
Chung Yuan Christian University, Taoyuan, Taiwan
mhyang@cycu.edu.tw

Abstract. In response to the rapid development of the Internet in recent years, numerous new Internet services have been developed to satisfy user needs. However, numerous security issues were also emerged. Because of current Internet protocols, attackers can hide their IP addresses when initiating attacks on targets, especially on the Internet of Things (IoT) frameworks. As a result, discovering the true location of attackers is difficult, especially the attacks are initiates from the personal and private devices that previously lacked Internet connection. Numerous researchers have proposed various packet traceback schemes. Our proposed scheme is a packet marking scheme that uses a 32-bit space in the packet header to record attack paths and the time to live field to decrease the false positive rate of tracebacks. This enables single-packet tracebacks through packet marking and does not require additional storage space on routers for recording attack path data.

Keywords: Packet marking scheme · Packet logging scheme
Hybrid IP traceback · Distributed denial of service · IP spoofing

1 Introduction

In response to the rapid development of the Internet in recent years, numerous new Internet services have been developed to satisfy user needs. However, these services may be shut down by denial of service attacks. Two types of denial of service attacks exist: flood-based attacks and software exploit attacks [5,8]. Flood-based attacks send massive numbers of packets to overload a target's bandwidth or computational or storage capacities, thus rendering the server unable to accept packets from legitimate users. In contrast, software exploit attacks use fewer packets to attack vulnerabilities in a target system that can disable the system and render it unable to provide services. In addition, most routers do not verify the authenticity of the source IP address, and attackers can forge the source IP address to hide their true locations. Therefore, the development of a traceback scheme to determine the true IP address of attacks is crucial.

© ICST Institute for Computer Sciences, Social Informatics and Telecommunications Engineering 2018
Y.-B. Lin et al. (Eds.): IoTaaS 2017, LNICST 246, pp. 177–184, 2018.
https://doi.org/10.1007/978-3-030-00410-1_21

Traceback schemes can be classified based on the type of attack they can respond to [3,7]. Some can only trace the true source of flood-based attacks [1,2,9,11], but others can trace the true source of both flood-based and software exploit attacks [13,14].

Packet logging traceback schemes [4,15] were developed to trace the source of software exploit attacks. In these schemes, each router traversed by a packet records unaltered information from the packet. This resolves the issue of not being able to trace the source from a single packet because of insufficient packet data space. A router's internal logs can be consulted to determine whether a specific packet passed through a specific router. However, if too many packet digests are stored on a Bloom filter, two separate packets can correspond to the same field and cause false positives. Another problem with packet logging schemes is that they require too much storage space on the router to store packet information. To address this issue, hybrid IP traceback schemes were developed [2,13,14]. In this type of scheme, unused header fields are used to record a packet's path information. After all header fields have been filled, path information is stored on the router. In 2014, Yang [14] proposed using multiple tables rather than a single table to reduce the router storage space required by the HAHIT scheme. However, an additional burden is still placed on routers because of the need to store overflow data on the routers.

In this paper, we proposed a single packet traceback method that allows the source of an attack to be accurately determined with zero router storage load. We used skitter data [12] from the Center for Applied Internet Data Analysis (CAIDA) to perform network topology tests of this traceback scheme. The key contributions of this paper are as follows:

1. Tracebacks can be completed using a single packet.
2. Attacks from multiple sources can be traced simultaneously.
3. No additional router storage capacity is required.
4. The traceback scheme has a zero false negative rate, defined as $\frac{\text{number of unidentified attack paths}}{\text{total number of attack paths}}$.
5. The traceback scheme has a low false positive rate, defined as $\frac{\text{number of wrongly identified attack paths}}{\text{total number of attacks}}$.
6. CAIDA's skitter data from 1998 to 2008, comprising network topology constructed from route information obtained by sending packets from a single origin to multiple destinations, were used to validate our method.

2 Improved Single Packet Traceback Scheme with Bloom Filters

Our scheme assumes that attackers initiate multiple software exploit attacks or one or more distributed denial of service attacks on a single target. Thus, the proposed scheme must be able to simultaneously trace multiple attack sources. In addition, only the final destination of the packet is considered when routers determine which downstream router to forward a packet to; the packet's originating IP is not authenticated. Attackers can spoof the source IP to hide their location, thus allowing all attacks to reach the victim. Furthermore, because we assume our traceback scheme is openly accessible, attackers can disguise their location by designing a forged mark in packet headers in an attempt to mislead the traceback.

To be able to perform tracebacks on attackers with these qualities, and to define the scope of problems that can be resolved by the proposed traceback scheme, our traceback scheme can only work if the following conditions are met:

- Routers are safe from intrusions.
- Routers can identify whether a packet was forwarded from another router or from a local area network.
- All routers support this traceback scheme.
- The target has an intrusion detection system because an attack must be identified before a traceback can begin.

To simplify assumptions and focus on the main proposal of this paper, we assume that the victim has an intrusion detection system to detect when attacks occur, and we do not discuss how the intrusions are detected in the present study. To trace the source of an attack, a packet must have space to record the routers traversed by the packet. As shown in Fig. 1, we use the 32-bit space in the IP header occupied by the identification, flag, and fragment offset fields to mark and store path information. Because only 0.06% to 0.25% of all packets exceed the maximum transmission unit and must be fragmented [6,10], storing path information in these fields will not affect normal network functioning in most cases.

Bit offset	0-3	4-7	8-15	16-18	19-31
0	Version	Header length	TOS	Total length	
32	Identification field			Flag	Fragment offset
64	TTL		Protocol	Header checksum	
96	Source address				
128	Destination address				
160	Options				
160 Or 196+	Payload(first 8 bytes)				

Fig. 1. Packet marker field in the IP header

2.1 Packet Marking Scheme

When router R_i receives a packet P, the router first determines whether the packet came from a local area network. If so, router R_i sets packet P's marker field, $P.mark32$, to 0 and packet P's TTL field, $P.ttl$, to the maximum value (255). These values prevent passing a non-zero marker to the Internet, which would result in the inability to accurately determine when to stop tracing and the difficulty of determining whether a packet has exceeded the hot count caused by different initial TTL values. Table 1 lists all symbols used in this method.

Table 1. List of symbols

R_i	$\{R_1, R_2, ..., R_i, ..., R_n\}$; a router on the path between the origin and the destination
P	a packet on the Internet
$P.mark32$	A 32-bit marker field in packet P
$P.mark30$	A 30-bit marker field in packet P
$P.mark15$	A 15-bit marker field in packet P
$P.ttl$	The TTL field in packet P's IP header
IP_{R_i}	The IP address of router R_i
$h()$	Hash function
MSM	Maximum size of a mark
BF	Bloom filter
MS	A flag that indicates the marker field is full and no additional marks can be included in this field
$P.id$	An identifier that is identical for all fragments of packet P
$P.no$	The sequence of fragments with the same identifier
SF	A flag that indicates the marker field has been fragmented
$threshold$	The threshold for fragmenting packets
$\|\|$	OR operator
$\%$	Mod operator

As shown in the Algorithm 1, when R_i receives a packet P that is not from a local area network, the router hashes its IP address IP_{R_i} to calculate multiple indexes that need to be marked in $P.mark32$. A bitwise OR operation is performed on 1 and the bits referenced by those indexes in $P.mark32$, and packet P is forwarded to the next router. This process repeats until the packet P reaches its destination.

Algorithm 1. Packet marking algorithm

   Input : A Packet header P

1 **if** P comes from local network **then**
2     $P.mark32 = 0$
3     $P.ttl = 255$
4 **end**
5 $P.mark[h(IP_{R_i})\%MSM]\|\|1$
6 $P.ttl = P.ttl - 1$
7 Forward this packet to the next router

Figure 2 shows an example in which five senders send packets through eight routers to the same destination. The IP hash values for routers R_1 through R_8 are

5, 1, 3, 3, 7, 1, 5, and 6, respectively. From Fig. 2, we see that attack packet sent by Attacker 1 was passed to the Internet via router R_1 and traversed routers R_3 and R_6 to reach its final destination. Because this packet traversed three routers, its TTL value $P.ttl$ is 3 less than the maximum, or 252. The string in $P.mark32$, the packet marker field, is 10101000. Three bits were set to 1 to record that this packet has traversed three routers. Attacker 2's packet also traversed three routers, and its TTL value $P.ttl$ is also 3 less than the maximum, or 252. However, because the IP hash values of routers R_2 and R_6 are both 1, only the first and third bits were set to 1, and the string in this packet's $P.mark32$ is 10100000. Attacker 3's packet was passed to the Internet via router R_7 but then took the same path as attacker 2's packet to reach the destination. Thus, its TTL value is 1 less than attacker 2's packet, or 251. However, three bits were set to 1 in the packet marker field, and the string in its $P.mark32$ is 10101000. During packet marking, the router does not distinguish whether a packet is part of an attack. Thus, the target also receives legitimate packets. For example, in Fig. 2, the destination also received packets from Legitimate users 1 and 2 with $P.mark32$ strings of 10100100 and 10010000, respectively.

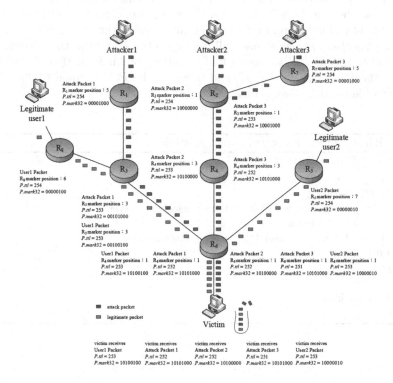

Fig. 2. An example of 3 attack and 2 legitimate packets forwarded to the same destination

When the target detects a successful denial of service attack from three attacking packets, the path reconstruction algorithm explained in the next section can be used to find the sources of these three attackers.

2.2 Path Reconstruction

When the victim detects an intrusion, the attack packet P is sent to the traceback server to find the source of the attack. The traceback server transmits the fields necessary for tracing the source, $P.mark32$ and $P.ttl$, to a router R_i that is one hop upstream from the victim for path reconstruction. As shown by the algorithm 2, after R_i receives $P.mark32$ and $P.ttl$, it uses its own IP address, IP_{R_i}, in a hash function to calculate its marker position in a BF. If R_i's marker position is unflagged (i.e., $P.mark32[h(IP_{R_i})] = 0$), then router R_i is not in the path of the attack packet P, and R_i no longer needs to assist with tracing the source of the attack. In contrast, if R_i's marker position is flagged (i.e., $P.mark32[h(IP_{R_i})] = 1$), then R_i transmits the BF that includes R_i's marker position to the traceback server. R_i also checks whether $P.ttl$ plus 1 is equal to the initialization value of 255; if so, then R_i is the boundary router for the attacker and the traceback is complete. If not, R_i transmits $P.mark32$ and $P.ttl$ to all other linked upstream routers to continue tracing the source of the attack. After the traceback server receives all attack packet BFs from the routers, the server integrates all BF values to find a router combination that completely matches the $P.mark32$ in the BF and in which the $P.ttl$ is equal to 255. This comprises the routing of an attack packet.

Algorithm 2. Path reconstruction algorithm

   Input : $P.mark32$, $P.ttl$

1   **if** $P.mark32[h(IP_{R_i})\%MSM] = 1$ **then**
2      $P.ttl = P.ttl + 1$
3   Send $((BF[h(IP_{R_i}\%MSM], P.ttl)$ to traceback server
4   **if** $P.ttl < 255$ **then**
5 | Send $P.mark32$ and $P.ttl$ to all upstream routers
6   **end**
7   **end**
8   **else**
9 | End trackback
10 **end**

---

3 Conclusion

Our proposed scheme, an improved packet traceback scheme with bloom filters, uses a 32-bit space in the packet header to record attack path information.

This enables single-packet tracebacks via packet marking and does not require additional storage space on routers for recording attack path data. Because no data is stored on routers, the router load is reduced compared to packet logging or hybrid IP traceback schemes. In addition, using the TTL field in packet headers decreases the false positive rate caused by marker field conflicts. We also proposed a dynamic marking space to further improve upon the traceback accuracy of the 32-bit marker field. Using 120-bit marking space results in a false positive rate of approximately 20%, which is 1/3 lower than the false positive rate observed in the scheme developed by Takurou et al.; using a 240-bit marking space results in a false positive rate of approximately 6%, which is five times lower than that observed in the scheme developed by Takurou et al. Furthermore, our proposed scheme has a 100% marker delivery ratio and only requires 16 packets to trace the source of an attack with 94% accuracy. Our proposed method successfully achieves the objectives of single packet traceback, zero router storage load, zero false negative rate, and low false positive rate.

Acknowledgements. The authors gratefully acknowledge the support from Ministry of Science and Technology under the grants MOST 105-2221-E-130-005 and 105-2221-E-033-051.

References

1. Aghaei-Foroushani, V., Zincir-Heywood, A.N.: Ip traceback through (authenticated) deterministic flow marking: an empirical evaluation. EURASIP J. Inf. Secur. **2013**(1), 5 (2013)
2. Cheng, L., Divakaran, D.M., Lim, W.Y., Thing, V.L.: Opportunistic piggyback marking for IP traceback. IEEE Trans. Inf. Forensics Secur. **11**(2), 273–288 (2016)
3. Cusack, B., Tian, Z., Kyaw, A.K.: Identifying DOS and DDOS attack origin: IP traceback methods comparison and evaluation for IoT. In: Mitton, N., Chaouchi, H., Noel, T., Watteyne, T., Gabillon, A., Capolsini, P. (eds.) InterIoT/SaSeIoT -2016. LNICST, vol. 190, pp. 127–138. Springer, Cham (2017). https://doi.org/10.1007/978-3-319-52727-7_14
4. Hilgenstieler, E., Duarte, E.P., Mansfield-Keeni, G., Shiratori, N.: Extensions to the source path isolation engine for precise and efficient log-based IP traceback. Comput. Secur. **29**(4), 383–392 (2010)
5. Hussain, A., Heidemann, J., Papadopoulos, C.: A framework for classifying denial of service attacks. In: Proceedings of the 2003 Conference on Applications, Technologies, Architectures, and Protocols for Computer Communications, pp. 99–110. ACM (2003)
6. John, W., Tafvelin, S.: Analysis of internet backbone traffic and header anomalies observed. In: Proceedings of the 7th ACM SIGCOMM Conference on Internet Measurement, pp. 111–116. ACM (2007)
7. Prakash, P.B., Krishna, E.P.: Achieving high accuracy in an attack-path reconstruction in marking on demand scheme. i-Manager's J. Inf. Technol. **5**(3), 24 (2016)
8. Prasad, K.M., Reddy, A.R.M., Rao, K.V.: DoS and DDoS attacks: defense, detection and traceback mechanisms-a survey. Global J. Comput. Sci. Technol. **14**(7) (2014)

9. Savage, S., Wetherall, D., Karlin, A., Anderson, T.: Network support for IP trace-back. IEEE/ACM Trans. Netw. **9**(3), 226–237 (2001)
10. Stoica, I., Zhang, H.: Providing guaranteed services without per flow management, vol. 29. ACM (1999)
11. Tian, H., Bi, J., Xiao, P.: A flow-based traceback scheme on an as-level overlay network. In: 2012 32nd International Conference on Distributed Computing Systems Workshops (ICDCSW), pp. 559–564. IEEE (2012)
12. UCSD, T.C.: The caida ucsd macroscopic skitter topology dataset. http://www.caida.org/tools/measurements/skitter
13. Yang, M.H.: Hybrid single-packet IP traceback with low storage and high accuracy. Sci. World J. **2014** (2014)
14. Yang, M.H., Yang, M.C., Luo, J.N., Hsu, W.C.: High accuracy and low storage hybrid IP traceback. In: 2014 International Conference on Computer, Information and Telecommunication Systems (CITS), pp. 1–5. IEEE (2014)
15. Zhang, L., Guan, Y.: Topo: a topology-aware single packet attack traceback scheme. In: Securecomm and Workshops, pp. 1–10. IEEE (2006)

Special Session: Wearable Technology and Applications (WTAA 2017)

Using Nonverbal Information
for Conversation Partners Inference
by Wearable Devices

Deeporn Mungtavesinsuk[1], Yan-Ann Chen[2(✉)], Cheng-Wei Wu[1], Ensa Bajo[1], Hsin-Wei Kao[1], and Yu-Chee Tseng[1]

[1] Department of Computer Science, National Chiao Tung University,
Hsinchu, Taiwan
{deeporn,cww0403}@nctu.edu.tw, bajoensa@gmail.com, scott02308@gmail.com,
yctseng@cs.nctu.edu.tw
[2] Department of Computer Science and Engineering, Yuan Ze University,
Taoyuan City, Taiwan
chenya@saturn.yzu.edu.tw

Abstract. In this paper, we propose a framework called conversational partner inference using nonverbal information (abbreviated as CFN). We use the wrist-based wearable device that has an accelerometer sensor to detect the user's hand movement. Besides, we propose three different methods, named *leading CFN*, *trainling CFN* and *leading-trailing CFN*, to integrate the detected movement behaviors with the sound data sensed by microphones to effectively infer conservational partners. In experiments, we collect real data to evaluate the proposed framework. The experimental results show that the accuracy of *leading CFN* is better than *trailing CFN* and *leading-trailing CFN*. Moreover, our approach shows higher accuracy than the state-of-the-art approach for conversational partner inference.

Keywords: Conversational partner inference
Nonverbal information · Social interaction analysis · Wearable devices

1 Introduction

Smartphone has become an essential tools for many people's daily life. With rapid advancement of smartphones, more and more types of sensors are embedded in smartphones. Among these sensors, the microphone is a common sensor that can be used to sense the sound around the user. Recently, various audio related applications on smartphones for inferring personal contexts have been proposed [1–4]. They use the sensed sound by smartphones to recognize ambient sounds [3], nearby speakers [1], the stress level of the user [2], and even the user's indoor location [4]. However, these applications mainly focus on individual users' contexts rather than conversation groups' contexts. Here are some of the recent studies that mainly focus on cell phone-based conversation. Socio-Phone is a mobile platform that proposed by [5] for conversational monitoring.

© ICST Institute for Computer Sciences, Social Informatics and Telecommunications Engineering 2018
Y.-B. Lin et al. (Eds.): IoTaaS 2017, LNICST 246, pp. 187–193, 2018.
https://doi.org/10.1007/978-3-030-00410-1_22

The main idea of their method is to use the volume of the phone to calculate and identify the speaker. However, this method assumes that the conversation group is known and does not propose a method to identify which speakers belong to the same conversation group. Socialweaver [6] uses a clustering-based approach to identify which speakers belong to the same conversation group by using a clustering algorithm. However, to achieve a considerable accuracy, it has to take approximately up to thirty minutes of conversation data, which requires a very high time cost. Afterward, a low time cost approach [7] for conversation partner inference is proposed. This approach uses the smartphone to detect the segments of speech from the speaker (also known as speaker turns [7]), and then uses associations between speaker turns of different speakers to infer conversational partners. The experimental results show that the approach has a good recognition rate. Although the above methods are committed to the study of conversation partner inference, they do not consider the speaker's body language to further enhance the inference performance. In view of this, we address the above research issue by proposing a new framework called *conversational partner inference using nonverbal information (CFN)*. In the proposed framework, we take the wrist-wearable device into consideration for capturing the acceleration information about the user's hand movements (called moving turns). We further incorporate moving turns and speaker turns into *action turns* for inferring conversational partners in a more effective manner. Based on the way of action turn composition, we propose three methods, namely *leading CFN*, *trailing CFN*, and *leading-trailing CFN*. Extensive experimental results show that the accuracy of *leading CFN* is better than *trailing* and *leading-trailing* ones. Moreover, the results show that the accuracy is approximately 2% to 6% higher than the current best approach [7].

2   Related Work

Several studies [5,8–11] have been conducted on developing novel applications for human's social interactions. Reference [11] designs an interesting social application called E-SmallTalker on mobile platform. It can efficiently compare the common interests and friends of two conversational partners and use such information to recommend users' some chat topics to begin a conversation. Reference [10] designs a wrist-based wearable device to detect the handshake behavior of two users. If a handshake behavior is detected by the developed system, the users' mobile devices will automatically exchange e-mail addresses and social network accounts, which avoids the inconvenience caused by the exchange of traditional business cards. Reference [9] proposes an application called High5, which uses wrist-based wearable devices to detect the clapping behavior between two or more people, which can be used to increase the times of interactions between employees in a company. Reference [12] uses a wearable device attached to the thigh of the user to analyze the movement direction and acceleration of the user, which allows to detect which users belong to which moving groups. Reference [8] analyzes human's nonverbal behaviors to understand the relationships of social interactions between people. Sociophone [5] is a an interaction monitoring platform, which uses the sound sensed by the microphone of the smartphone to know the identity of the speakers. It can be used to automatically record the user's daily conversation with others.

3   Conversation Partners Analysis

Figure 1 shows the workflow of our conversation inference mechanism. The smartphones of users form a proximity group via short-range communication. They continuously collect verbal information by recognizing their owners' speaker turns and emotions and nonverbal information from wearable sensors by understanding users' hand moving periods. After sharing information among these phones, they analyze self-conversational relationship with the others by investigating the fused data of verbal and nonverbal information. Figure 2 presents the proposed system architecture of this wearable sensing system for conversation partner inference. We then introduce components of the system architecture as follows.

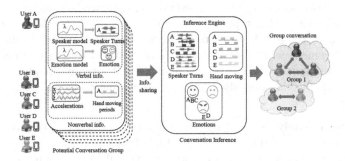

Fig. 1. The workflow of our analysis model.

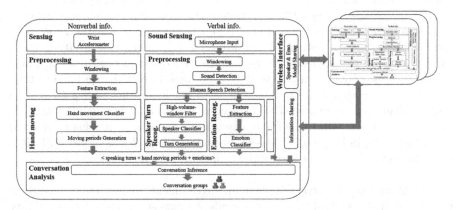

Fig. 2. The system architecture

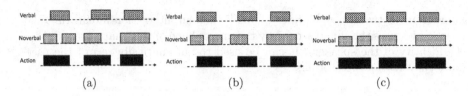

Fig. 3. Examples of (a) leading, (b) trailing, and (c) leading-trailing action turn composition.

Sensing, Processing, and Recognition Classifier. Here, we explain how to extract verbal and nonverbal information by this wearable sensing system. For verbal information, we follow the procedures of sensing, processing, and recognition in reference [7]. We then can obtain speaker turns and emotion of a user by analyzing user's voice in a conversation. For nonverbal information, we investigate user's hand movement during a conversation by analyzing accelerations from the sensor worn on the user's wrist. In the sensing component, thus, we simply measure wrist acceleration by a 3-axis accelerometer. Then, in the preprocessing component, we compute the total acceleration of 3-axis accelerations and extract 4 statistical features, *mean crossing rate, variance, average absolute deviation*, and *kurtosis*, within a period of window time. Next, the hand movement classifier utilizes these 4 features to build a recognition model to distinguish the hand movement which is caused by hand-gestures during a conversation. Finally, the component of conversation analysis will acquire a sequence of hand movement and speaking periods where we call moving turns and speaker turns, respectively.

Conversation Analysis. Through the wireless interface, one smartphone can acquire speaker turns and moving turns of nearby users. The conversation analysis component exploits these verbal and nonverbal information to infer conversation groups. The problem is how to do the data fusion with verbal and nonverbal information. Here, we define 3 methods, namely *leading CFN, trailing CFN*, and *leading-trailing CFN*, to compose the fused data called *action turns*. An action turn represents the period of time where a user dominates a conversation for interacting with others. The *leading CFN* is to model a situation where a speaker's hand-gesture leads a speaking sentence during a conversation. Thus, it composes an action turn by merging a speaker turn with the moving turn acted before it as shown in Fig. 3(a). On the other hand, the *trailing CFN* is to model a situation where a speaker's speaking sentence leads a hand-gesture. It composes an action turn by merging a speaker turn with the moving turn acted after it as shown in Fig. 3(b). Whereas, *leading-trailing CFN* is model both situations by merging a speaker turn with the moving turn acted around it as shown in Fig. 3(c).

To infer the group conversations in an environment, we analyze the relations among action turns of all the users. We adopt pairwise conversation possibility *Dialog Confidence(DC)* in [7] where we have a higher confidence that two people

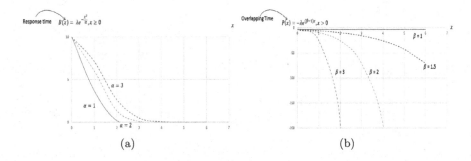

Fig. 4. (a) Bonus function (b) Penalty function.

have a conversation if their action turns are nearly close and hardly overlapping. We thus define two functions to evaluate the gap and overlapping of two adjacent turns. Given a gap x between one action turn of one user and that of the other user, the bonus function shown in Fig. 4(a) is defined as

$$f_b(x) = \lambda_1 e^{-\frac{x^2}{\alpha}} , \qquad (1)$$

where λ_1 and α are predefined constants to control the amplitude and the slope of the curve. The value $f_b(x)$ is inversely proportional to the gap x. On the contrary, given two turns with an overlapping period x, the penalty function shown in Fig. 4(b) is defined as

$$f_p(x) = -\lambda_2 e^{(\beta-1)x} , \qquad (2)$$

where λ_2 and β are predefined constants to control the amplitude and the slope of the curve.

Assume that there are users i and user j. we compute the DC by the following equation:

$$D_{i,j} = \frac{\sum\limits_{x_b \in B^{i,j}} f_b(x_b) + \sum\limits_{x_p \in P^{i,j}} f_p(x_p)}{|B^{i,j}| + |P^{i,j}|} , \qquad (3)$$

where $B^{i,j}$ and $P^{i,j}$ are sets of bonus and penalty cases between user i and j's actions turns. If the dialog confidence $D_{i,j}$ is above a threshold Δ_D, we determine that users i and j have a conversation in this interval. Therefore, we can infer that user i and j is in the same conversation group. Once we apply this DC computation for all 2-combinations of users in this environment, we will know the conversation partners of each user.

4   Performance Evaluation

In this section, we evaluate the performance of the conversation inference considering nonverbal information. We conduct experiments of having a conversation with 2 or 3 speakers while recording each speaker's voice and wrist acceleration.

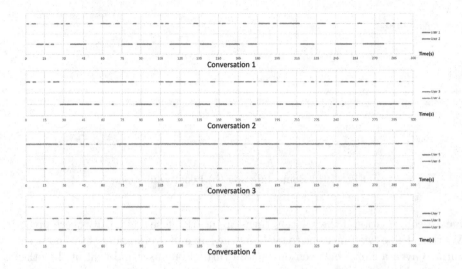

Fig. 5. Experiments of real-life conversations.

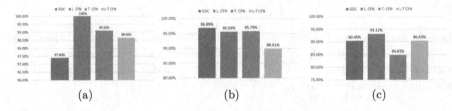

Fig. 6. Performance evaluation of scenario (a) 1, (b) 2, and (c) 3.

Figure 5 shows the domination of each speaker in the conversations where these turns are manually labelled. We define 3 scenarios of simulating concurrent group conversations in an environment from these conversation records. The scenario 1 simulates 2 concurrent group conversations by mixing the conversation 1 and 2; The scenario 2 simulates 3 concurrent group conversations by mixing the conversations 1, 2, and 3, each group has 2 speakers; Then, the scenario 3 simulates concurrent 2-speaker and 3-speaker conversation groups. Figure 6 shows performance of conversation inference while considering hand-gesture information. The performance matric is the accuracy of conversation inference which is computed by $\frac{TP+TN}{TP+FP+FN+TN}$. The TP, TN, FP, and FN represents the numbers of true positive, true negative, false positive, and false negative cases of conversation inference, respectively. The *leading CFN* can achieve better performance than the others. The reason is that the speaker may have some gestures before speaking and these gestures may enhance the continuity of action turns. However, the gesture behind a sentence may decrease the performance by overlapping with others' gesture or speaking.

5   Conclusion and Future Works

In this work, we propose a mechanism to infer conversation partner using non-verbal information with the assistance of wearable devices. We utilize wrist accelerometer to detect the movement of hand-gestures in a conversation. We observe the correlation of action turns, which are composed by verbal and non-verbal information, among speakers to enhance the performance of *Dialog Confidence* Finally, we show that the leading method of action turn composition can have 2% to 6% improvement of conversation inference.

References

1. Lu, H., Bernheim Brush, A.J., Priyantha, B., Karlson, A.K., Liu, J.: SpeakerSense: energy efficient unobtrusive speaker identification on mobile phones. In: Lyons, K., Hightower, J., Huang, E.M. (eds.) Pervasive 2011. LNCS, vol. 6696, pp. 188–205. Springer, Heidelberg (2011). https://doi.org/10.1007/978-3-642-21726-5_12
2. Lu, H., et al.: Stresssense: Detecting stress in unconstrained acoustic environments using smartphones. In: Proceedings of ACM International Conference on Ubiquitous Computing (UbiComp) (2012)
3. Rossi, M., Feese, S., Amft, O., Braune, N., Martis, S., Troster, G.: Ambientsense: a real-time ambient sound recognition system for smartphones (2013)
4. Tarzia, S.P., Dinda, P.A., Dick, R.P., Memik, G.: Indoor localization without infrastructure using the acoustic background spectrum. In: Proceedings of International Conference on Mobile Systems, Applications, and Services (MobiSys) (2011)
5. Lee, Y., et al.: Sociophone: everyday face-to-face interaction monitoring platform using multi-phone sensor fusion. In: Proceedings of International Conference on Mobile Systems, Applications, and Services (MobiSys) (2013)
6. Luo, C., Chan, M.C.: Socialweaver: collaborative inference of human conversation networks using smartphones. In: Proceedings of ACM Conference on Embedded Networked Sensor Systems (SenSys) (2013)
7. Chen, Y.A., Chen, J., Tseng, Y.C.: Inference of conversation partners by cooperative acoustic sensing in smartphone networks. IEEE Trans. Mob. Comput. 15(6), 1387–1400 (2016)
8. Basu, S.: Social signal processing: understanding social interactions through nonverbal behavior analysis. In: Proceedings of IEEE Conference on Computer Vision and Pattern Recognition Workshops (2009)
9. Kim, Y., et al.: High5: promoting interpersonal hand-to-hand touch for vibrant workplace with electrodermal sensor watches. In: Proceedings of ACM International Joint Conference on Pervasive and Ubiquitous Computing (UbiComp) (2014)
10. Wu, F.J., Chu, F.I., Tseng, Y.C.: Cyber-physical handshake. In: Proceedings of ACM Special Interest Group on Data Communication (SIGCOMM) (2011)
11. Yang, Z., Zhang, B., Dai, J., Champion, A.C., Xuan, D., Li, D.: E-SmallTalker: a distributed mobile system for social networking in physical proximity. In: Proceedings of International Conference on Distributed Computing Systems (ICDCS) (2010)
12. Gordon, D., Wirz, M., Roggen, D., Tröster, G., Beigl, M.: Group affiliation detection using model divergence for wearable devices. In: Proceedings of International Symposium on Wearable Computers (ISWC) (2014)

Enabling Over-The-Air Provisioning for Wearable Devices

Wei-Han Chen, Fuchun Joseph Lin[⊠], and YaHua Lee

Department of Computer Science, National Chiao Tung University,
Hsinchu, Taiwan
{alwayschoco.cs04g, fjlin, yahua.cs05g}@nctu.edu.tw

Abstract. The Internet of Things (IoT) is growing rapidly with more and more devices connected to the Internet. Among IoT devices, wearable devices have become an important category due to their wide applicability. However, most of the wearable products are designed to provide fixed services; once they are deployed, their functionality is difficult to change. In this research we develop new technologies that would enable the OTA (Over-The-Air) provisioning over BLE for the wearable devices. We use the method of Interworking Proxy Application Entity (IPE) defined in oneM2M to enable the OTA provisioning. Our experimental results show that the IPE method is an effective mechanism to support the OTA provisioning for wearable devices.

Keywords: OTA provisioning · Wearable devices · oneM2M
BLE · IPE

1 Introduction

In the recent years, the Internet of Things (IoT) has been growing rapidly with a large number of devices connected to the Internet. The Gartner forecasts that 20.4 billion connected devices will be in use by 2020 [1]. Among these devices, wearable devices which can be worn on the human body takes a great portion and brings great convenience to people's life. They are adopted in many IoT application areas such as healthcare and smart home [2]. However, most of the wearable products are not programmable. Consequently, it is very difficult to upgrade or change their service functions once they are deployed.

Over-The-Air (OTA) provisioning describes the ability to update firmware or install new applications for mobile devices via wireless networks. To enable the OTA provisioning for the wearable devices, we need to take their limited capabilities such as storage and battery life into consideration [3]. Bluetooth Low Energy (BLE) is an emerging wireless standard suitable for wearable devices due to its features of low power consumption and low storage requirement [4, 5].

In this research, we enable the OTA application provisioning for BLE devices based on oneM2M Interworking Proxy Application Entity (IPE) [6, 7]. To evaluate the effectiveness, we adopt four criteria including power consumption, system performance, transmission efficiency and software complexity and take the application size as the parameter to evaluate its impact on the performance.

© ICST Institute for Computer Sciences, Social Informatics and Telecommunications Engineering 2018
Y.-B. Lin et al. (Eds.): IoTaaS 2017, LNICST 246, pp. 194–201, 2018.
https://doi.org/10.1007/978-3-030-00410-1_23

The rest of the paper is organized as follows: Sect. 2 gives some background knowledge of OTA provisioning, BLE protocols and oneM2M technologies. Section 3 introduces the related research works in OTA provisioning. Section 4 describes the tools, architecture design and implementation results. Section 5 explains the evaluation criteria and analysis results. Finally, in Sect. 6 we present our conclusion and future work.

2 Background

2.1 Over-The-Air Provisioning

OTA is a standard for transmitting application-related information to the devices wirelessly. As the smartphones provide more functionalities, OTA has been used to distribute the new applications to smartphones via cellular networks. Recently, with the growing of wireless sensor networks and IoT, OTA is being realized by using low power consumed protocols such as 802.15.4, Zigbee, and BLE.

2.2 Bluetooth Low Energy

BLE is part of the Bluetooth core specification 4.0 or later releases developed by the Bluetooth Special Interest Group (SIG). It is designed with low power consumption and low complexity suitable for constrained devices and IoT applications. Due to its low cost compared to other similar wireless technologies, it is rapidly and widely implemented in smartphones, wearable devices, sensors, and other devices.

2.3 oneM2M Technologies

The oneM2M is the global standard for M2M/IoT platforms. In addition to addressing the requirements for M2M Service Layer, it defines the architecture, protocols, APIs, interfaces and security for M2M/IoT services. In our research, we use an oneM2M-based platform, OpenMTC, developed by FOKUS [8] as our provisioning server that accepts users' requests and interacts with the BLE devices.

3 Related Work

Fjellheim [9] designed an adaptive platform to support customized application delivery via various protocols according to required metadata. They also implemented an adaptable Web server to support OTA over HTTP. Vo and Torabi [10] proposed a framework for OTA provider-initiated software update on mobile devices subscribed to the service. Ndie et al. [11] came up with a method of provisioning mobile applications via Bluetooth between two mobile devices. Though there are some interesting OTA provisioning ideas reported in these papers, few of them use BLE as the communication method. In addition, none of them are designed specifically for wearable devices or based on an IoT platform. Moreover, most of them require subscription to the providers. In our research, we propose OTA provisioning for the wearable devices over oneM2M and BLE that differs from existing works.

4   Architecture Design and Implementation

4.1   Tools for Architecture Design

- Nordic Device Firmware Update (DFU) Mechanism for nRF5 SDK v11.0.0

In order to support OTA provisioning, Nordic provides OTA DFU mechanisms in their Software Development Kit (SDK). The DFU Service exposes necessary information to perform provisioning for the devices. The high level architecture is depicted in Fig. 1 where two devices are required for its operations: (1) DFU Controller, which triggers the DFU procedure and transfers the application images, and (2) DFU Target on which a bootloader is needed to start the DFU mode, manage the DFU procedure and activate the new firmware.

- oneM2M Interworking Proxy Application Entity

The oneM2M defined IPE in TS-0001 [6] as the solution for interworking with non-oneM2M entities. Figure 2 shows that it is designed as an AE (Application Entity) that enables different level of interworking between non-oneM2M and oneM2M interfaces including protocol interworking, semantic information exchange and data sharing. For OTA provisioning, we use IPE to translate BLE protocol messages to oneM2M RESTful operations such as HTTP and to exchange the data models between BLE devices and oneM2M-based platforms.

4.2   Architecture Design of Over-The-Air Provisioning with IPE

In our research, we use nRF52 DK as our BLE device and a Raspberry Pi 3 model B running Linux-like Raspbian as our provisioning server. In addition, a CSR Bluetooth USB dongle adapter is installed in the Raspberry Pi 3 to enable BLE communications. Bluez [12] is installed to control the Bluetooth dongle adapter in the Raspberry Pi for supporting BLE layers and protocols on Raspbian. As OpenMTC Release 4 is implemented in Python while Bluez only provides APIs in C language, we have to adopt another open source, Bluepy [13], in order to use Python APIs for BLE communications on OpenMTC.

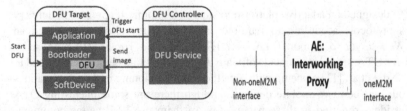

Fig. 1. Device Firmware Update architecture   **Fig. 2.** Interworking Proxy Application Entity

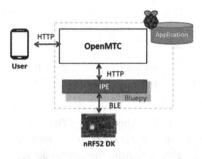

Fig. 3. System architecture

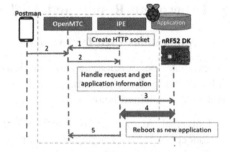

Fig. 4. Provisioning process

Our system architecture consists of four components as shown in Fig. 3.

1. OpenMTC: It is the provisioning server used to store the information of available applications and to forward the user's provisioning requests to the BLE device via IPE by subscription/notification mechanisms of oneM2M.
2. User: In our architecture, the user needs to send HTTP requests to retrieve the available application list and initiate application provisioning. We use Postman [14] to simulate the user's application for sending related HTTP requests.
3. BLE Device: This is nRF52 DK used as the provisioning target. The nRF52 DK is installed with s132 SoftDevice and the bootloader and is thus capable of supporting the DFU functionality.
4. IPE: Our IPE, which acts as the DFU controller and gateway application entity on the platform side, takes responsibility for interworking with the nRF52 DK and OpenMTC to achieve the provisioning functionality. It handles the HTTP requests from the platform, and manages the provisioning process with the BLE device.

4.3 Implementation of OTA Design

Figure 4 shows the step-by-step IPE provisioning process as follows.

1. First, we starts OpenMTC and IPE. The IPE will create a HTTP socket and subscribe to OpenMTC to receive the notification about the provisioning request.
2. When the user sends a provisioning request including the device address and the application to be provisioned, OpenMTC will notify IPE of the request. IPE then parses the request and gets the application path from the available application list.
3. Next, IPE uses APIs provided by Bluepy to connect to the nRF52 DK according to the device address in the request and triggers the DFU procedure.
4. IPE will carry out the DFU operations with nRF52 DK as defined in DFU Service by Nordic.
5. At the end of the process, nRF52 DK will reboot with the new application and IPE will create a resource in the platform to record the provisioning result.

Table 1. Sizes of applications.

Method/application	UART application	Proximity application	HRM application
IPE	26,566 bytes	35,040 bytes	23,180 bytes

5 Experiment Results and Analysis

5.1 Applications Used for Evaluation

To evaluate the effectiveness of our design of OTA provisioning, we create three different kinds of applications. Table 1 shows the sizes of these applications and each of them is explained below.

- Universal Asynchronous Receiver/Transmitter (UART) Application. The basic concept of UART is using one channel to transmit data and the other one to receive data between two devices. This application will receive data from the central device and print it on the monitor over serial connection on the nRF52 DK.
- Proximity Application. This application implements the Proximity Profile that alerts the user by the LEDs on the nRF52 DK when the connected device are too far apart. The blinking frequency will increase with the distance between the nRF52 DK and the central device connected.
- Heart Rate Measurement (HRM) Application. HRM is an implementation of the Heart Rate Service profile. When the notification is enabled, the simulation of heart rate value will be sent to the central device.

We need to integrate DFU Service into these applications, and propagate the BLE stack events to DFU Service. Besides, the applications have to support sharing bonding information which enables the device to advertise directly after entering the DFU mode.

5.2 Evaluation Criteria

Below we describe our evaluation criteria.

- Power Consumption. It is one of the critical issues in the design of wearable devices and their applications due to their inherent limit of battery-supplied power. As the nRF52 DK provides power measurement functionality, we can use the ampere-meter to directly monitor the current and derive power consumption during the DFU process.
- Transmission Efficiency. This is an important metrics to measure the efficiency of the connection method design for data transmission. We use Wireshark to capture the relevant packets and investigate the transmission time and average rate of application image transmission.
- System Performance. As the number of connected devices keeps growing, the system performance of the M2M platform becomes more and more important. We investigate the CPU utilization of the oneM2M platform while executing the application provisioning with the device. To profile our implementations more precisely, we adopt psutil, a Python program profiling tool, into our implementations instead of using the traditional tools in Linux environment (e.g. ps, top).
- Design Complexity. Finally, we analyze the design and implementation complexity of our architecture based on the system requirements including protocol support, prerequisite knowledge, device and firmware design etc.

5.3   Experiment Results and Analysis

The experiment environment is set up as follows. First, we use OpenMTC as our oneM2M platform and install it on a Raspberry Pi 3 Model B. For wearable devices, we adopt the nRF52 DK with s132 SDK and bootloader as the target device. Since the connection intervals of BLE connections will affect the performances of power consumption and transmission efficiency, we set the minimum as 7.5 ms and the maximum as 30 ms to reduce this influence. Below we report the results for each evaluation criteria.

- Power Consumption. The current of the nRF52 DK changes according to different operations in the DFU procedure. Consequently, we record all the values for analysis. Take the provisioning UART application for example (See Fig. 5), the average current is between 1 and 1.5 mA during the file transmission and the curve is stable. The analyses of provisioning three applications indicate that the power consumption will be affected by the application size (See Tables 2 and 3).
- Transmission Efficiency. For the transmission efficiency, we use Wireshark to catch the packet information during the provisioning process. The analysis results are shown in Table 3. Due to the limited payload of BLE, each packet can contain only 20 bytes of data at most. However, we can modify the connection intervals to achieve high throughput. In our experiment, the Proximity application has the largest packet which is about 35000 bytes but it only takes 20 s to transmit, which is acceptable for the users.
- System Performance. The platform CPU utilization of provisioning three applications respectively are shown in Fig. 6. We have marked the important timestamps for each, such as managing HTTP request, establishing connection with the device and transmitting the application images. We found that if the application size is bigger, then it will consume more CPU resource during the transmission procedure.

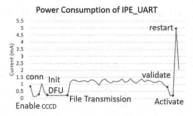

Fig. 5. Power consumption results of UART application

Table 2. Analysis results of power consumption.

	UART	Proximity	HRM
Image transmission (mA)	18.25	21.55	13.92
Whole procedure (mA)	23.71	26.07	18.32

Table 3. Analysis results of transmission efficiency.

	UART	Proximity	HRM
Process time (s)	25.89	34.10	20.72
Image transmission (s)	14.82	20.19	13.17
Average rate (bytes/s)	1792.67	1735.57	1760.24

- Design Complexity. The analysis results of the proposed method are shown in Table 4. The results show that our method is easy for development because we don't need to implement the whole system by ourselves like other OTA systems. In addition, it can be adopted for any BLE devices equipped with Nordic nRF51 SoC and later models.

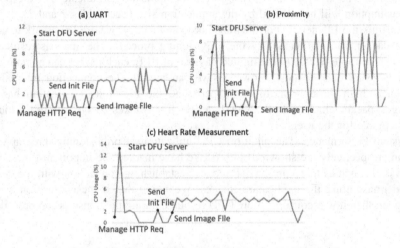

Fig. 6. Analysis results of system performance (CPU utilization)

Table 4. Design complexity analysis results

Items	IPE method
Support protocol stack	BLE 4.0 and above
Prerequisite knowledge	BLE, Nordic DFU Mechanism, oneM2M
Device requirement	Nordic nRF51 DK and above (nRF52 here)
Firmware requirement	nRF51/nRF5 SDK, SoftDevice + Bootloader
Enable OTA in application	Include DFU Module and Device Manager Library
Programing in oneM2M platform	IPE
Programming language	Python + ARM C
Third-party package/library	Bluez, Bluepy, OpenMTC

6   Conclusion and Future Work

This research proposed the architecture of the OTA application provisioning over BLE for the wearable devices based on oneM2M IPE. We have shown that our architecture is a flexible and effective method for OTA provisioning. With our architecture, the users can upgrade their wearable devices wirelessly by sending HTTP requests via the smartphones or the computers.

As the number of devices grows rapidly, IPv6 is an ideal protocol with more available addresses and stateless address auto-configuration tools for IoT network applications. 6LoWPAN over BLE recently defined by IETF describes the details of IPv6 over BLE links. In our future work, we plan to enable OTA provisioning via 6LoWPAN over BLE and compare it with the IPE method.

Acknowledgment. The research in this paper is funded by Ministry of Science and Technology (MOST) of Taiwan Government under Project Number MOST 105-2218-E-009-004.

References

1. Gartner: 8.4 billion Connected "Things" Will be Use in 2017, Up 31 Percent from 2016, 7 February 2017. http://www.gartner.com/newsroom/id/3598917
2. Lee, S.Y.: Situation Awareness in a smart home environment. In: IEEE 3rd World Forum on Internet of Things, pp. 678–683 (2016)
3. Patel, M., Wang, J.: Applications, challenges, and prospective in emerging body area networking technologies. IEEE Wirel. Commun. **2010**(17), 80–88 (2010)
4. Dementyev, A., Hodges, S., Taylor, S., Smith, J.: Power consumption analysis of Bluetooth Low Energy, Zigbee and ANT sensor nodes in a cyclic sleep scenario. IEEE Int. Wirel. Symp. **2013**, 1–4 (2013)
5. Gomez, C., Oller, J., Paradells, J.: Overview and evaluation of bluetooth low energy: an emerging low-power wireless technology. Sensors **12**(9), 11734 (2012)
6. oneM2M: TS 0001 v2.10.0, Functional Architecture
7. Ting, Y.Y.: A Comparison and Evaluation of Different BLE Connection Methods for Wearable Devices. National Chiao Tung University, Hsinchu (2016)
8. Fraunhofer Fokus: OpenMTC. http://www.open-mtc.org
9. Fhellheim, T.: Over-the-air deployment of application in multi-platform environments. In: Australian Software Engineering Conference (2006)
10. Vo, C.C., Torabi, T.: A framework for over the air provider-initiated software deployment on mobile devices. In: 19th Australian Software Engineering Conference, pp. 633–638 (2008)
11. Ndie, T.D., Tangha, C., Sangbong, T., Kufor, A.F.: Mobile application provisioning using Bluetooth wireless technology. J. Softw. Eng. Appl. **4**, 95–105 (2011)
12. Bluez. http://www.bluez.org
13. Bluepy. https://github.com/IanHarvey/bluepy
14. Postman. https://www.getpostman.com

Multiple User Activities Recognition in Smart Home

YaHua Lee, Fuchun Joseph Lin[✉], and Wei-Han Chen

Department of Computer Science,
National Chiao Tung University, Hsinchu, Taiwan
{yahua.cs05g, fjlin, alwayschocol213}@g2.nctu.edu.tw

Abstract. In this paper, we investigate the problem of recognizing multiuser activities using wearable devices in a home environment. Our research objective is to provide situation awareness so that a smart home can respond to the needs of its residents based on the accurate detection of their activities. In this research, we compare applying artificial neural network, decision tree and simple logistic regression for model construction and activity detection. Moreover, we also evaluate different architectural alternatives of our smart home system in order to discover the best system configuration. Our unique contribution lies on the low cost of the proposed system design.

Keywords: Wearable device · Internet of Things · Multiple user activities
Artificial neural network · Decision tree · Simple logistic regression

1 Introduction

With proliferation of the IoT technology, our lives are now closely related to smart devices. Many of these devices such as smart phones and wearable devices greatly improve the quality of our life. In particular, wearable devices are becoming more and more ubiquitous. The advances of wearable sensors and wireless networks enable the recognition of human activities based on the continuous readings from various sensors.

Our research objective is to exercise better control in a smart home environment by recognizing multiple user activities based only on data from BLE wearable sensors. We assume these multiple user activities occur in a living room of the smart home environment where the user may watch TV, read newspaper, take a nap on the sofa and do exercising.

We have developed a prototype system based on our research results. In our system, each user is only required to wear a wearable device equipped with accelerometer and gyroscope on his/her waist for activity detection. This wearable device will collect the data from the accelerometer and gyroscope and transmit the data collected to our system via a BLE-paired smartphone. Our system will then derive situation awareness in a living room environment by consolidating multiple users' activities thus recognized. To evaluate various design options for our prototype system, four different activity recognition methods and three different architectural configurations are explored in our experiments.

The rest of the paper is organized as follows: Sect. 2 surveys related work for activity recognition algorithms. Section 3 introduces our system architecture including

© ICST Institute for Computer Sciences, Social Informatics and Telecommunications Engineering 2018
Y.-B. Lin et al. (Eds.): IoTaaS 2017, LNICST 246, pp. 202–209, 2018.
https://doi.org/10.1007/978-3-030-00410-1_24

both its hardware and software components. Sections 4 and 5 respectively present our experimental results under different detection methods and architectural configurations. Finally, in Sect. 6 we provide our conclusion and future work.

2 Related Work

To accomplish activity recognition, we adopted several commonly used methods including simple logistic, artificial neural network (ANN) and C4.5 decision tree methods.

- Simple Logistic concerns two-dimensional sample points with one independent variable and one dependent variable (conventionally, the x and y coordinates in a Cartesian coordinate system) and finds a linear function (a non-vertical straight line) that, as accurately as possible, predicts the dependent variable values as a function of the independent variables [1, 2].
- Artificial Neural Network is based on a large collection of neural units, loosely modeling the way a biological brain solves problems with large clusters of biological neurons connected by axons [3, 4].
- C4.5 is an algorithm used to generate a decision tree [5]. This process can be repeated on each derived subset in a recursive manner called recursive partitioning. The attribute with the highest normalized information gain is chosen to make the decision.

Our previous research proposed several methods for the single user activity recognition based on the wearable device [6] including methods of decision tree, hidden Markov model and Viterbi algorithm. These methods also used the assistance of location data derived from Beacons. Our previous research also compared several different architectural configurations for performance evaluation. However, in order to realize a smart home environment, the previous effort on the single user activity recognition is not enough.

Consequently, there have been research efforts in multiple user activity recognition. For example, Rong et al. [7] defined the "combined label states" during model construction with the help of data association. Liang et al. [8] developed a multi-modal, wearable sensor platform to collect sensor data from multiple users, then used Coupled Hidden Markov Model (CHMM) and Factorial Conditional Random Field (FCRF) to model interacting processes in a sensor-based, multiuser scenario. Markus et al. [9] used the ARAS dataset which is a real-world multi-resident dataset stemming from two houses in order to evaluate the proposed algorithm.

In addition to related work mentioned above, we also surveyed other research efforts in activity identification. Overall, the accuracy of activity recognition reported so far is about 83%.

3 System Architecture and Its Components

We explain sensors, processing hardware and mining tools required by our system in the following.

A. Wearable Device

We used a wearable device "Koala" designed by our project team to construct our system. Koala is equipped with two sensors: a 3-axis accelerometer and a 3-axis gyroscope. It uses Bluetooth Low Energy (BLE) as the wireless communication protocol. The specification of Koala is shown in Fig. 1.

The smart phone can establish connection with Koala and receive approximately 30 sets of acceleration and gyroscope data per second. We set the window size used for activity recognition at 60 sets of data and the window movement at every 15 sets of data due to the frequency of motion data.

Whenever the window is full, the system will execute the activity recognition algorithm to identify the user's current activity, then move the window to collect the next 15 sets of motion data. Under this experiment, Koala is worn by a user at his/her waist as depicted in Fig. 2.

B. Smartphone

In our system, the smartphone acts as a gateway between Koala and the backend server. We used a Samsung Note 3 with Android 5.0 as the gateway. It has an Octa-core CPU (4 × 1.9 GHz Cortex-A15 & 4 × 1.3 GHz Cortex-A7) and 3 GB of RAM. Samsung Note 3 uses BLE to communicate with Koala and Wi-Fi to communicate with the M2M server such as Python or oneM2M server. Sensors on the phone include Compass Magnetometer, Proximity sensor, Accelerometer, Ambient light sensor, Gyroscope and Barometer.

C. Backend Server

Both Python and oneM2M servers reside in a Raspberry Pi 3 running Raspbian with 1.2 GHz 64-bit quad-core ARMv8 CPU and 1 GB RAM. We developed the former from scratch while adopted OpenMTC from FOKUS for the latter.

D. Smart Home

We use Philips Hue [10] smart lights as the representative appliances in our smart home environment. As depicted in Fig. 3, the M2M server such as Python Server can send RESTful control signals to a Hue bridge in order to control a Hue bulb through ZigBee.

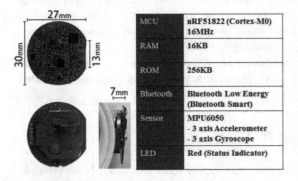

Fig. 1. Koala hardware and specification   **Fig. 2.** Koala worn on the waist

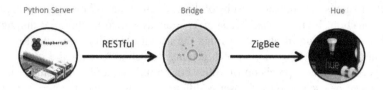

Python Server   Bridge   Hue

RESTful   ZigBee

Fig. 3. Hue control flow with Python server

E. Mining Tool

We utilized Weka (Waikato Environment for Knowledge Analysis) as our data mining and machine learning software. Weka supports many machine learning algorithms including artificial neural network, decision tree and simple logistic regression [11].

4   Experimental Results Under Different Detection Methods

We compare the performance of applying artificial neural network, decision tree and simple logistic regression for model construction and activity detection.

After collecting the input data from 10 people, we analyzed 17580 sets of data and derived 293 features based on a window size of 60. These features are used to train and construct the models for activity detection. The IPO diagram is shown in Fig. 4. The dataset was collected from Koala, then via feature extraction was further processed into mean, maximum, minimum and standard deviation for use in activity recognition.

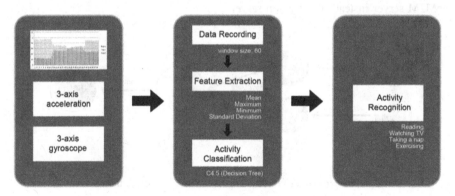

Fig. 4. Input-Process-Output (IPO) diagram

Table 1. Precision results of different algorithms

	Proportion of datasets	Simple logistic	Artificial neural network	Decision tree
Reading	0.300	0.667	0.798	0.944
Watching TV	0.283	0.696	0.871	0.928
Taking a nap	0.185	0.964	0.964	0.981
Exercising	0.232	1.000	1.000	1.000
Weighted avg.		0.807	0.896	0.959

Table 1 shows the precision results of three different algorithms we have applied in activity detection. It shows that Decision Tree always performs the best among three algorithms. In addition, it also shows that the activity "reading" gets the lowest precision due to its confusing motion with activity "watching", while the activity "exercising" gets the highest precision of 100% due to its unique distinguishable features. Since the size of each activity dataset is different, the weighted average is calculated according to the proportional size of each collected activity dataset. Overall, all algorithms could achieve at least 80% of the weighted average precision.

5 Experimental Results Under Different Architectural Configurations

We also evaluate four different architectural alternatives of the system design in order to find out the best system configuration that includes wearable devices, smartphone gateway and backend server.

These four system architectural alternatives are depicted in Figs. 5 and 6. Their differences lie in where the feature processing and activity detection procedures are carried out and what server is used to process the conflict resolution algorithms. The backend is a Python server in both Alternatives 1 and 2; in Alternative 1, the smartphone won't do feature processing but just relay the raw data to the server; on the other hand, in Alternative 2 feature processing is done on the smartphone. Likewise, these are also the differences between alternatives 3 and 4 except now the server is an oneM2M server instead of a Python server.

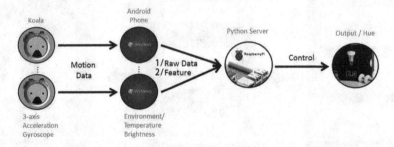

Fig. 5. System architectural alternatives 1 and 2 with Python server

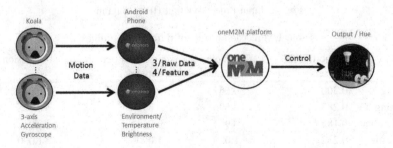

Fig. 6. System architectural alternatives 3 and 4 with oneM2M Server

Alternative 1. No processing by smart phone with Python server as backend
In our first architecture, we send the raw data from the smart phone to the Python server. This means that the Python server will do all the processing including extracting features from these 3-axis acceleration and gyroscope data and carrying out the activity detection and the conflict resolution algorithm.

Alternative 2. Feature processing by smartphone with Python server as backend
In the second architecture, the smartphone will perform feature extraction on the raw data collected from the wearable device with a frequency of once every 2–3 s. The extracted features then will be sent to the Python server for activity recognition and conflict resolution.

Alternative 3. No processing by smartphone with oneM2M server as backend
In the third architecture, we replace the Python server with an oneM2M server. This means the communications between the smart phone and the oneM2M server will follow the oneM2M RESTful standards to post and get the data to and from the server. Feature processing, activity detection and conflict resolution will all be performed on the oneM2M server.

Alternative 4. Feature processing by smartphone with oneM2M server as backend
In the fourth architecture, feature processing will be done in the smart phone. The oneM2M platform only needs to store the features from the RESTful posts and carry out both activity detection and conflict resolution algorithms based on the received features.

To discover which architecture can perform the best, these four architectural alternatives are evaluated based on a set of metrics including memory usage, processing time and CPU utilization.

- **Memory Usage**
The measurement results of memory usage for four architectural alternatives are shown in Fig. 7. Both architectures based on Python server consume a similar size of memory at 1%. On the other hand, the two based on oneM2M demands much more memory resource, especially the architecture starting from raw data; it has 2.8% of memory usage as compared to 1%.

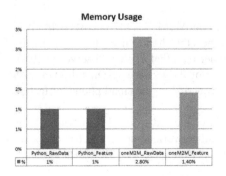

Fig. 7. Memory usage percentage

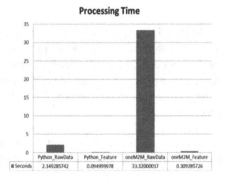

Fig. 8. Processing time result

- **Processing Time**

The processing time results are shown in Fig. 8. It indicates that both architectures starting from raw data will take more processing time than the others starting from feature data. We can reach around 22 times faster in the case of Python server and 107 times faster in the case of oneM2M server. On the other hand, between the Python server and the oneM2M server the former can achieve 3 times faster than the latter; especially in the case of the server starting from raw data, the Python server can obtain 15.5 times faster than the oneM2M server.

- **CPU Utilization**

The CPU utilization is affected by the efficiency of both architecture and algorithm. Here we focus only on the perspective of architecture so all our experiments are based on Decision Tree algorithms. Figure 9 illustrates the CPU utilization results of four architectural alternatives. It indicates the same rising and falling trend in both Python Raw Data and Python Feature systems with a higher CPU utilization by the former. Since processing feature from raw data takes 2 to 3 s, the highest point of CPU utilization appears on the basis of this frequency. It also shows that the oneM2M systems have to spend much more CPU cycles due to the effort on storing and getting data through the platform once every 2 to 3 s. The high rising points of CPU utilization follow this frequency very well. However, in the case of the oneM2M Raw Data system, the CPU utilization not only exhibits an irregular pattern but also stays very busy due to the processing of raw data.

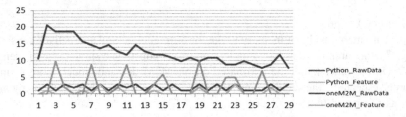

Fig. 9. CPU usage result of different architectures

In Raw Data systems, the CPU utilization of oneM2M (11.997 s) costs 6.48 times more than that of Python server (1.85 s). On the other hand, in Feature systems the loading in oneM2M (2.51 s) is 5.12 times heavier than that of Python server (0.49 s). Also, it is worth noting that the CPU utilization of the Feature systems drops to 0% during a large portion of the time due to the load sharing by the smart phone for feature processing.

As there will be a large number of devices connected to the IoT networks, it is better that work load is distributed among different network components. Therefore, we believe that Feature systems will provide better performance than Raw data systems.

6 Conclusions and Future Work

In this research, we have developed a situation awareness system for smart home based on multiple user activities recognition with four different architectures. Our activity recognition is based on three Machine Learning (ML) algorithms: Simple Logistic, Artificial Neural Network and Decision Tree.

Among three ML algorithms, we conclude that the Decision Tree algorithm at up to 96% of accuracy is the best algorithm for activity recognition. Moreover, among four architectural alternatives, using Python Server with feature processing done on the smartphone will provide a better average performance than the others.

Our unique contribution lies on providing a low-cost solution to activity recognition based on a simple wearable device Koala and a smart phone. Via detecting multiple user activities at home, smart home can be enabled with situation awareness and provide a more convenient and comfortable living environment for home users through the control of lighting, temperature and music. In the future, we plan to address the scalability issues of python and oneM2M servers. We expect better scalability can be achieved by oneM2M server than by Python server when there are numerous devices.

Acknowledgment. The research in this paper is funded by Ministry of Science and Technology (MOST) of Taiwan Government under Project Number MOST 105-2218-E-009-004.

References

1. Friedman, J., Hastie, T., Tibshirani, R.: Additive logistic regression: a statistical view of boosting. Ann. Stat. **28**(2), 337–407 (2000)
2. Simple linear regression. https://en.wikipedia.org/wiki/Simple_linear_regression. Accessed Feb 2017
3. Bataineh, M.H.: Artificial neural network for studying human performance. MS (Master of Science) thesis, University of Iowa (2012)
4. Artificial neural network. https://en.wikipedia.org/wiki/C4.5_algorithm. Accessed Feb 2017
5. Decision Tree C4.5. https://en.wikipedia.org/wiki/C4.5_algorithm. Accessed Feb 2017
6. Lee, S.-Y., Lin, F.J.: Situation awareness in a smart home environment. In: IEEE WF-IoT 2016, Reston, Virginia, USA, 12/12-14/2016
7. Chen, R., Tong, Y.: A Two-stage method for solving multi-resident activity recognition in smart environments. College of Information Science and Technology, Dalian Maritime University, Dalian, China (2014)
8. Wanga, L., Tao, G., Tao, X., Chen, H., Jian, L.: Recognizing multi-user activities using wearable sensors in a smart home. Pervasive Mobile Comput. **7**, 287–298 (2011)
9. Prossegger, M., Bouchachia, A.: Multi-resident activity recognition using incremental decision trees. In: Bouchachia, A. (ed.) ICAIS 2014. LNCS (LNAI), vol. 8779, pp. 182–191. Springer, Cham (2014). https://doi.org/10.1007/978-3-319-11298-5_19
10. Hue, P.: Philips. http://www2.meethue.com/. Accessed Feb 2017
11. Weka (machine learning), January 2017. https://en.wikipedia.org/wiki/Weka_(machine_learning). Accessed Feb 2017

Special Session: Building Smart Machine Applications (BSMA 2017)

D2D-Based Resource Saving and Throughput Enhancement for Massive Smart Devices in LTE eMBMS

Jeng-Yueng Chen[1(✉)] and Yi-Ting Mai[2]

[1] Department of Information Networking Technology,
Hsiuping University of Science and Technology, Taichung, Taiwan
jychen@hust.edu.tw
[2] Department of Sport Management, National Taiwan University of Sport,
Taichung, Taiwan
wkb@ntupes.edu.tw

Abstract. With the development of Internet of Thing (IoT) technologies, more and more intelligent devices can detect many kinds of environmental conditions, and send collected data or alarm back to application system automatically. If those massive IoT devices are connected via LTE network and the system need to send instructions to those IoT devices, the amount of data transmission in LTE would be raised quickly. To reduce the transmission load, multicasting provided by LTE evolved Multimedia Broadcast Multicast Services (eMBMS) service is one of solutions. However, the eMBMS service is dominated by the device with lowest signaling quality resulting in poor efficiency. A Device-to-Device (D2D) based mechanism was proposed to improve transmission efficiency of eMBMS service in this paper. Simulation results have shown that the proposed D2D-based mechanism can reduce the number of allocated resource blocks.

Keywords: LTE · eMBMS · D2D

1 Introduction

Thanks to the development of wireless communicating technologies, mobile computing becomes more and more popular in recent years. People send messages or share information to each other through the Internet even if they are moving. With the development of Internet of Thing (IoT) technologies, many newly applications are developed and changing people's daily life. Traditional human-to-human (H2H) communications had been extended to a new era of machine-to-machine (M2M) style. In M2M, devices communicated with each other without human participated. The IoT devices such as smart meters, smart medical healthcare devices, earthquake monitoring systems, etc., are also M2M applications.

Long Term Evolution (LTE) is developed by the 3rd Generation Partnership Project (3GPP), it has been designed to support all IP packet-switching services and is competing access network technologies in the fourth generation of mobile phone mobile communication technology standards (4G) wireless networks with IEEE 802.16 Worldwide Interoperability for Microwave Access (WiMAX) [1, 2]. LTE not only can

© ICST Institute for Computer Sciences, Social Informatics and Telecommunications Engineering 2018
Y.-B. Lin et al. (Eds.): IoTaaS 2017, LNICST 246, pp. 213–220, 2018.
https://doi.org/10.1007/978-3-030-00410-1_25

offer traditional voice telephony service, but also can provide cost effective broadband communication services. 3GPP formally approves the LTE to be the standard technology for the wireless communication. Since LTE is defined and developed by telecom vendors and is backward compatible with previous cellular systems such as GSM/UMTS, this makes LTE deployment much easier than WiMAX.

The Service & Systems Aspects (SA) working group of 3GPP also develops a new M2M technology, called Machine Type Communications (MTC), which is operated without interactive with human and can transmit data directly to servers located in LTE core network [3]. LTE-enabled IoT devices is similar to MTC devices. They need access network service in order to send their collected data to management servers located in LTE core network. Thus, the communications between massive deployed IoT devices and server may cause the system load of LTE increased largely.

To reduce the transmission load, the LTE evolved Multimedia Broadcast Multicast Services (eMBMS) is developed to provide broadcast and multicast services [4]. However, there are two problems found in current LTE eMBMS mechanism. The first one is about resource allocation issue. Since LTE will allocate the whole resources to eMBMS, it may cause a waste of radio resource when lower traffic transmission. The other one is about coding efficiency issue. Since eMBMS service is dominated by the device with lowest Modulation and Coding Scheme (MCS). In the paper, a Device-to-Device (D2D) based mechanism was proposed to improve the resource allocation and coding efficiency. The eMBMS service area is reduced in order to provide better radio link quality and higher channel coding rate. Devices outside the reduced eMBMS service area still can receive data by using D2D relay-connection from devices inside the eMBMS service area. Simulation results have shown that the proposed D2D-based mechanism can reduce the number of allocated resource blocks.

The remainder of the paper is organized as follows. In Sect. 2, a survey of the eMBMS and D2D communications in LTE is presented. Proposed D2D-based mechanism for LTE eMBMS is presented in Sect. 3. Results of performance evaluation are presented in Sect. 4. Finally, Sect. 5 concludes this paper.

2 Literature Review

2.1 LTE and LTE-Advanced

LTE was proposed by 3GPP which can use OFDM, OFDMA or SC-FDMA access technologies. It also can use 2×2 or 4×4 Multi-Input Multi-Output (MIMO) antenna systems and provide either frequency division duplex (FDD) or time division duplex (TDD) mode. Moreover, LTE not only offers traditional voice telephone service, but also can also provide cost effective broadband communication services. Since LTE is defined and developed by telecom vendors and is backward compatible with GSM/UMTS cellular systems. This makes LTE deployment much easier than WiMAX. Furthermore, LTE can combine OFMDA, MIMO and HARQ technologies. This means LTE can dynamically configure its bandwidth according to available frequencies and can support a high mobility environment. This is a desirable solution for high speed rail which moves at speeds up to 350 km/h.

In the enhanced LTE version, LTE-Advanced, the transmission bandwidth is further increased. The downlink transmission rate can go up to 1 Gbps if UEs are in low mobility status. Even when UEs are in high mobility status, the transmission rate can still reach 100 Mbps. Therefore, ITU has been certified that LTE-Advanced conforms to the requirements of IMT-Advanced for 4G. The major difference between 3GPP Rel. 10 LTE-Advanced and original LTE is a new entity called Relay Node (RN) introduced in LTE-Advanced. Each base station, namely evolved Node B (eNB), has a limited serving area. It is more difficult to deploy a new eNB since residents have expressed much concern about the electromagnetic waves impact on health. Thus, the idea of signal relaying by RN has been proposed and becomes an LTE-Advanced specification. A Donor eNB (DeNB) can expand its serving area by using RN to relay signal.

2.2   Device-to-Device Communications

When two nearby user equipments (UEs) served by the same eNB and exchanging data, the packets issued by sender UE have to route through LTE core network and back to receiver UE via same eNB. Even if those communicating UEs are close enough, the transmission still need to go through core network due to standard specification. If two nearby UEs can communicate directly without passing through the core network, it can significantly reduce the burden on the core network. This type of directly transmission was called Device-to-Device (D2D) communications [5]. Thanks to the largely development of hand-held devices and IoT technologies, the D2D scenario becomes more and more important.

When a UE (Sender UE) wants to send packet to another UE (Receiver UE) served by same eNB, they have to find each other by using D2D discovery mechanism. After confirming that the UE pair can use the D2D transmission mode, the eNB will allocates resources used for the D2D link. Then, those two UEs can use the D2D link for direct transmission.

2.3   LTE eMBMS

The eMBMS is used to provide broadcast and multicast service for LTE networks [6, 7]. The system architecture of eMBMS is illustrated in Fig. 1. An additional control entity called Multi-cell/Multicast Coordination Entity (MCE) is embedded within eNB. Also, two additional entities, namely e-MBMS-GW and e-BM-SC, are added in the EPC core network.

In LTE system, the resource scheduling interval is 1 ms namely TTI (Transmission Time Interval) which further divided into two resource blocks (RBs) and each RB contains 84 resource elements (REs). Each RE may use different channel coding mechanism allocated to single UE for transmitting or receiving. However, the allocation unit is TTI but not RE in eMBMS service. When the broadcast/multicast traffic is small, the unused REs are wasted. Even in highly broadcast/multicast traffic scenario, the unused REs may still happen resulting in poor transmission efficiency. Furthermore, the broadcast/multicast is one-to-all or one-to-many style of transmission. In order to achieve the broadcast/multicast service, the channel code scheme need to fit the farthest UE with lowest channel quality. Thus, the channel coding efficiency is quite poor.

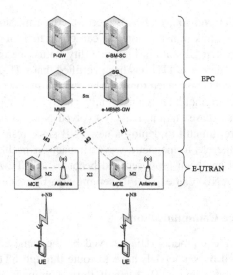

Fig. 1. LTE eMBMS Network Architecture.

3 Proposed D2D-Based eMBMS Service

As mentioned, the eNB can only transmit broadcast/multicast messages with worst channel coding technique in order to guarantee packet reception for all serving UEs. The transmission efficiency is quite poor. An interesting idea raised. If the UEs located in signal edge can be temporarily ignored and only UEs with well channel quality will receive the broadcast/multicast messages then the coding efficiency can be improved. The UEs that already receive broadcast/multicast messages can further forward to those temporarily ignored UEs via D2D communications with higher signal quality. The overall system throughput may be also improved. Based on this idea, the D2D-Based eMBMS service was proposed in this paper.

In order to achieve objectives of the proposed mechanism, there are three issues should be solved. First of all, which UEs can be temporarily ignored? A suitable evaluation mechanism should be developed. For a temporarily ignored UE, which relay UE can forward its received message via D2D? A suitable D2D selection mechanism should also be developed. If there is no any suitable relay UE found, how can the temporarily ignored UE receive its message? Therefore, a correction procedure should also be defined. Since no suitable UE can forward traffic, unicast delivery is used for the correction procedure. The eNB will send the missing data to edge UEs directly by unicast transmission. The remaining two issues are explained in the following sections. Figure 2 illustrated the basic idea of D2D-Based eMBMS service.

3.1 eMBMS Zone

Since only UEs with LTE Channel Quality Indicator (CQI) values lower than six may benefit on D2D transmission [8]. Therefore, the broadcast/multicast coverage area, namely eMBMS zone, can be bounded among CQI values smaller than six. The LTE

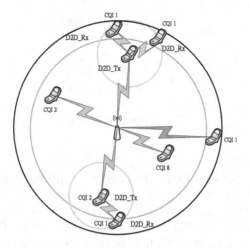

Fig. 2. Proposed D2D-Based eMBMS service.

serving area outside the eMBMS zone is called D2D zone. However, only benefit on the throughput enhancement and used RB reduction, the shirking down of eMBMS zone can be triggered. Therefore, RB usage calculation should be perform before making eMBMS zone decision. The RB usage can be calculated by Eq. 1:

$$\#RB = \left\lceil \frac{data\_eMBMS}{TBS(CQI_k)} \right\rceil \tag{1}$$

where *data_eMBMS* is the traffic would like to be sent by eMBMS, *TBS(CQI_k)* is the payload in a single RB with CQI value k. Thus, the RB needed for traditional eMBMS mechanism can be calculated by Eq. 2:

$$RB_{ori\_eMBMS} = \left\lceil \left(\left\lceil \frac{data\_eMBMS}{TBS(CQI\_lowest)} \right\rceil \right) / N_{TTI}^{RB} \right\rceil \times N_{TTI}^{RB} \tag{2}$$

where *CQI_lowest* is the lowest CQI value among all serving UEs. N_{TTI}^{RB} is the number of RB in a single TTI interval.

The goal of proposed mechanism is try to minimize the RB used:

$$Min(RB_T = RB_{adj\_eMBMS} + RB_{D2D} + RB_U) \tag{3}$$

RB_T is the number of RB used in the proposed mechanism. RB_{D2D} is the number of RB used in the D2D transmission portion while RB_U is the number of RB used in the correction procedure.

$$RB_{adj\_eMBMS} = \left\lceil \left(\left\lceil \frac{data\_eMBMD}{TBS(CQI\_eMBMS)} \right\rceil \right) / N_{TTI}^{RB} \right\rceil \times N_{TTI}^{RB} \tag{4}$$

$$RB_{D2D} = \sum_{i=1}^{K} \left\lceil \frac{data\_eMBMS}{TBS(d_i)} \right\rceil \tag{5}$$

$$RB_U = U \times \left\lceil \frac{data\_eMBMS}{TBS(CQI\_lowest)} \right\rceil \tag{6}$$

$$RB_{adj\_eMBMS} < 6 \times N_{TTI}^{RB} \tag{7}$$

$$RB_T < RB_{ori\_eMBMS} \tag{8}$$

CQI_eMBMS is the new CQI value that the eMBMS used to limit the new broadcast/multicast zone. Since the proposed D2D transmission adopt the spatial reuse techniques, there are K group of D2D pairs and each pair in a same group can send their traffic simultaneously [9]. The Eq. 7 shows that no more than six TTIs can be used by eMBMS as defined in LTE standard. If those equations are true, D2D-based eMBMS service is triggered. Otherwise, the standard eMBMS service is used.

3.2 Relay Selection

The proposed mechanism use smaller eMBMS serving zone in order to improve transmission efficiency. D2D is used to serve UEs outside the eMBMS zone. Moreover, the D2D transmission adopt the spatial reuse techniques to reduce totally RB used. Therefore, the selection of relay UE and D2D transmission scheduling should be carefully arranged.

Assume eNB has location information of all serving UEs. eNB firstly sort the UEs inside D2D zone by location information. Begin with the nearest UE, find an appropriate UE located in eMBMS zone and inside its signal coverage with highest signal quality (CQI value). This UE is chosen to act as relay. The next UE in the sorted list follows the procedure until all UEs are finished the relay selection. Beside, when a UE already act as relay, it will serve UEs as many as possible. The priority of the relay UE is much higher than other candidates. This can further reduce the number of D2D transmission pairs.

4 Performance Evaluation

Table 1 shows the simulation parameters used in the simulation program. In addition, the signal quality is measured by Signal-to-Interference-plus-Noise Ratio (SINR). Each UE will periodically report a Channel Quality Indicator (CQI) value to the eNB based on the signal quality. The SINR can be retrieved from the Eq. 9.

$$\frac{P_{eNB} - Path\_Loss}{Interference + Noise} \tag{9}$$

Table 1. Simulation parameters

Parameter	Value
LTE bandwidth	100 MHz
eNB signal diameter	3400 m
Path loss between UE and eNB	128.1 + 37.6log10(R) dB, R in km
Path loss between D2D UEs	140.7 + 36.7log10(R) dB, R in km
e-NB power	46 dBm
UE power	19 dBm
PRB size	12 sub-carrier per PRB
Data rate	1100 kbps
UE number	50–500
UEs distribution	Uniform

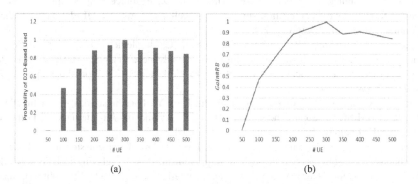

(a)   (b)

Fig. 3. Simulation results. (a) Shows the probability of adopting proposed mechanism while (b) shows the RB reduction as number of UE increased.

Figure 3 shows the simulation results. The probability of adopting D2D-Based eMBMS service increased as number of UE increase. More opportunity to trigger the D2D-based mechanism, resulting in more RB saving. When the number of UE larger than 300, the probability of adopting D2D-Based eMBMS service decreased due to the D2D spatial reuse difficulty.

5   Conclusion

A Device-to-Device based mechanism was proposed to improve transmission efficiency of eMBMS service in this paper. An idea of smaller eMBMS zone is used to improve transmission efficiency while D2D and unicast transmission are used to serve UEs located in D2D zone. A suitable zone size decision mechanism and a D2D relay UE selection algorithms are also proposed. Simulation results have shown that the proposed D2D-based mechanism can reduce the number of allocated resource blocks.

Acknowledgments. This work was supported in part by the Taiwan Mobile Co., Ltd., Taiwan, R.O.C., under grant no. 106-09-031.

References

1. Sesia, S., Toufik, I., Baker, M.P.J.: LTE – The UMTS Long Term Evolution: From Theory to Practice. Wiley, Hoboken (2009)
2. 3GPP TS 36.300: Evolved Universal Terrestrial Radio Access (E-UTRA) and Evolved Universal Terrestrial Radio Access Network (E-UTRAN). Rel. 10, v10.12.0 (2014)
3. Taleb, T., Kunz, A.: Machine type communications in 3GPP networks: potential, challenges, and solutions. IEEE Commun. Mag. **50**(3), 178–184 (2012)
4. 3GPP TS 23.246: Technical Specification Group Services and System Aspects; Multimedia Broadcast/Multicast Service (MBMS); Architecture and Functional Description. Rel. 12, v12.4.0 (2014)
5. Yu, C.-H., Doppler, K., Ribeiro, C.-B., Tirkkonen, O.: Resource sharing optimization for Device-to-Device communication underlaying cellular networks. IEEE Trans. Wirel. Commun. **10**(8), 2752–2763 (2011)
6. Nguyen, N.-D., Knopp, R., Nikaein, N., Bonnet, C.: Implementation and validation of multimedia broadcast multicast service for LTE/LTE-advanced in OpenAirInterface platform. In: 38th Conference on Local Computer Networks Workshops (LCN Workshops), pp. 70–76, Sydney, NSW (2013)
7. Bataa, O., Chuluun, O., Orosoo, T., Lamjav, E., Kim, Y., Gonchigsumlaa, K.: A functional design of BM-SC to support mobile IPTV in LTE network. In: 7th International Forum on Strategic Technology (IFOST), Tomsk, pp. 1–5 (2012)
8. Chen, J.-Y., Mai, Y.-T., Yang, C.-C., Young, F.F.: Design of transmission and scheduling mechanisms with fairness and throughput improvement for D2D relaying in LTE networks. In: 2017 International Conference on Innovation and Management (IAM 2017 Winter), Japan, pp. 681–92 (2017)
9. Doppler, K., Rinne, M., Wijting, C., Ribeiro, C.B., Hugl, K.: Device-to-Device communication as an underlay to LTE-advanced networks. IEEE Commun. Mag. **47**(12), 42–49 (2009)

Intelligent Trashcan Applications Relying on Internet of Things Technologies

Ye Chin Kiong[1], Chow-Yen-Desmond Sim[1], Ang Sinn[2],
Ming-Fong Tsai[3(✉)], and Lien-Wu Chen[2]

[1] Industrial Ph.D. Program of Internet of Things, Feng Chia University,
Taichung, Taiwan
[2] Department of Information Engineering and Computer Science,
Feng Chia University, Taichung, Taiwan
[3] Department of Electronic Engineering, National United University,
Miaoli, Taiwan
mingfongtsai@gmail.com

Abstract. Trashcans are the basic unit in the garbage-collecting procedure. This paper proposes an intelligent trashcan with flexible features, which is associated with a smart device application. The trashcan is able to detect RFID tags to decide whether to open its lid or not. The trashcan is also capable of moving around when it receives instructions from the remote application, and it has the ability to move according to a planned path. Different settings of the smart trashcan can be configured via the remote application. The proposed system has been implemented, and it is shown that the proposal is applicable.

1 Introduction

Waste management is an issue that concerns both developing and developed countries due to the fact that every individual produces solid waste every single day, which accumulates into a significant total amount of waste over a period of time. According to a recent article, 190 kilos of waste are produced every second across the world, which will be disastrous if not managed properly. The fundamental step of waste management is to gather the disposed-of garbage, and the common method involved is the trashcan. Various researchers have given impetus to the development of a clean city. The cleanliness of a city is highly relevant, as poor cleanliness causes foreigners to have a poor impression of a city, further leading to a negative impact on the nation's image.

The researchers of paper [1] proposed the use of a GSM (Global System for Mobile communication) module in Arduino Uno to report on the percentage of garbage in trashcans. Paper [2] proposed to use an IR module in Arduino Uno to detect the percentage of garbage in trashcans. The researchers of paper [3] suggested system architecture to find a time-optimal dynamic route for garbage trucks to support the 'Smart Clean City' project, which contributed to the time optimization of garbage collection. To enhance further the removal procedure of solid waste from trashcans, the authors of [4] proposed an e-monitoring garbage alert system based on IOT (Internet of Things) technology.

© ICST Institute for Computer Sciences, Social Informatics and Telecommunications Engineering 2018
Y.-B. Lin et al. (Eds.): IoTaaS 2017, LNICST 246, pp. 221–229, 2018.
https://doi.org/10.1007/978-3-030-00410-1_26

The level of garbage in a dustbin is detected by an ultrasonic sensor, which is interfaced with Arduino Uno. By creating alerts when the garbage bin is full, the proposed system reduces the manual process involved in the garbage management of a public area. Further research [5] on solid waste monitoring has also been undertaken, and the proposed system is an integration of popular communication technology such as RFID, GPS (Global Positioning System) and GIS (Geographic Information System).

The method of estimating the garbage fill level is to interpret the image taken by a camera attached to the garbage collection truck. Indeed, the mentioned works contribute substantially to the waste management process. However, none of the mentioned works focuses on the ownership of a non-public trashcan. In Taiwan it is easily noticeable that some trashcans are secured with a substantial lock, such that unauthorized access to them is prohibited. Unauthorized use of a trashcan is troublesome to the owner, as it will be filled quickly and the garbage involved will mostly be unsegregated waste [6]. In this paper a smart, automated trashcan is proposed. The trashcan is fitted with intelligent features, such as automatic lid opening, movement ability and obstacle detection. The smart trashcan can be accessed by directing an RFID tag to the RFID reader attached to it. In this case the user does not need to unlock the trashcan manually during each garbage disposal session. The trashcan is also able to move according to a planned route formed by tapes. Aside from being an automated trashcan, it can also serve as a form of remote controlled appliance. A mobile device application is constructed to serve as the remote controller of the smart trashcan. The user can instruct the smart trashcan to open and close the lid, move around or simply switch to automatic mode. The rest of the paper will be divided into three main parts: the system architecture, the implementation result and the conclusion.

2 System Architecture

This section is divided into three main parts, which are the system structure, the smart trashcan and the remote control application for the trashcan. First we will examine the overall structure of the proposed system, which includes the smart trashcan, the smart device application and the database server. Next the smart trashcan will be explained. Finally we will consider the remote control application for the smart trashcan.

2.1 System Structure

Figure 1 illustrates the overall system of the smart trashcan communication mechanism. The proposed system is composed of the smart trashcan itself, a mobile device application and a server. The main feature of the smart trashcan is the ability to lift up the lid and give access to the tag owner when the attached RFID reader reads the tag. The communication between the smart trashcan and the user involves data transmission through a Bluetooth module. The data involved are the instructions given to the smart trashcan during the remote controlled session and the trashcan's utilization of the information that is accumulated when the RFID reader scans a tag. Since the smart trashcan itself is not able to connect to the Internet, the information will be sent to the server database through the mobile application. The data in the server database can be accessed on request through a computer.

Fig. 1. System overview

2.2 Smart Trashcan

The smart trashcan is a trashcan integrated with the following: Arduino Mega 2560, a Bluetooth module, an RFID reader, a servomotor, a drive motor and wheels, a track sensor module, an L298N motor module and an ultrasonic sensor. Two main features are implemented: automatic lid opening after a tag is detected and movement according to a planned track. The smart trashcan will open its lid to give access whenever the RFID reader reads a tag. Figure 2 illustrates the lid-opening process to present a clearer concept. First of all the smart trashcan must be fitted with a power supply so that it can function properly.

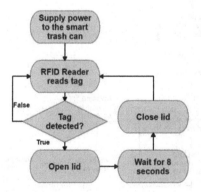

Fig. 2. Flow diagram of smart trashcan lid opening

The RFID reader mounted on the trashcan will start to detect tags. When a tag is detected, the smart trashcan will open its lid. The lid will stay open for eight seconds before it closes automatically. Then the smart trashcan will continue to read tags. In Sect. 1 it is mentioned that the smart trashcan can be controlled remotely by a smart device application. The remote control feature includes control of the lid.

When the lid is opened through the remote control application, it will not close automatically after eight seconds. Instead, the smart trashcan will wait for an order from the application. There are two ways in which the smart trashcan will move: first through remote control and second by following a planned track. The first method is performed by receiving instructions from the smart device application through a Bluetooth module. The smart trashcan is able to move forwards, move backwards, turn left and turn right. To avoid a collision, an ultrasound sensor is also installed in the smart trashcan. Whenever an obstacle is detected, the trashcan will turn right to avoid it. Next, we proceed to the second method, in which a path is planned for the smart trashcan and formed by black tapes. To enable the smart trashcan to move according to the track, a track sensor module is installed at the bottom of the trashcan. The track sensor module contains an IR infrared reflection sensor, which can be used for line following and edge detection. In a track sensor module, the infrared reflection sensor detects black lines and enables the object to move according to the lines.

2.3   Remote Controlling Application

The aim of the remote control application is to control the smart trashcan remotely. In our work the application is developed for an Android environment. The application has the ability to pair with the smart trashcan via a Bluetooth connection. Once they are paired, the application may control the lid, the motion and the interchange between the different modes of the smart trashcan. As mentioned in the previous sections, the opening and closing of the lid can be triggered by an RFID tag or by remote control. Through the remote control application, the user can decide which lid mode the smart trashcan will adopt.

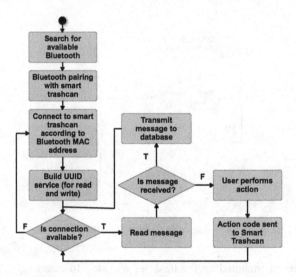

Fig. 3. Remote control application flow diagram

As the default setting, the smart trashcan remains static unless it is commanded to move around. Using the remote control application, the user may switch to the automatic routing mode in which the smart trashcan moves according to the black tapes.

The application also serves as the agent to transmit utilization data of the smart trashcan to the server database. Whenever the RFID reader reads a tag, the information is interpreted and stored in the Arduino module.

The information cannot be sent directly to the server, as the smart trashcan does not have the ability to connect to the Internet. Hence, when it is paired with a smart device that has the related application installed, the information will be passed to the application through a Bluetooth connection. Then the application will play its role by transmitting the received information to the server database if the smart device is connected to the Internet.

The flow diagram of the remote control application is shown in Fig. 3. Bluetooth plays an important role in enabling the communication between the smart trashcan and the application. Before the connection is established, the application will search for available Bluetooth devices. Then the smart trashcan is selected and a password is required to pair with the smart trashcan. The password is set to restrict unrelated people from accessing the smart trashcan. After successful Bluetooth pairing, the application and the smart trashcan are connected by the Bluetooth MAC address. A UUID service, which enables read and write communication, is built. If a connection is available, the application will start to read messages from the paired smart trashcan. If a message is received, for example RFID tag information, the message will be transmitted and stored in the server database. On the other hand, if the user performs any action, the action code will be sent to the smart trashcan. The smart trashcan will interpret the action code and adjust itself.

3   Implementation Results

A regular, plain indoor trashcan is selected as the basis of the smart trashcan. Figure 4 shows the implementation result of the smart trashcan. The trashcan is colourfully painted for a better visual effect. The components used are Arduino Mega 2560, an HC-06 Bluetooth module, an RFID RC522, a servomotor, a drive motor and wheels, a track sensor module, an L298N Dual H-Bridge Motor Controller, an ultrasonic sensor and a battery case, which are shown in Fig. 5. The components, except the servomotor, are installed at the bottom of the trashcan, and the implementation result is shown in Fig. 6. The smart trashcan is then attached to the base shown in Fig. 6. To move the lid, the servomotor is installed in the trashcan near the lid, as shown in Fig. 7, which illustrates the trashcan with an open lid. The installation functions to hold up the lid when required. Figure 8 illustrates the flow diagram of the smart trashcan. Once supplied with electricity, the pins of the component's input and output are initialized. The Bluetooth server service is also initialized and prepares to be connected. The Bluetooth server waits for a connection request from the remote control application. Once paired and password verified with the application, a connection will be established. The smart trashcan will read the instruction message from the application. At this point the user can control the smart trashcan by interacting with the interface provided by the remote control application. If any action is performed, an action code will be transmitted to the smart trashcan via the Bluetooth connection. If a message is received by the smart trashcan, it will interpret it and switch the trashcan mode according to the received action code. The remote control application will be discussed in the next paragraph.

Fig. 4. Smart trashcan

Fig. 5. Components of the smart trashcan

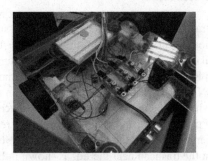

Fig. 6. Base of the smart trashcan

Fig. 7. Lid structure

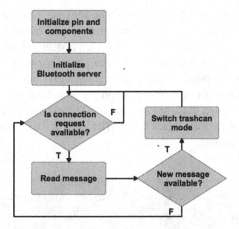

Fig. 8. Smart trashcan flow diagram

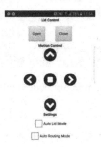

Fig. 9. Remote control application

Figure 9 presents the remote control application of the smart trashcan. The smart device application is developed for an Android environment using Android Studio 2.0. The application is able to pair with the smart trashcan Bluetooth module and control the smart trashcan remotely. The application features are divided into three sections on the screen. The top section is the lid control section, and two buttons are provided for the user to command the lid to open or close. Note that if the lid is opened using the button, it will not close automatically. Instead, the motor is programmed to wait for an instruction from the close button. The second section is the motion control section. The four buttons enable the smart trashcan to move forwards, turn right, move backwards and turn left. The button in the middle is the stop button. The stop button is available because the smart trashcan is programmed to move continuously once a direction button is pressed. Once a direction button is pressed, the trashcan will move in the desired direction until another direction button or the stop button is pressed. This purpose of this design is to avoid the user being obliged to press down the button continuously when the trashcan is required to move for a long distance. The bottom section is for the settings. In this section two options are provided: the automatic lid mode and the automatic routing mode. The automatic lid mode grants permission for the smart trashcan to open its lid when an RFID tag is detected. This means that, if the corresponding checkbox is left unchecked, the smart trashcan is considered to be locked, and it will not respond to any approaching RFID tag. The automatic routing mode enables the smart trashcan to move according to the planned path. This feature is operated using the mounted track sensor module. The expected path is a route formed using black tapes, which form black lines. The path is built prior to the automatic routing mode being enabled.

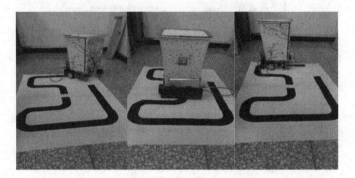

Fig. 10. Automatic routing mode implementation results

Table 1. Relation between s1, s2 and s3 and trashcan movement

S1 (left)	S2 (middle)	S3 (right)	Movement
HIGH	HIGH	HIGH	Forward
LOW	LOW	LOW	Stop
LOW	HIGH	HIGH	Right
LOW	LOW	HIGH	Right
HIGH	HIGH	LOW	Left
HIGH	LOW	LOW	Left
LOW	HIGH	LOW	Forward
HIGH	LOW	HIGH	Backward

Figure 10 shows the implementation result of the trashcan's automatic routing mode. A black path is formed using black tapes, and the smart trashcan is placed at the starting location. The smart trashcan is then switched to the automatic routing mode. Figure 10(a)–(c) show the movement of the trashcan. It follows the route and is able to turn around at the turning points. This function is performed by the track sensor module. The track sensor module senses three values, which represent the colour of the ground. The three values are s1, s2 and s3, which indicate left, middle and right, respectively. They help the smart trashcan to identify the next movement. For a clear depiction, the relation between the values of s1, s2 and s3 and the movement of the smart trashcan is shown in Table 1. A database is constructed on a lab server to receive data from the smart trashcan via the remote application. The database is a MySQL database, which is one of the built-in features of XAMPP, a free and open-source cross-platform web server solution stack package developed by Apache Friends. In our implementation the database is able to receive transmitted data successfully. The main utilization of the received data is to monitor the behaviour of each user.

4   Conclusion

In this paper a smart trashcan associated with a remotely controlled smart device application is proposed. The smart trashcan is integrated with an Arduino module, a Bluetooth module and RFID technology. The smart trashcan has the ability to control the opening and closing of its lid manually or based on an RFID tag, to follow a planned path and to move around. The remote application is able to pair with the smart trashcan via Bluetooth. The implementation results prove that the proposed ideas and features are applicable. In the future we will attempt to take further advantage of Internet of Things technology and implement more features, such as detecting the garbage fill level and creating alerts when the trashcan requires emptying.

References

1. Yusof, N., Jidin, A., Rahim, M.: Smart garbage monitoring system for waste management. In: MATEC Web of Conferences, pp. 1–5 (2017)
2. Parkash, Prabu, V.: IoT based waste management for smart city. Int. J. Innov. Res. Comput. Commun. Eng. 4(2), 1267–1274 (2016)
3. Borozdukhin, A., Dolinina, O., Pechenkin, V.: Approach to the garbage collection in the smart clean city project. In: IEEE International Colloquium on Information Science and Technology, pp. 918–922 (2016)
4. Kumar, N., Vuayalakshmi, B., Prarthana, R., Shankar, A.: IOT based smart garbage alert system using Arduino UNO. In: IEEE Region 10 Conference, pp. 1028–1034 (2016)
5. Arebey, M., Hannan, M., Basri, H., Begum, R., Abdullah, H.: Solid waste monitoring system integration based on RFID, GPS and Camera. In: International Conference on Intelligent and Advanced Systems, pp. 1–5 (2010)
6. Anagnostopoulos, T., et al.: Challenges and opportunities of waste management in IoT-enabled smart cities: a survey. IEEE Trans. Sustain. Comput. 99, 1–16 (2017)

A Local Customizable Gateway in General-Purpose IoT Framework

Wen-Hsing Kuo[1] and Min-Zheng Shieh[2(✉)]

[1] Department of Electrical Engineering, Yuan Ze University, Taoyuan, Taiwan
whkuo@ee.yzu.edu.tw
[2] Information Technology Service Center, National Chiao Tung University,
Hsinchu, Taiwan
mzshieh@nctu.edu.tw

Abstract. In the emergence of the Internet of Things, the local gateway plays an important role because it connects devices over heterogeneous networks and provides local intelligence. In this paper, we propose a structure of a general-purpose gateway which provides customizable connectivity for a wide range of devices and services such as home appliances, environment sensors, and web-page parsers. In addition, the gateway has an interface to communicate with the IoTtalk platform which has a graphical user interface for device management and enables users create new network applications by programming in Python. The gateway is also implemented on Android platform.

Keywords: Customizable gateway · IoT framework

1 Introduction

The Internet of Things can link different kinds of devices and services including sensors, wearables, home appliances, vehicles, servers and databases. Various intelligent systems such as smart home, smart city, digital healthcare, etc., and be constructed in this way. Since the application scenarios are variant, the access technologies and communication protocols for IoT are quite diverse. As such, devices using different protocols cannot directly communicate with each other even if they are physically approximate. Therefore, a gateway is often deployed to break the barrier.

In addition to providing connectivity, such a gateway plays important roles in IoT eco-system because it has various functions: (1) provides the intermediate connection to the Internet for low-cost and low power devices; (2) acts as an access filter for those have security concerns and thus cannot directly connect to IP networks; and (3) provides the local intelligence and preprocessing of sensors' raw data.

There are numerous existing works [2] discussing different aspects of IoT. Some works [3–5] focus on local gateways. Zhu et al. [3] proposed a prototype bridging wireless sensor networks into IoT. Guoqiang et al. [4] designed and implemented a more flexible gateway. Wu et al. [5] aimed to network application development.

To our best knowledge, there is no existing works that consider a structure of a general purpose IoT gateway. Therefore, this paper proposes an architecture that can connect Physical devices, internal sensors, remote information and a powerful IoT

© ICST Institute for Computer Sciences, Social Informatics and Telecommunications Engineering 2018
Y.-B. Lin et al. (Eds.): IoTaaS 2017, LNICST 246, pp. 230–233, 2018.
https://doi.org/10.1007/978-3-030-00410-1_27

management platform, IoTtalk [1] altogether. IoTtalk is a IoT cloud platform which allows users to create various IoT automation links in Python. Combining the gateway and the cloud service together, many innovative applications such as voice-based remote control, or a cloud-based health monitoring system collecting data from wearable devices become possible.

The rest of the paper is organized as follows. Section 2 details the architecture and the functions of each component. Section 3 shows the implementation case. The whole paper is concluded in Sect. 4.

2 System Architecture

This section describes the system architecture of the proposed general-purpose IoT gateway. We first present the components and their functions, and then an example shows how the gateway works as a voice-based remote control system.

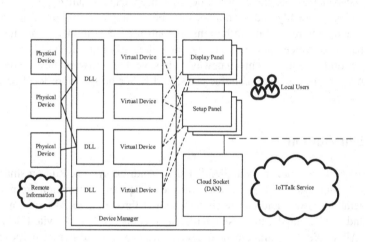

Fig. 1. The proposed architecture of a local customizable gateway in generate-purpose IoT framework.

2.1 Functions of Components

As shown in Fig. 1, the detail operation of each component is as follows. Physical devices, remote information or internal sensors are accessed by the gateway's dynamic linking libraries (DLLs) which implement the communication and data-fetching processes. DLLs are accessed by virtual devices (VDs), which provides a unified standardized APIs for higher-level management. They inherit an identical prototype object which contains common functions (e.g., start, stop, pause, resume, etc.) for Device Manager (DM) to control the operations and lifecycles. Based on the requirement of users, DM activates different VDs and their respective Setup-Panels and Display-Panels. These two Panels serve as the user interface and respectively provide the setup and the visualization interfaces of each VD. These two types of panels can be designed specifically to reflect different conditions and characteristics of VDs, or choose from existing components. Finally, the cloud socket access the information of VDs and synchronize them with the cloud services. By connecting to the IoTtalk platform, local physical devices can exchange data with remote services over the internet. Device users and service providers can easily develop different kinds of network applications using the Python programming language. The information can be further processed, which makes automation, big-data analysis and other broader applications possible.

2.2 Lifecycle and Mechanism

The following example shows the operation of the general purpose IoT gateway. Assume that the gateway is run on a setup box to provide, say, an intelligent smart-home application. The setup box uses standard Bluetooth library to connect local home appliances such as smart plugs, utilizes internal function to fetch the voice commands from users, and uses TCP/IP sockets to acquire current air quality condition from the Internet. Encapsulated into three virtual devices, users can customize the visualization of each VD independently and form a console. For example, using line graph to show the current temperature, and using buttons to control air-conditioners. Through DAN, the information of voice-command can be submitted to online IoTtalk services, and then trigger other devices. This gateway can save the software development and integration effort from device manufacturers, and better bridge more local sensors to cloud IoT services.

3 Implementation

The prototype of the gateway is implemented on Android system. Run on smartphone or setup box, our system supports BLE devices, acquires information from internal GPS/accelerator sensors, and can fetch information through web API such as Yahoo weather and XML standardized standards, and connects IoTtalk via HTTP-based RESTFul APIs. We have implemented several UI panels for different purposes. The sensed value can be represented by texts, line graphs or different graph icons. The physical setup, the UI and some network applications of the implemented system are shown in Fig. 2. The 5 VDs are a light bulb, a proximity sensor, a fan, a carbon monoxide sensor and an RFID reader labeled from 1 to 5, respectively. Their information is displayed on the UI panel and transferred to the IoTtalk platform via the gateway. On the IoTtalk platform, we build models and create corresponding devices features for each VD. Using several lines of Python codes, we develop 3 network applications: (1) If the proximity sensor detects an object nearby, then turn on the light; (2) If the concentration of carbon monoxide rises, then increase the speed of the fan; (3) When the RFID reader recognizes an ID, log the ID and time to the cloud.

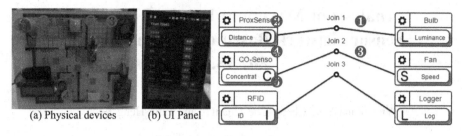

Fig. 2. The implemented system.

4 Conclusion

This paper discusses the structure of a general-purpose gateway for integrating local devices into a universal IoTtalk cloud services. By encapsulating different local devices, local sensors and remote resources into virtual devices, the gateway can provide an organized and customizable interface for users and remote cloud services. This structure can be applied on different IoT areas, such as healthcare, smart-home and smart cities.

Acknowledgements. The authors would like to thank Prof. Yi-Bing Lin and Dr. Yun-Wei Lin for their various supports including an early access version of the IoTtalk platform.

References

1. Lin, Y.B., Lin, Y.W., Huang, C.M., Chih, C.Y., Lin, P.: IoTtalk: a management platform for reconfigurable sensor devices. IEEE Internet Things J. (to appear)
2. Al-Fuqaha, A., Guizani, M., Mohammadi, M., Aledhari, M., Ayyash, M.: Internet of Things: a survey on enabling technologies, protocols, and applications. IEEE Commun. Surv. Tutor. **17**(4), 2347–2376 (2015)
3. Zhu, Q., Wang, R., Chen, Q., Liu, Y., Qin, W.: IOT gateway: bridging wireless sensor networks into Internet of Things. In: Proceedings of the IEEE/IFIP 8th International Conference on EUC, pp. 347–352 (2010)
4. Guoqiang, S., Yanming, C., Chao, Z., Yanxu, Z.: Design and implementation of a smart IoT gateway. In: 2013 IEEE International Conference on Green Computing and Communications and IEEE Internet of Things and IEEE Cyber, Physical and Social Computing, Beijing, pp. 720–723 (2013)
5. Wu, L., Xu, Y., Xu, C., Wang, F.: Plug-configure-play service-oriented gateway - for fast and easy sensor network application development. In: Proceedings of the 2nd International Conference on Sensor Networks - Volume 1: SENSORNETS, pp. 53–58 (2013)

Analysis of Maximum Depth of Wireless Sensor Network Based on RPL and IEEE 802.15.4

Yun-Shuai Yu[1], Cheng-Che Huang[2], and Chih-Heng Ke[2(✉)]

[1] Department of Electronic Engineering,
National Chin-Yi University of Technology, No. 57, Sec. 2, Zhongshan Road,
Taiping District, Taichung 411, Taiwan (R.O.C.)
yys@ncut.edu.tw
[2] Department of Computer Science and Information Engineering,
National Quemoy University, No. 1, University Road, Jinning Township,
Kinmen 892, Taiwan (R.O.C.)
neol_d2022@outlook.com, smallko@gmail.com

Abstract. The nodes in wireless sensor networks (WSN) are typically resource constrained so that they can maintain only a few routes. More-capable nodes can insert extra routing information, i.e. source routing header (SRH), into packets to instruct the resource constrained ones to route the packet. A WSN with deeper depth requires longer SRH, thus leaving less space of a packet for the user data. We analyze the relationship between the length of the user data and the maximum depth of a WSN based on RPL and IEEE 802.15.4. The results can guide the application designers and the network administrators in selecting a suitable length of user data to guarantee that the data can be routed to each sensor nodes. Simulation results prove the correctness of our analysis.

Keywords: Wireless sensor network · RPL · IEEE 802.15.4 · Depth
Source routing header

1 Introduction

In the last decade, wireless sensor networks (WSN) [1–4], have gained a tremendous attention due to the fourth industrial revolution or Industry 4.0. In a WSN, most nodes are constrained in resources such as processing capacity, energy capacity, and memory. Due to the resource constraints on the nodes, IETF proposes IPv6 Routing Protocol for Low-Power and Lossy Networks (RPL) [5] to address the routing problem. Within an RPL routing domain, a sensed environmental datum will be routed upward from a node to the root of the WSN. Typically, the root node relays the sensed data to a process automation controller or a computer via a wired link. Messages, such as queries or configurations, may be sent from the process automation controller or the computer to the sensor nodes. Those messages, at first, are relayed to the root node and then routed downward to the destination nodes. In an RPL domain, each sensor node records at least one parent node which is one of the immediate successors of the node on a path towards the root. Each node forwards the data packets to its parent node, thus achieving the

© ICST Institute for Computer Sciences, Social Informatics and Telecommunications Engineering 2018
Y.-B. Lin et al. (Eds.): IoTaaS 2017, LNICST 246, pp. 234–239, 2018.
https://doi.org/10.1007/978-3-030-00410-1_28

upward routing. In contrast to the upward routing, less-capable nodes are limited to maintain routes to other deeper nodes. So the process automation controller, the computer, or the root has to insert a source routing header (SRH) into the packets to instruct the resource constrained ones to route the packets. Therefore, downward routing consumes more space of a packet so that a user message may be too large to fit the packet.

A straightforward workaround is to be aware of the actual available space for user message and then the user can regulate the message to conform to the space limitation. In another way, the network administrator has to reconfigure the network topology to ensure that the depth of the WSN is not too deep since there should be a longer SRH for deeper nodes. Usually, it is expensive to design a flexible application which can accommodate the user messages to the topology of a WSN. Thus, network depth adjustment is a more economic solution. So the network administrator should be able to predict the maximum depth of the WSN when the maximum length of the user messages can be known in advance. One challenge is that WSNs based on RPL usually adopts IEEE 802.15.4 [6] as its physical layer and data link layer. IEEE 802.15.4 only supports frames of up to 127 bytes. It means that an adaptation layer is required to be above the IEEE 802.15.4 to compress/decompress the network layer protocol data units. Apparently, the performance of the adaptation layer affects the available space for user messages, which further affects the maximum depth of the WSN. To this end, this paper discusses how to determine the maximum depth of a WSN in given network topologies. For a better understanding of the analysis of the maximum network depth, OpenWSN [1] is used as an example WSN throughout this paper to explain how the above-mentioned factors consume the space. OpenWSN currently adopts 6LowPAN [7] as the adaptation layer and uses 6LoRH [8] to generate SRH. We adopt the simulator of OpenWSN to conduct experiments for the validation of our analysis.

The remainder of this paper is organized as follows. Section 2 describes the analysis of the maximum depth of a practical WSN. Section 3 describes the experimental methodology and results. Finally, Sect. 4 concludes this study and indicates the intended direction of future research.

2   Analysis of Maximum Depth of WSN

When a source host outside a WSN sends a user message to a sensor node inside the WSN, downward routing is performed to forward the message from the root of the WSN to the sensor node. In OpenWSN, the structure of a data frame for the above-mentioned user message is shown in Fig. 1. According to all the related standards and specifications, only the MAC footer field has a fixed length of 2 bytes. The lengths of all the remaining five fields in Fig. 1 should be variable. Thus, it is difficult to derive the maximum length of the SRH, which further determines the maximum depth of the WSN. However, the lengths of the UDP header and the compressed IPv6 header are currently fixed due to the simplified implementation of OpenWSN. When routing downwards, the UDP header is not compressed and the IPv6 header is compressed from 40 bytes to 36 bytes. In addition, the length of the MAC header is also fixed to 21 Bytes due to the simple network configuration. Since all nodes join the same PAN, i.e. personal area network, the addressing mode of the MAC header remains identical.

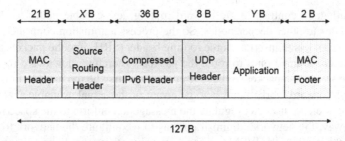

Fig. 1. The structure of a data frame using downward routing. Its source is a host outside a WSN and its destination is a node inside the WSN.

Now, only the SRH filed and the application protocol data unit (APDU) have variable lengths. Since the maximum length of the APDU can be determined by the manual of the WSN application, the maximum length of SRH can be calculated by the following equation where X is the length of the SRH and Y is the length of the APDU.

$$X = 127-21-36-8-Y-2 = 60-Y. \tag{1}$$

After determining the maximum length of the SRH, the maximum depth of the WSN can be derived based on the collected network topology and the SRH structure as shown in Fig. 2. The first byte of the SRH is a 6LoWPAN dispatch indicating the following values have to be parsed according to 6LoRH. One or several *Type-Length-Value* (TLV) field(s) will follow the dispatch. The Length field consists of a *Critical Format* field and a *Type Specification Extension* (TSE) field. In OpenWSN, TSE field is used as a Size, which will be explained later. The *Type* field can have five different values, which are 0, 1, 2, 3, and 4. The length of the *Value for the type* field is determined by the TSE value and the Type value.

Name	6LoWPAN Paging Dispatch	Critical Format	Type Specific Extension	Type	Value for the type	
Length	1 Byte	3 bits	5 bits	1 Byte		...
Value	F1H	100_2		0, 1, 2, 3, 4		...

Type-Length-Value (TLV) field   Other TLV fields

Fig. 2. The structure of the source routing header specified by 6LoRH.

The value of the *Type* field indicates the similarity of the IPv6 addresses of two consecutive nodes, i.e. two nodes of one hop, on the path towards the destination node.

If the most significant 15 bytes of their IPv6 addresses are the same, the value of the *Type* field is 0. If the length of the identical parts is 14, 12, or 8 bytes, the value will be 1, 2, or 3 respectively. For the remaining cases, the value will be 4.

The *TSE* field encodes the number of hops with the same type minus 1. Figure 3 shows an example network to explain how to determine the value of the *TSE* field. In the example, the PC sends a message to mote 5. Since the compressed IPv6 header can teach the mote 4 to forward the packet to the mote 5, the SRH should contain only the routing rules for three hops: (1) one from the PC to the mote 2; (2) one from the mote 2 to the mote 3; and (3) one from the mote 3 to the mote 4. Note that the wired link connects the data link layers of the PC and the root. Hence, the first hop should be from the PC to the mote 2. Usually, the IPv6 address of the PC differs a lot from the nodes of the WSN. So, the type of the first hop is usually 3 or 4. Since only the least significant one byte of the nodes of the second hop and the third one is different, the type of the other two hops is 0. Therefore, the *TSE* fields of the first TLV field should be 0, which is 1 minus 1. The *TSE* fields of the second TLV field should be 1, which is 2 minus 1.

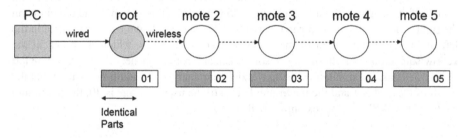

Fig. 3. Example network for describing the value of the TSE field. The mote 5 is the destination node while the PC is the source node. The most significant 15 bytes of the IPv6 addresses of all the wireless nodes are identical. They only differ in the least significant one byte.

The *Value for the type* field records the compressed IPv6 addresses of the destination nodes of the hops of the same type in the same *TLV* field. For example, assume that the IPv6 address of the PC is bbbb::1 and the one of the mote 2 is bbbb::1415:92cc:0:2, the *Value for the type* field of the first *TLV* field is 1415:92cc:0:2. For the second *TLV* field, the *Value for the type* field contains one byte of value 0x03 followed by one byte of value 0x04.

3   Experiments

We adopt the simulator, OpenSim, provided by OpenWSN to validate our analysis. The network topology and the IPv6 address configuration is shown in Fig. 3. Besides, the PDR (Packet Delivery Ratio) of each wireless link is set as 1. That is, all frames can be successfully transmitted except collision occurs. Figure 4 shows the network topology displayed in the user interface of the OpenWSN simulator.

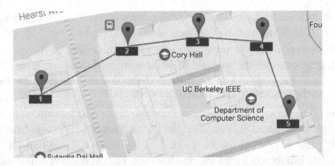

Fig. 4. Topology displayed in the user interface of the OpenWSN simulator. There are five wireless nodes. Besides, the PC is not shown in the user interface.

After all the nodes join the WSN, we send some messages from the PC to the mote 5. According to our analysis, the length of the SRH will be 15. Thus, the maximum available space for user messages will be 45 bytes. Figure 5 shows the simulation results. If the length of the user message is 45 bytes, which is shown in the red circle on the right of Fig. 5, the mote 5 can receive the message, as shown in the red circle in the left of Fig. 5. If the length of the user message is 46 bytes, which is shown in the yellow square on the right of Fig. 5, some critical errors happened, as shown in the left of Fig. 5. Thus, the simulation results validate our analysis. In addition, assume that the depth of the root is 1 and the maximum length of the user message is 40, the maximum depth of the WSN, in this example, will be 10.

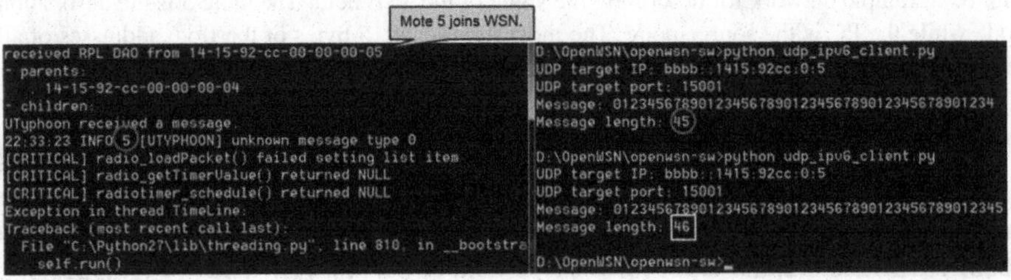

Fig. 5. Simulation results.

4   Conclusions

In this paper, we analyze the relationship between the maximum depth of a wireless sensor network and the maximum length of user messages. The knowledge is helpful for network administrators to configure their network topology. The simulation results prove the correctness of our analysis.

Acknowledgements. The authors would like to thank the Ministry of Science and Technology, Taiwan, R.O.C., for supporting this research under grant MOST 105-2221-E-167-035.

References

1. Watteyne, T., et al.: OpenWSN: a standards-based low-power wireless development environment. Trans. Emerg. Tel. Tech. **23**, 480–493 (2012)
2. Song, J., Han, S., Mok, A.K., Chen, D., Lucas, M., Nixon, M.: WirelessHART: applying wireless technology in real-time industrial process control. In: 2008 IEEE Real-Time and Embedded Technology and Applications Symposium, pp. 377–386 (2008)
3. Yu, Y.S.: A framework supporting centralized routing in multi-hop TSCH networks. IJ3C **4**, 27–34 (2015)
4. Contiki: The Open Source OS for the Internet of Things. http://www.contiki-os.org/
5. Winter, T., et al.: RPL: IPv6 routing protocol for low-power and lossy networks. RFC 6550 (2012)
6. IEEE Std 802.15.4TM-2006: Wireless Medium Access Control (MAC) and Physical Layer (PHY) Specifications for Low-Rate Wireless Personal Area Networks (LRWPANs) (2006)
7. Hui, J.W., Thubert, P.: Compression format for IPv6 datagrams over IEEE 802.15.4-based networks. RFC 6282 (2011)
8. Thubert, P., Bormann, C., Toutain, L., Cragie, R.: 6LoWPAN routing header. draft-ietf-roll-routing-dispatch-05 (2016)

Poster and Demo

Lightweight, Low-Rate Denial-of-Service Attack Prevention and Control Program for IoT Devices

Chi-Che Wu[1]([⊠]), Wei Yang Wang[2], and Rung-Shiang Cheng[3]

[1] Department of Electrical Engineering,
National Kaohsiung University of Applied Sciences, Kaohsiung, Taiwan
jerry@gm.kuas.edu.tw
[2] Department of Information Management,
National Kaohsiung University of Applied Sciences, Kaohsiung, Taiwan
wyang@gm.kuas.edu.tw
[3] Department of Computer and Communication, Kun Shan University,
Tainan, Taiwan
rscheng@mail.ksu.edu.tw

Abstract. As information technology has become more advanced, the Internet of things (IoT) has evolved from being a mere concept to becoming a part of everyday life. IoT-based home appliance applications have matured, and numerous relevant software programs have been made commercially available. Therefore, IoT-created security issues have become an issue that must be addressed. Although DoS attacks are one of the most commonly used methods by hackers to attack target hosts, most mainframe computers are equipped with excellent DoS attack prevention and control programs. Nevertheless, most IoT devices do not have high computing power and are thus prone to DoS attacks. Therefore, this study examined the feasibility of using a lightweight, low-rate DoS attack prevention and control program in IoT devices with low computing power. The objective is to enable these devices to prevent and control DoS attacks.

Keywords: HTTP/2 · Denial-of-service attacks
Low-rate denial-of-service attacks · Information security

1 Introduction

In recent years, the Internet of things (IoT) has been widely used in smart homes and in the field of industrial control. IoT embodies the concept of creating a network in which everything is connected. For users, the IoT provides a novel way of interacting with devices. The interaction process includes collecting relevant data; The use of IoT in the field of industrial control is even more prevalent than that in smart homes. For instance, smart factories add numerous sensors to relevant equipment. When the equipment malfunctions, the networking devices send warning messages through wireless transmission to inform users of the abnormal situation, achieving early disaster prevention.

In general, devices connected to an IoT-based network contain a network component with data transmission capability. In addition, several sensors that have

© ICST Institute for Computer Sciences, Social Informatics and Telecommunications Engineering 2018
Y.-B. Lin et al. (Eds.): IoTaaS 2017, LNICST 246, pp. 243–247, 2018.
https://doi.org/10.1007/978-3-030-00410-1_29

dissimilar goals or purposes are installed. These sensors are comparable to human senses and can be used to collect relevant data in surrounding environments.

2   Background Information

2.1   From the IoT to the WoT

The conventional IoT involves the use of numerous sensors that transmit related data to a cloud platform through a network device. Users who need to control or access relevant data can do so by connecting to the cloud platform and accessing inquired data. The Physical Web program introduced by Google in 2014 specified that all sensors and devices have URLs, which are the basis of connection in the web environment; these URLs are connected to physical devices to allow users to quickly control and use the devices.

2.2   Hypertext Transfer Protocol 2

The HTTP/2 request process differs from that of HTTP/1.1. For instance, HTTP/1.1 establishes 6–8 TCP connections to speed up the inquiry time, whereas HTTP/2 establishes only one TCP connection so as to reduce the burden on servers. After a TCP connection is established, browsers can establish multiple noninterfering streams and use the smallest unit frame to allocate the request content, facilitating browser–server communications (Fig. 1) [3–5].

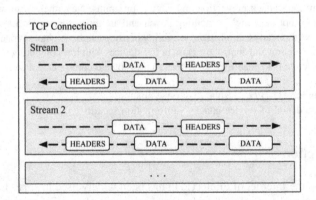

Fig. 1. HTTP/2 request submission process

2.3   DoS Attacks

Low-rate DoS attacks are a variation of DoS attacks; they attack by continuously sending a small number of network packets to attack server response times or buffer zones, causing depletion of server resources, resulting in service termination [6–8].

A study on low-rate DoS attacks on HTTP/2 services [1] confirmed that HTTP/2 security is at risk of low-rate DoS attacks. In such attacks, a virtual host using a type 1 ping and WINDOW_UPDATE frame defined by HTTP/2 attacks the virtual server. In the experiment of the aforementioned study, the degree of CPU depletion, size of the network packets received per second, and number of network packets received per second were used as a basis for assessing low-rate DoS attacks [1].

3   System Framework and Design

This study designed lightweight DoS-attack prevention and control programs for IoT devices that support WoT functions. Because RESTFul is the primary method for facilitating communication between devices, this study focused on designing a program that protects HTTP from low-rate DoS attacks.

HTTP/2 is the latest version of HTTP. Compared with HTTP/1.1, it has superior transmission capacity and lower power consumption. However, HTTP/2 is prone to low-rate DoS attacks. Thus, this study designed a defense mechanism in which the server firewall records the frames requested by users within a set time period (10 and 20 ms in this study) and identifies whether the frames are repeats and thereby pose a risk of a low-rate DoS attack. If the two criteria are met, the firewall initiates a filtering process (Fig. 2), which reduces the impact of the attacks on other users.

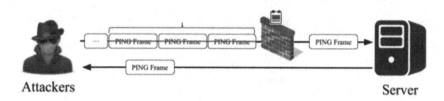

Fig. 2. Defense procedure

4   Performance Assessment

4.1   Average Time Required to Send and Receive Network Packets and the Final Network Packet Return Time

In this experiment, users were divided into two groups: attackers and legitimate users. The attackers initiated their attacks by continuously sending PING frames, whereas the legitimate users browsed webpages of all five types. A TCP connection was established every time a user visited a webpage. Once a connection was established, ten header frames were sent, which were then received and responded to in order to establish a new TCP connection. To prevent unclosed TCP connections from affecting the experimental results, signals indicating a closed TCP connection were sent to servers prior to completing new TCP connections. Users were required to wait 1 s before browsing the next webpage. Each experiment was performed 30 times (Fig. 3).

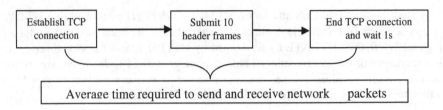

Fig. 3. Experiment procedure

4.2 Experiment Results

Experiment was performed to verify whether introducing the defense mechanism could effectively reduce the effect of attackers on legitimate users' usage experience. Similarly to Experiment 1, measurements from the experimental trials were listed in ascending order, and the 10 middle values were averaged to plot Fig. 4. The two graphs reveal that the defense mechanism effectively lowered the risk of a successful attack.

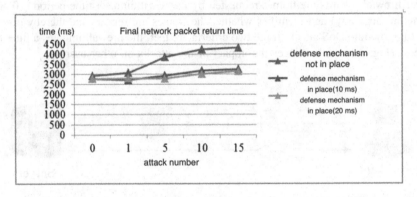

Fig. 4. Final network packet return time, with the defense mechanism used

5   Conclusion

HTTP/2 has special functions such as multiplexing and stream prioritization. However, although HTTP/2 has numerous advantages, studies have revealed that it also has several problems, one of which is its security. Therefore, this study conducted a series of experiments to explore this issue. The first experiment confirmed the existence threats to HTTP/2 security, which have also been identified in previous studies. Thus, the experimental results of this study offered two major contributions. The first is the revelation that the higher the number of attackers, the longer the amount of time is required for legitimate users to load webpages and that the effect is strongest when loading high-performance webpages. The second major contribution is the proposed defense mechanism that was verified in the second experiment; this mechanism can effectively reduce the effect of attackers on the usage experience of legitimate users.

References

1. Adi, E., et al.: Low-rate denial-of-service attacks against HTTP/2 services. In: 2015 5th International Conference on IT Convergence and Security (ICITCS), pp. 1–5. IEEE (2015)
2. Kuzmanovic, A., Knightly, E.W.: Low-rate TCP-targeted denial of service attacks: the shrew vs. the mice and elephants. In: Proceedings of the 2003 Conference on Applications, Technologies, Architectures, and Protocols for Computer Communications, pp. 75–86. ACM (2003)
3. Berners-Lee, T., Fielding, R., Frystyk, H.: Hypertext Transfer Protocol – HTTP/1.0, RFC 1945 (1996)
4. Fielding, R., et al.: Hypertext Transfer Protocol – HTTP/1.1, RFC 2616 (1999)
5. Chowdhury, S.A., Sapra, V., Hindle, A.: Is HTTP/2 more energy efficient than HTTP/1.1 for mobile users? PeerJ PrePrints **3**, e1571 (2015)
6. Grigorik, I.: Making the web faster with HTTP 2.0. Commun. ACM **56**(12), 42–49 (2013)
7. Varvello, M., et al.: To HTTP/2, or not to HTTP/2, that is the question. arXiv preprint arXiv: 1507.06562 (2015)
8. Belshe, M., Thomson, M., Peon, R.: Hypertext Transfer Protocol Version 2 (HTTP/2), RFC 7540 (2015)

Special Session: Security and Privacy in Internet of Things, Services and People (SP-IOTSP 2017)

An Optimized Implementation of Speech Recognition Combining GPU with Deep Belief Network for IoT

Weipeng Jing[1,2(✉)], Tao Jiang[1], Mithun Mukherjee[2], Lei Shu[2,3],
and Jian Kang[1]

[1] College of Information and Computer Engineering, Northeast Forestry University,
Harbin, China
{weipeng.jing,taojiang920619,laurelkang}@outlook.com
[2] Guangdong Provincial Key Laboratory on Petrochemical Equipment Fault
Diagnosis, Guangdong University of Petrochemical Technology, Maoming, China
{m.mukherjee,lei.shu}@ieee.org
[3] School of Engineering, University of Lincoln, Lincoln, UK

Abstract. With the advancement in Internet of Things (Iot), the speech recognition technology in mobile terminals' applications has become a new trend. Consequently, how to accelerate the training and improve the accuracy in speech recognition has attracted the attention of academia and industry. Generally, Deep Belief Network (DBN) with Graphic Processing Unit (GPU) is applied in acoustic model of speech recognition, critical research challenges are yet to be solved. It's hard for GPU to store the parameters of DBN at one time as well as GPU's shared memory is not fully used. And parameters transmission have become a bottleneck in multi-GPUs. This paper presents a new method in which the weight matrix is divided into sub-weight matrices and established a reasonable memory model. To eliminate the inefficient idle-state during data transfers, a stream process model is proposed in which the data transfer and kernel execution are performed simultaneously. Further, apply the optimized single GPU implementation to multi-GPUs and is intend to solve the parameters transmission. Experimental results show the optimized GPU implementation without violating the size limitation of GPU's memory.

Keywords: IoT · Speech recognition · DBN · GPU
Parallel computation · Mobile computing

1 Introduction

Internet of things (Iot)[1] has obtained grateful development, it has been applied in various fields. Mobile computing, as a important part of IoT, has attracted many people. Speech recognition of mobile computing is especially important for IoT. Therefore how to improve the training speed of speech recognition has

© ICST Institute for Computer Sciences, Social Informatics and Telecommunications Engineering 2018
Y.-B. Lin et al. (Eds.): IoTaaS 2017, LNICST 246, pp. 251–260, 2018.
https://doi.org/10.1007/978-3-030-00410-1_30

become one of important research topics in IoT. The traditional Gauss Mixture Model and Hidden Markov Model (GMM-HMM) [2] is a typical shallow learning structure and its performance is limited under the massive data. Deep learning which was pointed by Hinton et al. [3] is useful when training massive data by "layer-by-layer initialization". Deep Belief Network (DBN), a deep neural network, consists of Restricted Boltzmann Machine (RBMs) and is widely used in speech recognition. Microsoft researchers applied the RBM and DBN into the training of speech recognition's acoustic model, and have made great success on large scale vocabulary continuous recognition task [4]. However, training complexity limits its application in the mobile computing.

Graphic Processing Unit (GPU) has advantages of higher computing density and smaller size, which has been widely used in the field of speech recognition. GPU is applied to large vocabulary continuous speech recognition in [5] and has achieved better acceleration effect compared to Multi-CPUs. CuBLAS is used for training RBM to accelerate and has achieved good results in [6]. The GPU kernels are written in [7] to accelerate the training speed of RBM, but it's too complex and the scalability is not strong. Moreover, there are a large number of parameters in RBM model.

In summary, this paper is mainly focused on the training of speech recognition based on DBN using single GPU without the limitation of DBN model's parameters and the method is applied to multi-GPUs. In addition, a suitable memory model of GPU is designed utilizing the full computing capability of GPU to accelerate the DBN training speed with low word-error-rate.

2 DBN Training

The training process of DBN model in speech recognition mainly contains layer-wise greedy unsupervised learning in pre-training and supervised learning in fine-tuning.

2.1 Pre-training of DBN

Contrastive Divergence (CD) algorithm [8] is used for unsupervised training in each layer of RBM. Each layer of RBM receives the output values of the previous layer as the input value, then the output values are propagated in RBM. Finally the output values are used as the input value of the next layer RBM. The main objective of the pre-training is to retain the characteristic information of the training speech data's feature vectors while they are mapped to the different feature spaces.

Restricted Boltzmann Machine (RBM). RBMs are the key components of the DBN with a greedy learning algorithm. A RBM is an energy-based generative model that consists of two layers: (1) a layer of binary *visible* units and (2) a layer of binary *hidden* units, with symmetrical connections. Any unit in one layer is connected to all units in the other layer and has no connection with units in the same layer.

Considering RBM's special structure, given a particular random input configuration v_i, all the hidden units h_j, are independent of each other. As a result, the probability of h_j given v_i becomes

$$P(h_j = 1|v) = sigm \left(\sum_{i=1}^{m} W_{ij}v_i + b_j \right), \tag{1}$$

where $sigm(\cdot)$ is the sigmoid function. Similarly, the probability of v_i given a specific hidden state h_j is

$$P(v_i = 1|h) = sigm \left(\sum_{j=1}^{n} w_{ij}h_j + a_i \right). \tag{2}$$

Contrastive Divergence (CD) Algorithm. Pre-training is used to adjust the trained speech data. To obtain the value of θ in RBM, a much faster method, Contrastive Divergence (CD-k) algorithm [9] is used with k-parameter as 1. According the CD-k algorithm, the update rules are used as follows:

$$\Delta W_{ij} = \varepsilon(\langle v_i^{(0)}, h_j^{(0)} \rangle, \langle v_i^{(k)}, h_j^{(k)} \rangle), \tag{3}$$

$$\Delta a_i = \varepsilon(\langle v_i^{(0)}, v_i^{(k)} \rangle), \tag{4}$$

$$\Delta b_j = \varepsilon(\langle h_j^{(0)}, h_j^{(k)} \rangle), \tag{5}$$

Taking into account the scale of the trained speech data, part of trained speech data are taken as mini-batch [7] rather than every sample of trained speech data. To reconstruct v_i using CD algorithm, it is important to consider binary hidden states.

2.2   Fine Tuning of DBN

Initial values of the entire DBN model's parameters are obtained after pre-training. The fine tuning is performed on the speech data in which each frame is labeled with a target class label. The fine-tuning process is divided into two steps as: firstly, the extracted features of speech-data from the last layer of RBM are used as input values to the BP neural network, afterward, the output values are classified by the `softmax` function; secondly, cross-entropy [10] is used as the loss function for error calculation in BP algorithm that adjusts the parameters of whole DBN model.

As BP algorithm needs a long time to update θ, SGD algorithm is used to reduce the time. After completing the speech features' classification of a mini-batch, θ is directly updated using the calculated error to accelerate the training speed in DBN.

3   GPU Implementation of Proposed Algorithm

The proposed CD-k algorithm for large-scale RBMs was implemented on Compute Unified Device Architecture (CUDA)[1] of NVIDIA GPU, which benefits graphic rendering with massive parallelism. Although GPU can achieve remarkable performance for DBN under reasonable task decomposition of RBM and memory optimization [12], advantages of GPU's memory architecture are still not fully exploited for parallel DBN. To use the GPU to accelerate the training of DBN model, the optimization of RBM's training using GPU is implemented for three aspects: based on (1) memory model with sliced weight matrix, (2) multi-streams processing model on single GPU and (3) the multi-GPUs implementation.

3.1   Memory Model Based on Sliced Weight Matrix

The training speed of RBM can be improved by training the data with size of l. However, there still exists a problem that the large size of l will hurt the overall efficiency of learning. So in the training process, the size of l chosen is much smaller than the m, n, v_i, h_j, bias a_i and bias b_j are small so that they can store in the GPU device memory. However, the weight matrix is so large due to interconnection between any two units, it is likely to occur the phenomenon the weight matrix cannot store in GPU device at one-time. Also there are also other parameters in RBM especially the some speech signals will be trained at one time rather than one. So weight matrix is divided into many sub-weight matrices $W_i \in R^{m\prime \times n}$ where $m\prime << m$ such that every W_i could be stored in the GPU device memory. The sub-weight matrices will be determined by experiments, which also means the size of $m\prime$.

The trained DBN model's parameters are copied from CPU to GPU after having divided the weight matrix into sub-weight matrices. Using (1) and (2), $h_j^{(0)}$ and $v_i^{(k)}$ are calculated. When calculating $h_j^{(0)}$ with GPU, in order to hide the global memory latency, threads are needed to use at a much finer granularity to take full use of the GPU computing resources. Hence, the connection $w_{ij} \in W_i$ is taken as the smallest unit of computation which is called thread performing a function that multiples the v_i by its weight. Every block can be represented a unit by this way. Then, $h_j^{(0)}$ is calculated.

As for the calculation of $v_i^{(k)}$, the weight matrix is divided into W_i and transferring W_i one by one on demand. However, the transfer of W_i would cost lots of time, a method is adopted that avoids the undesirable memory transfer of W_i. Because the calculation of $v_i^{(k)}$ and $h_j^{(0)}$ use the same W_i, the $v_i^{(k)}$ will be

---

[1] In 2006, a parallel computing platform and programming model for NVIDIA GPUs named CUDA [11] was introduced aiming to make full use of computing power of GPUs to achieve general purpose computation. CUDA also enables programmers without any knowledge about graphic APIs to write C/C++ code for high performance scientific computation by using NVIDIA GPUs. Therefore, it is widely used in speech recognition based on DBN model.

calculated immediately after the calculation of $h_j^{(0)}$. In this way, $v_i^{(k)}$ calculation is done along with $h_j^{(0)}$ using the W_i that are already loaded and the second transfer is no longer needed, also it reduces the time of thread synchronization, accelerating the speed of RBM's training.

The same method is used to calculate $h_j^{(k)}$. After $h_j^{(k)}$ is finished, W_i is updated immediately as the updating W_i needs the corresponding $v_i^{(k)}$ and $h_j^{(k)}$ according to (3), saving another transfer of W_i for updating current W_i. Also the updating of W_i needs $h_j^{(k)}$, $h_j^{(0)}$, $v_i^{(k)}$, $v_i^{(0)}$ matrices.

3.2 Parallel Processing Based on Streams Process

The GPU implement of RBM using memory model based on sliced weight matrix has accelerated the speed. But the memory transfer becomes a major problem to reduce the training speed. For example, updating every W_i requires two memory transfers of CPU to GPU and one memory transfer of GPU to CPU. However, GPU simply keeps idling when these memory transfers occur, as a result, the GPU does not use the threads to calculate the task to be executed.

To make full use of GPU's computing resources and eliminate this inefficient idle-state, the streams process of CUDA are used to do concurrent execution of threads. There are two aspects in streams process: firstly, data transfers and kernel executions are executed concurrently in the same stream; secondly, launch multiple streams and overlapping CUDA operations in different streams to achieve concurrency execution. In our algorithm, potential concurrency exits in the two for-loops. With multiple streams launched and each responsible for a subset of W_i. The process of training RBM in opCD-k algorithm has following steps:

- *Step 1:* Copy the data from CPU to GPU,
- *Step 2:* Calculate $h_j^{(0)}$,
- *Step 3:* Calculate $v_i^{(k)}$ after k iterations of Gibbs sampling,
- *Step 4:* Calculate $h_j^{(k)}$,
- *Step 5:* Update the parameters $\theta = \{w_{ij}, a_i, b_j\}$, and
- *Step 6:* Transfer the results from GPU to CPU.

Combining the stream process of CUDA and opCD-k algorithm, it is evident that Step 1 and Step 2 could achieve concurrency execution in a stream; Step 2 and Step 3 could run concurrently as long as the computing resources on GPU allows; Step 1 and Step 6 can be performed concurrently in different streams.

3.3 Multi-GPUs Implementation

The two methods proposed above will improve the DBN's training speed. But single GPU's computation is limited. So in order to improve the speed of DBN's training, the multi-GPUs will be used. In Speech Recognition, due do the full connection of DBN model, it would cost much time to use model parallelism,

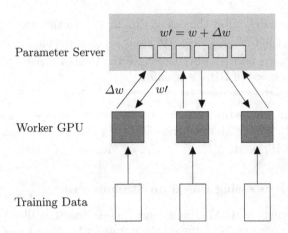

Fig. 1. Data parallelism with parameter server in multi-GPUs.

so the data parallelism is widely used. In this paper, we use parameter server to do DBN's training with multi-GPUs which are in a machine. As shown in Fig. 1, it is the data parallelism with parameter server in multi-GPUs. One GPU is chosen as parameter server. It receives one iteration's result of the parameters of DBN model from other GPUs, and it will do the update of the parameters and transfer them to the GPUs, so that the GPUs could do other iteration calculations. Under this circumstance, the bandwidth of the parameter server becomes a bottleneck.

So the total communications should be reduced. We can reduce the communication frequency by large the size of batch. But when the size of batch is too large, the data cannot store in GPU device. So we divide the batch with fetch × mini-batch. The size of mini-batch data will be copied to GPU, and copied fetch times. The result will not transfer to the parameter server instead they will be added at the local GPU. After fetch times, the final summation will be transferred to the parameter server. When deciding the size of fetch, the method of hot start is adopted. By this way, the communication frequency can be greatly reduced.

4　Experimental Results and Analysis

To verify the acceleration effect of DBN using the optimized GPU method. The input data are the 440-dimensional speech features which are spliced by 40-dimensional fMLLR features. The fMLLR features are obtained by the process of speech recognition toolkit Kaldi [13].

There are six layers of RBM in DBN model. The parameters in the two different stages of DBN model are different. The first layer of RBM is Gaussian-Bernoulli distribution, and others are Bernouli-Bernouli distributions. The Intel(R) Xeon(R) CPU E5-2620 v2 has 128G memory with a frequency of

2.10 GHZ, four GPUs which is called Tesla K20m which has 5G memory are used in the multi-GPUs. The version of operation system is Red Hat Enterprise Linux Server release 6.4, the CUDA Tookit is 7.0.

4.1   Parameters Tuning of OpCD-K Implementation

opCD-k implementation relies on weight slicing technique requiring a second transfer of W_i. In addition, stream synchronization and scheduling will introduce more overhead. All these new features of opCD-k may cause low performance. So the parameters must be set reasonable.

The Size of slice_size. The relations of the parameters in opCD-k algorithm can be described as:

$$s \times slice\_size \times n \times sizeof(float) \leq GPU\_memory \qquad (6)$$

where dev_meme is GPU memory available for storing weight matrix W_i and slice_size is the rows of each W_i. We explored different combinations of these parameters. Assuming a fixed amount of device memory, which is a common case given a particular GPU, an optimal combination of s and slice size is desirable. In this experiment, we assume the device memory limits us to load only one forth of a weight matrix $W^{1024 \times 1024}$. Multiple configurations satisfying s × slice_size = 1024/4 are valid such as 3×100, 4×75 and 5×60. The chosen value is that 300 is about equal to 1024/4 for calculation. We tried a set of configurations and draw a conclusion from the result in Fig. 2 that neither large slice with few streams nor small slice with numerous streams is a good choice. From the figure we can clearly observe the training time with the configurations change. And the 4×75 is the best choice for the experiment.

4.2   RBM Training Time Evaluation

We conduct an experiment to evaluate the training time of RBM. Results of the experiment can visually reflect the performance of DBN with optimized single GPU implementation.

RBM Training Time. Experiments are conducted to compare the training time spent on one iteration of RBM with the 440 visible units and different hidden units in three different ways as follows: (1) the optimized GPU implementation with 1/4 memory usage and five streams, (2) the implementation with single GPU as in [7], and (3) the implementation of Kaldi with single GPU. Figure 3 illustrates the training time with various number of hidden units for three cases. It is observed that the cost increases with the increase of hidden units. At first, the first way spends the most time because it need more time to exchange the weight matrix and streams synchronization. however, with the increment of the number of hidden units, the first way costs less time than the others. The reason is that the first way uses reasonable memory model and streams process. The first way achieves acceleration with a maximum time of 1.7 than the third way when the number of hidden units is 2^{13}.

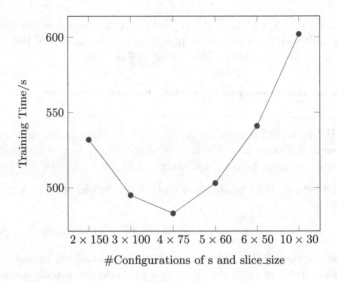

Fig. 2. Performance of different configurations of s and slice_size given $s \times slice\_size = 300$ on a RBM of 1024×1024.

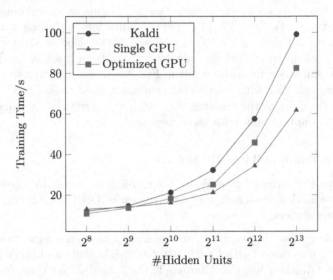

Fig. 3. RBM's training time after one iteration.

4.3 Performance of OpCD-K on DBN with Multi-GPUs

Training Time and word error rate are another two important factors to evaluate the performance of DBN. So we conduct the following experiments.

Training Time and Word Error Rate of DBN with Multi-GPUs. DBN training time is evaluated in four different ways listed in Table 1. It is observed that

Table 1. DBN'S training time with multi-GPUs

Model	Time/hour
Kaldi with single CPU	2.5
Kaldi with multi-GPUs	0.728
Multi-GPUs implementation in [14]	0.65
Optimized GPU implementation with multi-GPUs	0.54

the multi-GPUs implementation has greatly reduced the time of training DBN, which the time cost is only 0.52 h. It has achieved about 1.35 times and 1.2 times comparing with the Kali implementation and GPU implementation in [14]. Also it obtains the acceleration of 4.6 times than using the Kaldi with single GPU. Therefore, the optimized GPU implementation with multi-GPUs makes a great acceleration on training DBN model.

In the experimental part of the word error rate. It is observed from Table 2 that the optimized GPU implementation only has a 7% and 5% performance loss comparing with Kaldi with single GPU and multi-GPUs respectively.

Table 2. Training DBN's word error rate with multi-GPUs

Model	Error rate
Kaldi with single GPU	18.8%
Kaldi with multi-GPUs	19.3%
Multi-GPUs implementation in [14]	23.1%
Optimized GPU implementation with multi-GPUs	20.2%

5   Conclusion

This paper presents an efficient parallel algorithm to overcome the problem of huge parameters and unreasonable usage of GPU's memory model while accelerating the computation speed of speech recognition in wireless networks based on DBN. Aiming to fully utilize GPU's computing resources, we divide the weight matrix into sub-weight matrices to parallel the RBM's training for large parameters. In order to optimize the training of RBM, we adopt multi-streams processing model for single GPU. In addition, to cope with the limitations of a single GPU computing capability, We extend from single GPU to multi-GPUs to achieve better results. The future work includes to parallelize the computation of DBN on GPU-accelerated cluster to model large-scale problems under noisy environment.

Acknowledgement. The work described in this paper is supported by Guangdong Provincial Key Laboratory of Petrochemical Equipment Fault Diagnosis, Guangdong University of Petrochemical Technology (GDUPTKLAB201502) and Special Fund for Forest Scientific Research in the Public Welfare (201504307).

References

1. Gubbi, J., Buyya, R., Marusic, S., Palaniswami, M.: Internet of things (IoT): a vision, architectural elements, and future directions. Future Gen. Comput. Syst. **29**(7), 1645–1660 (2013)
2. Su, D., Wu, X., Xu, L.: GMM-HMM acoustic model training by a two level procedure with Gaussian components determined by automatic model selection. In: IEEE International Conference on Acoustics Speech and Signal Processing, pp. 4890–4893, Texas, USA, March 2010
3. Hinton, G.E., Salakhutdinov, R.R.: Reducing the dimensionality of data with neural networks. Science **313**(5786), 504–507 (2006)
4. Seide, F., Li, G., Yu, D.: Conversational speech transcription using context-dependent deep neural networks. In: Conference of the International Speech Communication Association (INTERSPEECH), Florence, Italy, pp. 437–440, August 2011
5. Sainath, T.N., Kingsbury, B., Ramabhadran, B., Fousek, P.: Making deep belief networks effective for large vocabulary continuous speech recognition. In: Proceedings of Automatic Speech Recognition and Understanding, pp. 30–35, December 2011
6. Raina, R., Madhavan, A., Ng, A.Y.: Large-scale deep unsupervised learning using graphics processors. In: Proceedings of International Conference on Machine Learning (ICML), Montreal, Quebec, Canada, pp. 873–880, June 2009
7. Lopes, N., Ribeiro, B.: Towards adaptive learning with improved convergence of deep belief networks on graphics processing units. Pattern Recogn. **47**(1), 114–127 (2014)
8. Hinton, G.E.: Training products of experts by minimizing contrastive divergence. Neural Comput. **14**(8), 1771–1800 (2002)
9. Swersky, K., Chen, B., Marlin, B., De Freitas, N.: A tutorial on stochastic approximation algorithms for training restricted Boltzmann machines and deep belief nets. In: Information Theory and Applications Workshop, pp. 1–10, January 2010
10. Deng, L., Togneri, R.: Deep dynamic models for learning hidden representations of speech features. In: Ogunfunmi, T., Togneri, R., Narasimha, M. (eds.) Speech & Audio Processing for Coding Enhancement & Recognition, pp. 153–195. Springer, Heidelberg (2015). https://doi.org/10.1007/978-1-4939-1456-2_6
11. NVIDIA. What is CUDA (2006)
12. Wang, Y., Tang, P., An, H., Liu, Z., Wang, K., Zhou, Y.: Optimization and analysis of parallel back propagation neural network on GPU Using CUDA. In: Arik, S., Huang, T., Lai, W.K., Liu, Q. (eds.) ICONIP 2015. LNCS, vol. 9491, pp. 156–163. Springer, Cham (2015). https://doi.org/10.1007/978-3-319-26555-1_18
13. Povey, D., et al.: The Kaldi speech recognition toolkit. IDIAP Publications (2012)
14. Xue, S., Yan, S., Dai, L.: Fast training algorithm for deep neural network using multiple GPUs. J. Tsinghua Univ. (Sci. Technol.) **53**(6), 745–748 (2013)

Invited Papers

An Adaptive Solution for Images Streaming in Vehicle Networks Using MQTT Protocol

Ming-Fong Tsai[1]([⊠]), Thanh-Nam Pham[2,3], Fu-Hsiang Ching[2], and Le-Hung Chen[4]

[1] Department of Electronic Engineering, National United University,
Miaoli, Taiwan
mingfongtsai@gmail.com
[2] Department of Information Engineering and Computer Science,
Feng Chia University, Taichung, Taiwan
[3] Department of Electronics and Communications Technology,
Thai Nguyen University of Information and Communications Technology,
Thái Nguyên, Vietnam
[4] Image Processing Section, Advanced Engineering Division,
Hua-chuang Automobile Information Technical Center Company,
Taichung, Taiwan

Abstract. In this study, we explored solutions to improve the quality of real-time image transmission in vehicle networks. We deployed multiple cameras in each vehicle to collect scene data on the road. Then, the collected data was transmitted to a streaming server through a gateway and using a 4G internet connection. We use the MQTT protocol to implement our system since this is a protocol designed specifically for Internet of Things technologies and has several advantages in terms of image streaming. In addition, in order to adapt to the change in bandwidth channel due to the movement of vehicles, we propose an algorithm to control the quality of image capture which is based on threshold levels. This algorithm is based on the current throughput of local network nodes, as compared with threshold values, to control the rate of sending data from each local node in subsequent transmissions. The results of simulation show that our proposed network significantly reduces both end-to-end delay and the delay in arrival of messages in the network when the number of nodes increases. The experimental results showed that the collected images are of high quality and allow accurate analysis of the surrounding environment of the moving vehicles.

Keywords: Internet of vehicles · MQTT protocol · 4G network
Image streaming

1 Introduction

In recent years, systems for driving assistance and the monitoring of vehicles have become increasingly prevalent, and now involve many types of applications, such as emergency vehicle notification systems, collision avoidance systems and car navigation systems. These systems are characterized by the use of Internet of Things (IoT) technology combined with wireless communication protocols. These protocols are generally

© ICST Institute for Computer Sciences, Social Informatics and Telecommunications Engineering 2018
Y.-B. Lin et al. (Eds.): IoTaaS 2017, LNICST 246, pp. 263–275, 2018.
https://doi.org/10.1007/978-3-030-00410-1_31

mobile ad hoc networks (VANET) or Mesh networking for short-range communications, and WiMAX (IEEE 802.16) or Global System for Mobile Communications 3G for long-range communications. These systems collect data from sensors and cameras placed on vehicles or roadside units and combined with the use of a GPS device can support driving safety applications and other related systems. However, these forms of communication have several disadvantages such as large delays and high rates of data loss. Today, fourth-generation telecommunications technology (4G) has been implemented which has high data transmission rates. This has enabled the development of a variety of services built for on-road users, particularly real-time video streaming services. The 4G network covers Taiwan, and in this country we have developed and implemented an intelligent system for monitoring vehicles, using a network of cameras installed on the vehicles. The captured images are transmitted to a cloud streaming server using the Message Queuing Telemetry Transport (MQTT) protocol. Unlike other implemented systems such as [1, 3], our system uses a Raspberry Pi platform as local nodes mounted on each individual vehicle; each node is connected to a camera, collects data from the camera and directly transmits these data to the cloud server using the 4G network. MQTT [7] is a publish/subscribe messaging protocol for constrained Internet-of-Things devices and unstable networks such as VANETs, which have high latency, low-bandwidth and unreliable channels. Thus, the MQTT protocol is an ideal approach for machine-to-machine applications, such as those reported in [4–7]. However, in contrast to these studies, we have used the MQTT protocol in VANETs for real-time image streaming, with Raspberry Pi modules functioning as IoT nodes.

In this study, we organized each vehicle as a local IoT network. In particular, the cameras as the IoT nodes are located at different locations on the vehicle to collect data surrounding the vehicle. In each local IoT network, nodes send data to a streaming server via a gateway and use the MQTT protocol. We deployed many Raspberry Pi modules to monitor and control the data collection at IoT nodes. To adapt to the changes of available bandwidth due to the constantly changing channels and movement of vehicles, we have developed an algorithm that enables the system to automatically control the quality of the captured image in the cameras, based on the current throughput of capturing nodes. The total throughput of all capturing nodes on a vehicle is divided into threshold levels. When the total throughput is small, corresponding to a low threshold level, the quality of the captured images is reduced accordingly; when the total throughput is large, corresponding to a high threshold level, the quality of capturing images is increased to match. This enables the system to constantly adapt to changes in the channel.

Since there are a high number of captured images from the cameras, the use of a traditional server by the system would require too much processing time, making it slow to respond in real time. However, the recent development of cloud computing technology allows the processing of large amounts of data and fast responses in real time. The proposed system uses a cloud streaming server to reduce response time and allow the expansion of the management system to larger numbers of vehicles. The remainder of this paper is organized as follows: Sect. 2 provides a description of the proposed system architecture and its components. Section 3 describes the analysis of the system and its performance parameters. Section 4 reports the implementation of the system and the results of simulation. The last section presents the conclusion

2 System Architecture

2.1 System Overview

Figure 1 describes the overview of the architecture of the proposed system. The system includes local MQTT client nodes installed in a vehicle, an MQTT broker (gateway) and a cloud server.

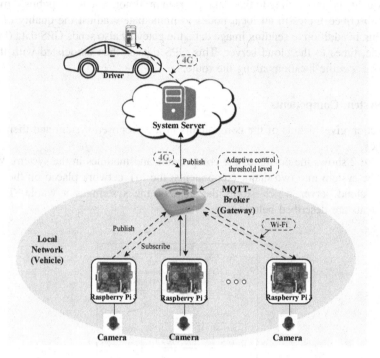

Fig. 1. Overview of the architecture of the proposed system.

In this system, each local node (MQTT Client) is connected to a camera. Cameras are mounted on the vehicle to capture images of the environment surrounding the vehicle. In our experiments, between one and six cameras were installed on a vehicle. The MQTT clients were connected to a MQTT broker through wi-fi connections. Each MQTT client registers a topic ID in the MQTT broker, and this registration process is referred to as subscribing. Each MQTT client sends data frequently to the subscribed topic in the MQTT broker. Our topic is formatted as vehicles/car-ip/node-ip, where each car has a unique identifier, and each MQTT client connected to a capturing camera also has a unique identifier. The MQTT broker acts as a gateway in this system. The MQTT broker receives real-time data from local nodes and forwards this to a cloud streaming server. When data is received, the cloud server checks its format; if correctly formatted, the server begins live-streaming data. When the user wants to view the real-time streaming data of the car, access to the streaming server follows the URI path of resources, and users can access the system resources through a web browser running on their smartphones. The system requires user's smartphone to have a 4G connection. In addition to the transmission of image data, the node also sends information about its data speed to the gateway. The gateway is responsive to the adaptive adjustments to the quality of image capturing at all connecting nodes. After receiving information on the data speed of all local nodes, the gateway calculates the total current data speed over these nodes and compares it with pre-defined threshold levels to determine whether the image quality corresponding to that data rate is high; if not, it sends a 'publish' message to all subscribed topics in all local nodes to immediately adjust the quality of image capturing. In addition to sending image data, the gateway also sends GPS data (latitude, longitude, time) to the cloud server. This GPS data is then associated with the live images of specific locations along the route.

2.2   System Components

This section gives details of the components in the proposed system and their related processes.

Figure 2 shows the details of the components and modules in the system. We can divide the system into two major components: the IoT network placed on the vehicle and the cloud server which stores the data of the system as a whole. The sub-components are described below.

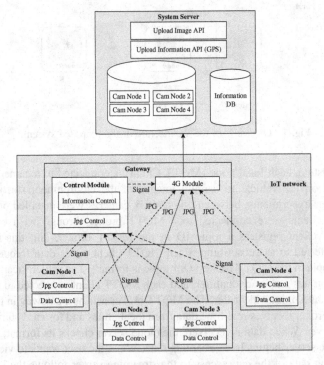

Fig. 2. Components/modules of the proposed system.

Cam Nodes. In the proposed system, the hardware platforms used to implement these cam nodes are the Raspberry Pi 3 and the Pi camera. First, a cam node connects to the gateway and initializes the environment variables. When ready, the system begins a routine periodic calculation, and the result returned is the threshold level of the subscribed channel. A cam node has two primary activities: listening and publishing. Initially, the value of threshold level is set to Level 4, which corresponds to the value of Level 95 in the JPEG image compression standard. In view of the characteristics of 4G channels, five threshold levels are used here to divide the quality of the input images into Levels 1 to 5, corresponding respectively to Levels 1, 25, 50, 95 and 100 of the JPEG standard. A greater value of the threshold level means a higher quality of image capture. When a cam node is informed of which threshold level to use, it acquires images with a size based on this threshold level. Finally, the local node begins publishing images to the subscribed topic ID in the MQTT broker. The number of images captured is also published to the MQTT broker, with an average of 8–10 images per second.

The gateway collects information about the speed of data streaming from these cam nodes and calculates the total amount of their data throughput from which to perform adaptive control. The control information will be sent back from the gateway to these nodes, and the cameras will proceed to adjust the quality of the collected image based on the control data.

Gateway. The gateway acts as a local wireless access point for the MQTT clients to connect to it via a wi-fi connection, and then connects to the cloud server via the 4G network. Thus, MQTT clients can send data to the online server. In addition, the gateway also acts as a controller which can make decisions on changing the rate of data transfer at each cam node. The hardware platform used in this system is a Raspberry Pi 3 combined with a 4G module.

The initialization processes of the gateway and the local nodes are very similar. Firstly, several environment variables are initialized and the data rate of each local node (node-rate) is subscribed. This subscription allows the gateway to monitor the current throughput of each node, indicated by the parameter node-rate. Following this, the gateway evaluates the information from all existing nodes, and determines whether the total throughput is higher or lower than the current threshold value. Following this, the new threshold level is decided based on this comparison. The gateway then publishes the new threshold level to all the connecting nodes. On receiving the new threshold level, local nodes adjust the image capturing based on this level. In addition to sending data to the server, the gateway also includes GPS data (latitude, longitude) to the MQTT server to provide information about the current location of the vehicle on the road.

System Server. The system server is a streaming server. Streaming server will receive data from the MQTT clients and display in real time to users through a web interface. The streaming server is composed of three functional components: the *blackhole* function, the *streaming* function and the *GPS* function. The *blackhole* function checks the format of the uploaded images. If the format is correct, these images will be saved in the storages. The *streaming* function is responsible for displaying real-time image data to the user with very small latency. The *GPS* function helps to store geographic information about the current location of the driver and of the network nodes to display combined with the image data.

2.3   MQTT Message Processes

The MQTT protocol primarily operates based on the exchange of data in the form of messages. It uses publish and subscribe methods to exchange these messages, which are similar to the response and request methods of the HTTP protocol. In this section, a detailed description is presented of the process of exchanging messages, as shown in Fig. 3. The message flows are divided into three links: the first is between cam node and gateway; the second is between gateway and server; and the third is between server and user.

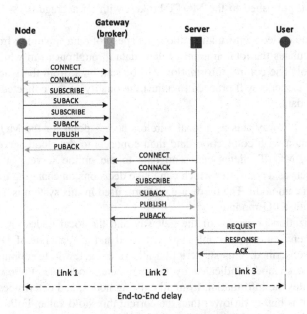

Fig. 3. Processes of message exchange in the proposed system.

When the cam node sends data to a subscribed channel, it can select one of three levels for quality of service (QoS) transmission: these levels are QoS0, QoS1 and QoS2. QoS0 means that the broker/client will deliver the message once, with no confirmation; QoS1 means that the broker/client will deliver the message at least once, with confirmation required; and QoS2 means the broker/client will deliver the message only once, using a four-step handshake [4]. The choice of QoS level will affect the performance of the system.

3 System Analysis

The performance of the system is analyzed based on metrics such as TCP end-to-end throughput, TCP end-to-end delay, arrival delay of messages (jitter), packet delivery ratio and packet drop rate.

3.1 Arrival Delay of Messages (Jiiter)

This section, we consider the arrival delay between messages generated by the cam nodes. Consider the case where the cam nodes, the gateway and the server are synchronized in time. The messages are generated using a generator with a constant rate and published to the MQTT broker (gateway). These messages arrive at the server with a varying delay depending on the network conditions. For two consecutive messages received by server, the arrival time of message n is denoted by t_n. The inter-message production period is denoted by T. With reference to [5], the inter-arrival jitter time J_n between message n and message $n - 1$ is given by:

$$J_n = t_n - t_{n-1} - T \tag{1}$$

Using the values of the inter-arrival timestamps in each message, the jitter value of two consecutive messages can be calculated. The proposed system is implemented in the 4G network, with a channel bandwidth of between 20 Mbps and 100 Mbps in the case of high mobility. The experimental results show that this jitter value is on the order of a few milliseconds and is therefore very close to zero, thus enabling high quality image streaming.

3.2 TCP End-to-End Delay

We define end-to-end delay as transmission delay denoting the time needed to transmit data from the cam node to the user. As shown in Fig. 3, assuming that data have been published on a given topic in the gateway:

$$t_{arr(i)\_topicID} < t_{req(i)\_topicID} < t_{arr(i+1)\_topicID} \tag{2}$$

where $t_{arr(i)\_topicID}$ is the time at which the ith data is published to this topic ID and $t_{req(i)\_topicID}$ is the time of the request for the ith data. This request should be made after the ith data is present; if the request is made before the data is available, the system waits for a short period, and this increases the end-to-end delay of the system. This delay arises from several factors such as packets being dropped in the queue or network congestion.

The end-to-end delay from the cam node to the user can be calculated as:

$$\Theta_{end-end} = \sum_{i=1}^{N} \left(D_{trans(i)} + D_{prop(i)} + D_{proc(i)} + D_{queue(i)} + D_{TA(i)} \right) \tag{3}$$

where N is the number of links. There are three links in our system. D_{trans} is the transmission delay, and is proportional to the length of the message. The transmission delay is considered here in the cam node, the gateway and the server. D_{prop} is the propagation delay, and depends on the physical length of the link. D_{proc} is the processing delay, which is the time required for processing the message header. We assume that D_{proc} is small compared with other network delays and can therefore be neglected. D_{queue} is the queuing delay, which is the time a message waits in a queue before being executed. In this system, the message waits in both the queue of the gateway and the queue of the server. D_{TA} is the turn-around time delay, which denotes the delay in adapting to a request for data from a specific topic ID. The queuing delay and the turn-around time delay depend on the size of the queue length.

The equation for computing the end-to-end delay can be rewritten to follow the flow of the message as:

$$\Theta_{end-end} = D^{N\text{-}G}_{CONNECT\text{-}TCP} + 2 \times D^{N\text{-}G}_{SUB\text{-}TCP} + D^{N\text{-}G}_{PUB\text{-}TCP} + D^{G\text{-}S}_{CONNECT\text{-}TCP}$$
$$+ D^{G\text{-}S}_{SUB\text{-}TCP} + D^{G\text{-}S}_{PUB\text{-}TCP} + D^{S\text{-}U}_{REQ\text{-}RES} + D_{queue} + 2 \times D_{TA} \tag{4}$$

where $D_{CONNECT\text{-}TCP}$, $D_{SUB\text{-}TCP}$ and $D_{PUB\text{-}TCP}$ form the round-trip TCP delay when the MQTT protocol is used. $N\text{-}G$, $G\text{-}S$ and $S\text{-}U$ are the connections between the cam node and gateway, gateway and server, and server and user respectively. $N\text{-}G$ is the Wi-Fi connection, and $G\text{-}S$ and $S\text{-}U$ are 4G connections. $D^{S\text{-}U}_{REQ\text{-}RES}$ is the round-trip TCP delay when the HTTP protocol is used to transmit data to the user from the server.

Considering the round-trip time delay (RTT) of TCP, with re-transmission if packet loss takes place, we can obtain:

$$\Theta_{end-end} = 4 \times RTT^{NG}_{TCP} + 3 \times RTT^{GS}_{TCP} + 2 \times RTT^{SU}_{TCP} + D_{queue} + 2 \times D_{TA} \tag{5}$$

3.3 TCP Throughput, Packet Delivery, Packet Dropped Rate

The TCP throughput represents the total amount of transmitted data per second from sources to the server. The TCP throughput is normally calculated in bit/sec, and depends on various parameters such as the error rate of the channel, the bandwidth of the channel, packet size, queue size and the number of cam nodes. The evaluation of TCP throughput is given in Sect. 4. Theoretically, the TCP throughput is calculated as follows:

$$TCPthroughput = \frac{Total\ number\ of\ received\ bits(N)}{period\ of\ time\ (\tau)} \tag{6}$$

where N is all the bits received at the destination node over a period of time τ. In this system, the value of throughput is based on adjusting the quality of image capturing in the source node, as described above.

The packet delivery ratio (PDR) denotes the ratio of total packets received by the destinations to those generated by the sources. It can be expressed by the following formula:

$$PDR = \frac{Total\,number\,of\,received\,packets\,(N_r)}{Total\,number\,of\,generated\,packets\,(N_g)} \tag{7}$$

Its value describes the state of the channel in terms of the error rate, network congestion and queuing overflow. The analysis of packet delivery ratio is also carried out in the following section, which describes the simulation results. Packet drop rate is a parameter that denotes the number of packets lost during end-to-end transmission. An M/M/1 queue, the probability of packet drop, is calculated by:

$$P = (1 - \rho)\rho^k \tag{8}$$

where $\rho = \frac{\mu_c}{\mu_s}$ is the system factor.

4   Implementation and Performance Evaluation

4.1   Experimental Results

In this implementation of image streaming using the MQTT protocol, MQTT Version 3.1.1 [8] was used. MQTT is an open-source message broker service that uses the MQTT protocol to send and receive messages from MQTT clients.

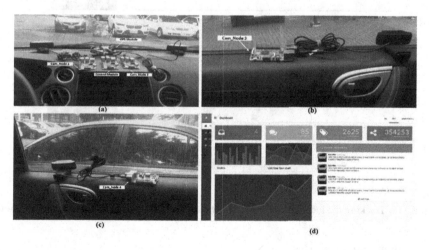

Fig. 4. Implementation of the proposed system: (a) cam nodes (Raspberry Pi 3) mounted at the front of the car; (b) a cam node mounted on the right side of the car; (c) cam node mounted on the left side of the car; (d) website interface.

Figure 4 illustrates the implementation of local nodes. Four Raspberry Pi 3 machines were mounted as cam nodes on a car. Each Raspberry Pi is connected to a camera to process the images captured by this camera. MQTT Mosquitto [8] was installed on each Raspberry Pi for image-streaming application. Figure 4(a) shows cam nodes 1 and 2, the GPS module and control module placed at the front of the car. Figure 4(b) shows cam node 3, placed at the right of the car; Fig. 4(c) shows cam node 4, placed at the left of the car; and Fig. 4(d) shows the website interface. The top-right corner of the web interface shows the storage for all the locations of and images from the vehicle; the middle of the web interface shows statistics on driving history; and the right-hand interface is the recent timeline history. Figure 5(a) shows the GPS route that the user has taken on Google maps. Figure 5(b) describes the normal view of the user web interface for two cam nodes placed at the front and back of the vehicle.

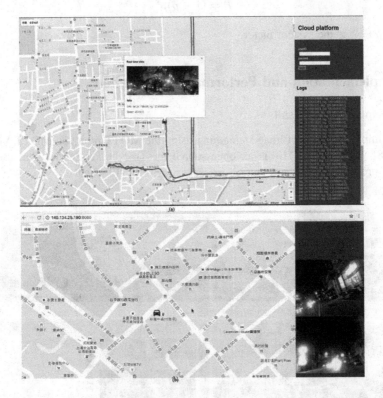

Fig. 5. (a) Tracking the location of the user on the road; (b) image streaming in the user's view.

4.2 Simulation Scenarios

To simulate the proposed architecture, we used the Network Simulation 2 (NS2.35) tool, and its configuration is shown in Table 1. The simulation scenario is described as follows: A local IoT network of cam nodes is connected to a 4G network for data transmission. Cam nodes in the local network will send data to the gateway through a Wi-Fi connection. The connection from the gateway to the server is a 4G connection. The gateway will connect to a base station called the eNB node, and this eNB node will be connected to the server via a wired connection with a delay of 2 ms. The simulation of our 4G network is based on the study in [9].

Table 1. Simulation settings.

Parameter	Value
Network area	1500 × 1500 m
Simulation time	100 s
Error model	Uniform random distribution
Number of nodes	{1, 2, 3, 4, 5, 6}
Channel	802.11
Bandwidth	11 Mb
Data rate	11 Mbps
Traffic type	Constant bit rate (CBR)
Packet size	1500 bytes
Routing protocol	AODV
Transport protocol	TCP Reno
Bandwidth AP – eNB	20 Mbps
Bandwidth eNB – server	100 Mbps
Propagation delay eNB – server	2 ms

To analyze the performance of the network, trace files were generated after each simulation scenario in the NS2 simulator. A traffic generator was used with constant bit rate (CBR) and was attached to each TCP flow with sending rate corresponding to the experimental values as described in Sect. 4.1. The results of the simulation show that the obtained TCP throughput of our network is very close to the experimental results. Figure 6(a) shows the total throughput of the network as the number of nodes is increased.

In Fig. 6(b), (c), we change the length of the queue and change the number of nodes to evaluate the performance of the system. Figure 6(b) describes a comparison of the end-to-end delay of the normal network and the proposed network when the number of cam nodes is increased. The TCP end-to-end delay is calculated as discussed in Sect. 3.2. From the simulation results, we can see that the end-to-end delay values of the proposed network and the normal networks are approximately the same when the number of nodes is small; when the number of nodes is increased, the proposed network has a significantly reduced end-to-end delay than the normal network. Because the normal network will have a high packet drop rate when the channel conditions change, thus leading to more retransmissions and increasing the latency. Figure 6(c) describes the analysis of the packet drop rate. It can be seen that the proposed network keeps a smaller packet drop rate than the normal network. That is because with the proposed network, we can adjust the arrival rate, thus reducing the congestion at the queues and leading to lower packet drop rate.

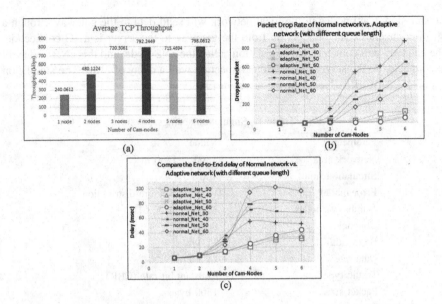

Fig. 6. (a) Network throughput for various numbers of cam nodes; comparison between the adaptive network and normal network for changes in queue length and number of cam nodes: (b) end-to-end delay; (c) packet drop rate.

5 Conclusion

The objective of this study is to introduce a system of smart monitoring cameras. Our system can automatically adjust the quality of streaming image capture to adapt to changes in the data rate of the channel due to the movement of vehicles. We propose dividing the uploading throughput into levels by which the quality of image capture can be controlled. An IoT network was set up in which each normal node was a Raspberry Pi, and these nodes were connected to a gateway to transfer data to a cloud streaming server using the MQTT protocol. Our implementation shows that this system consistently gives accurate information about the route through the captured images. This information can help enable driving safety applications such as risk warning and collision avoidance. The simulation results show that our adaptive control algorithm significantly reduced end-to-end delay by up to 65% when the number of nodes was increased and is thus very suitable for data streaming applications in intelligent transport systems. In the near future, we will focus on adding multi-hop functionality to the network architectures when considering the interaction between vehicles, improving the quality of images collected based on determining the optimal values of thresholds, and also extending the system with a greater number of nodes.

References

1. Wark, T., Corke, P., Karlsson, J., Sikka, P., Valencia, P.: Real-time image streaming over a low-bandwidth wireless camera network. In: 3rd International Conference on Intelligent Sensors, Sensor Networks and Information, pp. 113–118 (2007)
2. Bhatt, A., Patoliya, J.: Cost effective digitization of home appliances for home automation with low-power WiFi devices. In: International Conference on Advances in Electrical, Electronics, Information, Communication and Bio-Informatics, pp. 643–648 (2016)
3. Yaqub, M.A., Ahmed, S.H., Bouk, S.H., Kim, D.: FBR: fleet based video retrieval in 3G and 4G enabled vehicular ad hoc networks. In: IEEE ICC 2016 – Communication QoS, Reliability and Modeling Symposium (2016)
4. Tekin, Y., Sahingoz, O.K.: A publish/subscribe messaging system for wireless sensor networks. In: Sixth International Conference on Digital Information and Communication Technology and its Applications (DICTAP) (2016)
5. Luzuriaga, J.E., Cano, J.C., Calafate, C., Manzoni, P.: Handling mobility in IoT applications using the MQTT protocol. In: Internet of Things Technologies and Applications (2015)
6. Luzuriaga, J.E., Perez, M., Boronat, P., Cano, J.C., Calafate, C., Manzoni, P.: A comparative evolution of AMQP and MQTT protocols over unstable and mobile networks. In: 12th Annual IEEE Conference on Consumer Communications and Networking Conference (CCNC) (2015)
7. Govinda, K., Azad, A.P.: End-to-end service assurance in IoT MQTT-SN. In: 12th Annual IEEE Consumer Communications and Networking Conference (CCNC) (2015)
8. MQTT Mosquitto Version 3.1.1 Homepage. http://mosquitto.org/. Accessed 22 Dec 2016
9. Abed, G.A., Ismail, M., Jumari, K.: Traffic modeling of LTE mobile broadband network based on NS-2 simulator. In: 3rd International Conference on Computational Intelligence, Communication Systems and Networks (2011)

Development of Path Planning Approach Based on Improved A-star Algorithm in AGV System

Yan Zhang[1], Ling-ling Li[2], Hsiung-Cheng Lin[3(✉)], Zewen Ma[1],
and Jiang Zhao[1]

[1] School of Electrical Engineering,
Hebei University of Science and Technology, Shijiazhuang 050018, China
[2] Department of the Electronic Information Engineering,
Hebei University of Technology, Tianjin 300130, China
[3] Department of Electronic Engineering,
National Chin-Yi University of Technology, Taichung 41170, Taiwan
hclin@ncut.edu.tw

Abstract. Automate guide vehicle (AGV) has been widely applied in industry. Therefore, it is important to design a highly efficient AGV. The path planning is known as one of the key factor for AGV operation. Although typical A-star algorithm with a heuristic mechanism can be used in the shortest path searching, it may suffer from broken lines and redundant nodes. In this paper, an improved A-star algorithm is presented. Based on the initial path planned by A-star algorithm, traversing all the nodes on an initial path and deleting unnecessary nodes and connections, the proposed model can remove the superfluous inflection points and redundant nodes effectively so that no obstacles exist during AGV moving. The performance results reveal that the proposed method can provide more efficient path planning with a shorter route and less turn times.

Keywords: Automate guide vehicle (AGV) · A-star algorithm
Floyd algorithm · Path planning

1 Introduction

In recent years, AGV has been widely in a warehouse or other areas. It is known that the transport efficiency is determined by an effective path plan [1–3]. For this reason, it is an indispensable task to find the efficient path for AGV. It is found that one of the biggest challenge is how to eliminate the excess inflection points in the path and effectively improve the efficiency of transport. An algorithm for solving optimal path planning problems was reported based on parameterization method and fuzzy aggregation [1]. A genetic algorithm was also used to find an effective path planning in a mobile robot [2]. Another path planning for AGV transport system was studied in a manufacturing environment recently [3]. In this study, it is more focused on AGV system operated in a warehouse environment. An improved A-star algorithm is proposed to present an effective path planning than traditional methods.

Y.-B. Lin et al. (Eds.): IoTaaS 2017, LNICST 246, pp. 276–279, 2018.
https://doi.org/10.1007/978-3-030-00410-1_32

2 Algorithm Principle

A-star algorithm is a heuristic search algorithm to find the node with the least cost by traversing the surrounding nodes, and the target point can be achieved from next node searching [4–6]. Evaluation function $F(n)$

$$F(n) = G(n) + H(n) \tag{1}$$

Where n is the node that is currently being expand. $G(n)$ is the distance from the start node to the current node n along the planned path. Heuristic function $H(n)$, $H(n)$ is the minimum cost estimate from the node n to the end node, and less than the actual cost.

Define the coordinates of the current node n and target node to be (x_1, y_1) and (x_2, y_2)

$$H(n) = sqrt \left[(x_1 - x_2)^2 + (y_1 - y_2)^2 \right] \tag{2}$$

$$F(n) = G(n) + sqrt \left[(x_1 - x_2)^2 + (y_1 - y_2)^2 \right] \tag{3}$$

2.1 A-star Algorithm Flow

The open table and the close table are applied to store the information of nodes, which include the nodes in the planed path and surrounding nodes, the open table store the information of minimum cost and the close able store the node in the planed path.

(1) Place the start node into the open table and calculate $F(n)$. (2) Place the node with the minimum $F(n)$ in the open table and the $F(n)$ into the close table, if the node is the start node, place the start node and the its $F(n)$ into the close table. (3) Determine whether the current node in the close table is end node, if the node is end node, the A-star algorithm is finished, and if not, go to the step 4. (4) Expand the surrounding nodes by unit step, calculate their $F(n)$ and place the nodes and $F(n)$ of the nodes into open table. (5) Sort the surrounding nodes in the open table according to $F(n)$ and return to the step 2 (Fig. 1).

2.2 The Principle of Improved A-star Algorithm

In this paper, the nodes planned by A-star algorithm were quadratic programmed by Floyd algorithm which is used to smooth the A-star algorithm [3]. The improved A-star algorithm consists of two parts: the first one is traversing all the nodes from an initial path, merging the path node on the same line, and the last part is deleting the nodes which prolong the length of initial path with no obstacle existing on the line connected nodes.

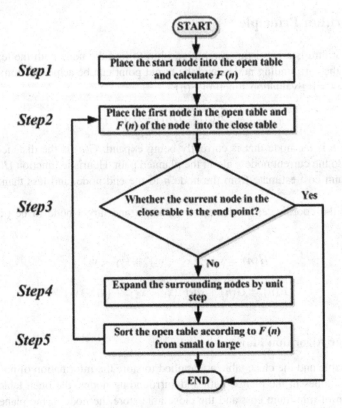

Fig. 1. A-star algorithm flow

3 Performance Results and Analysis

For this study, the warehouse map shown in Fig. 2 is simulated by MATLAB from an actual AGV warehouse environment, where the black grids represent the obstacles, and the red line is the path of AGV moving. The AGV paths planned by traditional A-star algorithm and improved A-star algorithm are shown in Fig. 2a, b, respectively. It is obvious that the proposed improved A-star algorithm indicates a better solution, i.e., shorter route. Also, the turn times from the A-star algorithm is 4, but the improved A-star algorithm requires only 3 times. The comparison of performance efficiency for AGV is shown in Table 1.

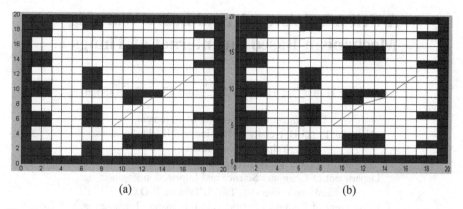

(a)   (b)

Fig. 2. Comparison of the path of A-star algorithm and improved A-star algorithm. (a) A-star algorithm (b) improved A-star algorithm

Table 1. The comparison of performance efficiency for AGV.

Algorithm	The length of path	Turn times
A-star	11.98	4
Improved A-star	10.78	3

4 Conclusions

In a warehouse environment, it is important for AGV to choose an effective path so that the transport efficiency can be increased. The proposed improved A-star algorithm proves that it can eliminate the excess inflection points in the path and provide more effective path plan than traditional A-star algorithm in the transport system. Therefore, the proposed model is feasible to be applied to AGV path plan in industry.

References

1. Zamiriam, M., Kamyad, A.V., Farahi, M.H.: A novel algorithm for solving optimal path planning problems based on parameterization method and fuzzy aggregation. Phys. Lett. A **373**(38), 3439–3447 (2009)
2. Panda, R.K., Choudhury, B.B.: An effective path planning of mobile robot using genetic algorithm. IEEE Int. Conf. Comput. Intell. Commun. Technol. **145**(15), 287–291 (2015)
3. Zhong, J.: Path planning of AGV transport subsystem in manufacturing environment. Mech. Des. Manuf. (2), 237–239 (2010)
4. Huating, T., Tao, L., Ying, Q.: Research on path search of four-way mobile robot based on improved A-star algorithm. Control Des. **6**, 1007–1012 (2017)
5. Jing, M., Jiabin, W., Xue, Z.: Application of A-star algorithm in vehicle path planning. Comput. Technol. Dev. **11**, 155–156 (2016)
6. Tan, Y., Li, Y.: Unmanned aerial vehicle path planning based on A-star algorithm in the complex environment. Syst. Eng. Electr. **6**, 1270–1273 (2017)

A Self-administered Healthcare Warning Mechanism Based on Internet of Things

Lun-Ping Hung[1]([✉]), Hsiu-An Lee[2], and Chien-Lian Chen[3]

[1] Department of Information Management,
National Taipei University of Nursing and Health Sciences,
Taipei, Taiwan, R.O.C.
lunping@ntunhs.edu.tw
[2] Department of Computer Science and Information Engineering,
Tamkang University, Taipei, Taiwan, R.O.C.
[3] Department of Computer Science and Information Engineering,
Aletheia University, Taipei, Taiwan, R.O.C.

Abstract. In view of today's society of advanced medical technology and popularity of social networking, remote home care will become the new stream of health care services. In this paper, the medical resources and information technology were combined to set up a self-administered healthcare warning mechanism. Through wireless transmission, patients' psychological status can be monitored at home. Under the event-driven mode, appropriate professional medical advice and response measures were proposed so that the subjects could safely and effectively engage self-care at home under the support of information technology. Depending on individuals' needs, information technology can reduce the care costs and enhance the medical service quality, thereby achieving the goal of seamless integration of the health care system both inside and outside the hospital.

Keywords: Home care · Electrocardiogram (EKG) · Vital sign
Internet of Things

1 Introduction

In the rapidly changing information society, the pace of life has rapidly accelerated. Long-term negligence of health is likely to lead to the happen of Cardiovascular diseases 0. In order to ensure a seamless integration of health care system for post-operative patients with cardiovascular disease and hospital care, doctors will recommend a healthcare mode outside the hospital based on the evaluation of patients' conditions. Subacute care is a comprehensive inpatient care and is designed for patients with acute illness, injuries, or aggravated diseases. It is a type of target-oriented treatment aimed at assisting patients through the stage of disease to recovery. Patients can return home or be admitted to nursing home when their conditions are stabilized.

Accompanied by the rising needs of mobile hospital and home nursing, the concept of telecare arises. The origin of this concept can be traced back to the term of eHealth that is defined as the application of Internet and other related technologies in the

Y.-B. Lin et al. (Eds.): IoTaaS 2017, LNICST 246, pp. 280–285, 2018.
https://doi.org/10.1007/978-3-030-00410-1_33

healthcare industry to improve the quality of clinical process [2]. Nowadays, equipments used in telecare adopt wireless sensor that enables users to collect vital signs including heart beat, pulse, glucose, and blood pressure and to transmit these information through mobile devices to medical institutions where doctors can grasp patients' current condition based on received information 00. Through the hard device to receiving the vital sign of patient, we develop an intelligent platform with the module of self-administered healthcare warning mechanism to warnings users when their health condition appears abnormal phenomenon and inform them their health require extra attention.

This paper is organized as follows. Section 2 describes the entire self-administered healthcare warning mechanism in detail. In Sect. 3, we describe the result of our simulation experiment. Discussion and conclusion are in Sect. 4.

2 Methodology

In order to monitor the condition of Cardiovascular diseases patient effective and abiding and offer the appropriate nursing process promptly. The application of information technology will be the most important part in this study.

This section will be distributed into three parts. The selection of hard device and the method of vital sign measurement and recording function will describe in Sect. 2.1. Section 2.2 will be the boundary of warning mechanism and the process will describe in Sect. 2.3.

2.1 Vital Sign Measurement and Recording Function

This research has applied the wireless vital sign receiver to grasp the condition of patient and transmit to the platform through the wireless. After measuring and uploading the vital signs, the user can self-inspect his health status. As shown in Fig. 1, if any figures were out of boundary, the system will show up the warning message below. After measuring the vital signs, the results were uploaded to the medical

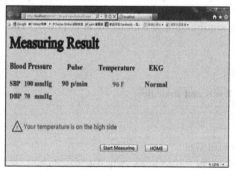

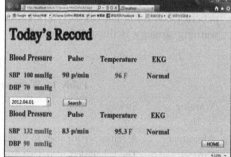

Fig. 1. Vital sign measuring and recording function – measuring result

Fig. 2. Vital sign measuring and recording function – health record

database in hospital, and the health record in the system was updated. As shown in Fig. 2. The user may also search the measurement records of the previous days through the system.

2.2 Critical Value Warning Function

In general, in addition to EKG monitoring, the postoperative home care patients' other vital signs such as: respiration, temperature, pulse, blood pressure, and blood oxygen should be measured. The vital signs are subject to changes due to the human health status and amount of activity and these vital signs are correlated. For instance, if a person experiences shortness of breath, this person's blood flow and oxygen supply capacity will be changed, resulting in the blood pressure and blood oxygen volume are not in the standard ranges. Therefore, to assess whether or not a person's physiological function is normal and healthy, depending on one type of vital sign value is not enough to make the right judgments. Clinically, multiple vital sign data is used to perform diagnosis. However, based on a person's physiological status, past medical history, and family medical history, the vital sign health standards and critical value ranges differed for every individual, no single standard value is sufficient for the respective monitors to determine whether the health of the patient is in "safe" or "critical" condition.

In view of this, the threshold values of the vital signs adopted for patient's discharge assessment on this platform are the warning threshold values for the previous month and based on the doctor's judgment after comparing the assessment setting values at the time of discharge and user's vital signs measured during the first month, patient's vital sign health standards were reset or adjusted. In the phase of system initialization, an emergency contact person was set and patient and contact person were notified of the possible conditions and disposal in consideration to the warning degree. The warning mechanism is divided into three degrees: abnormal, critical, and urgent. The "abnormal" warning tones sent out by the system is when patient's vital signs have not been received yet. It acts as a reminder for patients to measure their vital signs. The "critical" warning tones sent out by the system is when the patient's health status becomes severe, which may jeopardize patient's life if an immediate disposal is not done. Therefore, the critical warning degree is further divided into critical and urgent, the former is when the doctor deems it necessary for the patient to return to the hospital for checkup before the next scheduled appointment while the latter is when the patient's condition is extremely critical and requires immediate medical attention. The warning strategy is illustrated in Table 1.

Table 1. Warning levels and strategies

Warning levels	Strategy
Abnormal	A reminder for user to collect vital sign
Critical	The scheduled next-visit appointment shifted to an early date based on doctor's diagnosis
Urgent	Requiring immediate medical attention based on doctor's diagnosis

2.3　The Process of Warning Mechanism

The flowchart of warning mechanism process is shown in Fig. 3. If the system does not receive daily vital sign values, the receiving device hold by user will send out two short waning sounds that each lasts for three seconds to remind patient to measure vital signs. After receiving the measured data, the system will record the message received. If the data is not received within 15 min, the system will send SMS to the emergency contact person whom will be requested to check the patient's condition and confirm whether the patient has experienced severe physical discomfort or to further assist the patient in eliminating obstacles during the measurement, uploading data, or sending notification for emergency rescue. In case of severe physical discomfort, the healthcare system will immediately send SMS and transmit patient's medical records to the attending physician who will then determine if the patient required immediate medical attention and engaged in follow-up rescue. If the patient does not require immediate medical attention, the doctor will then make a decision based on the patient's condition to see if the patient needs an early next-visit or engage in simple emergency disposal at home.

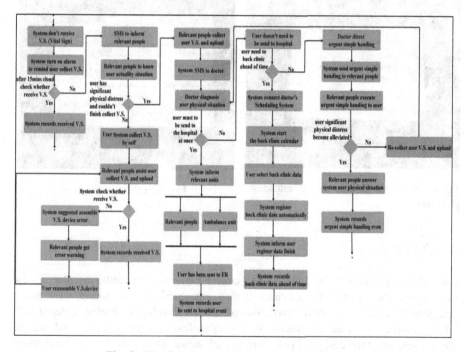

Fig. 3. The flowchart of warning mechanism process

3 Simulation

This section will simulate the situation when the system received an abnormal figure and triggered the process of warning mechanism. Also, we assumed the user's condition is not available to measuring the vital sign by themselves.

After 15 min system triggered the first time warning to patient and still don't receive the update figures. System will send a message to the relevant people. When relevant people upload the newest vital sign, the system will sent an order request to the attending physician to decide whether the patient should sent to the hospital at once. As shown as Fig. 4. Suppose the decision of physician is unnecessary, but the patient have to back to clinic ahead of the next appointment. System will check the appointment of physician and send the recommended schedule for patient to register. As shown as Fig. 5.

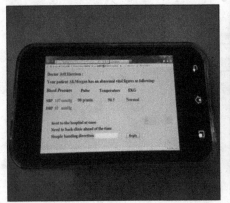

Fig. 4. An order request to the attending physician

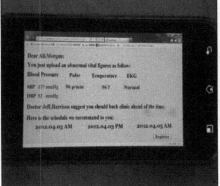

Fig. 5. Patient registration

4 Conclusions

After discharge from the hospital, postoperative patients with cardiovascular disease can resume their daily life activities if they can continue monitoring their health condition. Our research team devote themselves on developing a user-centered self-administrative healthcare mechanism involving professional medical staff and patients themselves. As to the design of risk warning, self-administrative healthcare mechanism for homecare patients establishes a personalized warning, reminder, and precaution function based on individual differed health status and can recommend proper measures. Regarding the warning setting strategy, we divide warnings into abnormal, critical, and urgent degree and dispatch follow-up works based on the degree of emergency. With the advanced technology, a new generation of the application of healthcare platform is engaged to perform remote care, to reduce the cost of medical resources, and to enhance the quality of medical care.

References

1. WHO: Cardiovascular diseases, CVDs (2009). http://www.who.int/mediacentre/factsheets/fs317/en/index.html. Accessed September 2009
2. Marconi, J.: E-Health: navigating the internet for health information healthcare. In: Advocacy White Paper. Healthcare Information and Management Systems Society (2002)
3. Lee, R.G., Hsiao, C.C., Chen, C.C., Liu, H.M.: A mobile-care system integrated with bluetooth blood pressure and pulse monitor, and cellular phone. IEICE Trans. Inf. Syst. **89**, 1702–1711 (2006)
4. Lin, C.-T., et al.: An intelligent telecardiology system using a wearable and wireless EKG to detect atrial fibrillation. IEEE Trans. Inf. Technol. Biomed. **14**(3), 726–733 (2010)

IoT Service Provider Recommender Model Using Trust Strength

Weiwei Yuan[1,2], Chenliang Li[1], Donghai Guan[1,2], Guangjie Han[3(✉)], and Feng Wang[4]

[1] College of Computer Science and Technology,
Nanjing University of Aeronautics and Astronautics, Nanjing 211106, China
{yuanweiwei,dhguan}@nuaa.edu.cn, lcljoric@gmail.com
[2] Collaborative Innovation Center of Novel Software Technology
and Industrialization, Nanjing 210093, China
[3] Deparment of Information and Communication Systems, Hohai University,
Changzhou, China
hanguangjie@gmail.com
[4] School of Information Science and Engineering, Changzhou University,
Changzhou 213164, China
wfeng@cczu.edu.cn

Abstract. Recommendation algorithms predict users' opinions towards IoT service providers, helping users finding things that might be of their interests. With the rapid development of IoT applications, various recommender models have been proposed for usage, trust-aware recommender models have been verified to have reasonable recommendation performances even in case of data sparseness. However, existing works did not consider the influence of distrust between users. They recommend items only base on the trust relations between users. We therefore propose a novel trust strength based IoT service provider recommender model which predicts ratings with recommendations given by recommenders with both trust and distrust relations with the active users. The trust strength also merges both local and structural information of users in the trust network. The experimental results show that the proposed method has better prediction accuracy and prediction coverage than the existing works. In addition, the proposed method is computational less expensive.

Keywords: Service provider recommendation
Trust-aware recommendation algorithm · Recommender systems

1 Introduction

Recommendation algorithms predict users' opinions towards service providers of IoT, helping users finding things that might be of their interests. With the rapid development of IoT [1], it is more and more important for IoT applications to find the reliable IoT service providers for users. Trust-aware Collaborative Filtering (TCF) [3, 4] improves the classical Collaborative Filtering (CF) [2] by exploiting users' trust to predict their ratings on service providers. TCF merges the recommendations according to the trust relations between the active user and the recommenders. Since trust is transitive, it is

© ICST Institute for Computer Sciences, Social Informatics and Telecommunications Engineering 2018
Y.-B. Lin et al. (Eds.): IoTaaS 2017, LNICST 246, pp. 286–293, 2018.
https://doi.org/10.1007/978-3-030-00410-1_34

possible to build up the relationship between users via trust propagations. This makes TCF have good recommendation performances in case of data sparseness.

However, existing TCF models recommend items only based on trust relations between users. They did not consider the influence of distrust between users. This is because trust relations is easier to be calculated than the distrust relations. Trust is transitive, while distrust is not transitive. Furthermore, it is also not easy to merge the trust relations and the distrust relations directly. Since trust relations always coexist with distrust relations in the real applications, ratings should be predicted with the recommendations given by users with both trust and distrust relations.

To solve the problems of existing works, we propose a novel trust strength based IoT service provider recommender model. The trust strength merges local information and structural information of the users in a social network with both trust relations and distrust relations. Logistic Regression is used to calculate the trust strength and the recommendations are then merged by the trust strength to give the prediction. The experimental results show that the proposed method has better prediction performances comparing with the existing works. In addition, the proposed method is computational less expensive.

The contributions of this work mainly lie in: (1) The proposed method involves both trust and distrust relations between users to predict ratings. This makes it more suitable to be applied in the real applications. (2) The proposed method considers both local and structural information of users in the trust network to predict ratings. This makes it more appropriate to reflect the real trust strength between users. (3) The proposed method is computational much less expensive than the existing works.

The rest of the paper is organized as follows: Sect. 2 describes the related works, Sect. 3 introduces the proposed method, Sect. 4 demonstrates the experiment results, and the last section concludes this paper and points out the future works.

2 Related Works

This paper proposes a trust strength based recommender model for IoT service provider recommendation. It is closely related to TCF [3, 4] which predicts ratings with only trust relations. The rating prediction mechanism of TCF is similar to that of CF [2]:

$$p_{act,i} = \overline{r_{act}} + \frac{\sum_{rec=1}^{k} w_{act,rec}(r_{rec,i} - \overline{r_{rec}})}{\sum_{rec=1}^{k} w_{act,rec}}, \tag{1}$$

where $p_{act,i}$ is the predicted rating of the active user act on item i, rec is one of the k recommenders who have rated i, $\overline{r_{act}}$ and $\overline{r_{rec}}$ are the average rating of act and rec respectively, $r_{rec,i}$ is the recommendation given by rec on i, and $w_{act,rec}$ is the weight of act on rec . $w_{act,rec}$ is calculated as:

$$w_{act,rec} = \frac{d_{\max} - d_{act,rec} + 1}{d_{\max}}, \tag{2}$$

where d_{max} is the maximum allowable trust propagation distance, and $d_{act,rec}$ is the trust propagation distance from *act* to *rec*, $d_{act,rec} \leq d_{max}$. As shown in (2), TCF only involves trust relationships between users.

There are also some other recommender models related to the proposed method including CF+TCF [4], which utilizes the basic model of CF while calculating the weight by combining users' similarities and trust relations; UPC [9], which uses a user preference clustering method to substitute the neighbor finding and weight assigning mechanism of CF; RTCF [10], which utilizes the basic model of TCF while uses the reliability score to reconstruct the trust network before finding neighbors; RDT [11], which combines user ratings and trusts as a neighbor finding mechanism.

The proposed method involves both trust and distrust relations in trust strength calculation. Since distrust cannot propagate, trust and distrust are merged according to the Structural Balance Theory [5] in this work. Structural Balance Theory focuses on the triad relations between users. It predicts social relations between users to keep the balance of triangles involved in trust networks. Structural Balance Theory considers the triad social relations between users as undirected networks. Two kinds of triad relations are regarded as balanced by the Structural Balance Theory, as shown in Fig. 1. The balanced triangles should have either three trust relationships or one trust relations and two distrust relationships. Other triangles are all regarded as unbalanced. The proposed method involves the distrust information to calculate the trust strength to keep the balance of triangles including the active users and the recommenders. Note that to simplify the calculation of trust strength, this work regards the involved triads as undirected triads.

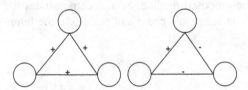

Fig. 1. Balanced triad relationships according to the Structural Balance Theory.

3 The Proposed Method

The architecture of the proposed method is given in Fig. 2. The proposed IoT service provider recommender model consists of three modules: the feature selection module, the trust strength calculation module and the rating prediction module. The details of the proposed method are as follows.

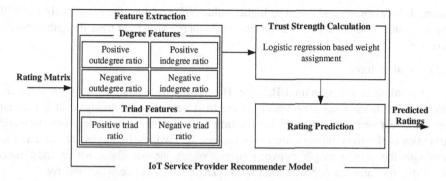

Fig. 2. The architecture of the proposed method.

(1) Feature Extraction

To calculate the trust strength between users, two kinds of features are extracted:

(A) Degree features

A user's degree represents its local trust relations with other users. Let *act* be an active user and *rec* be a recommender. Four degree features are extracted to evaluate a recommender's trust strength on the active user, which include the positive outdegree ratio of *act* POR(*act*), the negative outdegree ratio of *act* NOR(*act*), the positive indegree ratio of *rec* PIR(*rec*), and the negative indegree ratio of *rec* NIR(*rec*):

$$POR(act) = \frac{d_{out}^{+}(act)}{d_{out}^{+}(act) + d_{out}^{-}(act)} \tag{3}$$

$$NOR(act) = \frac{d_{out}^{-}(act)}{d_{out}^{+}(act) + d_{out}^{-}(act)} \tag{4}$$

$$PIR(rec) = \frac{d_{in}^{+}(rec)}{d_{in}^{+}(rec) + d_{in}^{-}(rec)} \tag{5}$$

$$NIR(rec) = \frac{d_{in}^{-}(rec)}{d_{in}^{+}(rec) + d_{in}^{-}(rec)} \tag{6}$$

where $d_{out}^{+}(act)$ is the positive outdegree of *act*, $d_{out}^{-}(act)$ is the negative outdegree of *act*, $d_{in}^{+}(rec)$ is the positive indegree of *rec*, and $d_{in}^{-}(rec)$ is the negative indegree of *rec*.

The higher value POR(*act*) has, the more likely *act* will trust other users, and the more likely there exists tight trust strength between *act* and *rec*. The higher value NOR(*act*) has, the more likely *act* will distrust other users, and the less likely there exists tight trust strength between *act* and *rec*. The higher value PIR(*rec*) has, the more likely *rec* will be trusted by other users, and the more likely there exists tight trust strength between *act* and *rec*. The higher value $NIR(rec)$ has, the more likely *rec* will be distrusted by other users, and the less likely there exists tight trust strength between *act* and *rec*.

(B) Triad features

According to the Structural Balance Theory, the trust relations between users are also related to the triad relationship of the trust network. The triangles in the social network represent the structural information related to the target user. The balanced triangles of the trust network are given in Sect. 2. Two triad features are extracted to evaluate the trust strength between users, which include the positive triad ratio $PTR(act, rec)$ and the negative triad ratio $NTR(act, rec)$ between *act* and *rec*:

$$PTR(act, rec) = \frac{\sum_{comNei \in C} I(Sign(act, comNei) * Sign(rec, comNei) = 1)}{|C|} \tag{7}$$

$$NTR(act, rec) = \frac{\sum_{comNei \in C} I(Sign(act, comNei) * Sign(rec, comNei) = -1)}{|C|} \tag{8}$$

where C represents the set of common neighbors between *act* and *rec*, $|C|$ is the number of common neighbors between *act* and *rec*, and $I(.)$ is an indicator function which equals to 1 if the equation inside is true.

Considering the triangle consisting the active user *act*, the recommender *rec* and one of their common neighbor *comNei*, if the sign of the social relations between *act* and *comNei* is the same as the sign of the social relations between *rec* and *comNei*, the social relation between *act* and *comNei* should be positive to keep the balance of the triangles. These triangles are named as positive triad in this work. While if the sign of the social relations between *act* and *comNei* is the opposite to the sign of the social relations between *rec* and *comNei*, the social relation between *act* and *comNei* should be negative to keep the balance of the triangles. These triangles are named as negative triad in this work. The higher value $PTR(act, rec)$ has, the more likely there exists a tight trust strength between *act* and *rec*; while the higher value $NTR(act, rec)$ has, the less likely there exists a tight trust strength between *act* and *rec*.

(2) Trust Strength Calculation

Based on the above features representing the degree information and the triad information, trust strength between the active user and the recommender is calculated. The influence of these selected features is calculated by a non-linear model:

$$s = \frac{1}{1 + e^{-(\mathbf{w}^T \mathbf{x} + b)}} \tag{9}$$

where s denotes the trust strength, $\mathbf{w}$ denotes the array of the weights assigned to the extracted features, $\mathbf{x}$ is the array of features, and b is a constant. The parameter $\mathbf{w}$ is calculated by Logistic Regression, which aims at optimizing the following objective function:

$$\min_{\mathbf{w},b} \alpha \|\mathbf{w}\|_2^2 + \sum_{i=1}^{n} \ln(e^{-y_i(\mathbf{w}^T \mathbf{x}_i + b)} + 1) \tag{10}$$

where y_i equals to 1 if the ith link of the training set is the trust relationship, y_i equals to 0 if the ith link of the training set is the distrust relationship, $\mathbf{w}^T \mathbf{w}$ is a regularizer, and α is a parameter determining the significance of the regularizer. The parameter $\mathbf{w}$ is then calculated by performing gradient descent method or Newton method.

(3) Rating Prediction

Using the trust strength calculated by (9), the active user's rating on the target item i is calculated as follows:

$$P_{act,i} = \frac{\mathbf{s} \cdot \mathbf{r}}{\|\mathbf{s}\|_1} \tag{11}$$

where $\mathbf{s}$ is the array of trust strength between the active user and the recommenders, and $\mathbf{r}$ is the array of recommendations on the target item.

4 Experimental Results

Experiments are held on two datasets to verify the performances of the proposed method. The datasets are extracted from the online review website Epinions. The Epinions dataset [8] has 13,668,320 user-item ratings. Users in the Epinions dataset connect to others by trust and distrust links in the user-user trust network. We randomly extract 300,000 ratings from the Epinions dataset as the basis of the experimental dataset. Trust between the users giving these ratings are then extracted from the Epinions dataset to measure the social relationship between users. This dataset is called the original dataset in the experiments. To examine the performances of the proposed method in case of sparse trust relations, a dataset named sparse trust dataset is extracted from the original dataset. In the sparse trust dataset, 70% of the social relations, which include trust and distrust, are randomly removed from the social relations of the original dataset. Two kinds of performances are examined for the proposed method. One is the prediction accuracy of the proposed method, which is calculate by the Mean Absolute Error (MAE). And the other is the prediction coverage of the proposed method.

Based on the experimental results, the prediction performances of the proposed method using the original dataset and the sparse trust dataset are given in Figs. 3 and 4 respectively. It is shown that the prediction accuracy of the proposed method is better than the prediction accuracy of the existing works by using both the original dataset and the sparse trust dataset. Though the prediction accuracy of UPC is slightly worse than that of the proposed method, the prediction coverage of the proposed method is significantly higher than UPC by using the original dataset and sparse trust dataset. The coverage of the proposed method is better than that of the existing works by using the original dataset and the sparse trust dataset. Among the existing works, the prediction coverage of RDT is the best, which is only slightly worse than the prediction coverage of the proposed method.

However, the prediction accuracy of the proposed method is significantly better than that of RDT by using the original dataset and sparse trust dataset.

The computational complexity of the proposed method is measured by the time consumption in this work. Figure 5 gives the time consumption of the proposed method comparing with that of the existing works. By using both the original dataset and the sparse trust dataset, the time consumption of the proposed method is significantly less than that of the existing work. This means the computational complexity of the proposed method is the lowest among all works.

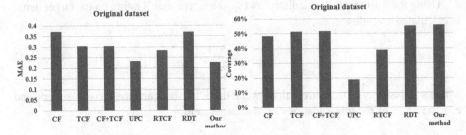

Fig. 3. The prediction performances of the proposed method by using the original dataset.

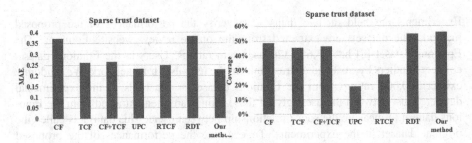

Fig. 4. The prediction performances of the proposed method by using the sparse trust dataset.

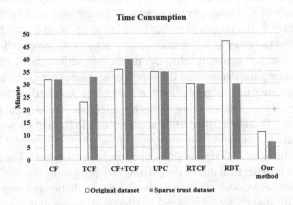

Fig. 5. The time consumption of the proposed method by using the original dataset and the sparse trust dataset.

5 Conclusion and Future Works

This paper aims at proposing an IoT service provider recommender model which would reliably recommend service providers to the users of IoT. This is achieved by recommending IoT service providers based on the trust strength between users. The proposed work involves both trust and distrust relations between users. It also involves both local and structural information of users in trust networks. Experiments results show that the proposed method has better prediction performances than existing works. Our future research will mainly focus on developing more high-performance recommendation algorithms exploiting trust and distrust information. We also plan to apply the proposed trust strength based recommender model in more application areas, e.g., in the applications mentioned [6, 7]. This would further improve the performances of the proposed model in real applications.

Acknowledgements. This research was supported by Nature Science Foundation of China No. 61672284, Natural Science Foundation of Jiangsu Province of China No. BK20171418, Open Project Foundation of Information Technology Research Base of Civil Aviation Administration of China No. CAAC-ITRB-201501 and No. CAAC-ITRB-201602, China Postdoctoral Science Foundation No. 2016M591841 and No. 2016M601707, and Changzhou Sciences and Technology Program No. CJ20160016.

References

1. Gubbi, J., Buyya, R., Marusic, S., Palaniswami, M.: Internet of Things (IoT): a vision, architectural elements, and future directions. Future Gener. Comput. Syst. **29**(7), 1645–1660 (2013)
2. Koren, Y., Bell, R.: Advances in collaborative filtering. In: Ricci, F., Rokach, L., Shapira, B. (eds.) Recommender Systems Handbook, pp. 77–118. Springer, Boston, MA (2015). https://doi.org/10.1007/978-1-4899-7637-6_3
3. Yuan, W., Guan, D., Lee, Y.K., Lee, S., Hur, S.J.: Improved trust-aware recommender system using small-worldness of trust networks. Knowl.-Based Syst. **23**(3), 232–238 (2010)
4. Yuan, W., Guan, D.: Optimized trust-aware recommender system using genetic algorithm. Neural Netw. World **27**(1), 77 (2017)
5. Qi, L., et al.: Structural balance theory-based E-commerce recommendation over big rating data. IEEE Trans. Big Data (2016)
6. Han, G., Que, W., Jia, G., Shu, L.: An efficient virtual machine consolidation scheme for multimedia cloud computing. Sensors **16**(2), 246 (2016)
7. Han, G., Chao, J., Zhang, C., Shu, L., Li, Q.: The impacts of mobility models on DV-hop based localization in mobile wireless sensor networks. J. Netw. Comput. Appl. **42**, 70–79 (2014)
8. http://www.trustlet.org/epinions.html
9. Zhang, J., Lin, Y., Lin, M., Liu, J.: An effective collaborative filtering algorithm based on user preference clustering. Appl. Intell. **45**(2), 230–240 (2016)
10. Moradi, P., Ahmadian, S.: A reliability-based recommendation method to improve trust-aware recommender systems. Expert Syst. Appl. **42**(21), 7386–7398 (2015)
11. Lee, W.P., Ma, C.Y.: Enhancing collaborative recommendation performance by combining user preference and trust-distrust propagation in social networks. Knowl.-Based Syst. **106**, 125–134 (2016)

Research on the Condition Monitoring of Transmission and Transformation Equipment Based on Improved Support Vector Machine in the Internet of Things

Chao Fu[1], Qing Lv[1(✉)], Chong Li[2], Yun Feng[1], and Xiao-li Li[1]

[1] Hebei Normal University, Shijiazhuang 050024, China
lvqing1017@163.com
[2] Hebei Electric Power Survey Design and Research Institute,
Shijiazhuang 050031, China

Abstract. The realization of smart grid is based on the real-time command of important operation parameters of power transmission and transformation equipment. The Internet of things has powerful capabilities of information collection and interactive, which can be used as the support for the condition monitoring of transmission and transformation equipment in the smart grid environment. This paper takes the power grid equipment as the center, takes intelligent on-line monitoring of equipment as the direction, starting from the equipment condition assessment and fault types, carried out the research about of grid equipment real-time state monitoring and fault diagnosis under the environment of Internet of things. Paper mainly includes: constructing the status evaluation framework and real-time evaluation model of power grid equipment from the angle of the status value of on-line monitoring of IoT, using support vector machine (SVM) for power transmission and transformation equipment condition monitoring, choosing a suitable kernel function by comparing the linear kernel function, polynomial kernel function, the radial basis kernel function and multi-layer perceptron kernel function of multiple parameters; by analyzing the traditional cross-validation method, this paper proposed the improved cross validation (K-CV) method, and we use Actual data of power grid field as the sample, finally obtain the fault classification result by constant parameter optimization. The experimental result shows that the support vector machine based on improved 10-CV cross-validation method in the Internet of things is able to monitor the condition of transmission and transformation equipment more rapidly and accurately.

Keywords: Internet of Things
Power transmission and transformation equipment
On-line monitoring · Support vector machines (SVM)

1 Preface

Content service net is the product of the information technology developing, its meaning is defined by the Ashton scholar at the Massachusetts institute of technology, they said the Internet of things is a network which uses A range of sensing devices such as RFID to realize the interconnection of objects and the Internet, this technology can realize objects' intelligent identification and real-time management [1]. The international telecommunication union launched a specific research report about the Internet of things in the early 20th century, the report makes a comprehensive description of the Internet of things, namely a network which can be applied to all items to realize the information interaction, Internet of things can also make a more effective application of wireless sensors, RFID radio frequency technology and other advanced technology.

At present, the Internet of things can be widely used in all sorts of objects. Through deploying different form of sensor devices at different positions, with the communication network specified in standard protocol, the Internet of things can realize the safe and reliable transfer of data, and also achieve objects like the uniformed services, collaborative processing, data association and real-time monitoring. The Internet of things makes many changes in technology from birth, from using the radio frequency identification technology to construct logistics network, to using the Internet technology, wireless sensor technology, nanotechnology, big data and cloud computing technology for data acquisition, data transmission and analysis, which implement the exchange of information between people and objects or objects and objects in wide-area scope. In fact, the basic network structure should include the perception layer, network layer and application layer according to the function implementation of the Internet of things platform, as shown in Fig. 1.

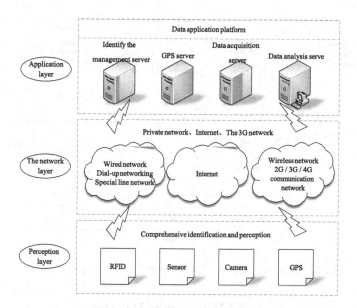

Fig. 1. Simple three-layer network structure diagram

The concept of IOTIPS (Internet Of Things In Power System) is apply the Internet of things platform too electric power system industry, which refers to using the sensors related to Internet of things to get monitoring information of power grid equipment, to transmit monitoring information of specific network, and process the information with certain means (Intelligent Methods, Data Mining, etc.), and finally realizes the intelligent data acquisition, fault diagnosis and maintenance decision support of power grid equipment. IOTIPS is applied in every link in smart grid, and also has been practicing and developing constantly, the application of Internet of things can not only promote the intelligent level of power system, but also realize the efficient management of the equipment operation, which promoting the combination of the informatization and the integration of power system.

During the period of power generation, using power Internet make a great improvement of the monitoring situation of equipment state. During the transmission phase, the Internet of things can realize the real-time monitoring of transmission equipment and lines, which ensures the safe equipment operation, and improve the efficiency and reliability of the equipment. In the stage of transformation, the Internet of things can accurately monitor the relevant parts of the substation and reduce the unnecessary loss of the equipment; In the stage of the power distribution, the Internet of things technology can monitor, diagnose and analyze the distribution network state, to ensure a safe and reliable operation of the distribution network, and enhance the level of power supply and reduce the risk of loss and maintenance equipment. The common application architecture for IOTIPS is shown in Fig. 2.

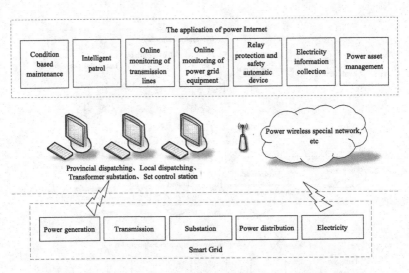

Fig. 2. Schematic diagram of network architecture of power Internet

2   State Monitoring and Maintenance Decision

There are two kinds of data collected by equipment condition monitoring which are online data and offline data. Real-time online data collection, relying on the Internet of things technology, is basis for equipment condition assessment, fault diagnosis and maintenance decision. State monitoring and timely key data acquisition can be done through some key technology in Internet of things, which can monitor the main equipment in power grid operation, such as power transformer, high voltage circuit breaker, transmission line. Such as the real-time data for transformers is transformer oil status and gas content, partial discharge and Operating Humidity; High voltage circuit breaker can use vibrating sensors to collect machinery vibration signal, combined with network transmission technology, the data can be uploaded to the server for processing. When there is abnormal vibration, warning can be sent; the online monitoring of transmission lines also has a certain development, which is constructing the correlation between the leakage current of the insulator surface and the degree of pollution, and estimate the operation state of the insulator by monitoring the leakage current of the device.

The maintenance decision of the power grid equipment's state is based on the condition monitoring and trend analysis of equipment, implementing condition-based maintenance requires timely monitoring of power grid equipment operation, and obtaining information such as the real-time running parameters [2]. In the Internet of things' environment, real-time monitoring can be used to detect the parameters of the relevant parameters of power grid equipment through intelligent sensing device, which can be used to acquire the status information of the component movement, vibration signal, loop current and real-time temperature of the equipment. By analyzing the data obtained from these sensors and the data of the off-line test, it can detect the running state and potential failure problems of the power grid equipment, so as to formulate a reasonable maintenance plan [3]. Based on the factors such as reliability, security and economy, introducing the expert decision-making system can guarantee these factors reach an acceptable level. In order to select the most suitable maintenance scheme for equipment maintenance, effectively reduce the loss and impact of blind routine maintenance to ensure timely and reliable power supply, improve the efficiency use of equipment and reduce maintenance risk.

3 Improved Support Vector Machine Status Monitoring

3.1 Support Vector Machine

Support Vector Machine (SVM) is a universal learning algorithm for realizing structural risk minimization principle, which is suitable for classification of small sample data [4]. The core idea is to transform nonlinear problems in low dimensional space into high dimensional linear problems through kernel functions, the kernel function is the key to the nonlinear transformation in SVM. SVM is a binary classifier, and it is necessary to construct multivariate classifier for fault diagnosis for multiple fault types.

According to the principle of SVM and the characteristics of the power transmission and transformation equipment condition monitoring, taking the most common hexafluoride high voltage circuit breaker as an example. The support vector machine condition monitoring method is proposed, and the system structure is shown in Fig. 3:

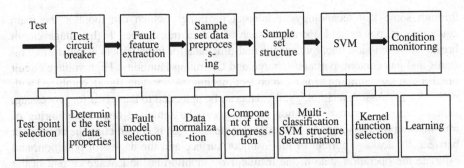

Fig. 3. The fault diagnosis structure of high voltage circuit breaker based on SVM

3.2 Sample Data Pretreatment

3.2.1 K-Means Clustering Algorithm Initialization

K-means clustering algorithm is an unsupervised machine learning algorithm, its essence is to group the data that people don't know beforehand, make the data in the same group as similar as possible and the data in different groups as different as possible, its purpose is to reveal the true status of the distribution of data [5]. K-means clustering algorithm is based on random clustering center, whose parameter K is the sampling frequency. Generally speaking, K takes 3–10 [6], and the overall square error criterion has converged. In this paper, the original data is preprocessed by this algorithm, and some data deviation is greatly removed, so it is not easy to have high dimensional partitioning in support vector machine operation.

Based on the data of actual case, the samples for the 4D of four types of data, normal and fault code expressed with N, P_1, P_2, P_3 respectively (As described in Sect. 4.1), the K-means clustering algorithm is used for data initialization, as shown in Fig. 4.

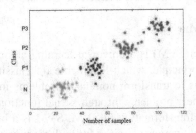

Fig. 4. K-means clustering algorithm preclassification

3.2.2 Sample Normalization

Based on the support vector machine theory, the focus of the high voltage circuit breaker status monitoring is how to convert the collected sample data into data suitable for support vector machine processing. When the sample value fluctuates a lot, it applies to all equally small data in the data group, which avoids difficult problems like the big data occupies the dominant position and calculation in support vector machine training, In the literature [7], why the scale transformation is elaborated, the ultimate goal is to use unified standard conversion to the same range of [0, 1] or [1, + 1], so the scale transform is also called the normalized and standardized [8]. The data is transformed to [a, b], as shown in Eq. 1:

$$\bar{x}_i = a + (b\,a) \times \frac{x_i \quad x_{min}}{x_{max} \quad x_{min}} \tag{1}$$

x_i is the sample data, x_{min} is the smallest data of sample concentration value, and x_{max} is the largest data of the sample concentration value.

3.3 Selection of Kernel Function and Its Parameters

The function of the kernel is to map the input space to the characteristic space of high dimensional [9], which means using different kernel functions can get different high-dimensional feature space, the kernel function parameter changes influenced the distribution of the sample data in the complexity of high dimensional feature space, thus, the generalization ability of the optimal classification hyperplane obtained in the feature space is affected.

Select the characteristic parameter of linear kernel function, polynomial kernel function, the radial basis function (RBF) and multi-layer perceptron kernel function (MLP), and a one-to-one method is used to train multi-classification support vector machines, The number and classification of support vectors for different kernel parameters are compared, and the training time and test time are compared respectively. The results are shown in Tables 1, 2, 3 and 4.

Table 1. Polynomial kernel function SVM diagnosis results (C = 10)

Nuclear parameter γ	The number of SV	Proportion of SV	Training time (s)	The test of time (s)	Classification accuracy
2	613	33.17%	2.73	0.52	91.31%
4	397	21.47%	3.06	0.43	93.25%
6	459	24.87%	4.25	0.49	87.38%

Table 2. SVM diagnosis result of gaussian kernel function (C = 10)

Nuclear parameter γ	The number of SV	Proportion of SV	Training time (s)	The test of time (s)	Classification accuracy
0.5	833	46.27%	2.85	0.48	80.13%
1	765	43.27%	1.73	0.82	93.37%
2	750	41.65%	2.11	0.38	89.32%

Table 3. Radial basis kernel function SVM diagnosis result (C = 10)

Nuclear parameter γ	The number of SV	Proportion of SV	Training time (s)	The test of time (s)	Classification accuracy
0.5	823	47.17%	2.56	0.99	96.53%
1	765	42.47%	3.45	1.21	97.85%
2	751	41.67%	1.30	0.81	92.34%

Table 4. The diagnostic result of SVM for multi-layer perceptron kernel function (C = 10)

Nuclear parameter ρ and b	The number of SV	Proportion of SV	Training time (s)	The test of time (s)	Classification accuracy
0.1, −1	1126	65.3%	5.78	1.98	84.78%
0.1, −1.5	1401	77.6%	5.26	1.23	93.21%
0.1, −2	1327	73.12%	4.98	2.03	84.36%

The experimental results (Tables 1 and 4) shows that the support vector machines with radial basis and polynomial kernel function are better than those of the other two kernel functions. Among them, the number of support vector machines with multinomial kernel is the least, and the multi-layer perceptron kernel has the most support vector, the longest training and testing time, and the shortest training time of gaussian kernel.

3.4 Improved K-CV Cross Validation Method

With regard to optimization of SVM parameters, there is no universally acknowledged best method in the world, and many of them are Cross Validation (CV) method. CV method is used to examine the effects of machine learning, its essence is to divide the sample data into training sets and validation sets, and with the training set to train a classifier and using validation set to test the classification accuracy of the model, and also test the performance of classifiers [10]. In most literatures, [11] the CV method is the original data were randomly divided into training set and validation set two groups, the first adopts the training set training classifier, and then using a validation set to test model, the classification accuracy is used as the criterion. This Method is called Hold-Out Method, the advantages of this method is obvious: random and simple classification, running fast, but essentially speaking, Hold-Out Method is not a cross-validation method, because this method does not meet the ideas of the cross, simply random grouping, therefore, the classification accuracy of the final verification set lacks relative independence, leading to the result is not convincing. This paper proposes a modified Hold-Out Method (K-CV Method) based on Hold-Out Method, Divide the original data into K groups evenly, Make a validation set of each subset data respectively, The rest of the k − 1 subset data is used as a training set, it will get K models, as shown in Fig. 5, the arithmetic mean of classification accuracy of K model was adopted, namely, $\frac{1}{C_K^{K-1}}\sum_{I=1}^{K} P_i$ as the K-CV Method under the performance of the classifier. K is generally greater than or equal to 2 (Only Take 2, When the Data Volume of the Original Data Collection is Very Small), during the actual operation, K is usually from 3, and in this paper K is 10. K-CV method abandoned the traditional random grouping method, it overcomes the difficulties of the classification accuracy of verification set is related to the original data grouping largely, which ensure the classification accuracy of the objective independence.

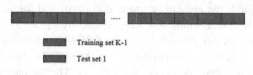

Training set K-1

Test set 1

Fig. 5. K-CV cross validation method

Table 5 using the 10-cv to match the difference between the different nuclear function and the sorting time. The best effect is adopted when using RBF kernel function, and when using the polynomial kernel function is basically lost the significance of identification, its error rate is much bigger, it shows that under the kernel mapping, the different categories of parametric mixed together, became highly inseparable. Gaussian kernel function and multi-layer perceptron kernel function are not suitable for sulfur hexafluoride high voltage circuit breaker fault classification, integrated all the above factors, the RBF kernel function is chosen as the kernel function.

Table 5. Comparison of different kernel function under 10-CV method

Kernel function	Recognition rate (%)	Classification of time (s)
Polynomial kernel function	77.48	10.32
Gaussian kernel function ($d = 3$)	91.7	13.57
Radial basis kernel function ($C = 10$)	97.56	13.6
Multi-layer perceptron kernel function	91.23	21.65

Penalty parameters C and γ are two important parameters of RBF kernel function, the impact on the accuracy of the SVM diagnosis is big, too large value or too small value of C, will make the generalization ability of the system become poor, γ reflects the characteristics of the training data, it also has great influence on the generalization ability of the system.

4 Status Monitoring Cases

4.1 Test Data Set Description and Data Visualization

In this paper, we use the data from the LW25-252/T4000-50 circuit breaker which is installed in the third set of the west Shijiazhuang substation of Hebei electric power company EHV transmission and substation branch and produced by Xi'an High voltage switch Co Ltd. Fault types are as follows: base screw loosening, shock absorbers with extra impacting and motion parts falling off (Fault Codes Are P_1, P_2, And P_3 Respectively Express). Each fault type detects the breaker contact stroke, the breaker vibration signal, the breaker action coil current, and the main loop current 4 attributes respectively (Dimensions Are Represented by x_1, x_2, x_3, x_4). The data collector collects 120 points per phase at the rate of 25 kHz when the circuit breaker is simulated, and the data is transmitted to the PC via the rs-232-C bus to be preprocessed, and the signal is soft threshold denoising respectively. The data are shown in Table 6.

Table 6. High voltage circuit breaker characteristics sample data

Fault type	x_1	x_2	x_3	x_4
N	175.9	163.15	1.955	14.6
	177.1	178.9	2.38	8.64
	183.1	173.6	2.7783	13.5
	......	......	......	......
P_1	192.2	156.55	2.635	12.2
	205.6	159.32	2.3375	12.4
	192.7	155.4	2.448	16.8
	......	......	......	......
P_2	190.4	134.3	1.325	7.2
	181.8	124	1.265	6.1
	185.2	136.4	2.0825	4.3
	......	......	......	......
P_3	190.4	145.7	1.377	14.2
	204.5	137.94	1.172	7.7
	178.2	148.8	1.5215	11.3
	......	......	......	......

In order to provide an overview of the data statistics feature, data visualization operation is performed for data after preprocessing, and its data "boxplot" is shown in Fig. 6, the 120 groups of data are divided into the training set and the test set according to the 10-cv cross test model of the previous text subsequently, and the results are shown in Fig. 7.

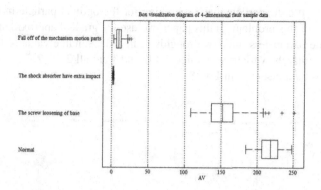

Fig. 6. 4-dimensional failure sample box diagram

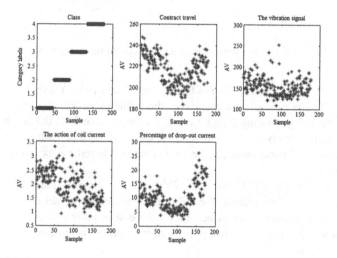

Fig. 7. Fractal dimension visualization diagram of fault samples

4.2 Parameter Optimization Based on RBF Kernel Function 10-CV Cross Validation Method

The original data was divided into 10 groups (Mean Points) to form the 10-cv cross validation method for parameter optimization. It usually uses a grid optimization algorithm or Particle Swarm Optimization (PSO—Particle Swarm Optimization) algorithm, although grid optimization can be used to find the highest classification accuracy in CV, which is the global optimal solution, But sometimes it takes a lot of time to find the best parameter C and γ, if you have a higher number of categories or in a larger range; the particle swarm optimization algorithm uses heuristic algorithm to avoid all the parameter points in the grid. And it is similar with genetic algorithm, which is a kind of based on iterative optimization algorithm, the system is initialized to a group of random solutions, It doesn't have the CV cross-thinking that the genetic algorithm uses. It's the particle that's searching for the optimal particle in the solution space. In view of this problem, in this paper, we use the gradual approximation method to optimize the parameters. First, we roughly search the suitable value of C and γ in a large range, so that the variation of values of C and γ are all 2^{-10}, 2^{-9}, ..., 2^{10} and the simulation results are shown in Fig. 8:

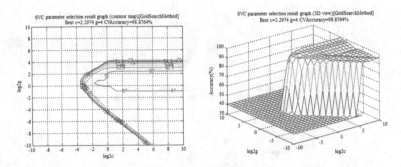

Fig. 8. Parameter optimization result graph (rough optimization)

In Fig. 8, The x axis is the value of the log base 2 of C, The Y-axis is the value γ of the log base 2, The contour line represents the accuracy of the 10-cv method corresponding to the corresponding C and γ value. As can be seen from the graph, the range of C can be narrowed down to 2^{-2}–2^4, and the range of γ can be reduced to 2^{-2}–2^4, so that the selection of parameters can be further refined based on the rough parameter selection above.

Change the value of C to: $2^{-2}, 2^{-1.5}, ..., 2^4$, change the value of γ to $2^{-4}, 2^{-3.5}, ..., 2^4$, and the change interval of the final parameter selection result graph is set to 0.9, so that the change of accuracy can be seen more clearly.

You can see that under the 10-cv method, the optimal parameter is C = 1.41421, γ = 1. As shown in Fig. 9.

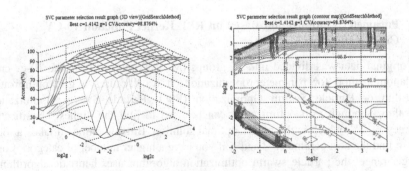

Fig. 9. Parametric optimization result graph (fine tuning)

4.3   Performance Evaluation and Analysis of Results

Receiver Operating Characteristic (ROC) is a visual evaluation of the performance of the classifier, which gives the competition relation between TPR and FPR of the classifier in the form of curve [12]. The horizontal axis in the ROC curve represents the false positive rate of FPR and the vertical axis represents real rate of TPR, and establish the two-dimensional plane rectangular coordinate system that at the origin, TPR = FPR = 0 [13]. Starting at the origin, if a sample is a positive sample of the correct classification, that is, a real data sample, TPR increases. In the ROC curve, move up and draw a point. In the ROC curve, move to the right and draw a point. If the classifier classifies a negative sample as positive, the false positive sample appears, then FPR increases. In the ROC curve, move to the right and draw a point. As the sample expands, so does the number of categories and negatives.

Figure 10 shows the ROC curve diagram of the test data set. In this data set, empirical parameters, rough parameter searching, and fine parameters are used respectively to correspond to three serrated curves of blue, green and red respectively, namely ROC curve. The diagonals in the graph are the ROC curves of random guesses. In general, If the curve is closer to the point (0, 1), the curve of TPR is higher, its classification performance the better. It can be seen that the classification performance is excellent as the parameters are optimized.

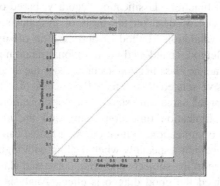

Fig. 10. The ROC curve quantifies schematic diagram (Color figure online)

After the parameters are optimized, and the SVM condition monitoring can be carried out on the field data. The results of the test set, as shown in Fig. 11, test classification accuracy to 98.8764%. As we can see from Fig. 11, although the classification effect is excellent, there are still outliers. This is associated with the selection of penalty parameter, although the classification accuracy is not 100%, but the purpose of parameter optimization is to find the best generalization properties, through a large number of field data validation, this method has good classification features, can be used in power transmission and transformation equipment condition monitoring.

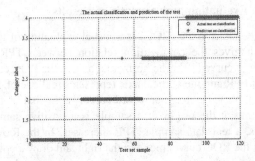

Fig. 11. Test set classification result graph

5 Conclusion

This article first expounds the relevant technology of the Internet of things, by analyzing the Internet of things monitoring technology and equipment condition monitoring, the relationship between construction of electric power of the Internet of things network architecture, which leads to the power grid equipment condition assessment and maintenance decision and the meaning of research and analysis. Then on the basis of support vector machine (SVM) theory, through the calculation of actual data to compare various kernel function classification accuracy, based on the analysis of traditional Method Hold-Out Method on the basis of in-depth study, put forward the modified 10-CV cross validation Method of optimization of support vector machine (SVM) classification Method, abandoned the traditional random grouping Method, the original data to overcome the classification accuracy with the original data of validation set grouping of excessive related this defect. Parameters of support vector machine (SVM) is put forward at the same time step by step optimization method, this method overcomes the grid optimization time consuming and the idea of particle swarm optimization algorithm optimization without crossing faults, can greatly accelerate the rate of parameter optimization, especially when dealing with high dimensional or large amount of data, and then to the subjects operating curve and classification accuracy as the criterion, has obtained the good diagnosis effect. Analysis results show that the proposed feature extraction method can effectively extract the fault signal characteristic, compared with the traditional methods, based on the radial basis kernel function is modified 10-CV cross validation method of support vector function is more rapid, accurate judgment high voltage circuit breaker mechanical fault type, and has good generalization.

Finally test validation tests, LW25-252/T4000-50 type sulfur hexafluoride high voltage circuit breaker condition monitoring, for example, in a normal state and base screw loosening, shock absorber, the mechanism motion parts have extra impact loss under three kinds of fault circuit breaker contact trip, breaker vibration signals, the main loop of the circuit breaker action coil current, current four properties of 120 groups of signals as the input sample set. The model parameters of support vector machine were optimized by using the improved 10-cv cross validation method, and the test results were obtained by using the operation curve and classification accuracy of the subject.

Test results meet the requirements of power transmission and transformation equipment condition monitoring design, test results coincide with theoretical analysis, compared with the traditional methods, based on improved support vector function is more rapid, accurate judgment power transmission and transformation equipment failure type, meet the power grid equipment under Internet real-time condition monitoring and fault diagnosis of demand.

References

1. Wu, C., Cheng, L., Tian, Z., et al.: Online monitoring system of substation based on the Internet of Things. New Technol. Electr. Electr. Power **32**(4), 110–114 (2015)
2. Yang, J., Fang, B., Zhai, L., et al.: Research on the security model of general control system for the Internet of Things. J. Commun. **33**(11), 49–56 (2014)
3. Huang, X., Zhang, Y., Zhu, Y., et al.: Research on transmission and transformation equipment monitoring system based on the Internet of Things. Power Syst. Prot. Control **41** (9), 137–141 (2016)
4. Li, L., Zhang, Z.: The application of support vector machine in mechanical fault diagnosis. Comput. Eng. Appl. **38**(19), 19–21 (2016)
5. Wang, S., San, Y.: A review of the training algorithms of support vector machines. J. Intell. Syst. (06) (2015)
6. Wu, J., Yang, S., Liu, C.: A short-term load forecasting method for support vector machines based on genetic algorithm optimization. J. Central South Univ. (Nat. Sci. Ed.) (01) (2007)
7. Wang, X., Wang, X., Wu, Y.: Rapid diagnosis and new knowledge acquisition methods in the fault diagnosis expert system of high voltage circuit breakers. J. China Electr. Eng. **27**(3), 96–99 (2016)
8. Gammermann, A.: Support vector machine learning algorithm and transduction. Comput. Stat. **15**(1), 31–39 (2016)
9. Lei, G., Wu, H.: Applying a novel decision rule to the sphere-structured support vector machines algorithm. Neural Comput. Appl. **18**(7), 675 (2013)
10. Wang, K., Cai, W., Deng, Y., et al.: Online monitoring system application and management platform of power transmission lines. High Volt. Technol. **38**(5), 1274–1280 (2014)
11. Han, M., Ding, J.: Improvement and implementation of BP algorithm based on cross-validation. Comput. Eng. Des. (14) (2011)
12. Zhang, D., Hu, J., Cui, T., et al.: Application of RF identification technology of sensor to the status information of electrical equipment in substations. High Volt. Technol. **39**(11), 2623–2630 (2015)
13. Li, X., Gong, Q., Qiao, H.: Application of the Internet of Things in power system. Power Syst. Prot. Control **38**(22), 232–236 (2015)

A Dynamic Detection Point Frame Length Adjustment Method for RFID Anti-collision

Xiaoning Feng[1](✉), Zhuo Wang[2](✉), Bijun Yan[1], Guangjie Han[3], Feng Wang[4], and Xue Song[1]

[1] College of Computer Science and Technology, Harbin Engineering University, Harbin 150001, China
fengxiaoning@hrbeu.edu.cn
[2] College of Shipbuilding Engineering, Harbin Engineering University, Harbin 150001, China
wangzhuo@hrbeu.edu.cn
[3] Department of Information and Communication Systems, Hohai University, Changzhou, China
hanguangjie@gmail.com
[4] School of Information Science and Engineering, Changzhou University, Changzhou 213164, China
wfeng@cczu.edu.cn

Abstract. The tag collision problem is an important issue that affects the efficiency of RFID system. A method of frame length adjustment based on dynamic detection points is proposed in this paper. The method calculates the size of the detection slot area in the frame according to the calculation of the sample size. And then it determines the location of the detection point in the frame. So, the detection point is dynamically adjusted with the length of the frame. Compared with the fixed detection point method, simulation results showed that the dynamic detection point method can adjust the frame length more accurately and improve the system throughput and speed the tag identification.

Keywords: RFID · Anti-collision algorithm · Frame length adjustment Detection point

1 Introduction

With the development of the identification methods, Radio Frequency Identification (RFID) technology has been widely used in various fields because of its advantages such as non-contact, rapid identification, small size and so on. Combined with Internet of Things, the 'EPC C1 Gen2' (EPC-C-G below) standard becomes the most widely used standard of RFID technology in recent years [1, 2]. In general, the RFID system consists of three parts: tags, readers and processing system. The tag collision occurs when a large number of tags simultaneously respond to one reader in RFID system. The problem of tag collision increases tag identification time, reduces tag identification rate and system throughput. Many anti-collision methods have been proposed to solve

© ICST Institute for Computer Sciences, Social Informatics and Telecommunications Engineering 2018
Y.-B. Lin et al. (Eds.): IoTaaS 2017, LNICST 246, pp. 308–315, 2018.
https://doi.org/10.1007/978-3-030-00410-1_36

the problem. Most of them can be divided into three categories: tree-based, ALOHA based and hybrid algorithms [3].

Tree-based anti-collision algorithms consist of multiple periodic for reader's query commands and tag's responses. The set of tags was divides into two branches according to each collision's tag bit. The process will loop until each branch has only one tag. And all the tags can be identified. The typical tree-based algorithms include dynamic binary tree search algorithm, backward binary tree search algorithm and query tree algorithm.

Hybrid algorithms have the advantages of ALOHA-based algorithms and tree-based algorithms. But tree-based and hybrid anti-collision algorithms cannot be implemented by the EPC-C-G standard because the reader based on this standard cannot effectively identify collision tags based on the collision bits. Therefore, we have focused on the ALOHA-based anti-collision algorithm in this paper.

The main idea of ALOHA-based anti-collision algorithms is to make the tags to select different time slot when responding to the reader in order to reduce the probability of tag collision. And the algorithms mainly are pure ALOHA algorithm, slotted ALOHA (SA) algorithm, framed slotted ALOHA (FSA) algorithm and dynamic framed slotted ALOHA (DFSA) algorithm [4]. DFSA algorithm is the most efficient and widely adopted by RFID standards. The improvement of DFSA anti-collision algorithm for EPC-C-G standard is time slot random anti-collision algorithm called Q-algorithm. The performance improvement for the Q-algorithm can be accomplished in two aspects. One is how to adjust the frame length, and the other one is how to estimate the number of remaining tags.

The problem of how to adjust the frame length can be divided into two parts. One is how to match the optimal frame length for the remaining tags. The other one is when to adjust the frame length. On the basis of when to adjust the frame length the existing algorithms can be divided into three categories. According to the frame length needs to be adjusted slot by slot, partial slots or all slots in the frame. The [5] proposed a novel algorithm, access probability adjustment based fine-grained Q-algorithm (APAFQ) algorithm. The APAFQ scheme is driven by updating Q value with two different weights, slot by slot. However, the frame length is adjusted slowly in the algorithm because the frame length is adjusted slot by slot. The [6] proposed an early adjustment of frame length (EAFL) algorithm. This algorithm adjusts the frame length by partial slots or all slots in the frame. However, if the selection of partial slots is not appropriate, the early adjustment of frame length is lost. The [7] introduced an improvised dynamic frame slotted ALOHA (ID-FSA) algorithm. The algorithm adjusts the frame length based on the inventory results of all the slots in previous cycles. But the reader takes too many collision slots and empty slots.

In this paper, we presented a new algorithm based on dynamic frame slotted ALOHA. To obtain the number of slots that can represent the distribution of tags in the whole frame, the algorithm uses the sample size to calculate the size of the detection slots area in the frame so that the position of the detection point is adjusted with the frame length dynamically.

2 Algorithm Description

2.1 Dynamic Detection Point Frame Length Adjustment Method

Combining the idea of the frame length needs to be adjusted by partial slots in the frame, a method of frame length adjustment based on dynamic detection points is proposed in this paper. We want to calculate the number of slots that can accurately represent the distribution of the tags in the whole slots of frame. Thus, we can determine the location of the detection points in the frame. The degree of dispersion of the tags distribution in the frame is an important factor that affects the size of the detection region and can be expressed in terms of variance of the number of tags in the frame.

In the RFID system, tags can obtain the frame length information for the current inventory cycle after receiving the Query(Q) command sent by reader. And then they randomly select any slot in the frame to respond their own identity information. To obtain the variance of the number of tags in slots we need to know how many slots in each case and how many slots have tags when there are n tags. The probability of selecting any slot for each tag is the inverse of the frame length $1/L$, under the condition of the inventory cycle with frame length L. Suppose n $-$ 1 tags have chosen A_{n-1} slots. There are two cases If adding a tag to choose those slots in the current frame. One case is that the tag selects those slots with tag success or collision. The probability is A_{n-1}/L. The other is that the tag choose idle slot. The probability is $1 - A_{n-1}/L$. Then the value of A_n is shown in (1), (2) and (3).

$$A_n = \frac{A_{n-1}}{L} \times A_{n-1} + \left(1 - \frac{A_{n-1}}{L}\right) \times (A_{n-1} + 1). \tag{1}$$

$$A_n = 1 + \lambda \times A_{n-1}. \tag{2}$$

$$A_n = \frac{1 - \lambda^n}{1 - \lambda}. \tag{3}$$

where n is the number of tags, L is the length of frame, and $\lambda = (L - 1)/L$.

The average slot number with x_i tags is shown in (4) and (5).

$$l_n^{x_i} = \left(1 - \frac{A_{n-1}}{L}\right) l_{n-1}^{x_i} + \frac{l_n^{x_i-1}}{L} \times \left(l_{n-1}^{x_i} + 1\right) + \frac{A_{n-1} - l_{n-1}^{x_i-1} - l_{n-1}^{x_i}}{L} l_{n-1}^{x_i} + \frac{l_{n-1}^{x_i}}{L}$$
$$\times \left(l_{n-1}^{x_i} - 1\right). \tag{4}$$

$$l_n^{x_i} = \frac{\lambda^n}{1 - \lambda} \binom{n}{x_i} \left(\frac{1 - \lambda}{\lambda}\right)^{x_i}. \tag{5}$$

where x_i represents the number of tags which select the same slot, $i = 0, 1, 2, 3, \ldots, n$. When i is 0, x_0 stands for slot without tag selected, $l_n^{x_0}$ represents the number of idle slots. When i is 1, x_1 stands for slots with only one tag selected, $l_n^{x_1}$ represents the number of successful slots. When the i is greater than or equal to 2, x_i stands for a slot with i tags selected, $l_n^{x_i}$ represents the number of collision slots containing x_i tags.

In this paper, the relation between the optimal frame length and the number of tags is obtained by the theoretical maximum of the system throughput. Then the average number of tags allocated in each slot is 0.5. Then, the variance of the slot distribution in the frame is shown in (6).

$$\sigma^2 = \frac{(x_1 - \bar{x})^2 l_n^{x_1} + (x_2 - \bar{x})^2 l_n^{x_2} + \cdots + (x_n - \bar{x})^2 l_n^{x_n}}{n}. \tag{6}$$

where $\bar{x}$ represents the average number of tags in slots.

The selection of partial slots from the current frame representing all slots is analogous to a sampling survey of the population in order to infer some property or feature of the population. The frame is population, and the partial slots is sample, called the sample slots. To determine the sample slots size, we need to consider the degree of dispersion of the slot distribution in the frame, as well as the estimation error and the confidence level of infer result. Therefore, the formula for calculating the sample size of the sample slots in the frame is as follows in (7).

$$s = \frac{L(z_{\alpha/2})^2 \sigma^2}{(L-1)d^2 + (z_{\alpha/2})^2 \sigma^2}. \tag{7}$$

where the confidence level is $1 - \alpha$, $z_{\alpha/2}$ is the standard error confidence level, d is the maximum allowable error, L is the frame length, which is population.

EPC-C-G standard specifies that frame length can only be the power of 2. The sample slots size in the frame is shown in Table 1.

Table 1. Time slots sample size in frame.

Q	3	4	5	6	7	8	9	10
Frame length L	8	16	32	64	128	256	512	1024
Sample slots size	6	10	12	16	24	34	56	64
Detection point		3/4	5/8	3/8	1/4	3/16	17/128	7/64	1/16

Reader determines whether the current frame length is optimal at the location of the detection point.

2.2 The Proposed Algorithm

In the process of identifying tags, reader first sends the Select command to select a set of specific tags that have been activated within its radio frequency range. After that, reader initializes the frame length by sending the Query(Q) command to those tags, where the frame length is 2Q.

Tags receive this command and get the frame length information. And then tags select a slot through its internal random number generator and send its Random Number 16 (RN16) when reader inventories this slot. Reader inventories slot, determines and records the type of slots. If there is a collision or empty slot, reader records the slot and continues inventorying. As for successful slot, reader not only needs to record the slot type but also needs to exchange data with the tag to get its information. Reader sends QueryRep command after each slot in order to reduce the random number of the tag. Thus, the tag is kept synchronous with the reader. In order to get the detection point i, reader should estimate the number of tags according to $n = (S + 2.17 \cdot C)L/i$ and obtains the Q value of the optimal frame length based on $Q_{opt} = round(log2(1.89 \cdot n))$. If the number of collision slots C equals 0, the tag identification is completed. Otherwise, there are tags which have not been identified and the reader continues to inventory.

The algorithm presented in this paper is described in pseudo code as followed.

```
Initialize Frame;
while (unidentified tags≠0)
Start inventory cycle and initialize different types of slot record values;
  while (slots without inventory≠0)
    Interrogate the tags in slot and record slot type;
    if Inventory the detection point
        then Estimate tags number and obtain the optimal frame length;
      if the current frame length optimal
        then Continue inventory;
      else Estimate remaining tags number, update Q and start a new inventory
cycle;
      end if
    else Continue inventory
    end if
  end while
end while
```

3 Simulation Results

We evaluated the number of collision slots and system throughput of the proposed algorithm and compared its performance with existing methods including DFSA, APAFQ and EAFL algorithm.

The simulation conditions in this paper are based on the EPC-C-G standard and referred to [7]. The main parameters used in the simulations are shown in Table 2. It also defines a basic duration for interrogator-to-tag signaling called Tari. The basic duration for interrogator-to-tag signaling to be 12.5 μs, this corresponds to a transmission speed of 80 kb/s. For the interrogator-to-tag link, the durations of data-0 and data-1 are one Tari and two Taris, respectively. On the other hand, the durations of data-0 and data-1 for tag-to-interrogator link are 6.25 μs, which corresponds to a link frequency of 160 kHz.

The number of collision slots is the quantities of all collision slots that are recorded by reader during the identification process for tags. Figure 1 displays the number of collision slots of four algorithms when the initial frame length is 128, which means the

Table 2. Simulation parameter values.

Parameters	Time interval (μs)
Reader-to-tag preamble	112.5
Reader-to-tag frame sync	62.5
Reader-to-tag data-0	12.5
Reader-to-tag data-1	25
Tag-to-reader preamble	112.5
Tag-to-reader data-0/data-1	6.25
Query(Q) command	412.5
QueryAdjust(Q) command	168.75
QueryRepeat command	75
ACK command	337.5
RN16 (preamble included)	212.5
PC+EPC+CRC16 (preamble included)	912.5
T_1	62.5
T_2	62.5
T_3	5
T_4	112.5

value of Q is 7. From Fig. 1 we can see our algorithm has the least number of collision slots among the algorithms. Since the location of judge whether the current frame length is optimal or not is fixed, the number of collision slots in EAFL is more than that of the proposed algorithm. APAFQ inventories more collision slots due to its slot by slot adjustment strategy. Since there is no early adjustment strategy for DFSA, the number of collision slots to be recorded is the largest compared to the other three algorithms.

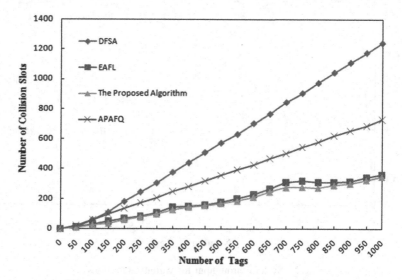

Fig. 1. Number of collision slots for various algorithms.

And we also compared the system throughput of the four algorithms with the same initial frame length 128 in Fig. 2. The system throughput is the ratio of the time spent by successful slots and the total time spent by reader to identify all tags. The total time spent in identifying tags includes the time taken by the successful time slot plus the time spent in the collision slot and the idle slot. The throughput formula is shown in (8).

$$Thr = \frac{S \cdot T_S}{S \cdot T_S + C \cdot T_C + E \cdot T_E}. \tag{8}$$

where S is the number of successful slots, E is the number of empty slots, C is the number of collision slots, T_S, T_C and T_E are the durations of successful, collision, and empty slot, respectively.

As shown in Fig. 2, the system throughput of those four algorithms is rapidly reaching its maximum and then fluctuates near the maximum. Among them, the system throughput of the proposed algorithm is better than all other algorithms. It maintained a steady state near its maximum after the number of tags reaches 50. EAFL will take inventory of excess collision slots and free slots when the current frame length is not optimal, so its performance is lower than the proposed algorithm. APAFQ is slow to adjust the frame length due to the slot by slot strategy, so the system throughput is lower than that of EAFL and the proposed algorithm. The performance of DFSA fluctuates greatly when the number of tags is small, because the influence of initial frame length is larger.

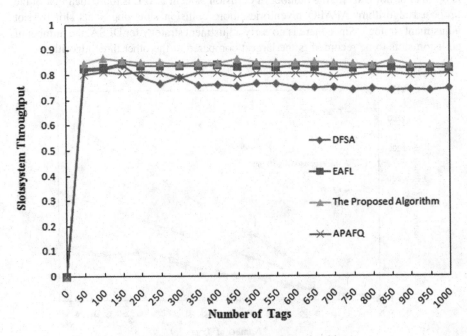

Fig. 2. System throughput for various algorithms

4 Conclusion

In order to adjust the detection point with the frame length dynamically, the paper presented an algorithm which uses the sample size to calculate the size of the detection slots area in the frame. Simulation results show the proposed algorithm has the advantages of less number of collision slots and higher system throughput.

Acknowledgements. This work was supported by The National Natural Science Foundation of China No. 61571150, Changzhou Sciences and Technology Program No. CJ20160016, General Financial grant from the China Postdoctoral Science Foundation No. 2016M601707.

References

1. EPC Radio-Frequency Identity Protocols Class-1 Generation-2 UHF RFID Protocol for Communications at 860 MHz–960 MHz, version 1.2.0
2. Floerkemeier, C.: Transmission control scheme for fast RFID object identification. In: IEEE International Conference on Pervasive Computing and Communications Workshops, p. 457. IEEE Computer Society (2006)
3. Chen, Y., Su, J., Yi, W.: An efficient and easy-to-implement tag identification algorithm for UHF RFID systems. IEEE Commun. Lett. **PP**(99), 1 (2017)
4. Šolić, P., Radić, J., Rožić, N.: Energy efficient tag estimation method for ALOHA-based RFID systems. Sens. J. IEEE **14**(10), 3637–3647 (2014)
5. Su, J., Zhao, X., Hong, D.: Q-value fine-grained adjustment based RFID anti-collision algorithm. IEICE Trans. Commun. **E99. B**(7), 1593–1598 (2016)
6. Chen, W.T.: Optimal frame length analysis and an efficient anti-collision algorithm with early adjustment of frame length for RFID systems. IEEE Trans. Veh. Technol. **65**(5), 3342–3348 (2016)
7. Dhakal, S., Shin, S.: Parametric heuristic schemes for performance improvement in Frame Slotted Aloha based RFID systems. In: International Conference on ICT for Smart Society, pp. 1–5. IEEE (2013)
8. Klair, D.K., Chin, K.W., Raad, R.: A survey and tutorial of RFID anti-collision protocols. IEEE Commun. Surv. Tutor. **12**(3), 400–421 (2010)
9. Schoute, F.C.: Dynamic frame length ALOHA. Mob. Commun. **31**(4), 565–568 (1983)
10. Cha, J.R., Kim, J.H.: Novel anti-collision algorithms for fast object identification in RFID system. In: Proceedings of the International Conference on Parallel and Distributed Systems, pp. 63–67. IEEE (2005)
11. Han, G., Que, W., Jia, G., Shu, L.: An efficient virtual machine consolidation scheme for multimedia cloud computing. Sensors **16**(2), article no. 246 (2016)
12. Han, G., Chao, J., Zhang, C., Shu, L., Li, Q.: The impacts of mobility models on DV-hop based localization in mobile wireless sensor networks. J. Netw. Comput. Appl. **42**(6), 70–79 (2014)
13. Han, G., Jiang, J., Shu, L., Guizani, M., Nishio, S.: A two-step secure localization for wireless sensor networks. Comput. J. **56**(10), 1151–1153 (2013)

Fault Diagnosis and Monitoring Device Design for the Electrical Life Test of Low Voltage Circuit Breaker

Jungang Zhou[1,2] and Zhigang Li[1(✉)]

[1] School of Electrical Engineering, Hebei University of Technology,
Tianjin 300130, China
zgli@hebut.edu.cn
[2] Shandong Institute for Product Quality Inspection, Jinan 250102, China

Abstract. In the electrical life test, the low voltage circuit breaker may have a variety of faults. At present, that lacks effective fault diagnosis method and monitoring device. To solve the above problem, the method of fault diagnosis and the design of monitoring device are proposed in this paper. The method of fault diagnosis includes the collection of test parameters and the model establishment of fault diagnosis. Based on the fault diagnosis model, the electrical life test monitoring device is designed. The device is used to collect the test data in real time, and analyzed the logic to determine whether the fault occurred during the test. When the fault occurred, the device will automatically take protective measures. In order to improve its intelligence, the intelligent monitoring device is designed based on Device net bus technology. It has been implemented in the Device net control network and has the function of Internet of things. So the real-time monitoring test process of remote network can be realized.

Keywords: Low voltage circuit breaker · Electrical life test · Fault diagnosis
Monitoring device · Device net

1 Introduction

At present, the research of fault diagnosis for circuit breaker is mainly focused on the high voltage circuit breaker (HVCB), but there are few researches of fault diagnosis for low voltage circuit breaker. The research method of fault diagnosis is signal analysis for HVCB. Firstly, collecting the vibration signal as HVCB opening and closing, and then these theories such as the particle swarm optimization (PSO) algorithm, support vector machine (SVM), empirical mode decomposition (EMD), wavelet transform, neural network, artificial immune network, fault diagnosis expert system and so on are applied to process the collected signal, so the fault type can be determined.

Based on PSO, combining algorithms such as least squares support vector machine (LSSVM) [1, 2], particle swarm fused kernel fuzzy C-means (P-KFCM) [2] and radial basis function (RBF) [3] neural network to research. In [1], the PSO algorithm is adopted to optimize the parameter of LSSVM algorithm, so the diagnosis speed and accuracy by PSO-LSSVM algorithm is better than traditional SVM algorithm. In [2], this method combined P-KFCM and SVM solves local optimum problem can

© ICST Institute for Computer Sciences, Social Informatics and Telecommunications Engineering 2018
Y.-B. Lin et al. (Eds.): IoTaaS 2017, LNICST 246, pp. 316–329, 2018.
https://doi.org/10.1007/978-3-030-00410-1_37

effectively improve reliability of diagnostic. In [3], the accuracy and precision of RBF network model based on PSO are higher than traditional neural network model. In [4], the EMD amount of energy and SVM theory are combined to identify the difference of vibration signals and fault type. In [6], based on the combined method of fast kernel independent component analysis (fast KICA) and the ensemble empirical mode decomposition (EEMD) decomposition, the signal is processed as input feature vector of SVM. The wavelet theory is combined with SVM theory, wavelet transform and wavelet packet analysis and applied for fault diagnosis. In [7], the empirical wavelet transform (EWT) and one-class support vector machine (OCSVM) are combined and proposed as new mechanical fault diagnosis method, that can diagnose the mechanical fault high reliability. In [8], the zero-phase filter time-frequency entropy is analyzed based wavelet packet and then the SVM classifiers are introduced for fault diagnosis under different conditions. In [10], the grey theory is applied in fault diagnosis, a new diagnostic model based on the grey relation analysis method (GRAM) is established and that can effectively diagnose the mechanical failure of circuit breaker. In [11], based on artificial immune network (ai Net), an on-line self-learning classifier artificial immune network (C-ai Net) is proposed for identifying mechanical failures. It can achieve more precise judgment than neural network method. The expert system is applied in fault diagnosis [12, 13]. In [12], the method based on the expert system and neural network, it can deal with the fault data that sent from on-line monitoring equipment and then discover the fault type. In [14], it is proposed for real-time fault diagnosis. In [15], a robust diagnosis method is proposed and that improves the anti-interference performance. In [16], a new analytic model is established to take into account of the possible malfunctions of protective relays and circuit breaker as well as the missing and false alarms. The research of fault diagnosis is less for low voltage circuit breaker. In [17], based on EMD and intrinsic mode function (IMF), the fault identification model of extreme learning machine is built. The research on the electrical life is another important aspect for the electrical equipment [18, 19]. In [19], it is the influence and experimental study on electrical life under different protected circuit conditions. In [20], it summarizes these methods that are typically used in industry to evaluate the service life of low voltage power circuit breaker and molded case circuit breaker. In [21], a new method is proposed for the life assessment of electrical components, that supports the decision-making in future deregulation of the electric energy market. In [22], it establishes a new comprehensive model based on cloud model that considers fuzziness and randomness of uncertainty at the same time for electrical life.

If those above research methods are applied in this paper, there are three problems: 1. the fault judgment of electrical life test may happen the erroneous judgment that may directly lead to accidents; 2. if those above methods are used to analyze and judge whether the fault occurs based on collected signal, there is time lag for the judgment of the fault; 3. it is a heavy work and no practical significance to analyze the signal of each waveform.

2 Method of Collecting Test Parameters

In the process of the electrical life test for the low voltage circuit breaker, there are specified parameters, such as the test voltage U, the test current I, the connection time T_j, the opening time T_f, and the test number N. The test has these characteristics: many times, long cycle and difficult to find fault. In the process of test, there may be various kinds of faults, such as the contact welding, the serious wear of the contact, the failure of the mechanical structure, the clamping of the auxiliary device and so on. When the fault occurs, it is possible to cause other accidents, so the test process needs to be monitored in real time. The traditional monitoring method is to collect waveforms of voltage and current, as shown in Fig. 1. The real-time waveform of voltage and current is observed by the tester, and the fault is judged based on the change of the waveform. On the one hand, this method generates a large number of invalid and non fault data records; on the other hand, it depends on the time and experience of the tester.

To solve the above problem, a method for collecting test parameters is proposed in this paper. This method selects five parameters that are the test voltage effective value, the test current effective value, the connection time, the opening time and the test number. The collection of these above parameters uses electronic devices that collect effective value, compared with the use of waveform collection equipment, and greatly reduces the cost.

The electrical life test of three-phase low voltage AC circuit breaker is taken as an example. The method of collecting test parameters is shown in Fig. 2 that is the electrical life test system. These symbols of A, B, C represent the A phase, B phase, C phase of power supply, respectively. The vacuum circuit breaker is connected in the system in series. If the vacuum circuit breaker is opened, the power supply of the test system is cut off. These symbols of I_A, I_B, I_C represent these current transformers of A phase, B phase, C phase, that are used to collect these current signals. Z_1 represents the short-circuit impedance of inlet end for the circuit breaker. Z_2 represents the electrical life impedance of the outlet end for the circuit breaker. These symbols of U_A, U_B, U_C represent the voltage collection signals between the ends of the inlet and the outlet of A phase, B phase, C phase for the circuit breaker. It is marked as "C", as the circuit breaker is closed. It is marked as "O", as the circuit breaker is opened. Each "C-O" operation in the electrical life test is recorded as the completion of a single test that is cycle. The voltage effective value is collected between the inlet end and outlet end of the contact. If the test is normal, as the contact state is closed, the contact resistance between the contact ends is almost zero, and so the voltage effective value is almost zero; as the contact state is opened, the inlet end is charged, the outlet end is suspended, and so the voltage effective value between the contact ends is the power phase voltage. The current effective value is collected with current transformer which primary side is hollow that achieves the effect of electrical isolation.

During the electrical life test, these values of normal state parameters are shown in Table 1. In the process of test, if the waveform of the parameters is collected, the normal test waveform is shown in Fig. 1.

In Fig. 1, there are I_A, U_A, I_B, U_B, I_C, U_C in waveform channels from top to bottom. The time that the voltage disappears but the current existences is the connection time

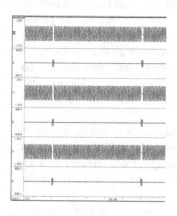

Fig. 1. The normal test waveform

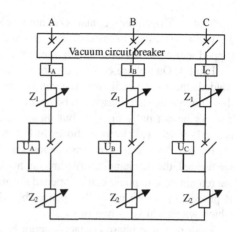

Fig. 2. The electrical life test system diagram

Table 1. The normal state parameter

U_A		U_B		U_C		I_A		I_B		I_C		T_{jA}		T_{jB}		T_{jC}		T_{fA}		T_{fB}		T_{fC}	
C	O	C	O	C	O	C	O	C	O	C	O	C	O	C	O	C	O	C	O	C	O	C	O
0	U	0	U	0	U	I	0	I	0	I	0	T_j	/	T_j	/	T_j	/	/	T_f	/	T_f	/	T_f

and marked as T_j. The time that the current disappears but the voltage existences is the opening time and marked as T_f. These effective values of I_A, U_A, I_B, U_B, I_C and U_C are measured from Fig. 1, as well as T_j and T_f.

3   Established Fault Diagnosis Model

3.1   Typical Fault Examples

In the process of the electrical life test, the three-phase low voltage AC circuit breaker may have the following typical faults in Fig. 2. The fault description and analysis are described as follows.

Fault 1. One phase contact cannot be closed normally, such as that the contact is worn seriously, the mechanical structure can not be closed normally, the contact tripped and other reasons, but these remaining two phases can be closed normally. For example, the A phase contact can not be normally closed, but these contacts of B and C phase can be normally closed, which waveform is shown in Fig. 3.

Fault 2. Two phase contacts cannot be closed normally, such as that these contacts are worn seriously, the mechanical structure can not be closed normally, the contact tripped and other reasons, but the remaining one phase can be closed normally. For example, these contacts of A phase and B phase can not be normally closed, but C phase contact can be normally closed, which waveform is shown in Fig. 4.

Fault 3. Three phase contacts cannot be closed normally, such as that these contacts are worn seriously, the mechanical structure can not be closed normally, the contact tripped and other reasons, which waveform is shown in Fig. 5.

Fault 4. One phase contact cannot be opened normally, such as that the contact is welded, the mechanical structure can not be opened normally and other reasons, but these remaining two phases can be opened normally. For example, the A phase contact can not be normally opened, but these contacts of B and C phase can be normally opened, which waveform is shown in Fig. 6.

Fault 5. Two phase contacts cannot be opened normally, such as that these contacts are welded, the mechanical structure can not be opened normally and other reasons, but the remaining one phase can be opened normally. For example, these contacts of A and B phase can not be normally opened, but C phase contact can be normally opened, which waveform is shown in Fig. 7.

Fault 6. Three phase contacts cannot be opened normally, such as that these contacts are welded, the mechanical structure can not be opened normally and other reasons, which waveform is shown in Fig. 8.

Fault 7. The connection time is a fault that connection time is longer than specified time, such as that the contact wears seriously, the test auxiliary device leads to the fault and other reasons. That waveform is relatively simple, compared to Fig. 1 can be understood, so it is not shown separately.

Fault 8. The opening time is a fault that opening time is longer than specified time, such as that the contact wears seriously, the test auxiliary device leads to the fault and other reasons. That waveform is relatively simple, compared to Fig. 1 can be understood, so it is not shown separately.

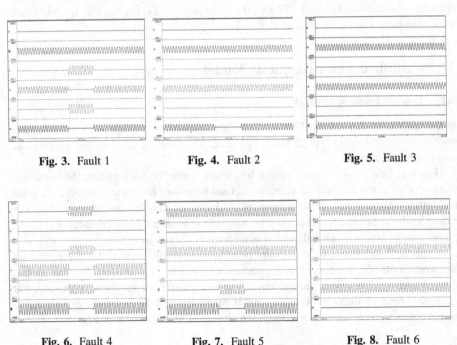

Fig. 3. Fault 1   **Fig. 4.** Fault 2   **Fig. 5.** Fault 3

Fig. 6. Fault 4   **Fig. 7.** Fault 5   **Fig. 8.** Fault 6

In Figures from 3, 4, 5, 6, 7 and 8, there are I_A, U_A, I_B, U_B, I_C, U_C in waveform channels from top to bottom. Compared Figs. 1, 3, 4, 5, 6, 7 and 8, can be found that these parameters change differently in different faults. Based on the above data analysis of fault waveform, the fault diagnosis model is established as follows.

3.2 Established Mathematical Model

The rated voltage and current of the circuit breaker are marked as Ue and Ie respectively. According to the electrical life test requirement, the test voltage is $U = [1, 1.05]Ue$, the test current is $I = [1, 1.05] Ie$, the test number is N. T_j and T_f have not test requirements, but according to long term test experience, this paper sets requirements: the connection time is within $1.1T_j$, the opening time is within $1.1\ T_f$. Those above five parameters change within a reasonable range as the test is normally carried out. Those above five parameters change beyond a reasonable range as the fault occurs during the test. These parameters collected by the monitoring device are the test voltage effective value U_1, the test current effective value I_1, the connection time T_{j1}, the opening time T_{f1}, the test number N_1. The mathematical relationship is established and shown in Table 2.

Based on the mathematical relationship in table, there are fault examples from 1 to 8, and the mathematical model is established with function. The normal state and fault state of these parameters can be represented by the truth value "0" and "1", respectively. The mathematical relationship of Table 2 is shown in the truth table as shown in Table 3. These parameters are measured independently, but that are related to each other. The relationship among these parameters is expressed with the algorithm "or" ($\oplus$).

Table 2. The mathematical relationship

Parameter	Normal	Fault
Voltage	$U_1 \in U$	$U_1 \notin U$
Current	$I_1 \in I$	$I_1 \notin I$
Connection time	$T_{j1} < 1.1T_j$	$T_{j1} \geq 1.1T_j$
Opening time	$T_{f1} < 1.1T_f$	$T_{f1} \geq 1.1T_f$
Test number	$N_1 \leq N$	$N_1 > N$

Table 3. The truth value table

Parameter	Normal	Fault
S_1	0	1
S_2	0	1
S_3	0	1
S_4	0	1
S_5	0	1

$S = \{s_1, s_2 \cdots s_m\}$ represents a parameter set that may fault, $s_m = 1$ represents the fault state of parameter m, $s_m = 0$ represents the normal state of parameter m, m represents the number of parameters. In this paper $m = 5$, s_1 represents the test voltage, s_2 represents the test current, s_3 represents the connection time, s_4 represents the opening time, s_5 represents the test number. In the circuit, n represents a phase in a three-phase circuit, $s_{mn} = \{s_{mA}, s_{mB}, s_{mC}\}$, A phase, B phase and C phase are expressed respectively with s_{mA}, s_{mB}, s_{mC}. The fault state of n phase of m parameter is expressed with $s_{mn} = 1$ and the normal state of n phase of m parameter is expressed with $s_{mn} = 0$. In the process of electrical life test, the contact is divided into two states: closed and opened that are expressed with s_{mnC} and s_{mnO} respectively. Those are expressed with set $s_{mn} = \{s_{mnC}, s_{mnO}\}$. Their fault states are expressed with $s_{mnC} = 1, s_{mnO} = 1$ and their normal states are expressed with $s_{mnC} = 0, s_{mnO} = 0$.

In summary, the relationship of these above parameters is represented in (1).

$$
\begin{cases}
S = \{s_1, s_2, s_3, s_4, s_5\} \\
\quad s_1 = \{s_{1A}, s_{1B}, s_{1C}\} = \{\{s_{1AC}, s_{1AO}\}, \{s_{1BC}, s_{1BO}\}, \{s_{1CC}, s_{1CO}\}\} \\
\quad s_2 = \{s_{2A}, s_{2B}, s_{2C}\} = \{\{s_{2AC}, s_{2AO}\}, \{s_{2BC}, s_{2BO}\}, \{s_{2CC}, s_{2CO}\}\} \\
= \; s_3 = \{s_{3A}, s_{3B}, s_{3C}\} = \{\{s_{3AC}, s_{3AO}\}, \{s_{3BC}, s_{3BO}\}, \{s_{3CC}, s_{3CO}\}\} \\
\quad s_4 = \{s_{4A}, s_{4B}, s_{4C}\} = \{\{s_{4AC}, s_{4AO}\}, \{s_{4BC}, s_{4BO}\}, \{s_{4CC}, s_{4CO}\}\} \\
\quad s_5 = \{s_{5A}, s_{5B}, s_{5C}\} = \{\{s_{5AC}, s_{5AO}\}, \{s_{5BC}, s_{5BO}\}, \{s_{5CC}, s_{5CO}\}\}
\end{cases}
\tag{1}
$$

Considering the logical relationship of the fault, the function expression of the fault diagnosis model is as follows:

$$s_{mn} = s_{mnC} \oplus s_{mnO} \tag{2}$$

$$s_m = s_{mA} \oplus s_{mB} \oplus s_{mC} \tag{3}$$

$$S = s_1 \oplus s_2 \cdots \oplus s_5 \tag{4}$$

s_1, s_2, s_3 and s_4 are real-time monitored of each cycle, s_5 is cumulatively counted once. According to the above logic operation, the result of logic operation $S = 1$ can be judged as a fault, as the truth value of one parameter is changed from "0" to "1".

3.3   Example Analysis of Fault Diagnosis

From fault 1 to fault 6, the test voltage effective value, the test current effective value, the connection time and the opening time have changed significantly, and the specific

Table 4. The specific change of parameters

Parameters	Fault 1		Fault 2		Fault 3		Fault 4		Fault 5		Fault 6	
	C	O	C	O	C	O	C	O	C	O	C	O
U_A	U	U	U	U	U	U	0	0	0	0	0	0
U_B	0	U	U	U	U	U	0	$\sqrt{3}$ U	0	0	0	0
U_C	0	U	0	U	U	U	0	$\sqrt{3}$ U	0	U	0	0
I_A	0	0	0	0	0	0	I	0	I	$\sqrt{3}$ I/2	I	I
I_B	$\sqrt{3}$ I/2	0	0	0	0	0	I	0	I	$\sqrt{3}$ I/2	I	I
I_C	$\sqrt{3}$ I/2	0	0	0	0	0	I	0	I	0	I	I
T_{jA}	0	/	0	/	0	/	$T_j + T_f$	/	$T_j + T_f$	/	$T_j + T_f$	/
T_{jB}	T_j	/	0	/	0	/	T_j	/	$T_j + T_f$	/	$T_j + T_f$	/
T_{jC}	T_j	/	T_j	/	0	/	T_j	/	T_j	/	$T_j + T_f$	/
T_{fA}	/	$T_j + T_f$	/	$T_j + T_f$	/	$T_j + T_f$	/	0	/	0	/	0
T_{fB}	/	T_f	/	$T_j + T_f$	/	$T_j + T_f$	/	T_f	/	0	/	0
T_{fC}	/	T_f	/	T_f	/	$T_j + T_f$	/	T_f	/	T_f	/	0

Table 5. The truth value of fault 1

s_{1AC}	s_{1AO}	s_{1BC}	s_{1BO}	s_{1CC}	s_{1CO}	s_{2AC}	s_{2AO}	s_{2BC}	s_{2BO}	s_{2CC}	s_{2CO}
1	0	0	0	0	0	1	0	1	0	1	0

s_{3AC}	s_{3AO}	s_{3BC}	s_{3BO}	s_{3CC}	s_{3CO}	s_{4AC}	s_{4AO}	s_{4BC}	s_{4BO}	s_{4CC}	s_{4CO}
1	0	0	0	0	0	0	1	0	0	0	0

change of parameters is as shown in Table 4. Based on the mathematical model, fault 1 is taken as an example to analyze, and the truth value table is shown in Table 5.

Based on the truth value in Table 5, the result is $S = 1$ that the logic relationship is calculated with (1)–(4), so it is judged for the test fault. In accordance with the same method, the fault truth table of the above fault example 2 to 8 is listed for logical calculation. The results show that the fault diagnosis model can be used to judge whether the fault occurred in the test process.

4   Design of Monitoring Device

4.1   General Idea

Based on the above fault diagnosis model, the overall design idea of the monitoring device is as follows.

Step 1. The fault diagnosis model is established. According to the test requirements, the fault diagnosis model is established, and the data of the fault diagnosis model is input into the monitoring device, which is the basis for judging whether the fault occurs in the test process.

Step 2. The real time data is collected. These characteristics of this test are long cycle, high operating frequency, high fault rate, so that need to collect real time data which is transmitted to the monitoring device.

Step 3. The data is judged. The collected real time data is calculated according to the fault diagnosis model to judge whether the fault occurs.

Step 4. The protective measure is taken. If there is no fault, the monitoring device will not take protective measure, and then the test continues. If there is a fault, the monitoring device will take protective measure (e.g., the vacuum circuit breaker is opened in Fig. 2). The test is stopped and the tester is informed to deal with the fault.

4.2   The Production of Monitoring Device

Based on the above fault diagnosis model, the monitoring device is made in this paper, which can effectively monitor the test process. The test voltage effective value is monitored with the voltmeter. The test current effective value is monitored with the ammeter. The connection time and opening time are monitored with the time relay. The test number is monitored with the counter. A simple circuit is used to realize the logic judgment and output, and has the function of automatic alarm and automatic protection when the fault is detected.

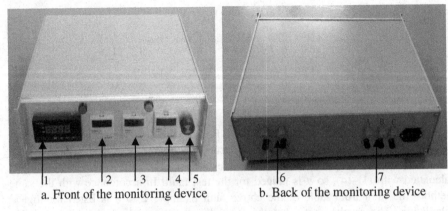

a. Front of the monitoring device   b. Back of the monitoring device

Fig. 9. a. Front of the monitoring device b. Back of the monitoring device

Where 1. voltmeter, 2. connection time relay, 3. opening time relay, 4. counter, 5. buzzer, 6. output contacts, 7. voltage signal input terminals

It can be seen from Figs. 3, 4, 5, 6, 7 and 8 that the change of voltage and current is mutual when fault occurs, so one parameter can be selected for monitoring. In this paper, the voltage type monitoring device and the current type monitoring device are designed respectively. Taking the voltage type monitoring device as an example, the front of the monitoring device is shown in Fig. 9a, and the back of the monitoring device is shown in Fig. 9b. The voltmeter has these functions of data storage and logic judgment, and can set the upper and lower limit of the voltage effective value. That is, the upper limit value is 1.05Ue, the lower limit value is Ue. When the upper and lower limits of the voltage effective value are collected, the logic output of the voltmeter is 0. In another condition, it is 1. Two time relays are used to collect the connection time and the opening time. They have these functions of data storage and logic judgment. When the time that the real time collected does not exceed the set time, the logic output of the time relay is 0. In another condition, it is 1. The counter is used to collect the test number, and it has these functions of data storage and logic judgment. When the number that the real time collected does not exceed the set number, the logic output of the counter is 0. In another condition, it is 1. The internal circuit structure is built to achieve the judgment function of fault diagnosis model. When a fault occurs, the buzzer sends out a sound warning that the test had fault; the output contacts action makes the vacuum circuit breaker automatically open and cut off the main circuit of the electrical life test system. These voltage signal input terminals collect U_A, U_B, U_C voltage effective value in Fig. 2.

4.3 The Working Flow Chart

Combined with Figs. 2 and 9, the electrical life test of the three-phase low voltage AC circuit breaker is taken as an example to illustrate the working flow chart of the monitoring device, as shown in Fig. 10.

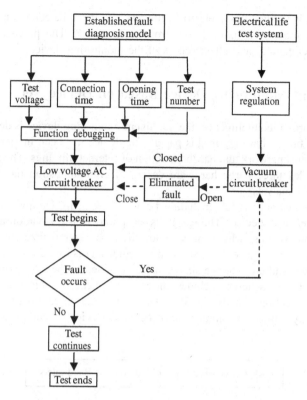

Fig. 10. The working flow chart of monitoring device

The working flow chart of the monitoring device is described in detail in Fig. 10. First of all, based on the fault diagnosis model of Table 2, these test parameters of test voltage value, connection time, opening time and test number are respectively set in the voltmeter, connection time relay, opening time relay and counter. And then, these faults of test voltage, connection time, opening time and test number are simulated in a simple circuit, the monitoring device can monitor the occurrence of the fault and then takes protective measure. All functions are normal and the monitoring device is connected to the low voltage AC circuit breaker. The electrical life test is carried out in the electrical life test system that is regulated and test parameters meet the requirements. The vacuum circuit breaker is connected with the low voltage AC circuit breaker in the main circuit of the test system. The open control of vacuum circuit breaker is connected with the output contact of the monitoring device, as part of the control circuit for the test system. As the electrical life test is carrying, the monitoring device monitors real time test data and analysis whether the fault occurs. If there is no fault, the test continues until the end of the test. If the fault occurs, the output contacts of the monitoring device move, so that the vacuum circuit breaker is opened, and the tester hears the alarm sound to eliminate the fault then the vacuum circuit breaker is closed.

The device is verified in the electrical life test, and it can detect and take protective measure when the typical fault occurs from fault 1 to 8. The practical application proves the practicability and effectiveness of the monitoring device.

5 Intelligent Monitoring Device Based on Device Net

In order to improve its intelligence, the intelligent monitoring device is designed based on Device net bus technology in this paper. The device has been implemented in the Device net control network and has the function of Internet of things. The main work of this part includes three parts: hardware design of communication module, software design and data analysis.

First, these external signals including I_A, U_A, I_B, U_B, I_C, U_C and status signal of vacuum breaker are selected. These signals are photoelectric isolation and D/A conversion as input signals, where the vacuum circuit breaker realizes remote wireless control through I/O interface. PIC18F458 microcontroller is used as the control chip for hardware design, and these above signals are transmitted to the microcontroller. Then, the software design scheme includes the establishment of object model and I/O information connection. Finally, the SST-DN3-PCU-1 master card is used as a network analyzer to analyze the data communication between Device net and the test progress in

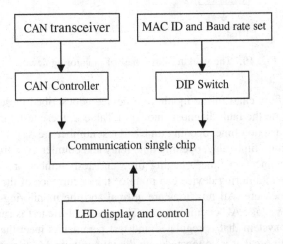

Fig. 11. The flow chart of hardware communication module design

detail. These operation parameters and status of intelligent monitoring device are uploaded to the network to realize remote monitoring and operation, and the real-time monitoring test process of remote network can be realized.

The flow chart of hardware communication module design is shown in Fig. 11, as follows

The hardware communication module design. The PIC18F458 is used as communication module control chip, and the chip is integrated with CAN controller.

The CAN transceiver chip uses the PCA82C250T as the bus driver. The main function of communication module is explained as follows.

(1) The CAN bus protocol is used to realize the basic functions of CAN communication transceiver and controller.
(2) The MAC ID and baud rate of the node are set by the DIP switch. The DIP switch sets the node address and can transmit data at three baud rates of 125K, 250K and 500K
(3) The SPI serial communication is used between the communication module MCU and the control unit to realize data exchange between the bus and the control unit
(4) The bus module communication status is displayed on LED display, according to the test needs, we can remote control, modify the test parameters, and transmitted to the monitoring device.

Software design. According to the functions that the data acquisition unit and the

Table 6. The object model

Object class	Message router	Device net	Connection	Analog input point	Discrete output point	Discrete input point
Data	1	1	1 explicit message 1 I/O message	6	1	1

control unit of the intelligent monitoring device can complete, these parameters that need to be transmitted in the network are defined. There are 8 I/O message data: I_A, U_A, I_B, U_B, I_C, U_C, N and vacuum breaker Open/Close control signal. There is 1 explicit message: vacuum breaker status signal. Thus, the object model of the intelligent monitoring device is defined, as shown in Table 6.

Data analysis. This article uses the Device Net Network Analyzer analysis component in SST-DN3-PCU-1 as the network analyzer to obtain the data transmitted online. According to the fault model calculation method established above, the obtained data is analyzed in real time to determine whether there is a fault during the process. The data analysis and process is the same between monitoring device and intelligent monitoring device so we will not repeat the description.

6 Conclusions

In this paper, through the method of collecting test parameters, establishing fault diagnosis model and the design of monitoring device, effectively solves the problem of fault diagnosis and monitoring device for low voltage circuit breaker in the electrical life test. This paper has these following advantages compared with the traditional electrical life test method.

1. Collected parameters real time, based on the established fault diagnosis model, to determine whether the fault occurred in a timely manner.
2. The design of the monitoring device achieves fault diagnosis through effective value collection. Compared with the waveform collection method, the monitor device has no data storage and waveform generation, so the cost of equipment is reduced.
3. The design of the monitoring device has the function of automatic alarm and protective measures. The fault diagnosis does not rely on the experience of the tester to judge. Do not need the tester in the test site in real time, which saves labor cost.

Acknowledgement. This work was supported in part by the National Natural Science Foundation (51377044), National Science and Technology Support Program (2015BAA09B01), Hebei province science and technology plan project (14214503D), Science and technology plan project of General Administration of Quality Supervision, Inspection and Quarantine of the P. R. C. (2016QK098).

References

1. Jia, R., Hong, G., Xue, J., Cui, J.: Application of particle swarm optimization-least square support vector machine algorithm in mechanical fault diagnosis of high-voltage circuit breaker. Power Syst. Technol. **34**(3), 197–200 (2010)
2. Mei, F., Mei, J., Zheng, J., Zhang, S., Zhu, K.: Application of particle swarm fused KFCM and classification model of SVM for fault diagnosis of circuit breaker. Proc. CSEE **33**(36), 134–141 (2013)
3. Xu, J., Zhang, B., Lin, X., Li, B., Teng, Y.: Application of energy spectrum entropy vector method and RBF neural networks optimized by the particle swarm in high-voltage circuit breaker mechanical fault diagnosis. High Volt. Eng. **38**(6), 1299–1306 (2012)
4. Sun, Y., Wu, J., Lian, S., Zhang, L.: Extraction of vibration signal feature vector of circuit breaker based on empirical mode decomposition amount of energy. Trans. China Electrotech. Soc. **29**(3), 228–236 (2014)
5. Huang, J., Hu, X., Gong, Y.: Machinery fault diagnosis of high voltage circuit breaker based on empirical mode decomposition. Proc. CSEE **31**(12), 108–113 (2011)
6. Shutao, Z., Pei, Z., Lu, S., Jing, G.: Vibration and acoustic joint mechanical fault diagnosis method of high voltage circuit breakers. Trans. China Electrotech. Soc. **29**(7), 216–221 (2014)
7. Huang, N., Zhang, S., Cai, G., Lu, D.: Mechanical fault diagnosis of high voltage circuit breakers utilizing empirical wavelet transform and one-class support vector machine. Chin. J. Sci. Instrum. **36**(12), 2773–2781 (2015)
8. Chang, G., Wang, Y., Wang, W.: Mechanical fault diagnosis of high voltage circuit breakers utilizing zero-phase filter time-frequency entropy of vibration signal. Proc. CSEE **33**(3), 155–162 (2013)
9. Lee, D.S.S., Lighgow, B.J., Morrison, R.E.: New fault diagnosis of circuit breakers. IEEE Trans. Power Deliv. **18**(2), 454–459 (2003)
10. Yang, Z., Liang, L., Li, X., Wu, S.: Application of the gray correlation model in fault diagnosis of high-voltage circuit breakers. Power Syst. Technol. **39**(6), 1731–1735 (2015)

11. Lv, C., Yu, H., Wang, L.: On-line self-learning fault diagnosis for circuit breakers based on artificial immune network. Proc. CSEE **29**(34), 128–134 (2009)
12. Wang, X., Rong, M., Wu, Y., Liu, D.: Method of quick fault diagnosis and new knowledge obtainment for high voltage circuit breaker expert system. Proc. CSEE **27**(3), 95–99 (2007)
13. Huang, J., Hu, X., Gong, Y., Yang, F.: Machinery fault diagnosis expert system for high voltage circuit breaker. Electricmach. Control **15**(10), 43–49 (2011)
14. Ni, J., Zhang, C., Yang, S.X.: An adaptive approach based on KPCA and SVM for real-time fault diagnosis of HVCBs. IEEE Trans Power Deliv. **26**(3), 1960–1971 (2011)
15. Mei, F., Mei, J., Zheng, J., Zhu, K.: The robust fault diagnostic method for circuit breaker based on KPCA and SVM. Trans. China Electrotech. Soc. **29**(1), 50–58 (2014)
16. Guo, W., Wen, F., Ledwich, G., Liao, Z., He, X., Liang, J.: An analytic model for fault diagnosis in power systems considering malfunctions of protective relays and circuit breakers. IEEE Trans. Power Deliv. **25**(3), 1393–1401 (2010)
17. Zhang, L., Shi, D., Miao, X.: Research on vibration signal feature analysis and its fault diagnosis. Electr. Mach. Control **20**(10), 82–87 (2016)
18. Wang, P., Zhang, J., Yu, Y., Lv, Z., Luo, C.: A new type of on-line monitoring system for electrical endurance of circuit breaker. Autom. Electr. Power Syst. **33**(17), 109–111 (2009)
19. Guo, F., Wang, Z., Li, Y., Liu, W., Yao, X., Fang, C.: Influence and experimental study on relay's electrical life under different protected circuits conditions. Proc. CSEE **27**(31), 77–82 (2007)
20. Sprague, M.J.: Service-life evaluations of low-voltage power circuit breakers and molded-case circuit breakers. IEEE Trans. Indust. Appl. **37**(1), 145–152 (2001)
21. Zhang, X., Gockenbach, E., Wasserberg, V., Borsi, H.: Estimation of the lifetime of the electrical components in distribution networks. IEEE Trans. Power Deliv. **22**(1), 515–522 (2007)
22. Hu, C., Tao, F., Yang, J., Liang, Y., Wang. Y.: An assessment method for electrical life of vacuum circuit breaker based on coud model. In: 2014 International Conference on High Voltage Engineering and Application, pp. 1–4 (2014)
23. Li, L., Han, Y., Chen, W., Lv, C., Sun, D.: An improved wavelet packet-chaos model for life prediction of space relays based on volterra series. PLoS ONE **11**(6), e0158435 (2016)

Mainland China

Sound-Wave Transmission System in Mobile Device

Ching-Lung Chang[✉], Meng-Lun Cai, and Yu-Shiang Shiau

Department of CSIE, National Yunlin University of Science and Technology,
Douliu, Taiwan, R.O.C.
{chang, M10217001}@yuntech.edu.tw

Abstract. Based on equipments of speaker and microphone in mobile device, we develop a sound wave transmission system. The digital data is encoded in the analogy sound wave, transmitted by speaker, received by microphone, and decoded by the mobile device to derive the original data. For enhance the accuracy, the functionalities of error correction and adaptive frequency response are consideration in the system. The throughput of the system is 72 bps with accuracy rate 90% under transmission distance 100 cm.

Keywords: Sound-wave transmission system · Fast Fourier Transform
Hamming code

1 Introduction

With the advance of VLSI design and communication technique, the smart phone and tablet PC are widely accepted as the major platform for mobile communication. Up to now, the major communication interfaces in mobile devices includes Bluetooth, WiFi, and NFC. The NFC only supports close communication. It needs pairing operations in Bluetooth to make a connection before data communication. In the WiFi, the IP address or some of setup operations for the Direct WiFi is required. These pairing or set up operations are difficult for general users. For providing a friendly user interface in mobile device communication, this paper develops a sound-wave transmission system based on the general speaker and microphone. If we want to start a communication between mobile devices, we can first send the pairing/setup information or IP address via the acoustics transmission system to the peer mobile device. Once the peer mobile device receives the configuration information, based on the received information, a connection between mobile devices via Bluetooth or WiFi interface can be established automatically for further data communication.

The sound-wave transmission system can be classified into digital audio transmission and analog audio transmission, as shown in Fig. 1. Most of the literatures target on the digital audio signal processing for embedding a copyright watermarking

This work is supported by the Ministry of Science and Technology, Taiwan, Republic of China, under grant number *MOST 103-2218-E-224-003-MY2*.

Y.-B. Lin et al. (Eds.): IoTaaS 2017, LNICST 246, pp. 333–339, 2018.
https://doi.org/10.1007/978-3-030-00410-1_38

[3, 4]. Most of researches in analog audio communication focus on the topics of underwater communication. The properties of underwater transceiver are very different from general speaker and microphone. Considering the human audible frequency, the frequency response of speaker and microphone is generally designed to less than 20 kHz [1]. Xiang et al. [2] consider the analog audio communication, such Fig. 1(a) depicts. In [2], it focuses on study the effect of AD/DA equipments. Thus, the wire-line is used to connect the line-out of transmission side to the line-in of receiving side for excluding the sound-wave distortion in the air communication.

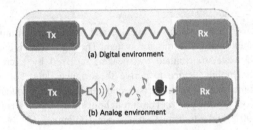

Fig. 1. The concept of sound-wave transmission system

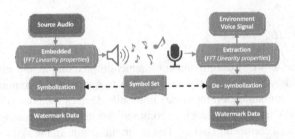

Fig. 2. Sound-wave transmission system architecture

Difference from the [2] consideration, we target on the sound-wave transmission system design based on the speaker/microphone transceiver, as Fig. 1(b) depicts.

2   The Design of Sound-Wave Transmission System

Figure 2 illustrates the sound-wave transmission system architecture. The digital data is embedded in the background audio under frequency domain. An inverse Fast Fourier Transform (IFFT) converts the frequency domain sound wave to the time domain and playout to the speaker. In the receiver side, the sound wave is received by the microphone and digitalized by the A/D converter. The digital sound waves are converted to the frequency domain by FFT for extracting the transmitted digital data.

2.1   Protocol Stack

For reducing the interference, we choose the frequencies of 17 kHz, 18 kHz, and 19 kHz as the elementary frequencies. Based on these three frequencies, we design four type of symbols, called *Bit0* symbol, *Bit1* symbol, *Gain* symbol, and *Guard* symbol. Figure 3 illustrates the protocol stacks of the proposed sound-wave transmission system. Herein, the application layer generates the transmission data called watermarking data which relies sound-wave to transmit. The data link layer composes the application data with *Sync-code* as data link frame. The purpose of *Sync-code* is used for frame delimitation. The pattern of *Sync-code* is binary pattern 0110. At the same time, the data link layer implements hamming code in application data for 1-bit error correction. The codec function of physical layer converts the analogy sound-wave to digital binary bits. Due to the frequency response in speaker/microphone is difference. This means the attenuation a sound frequency may difference in different speaker/microphone. Figure 3 depicts the attenuation of the three elementary frequencies against to distance. Thus, we design a *Gain* symbol which consists all of sound frequencies used in the system for amplitude adaption in receiving side. In the transmission side, the *Gain* symbol is transmitted with the fix power. In the receiving side, based on the receiving power of *Gain* symbol, we understand the attenuation rate of the used speaker/microphone pair. Therefore, depending on the attenuation rate of the *Gain* symbol, the receiver compensates the attenuation in the following *sync-code* and *data symbol*. The *Guard* symbol uses for avoiding the interference between *Gain* symbol and *Sync-code* (Fig. 4).

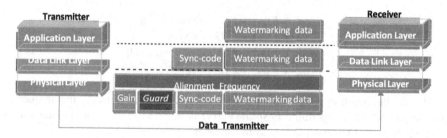

Fig. 3. The protocol stack of sound-wave transmission system

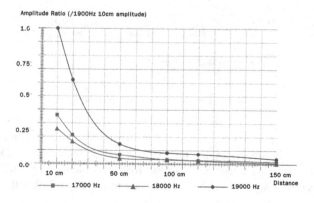

Fig. 4. The relationship between attenuation and distance

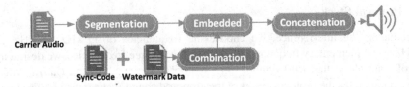

Fig. 5. The transmission of data link layer

2.2   System Implementation

Figure 5 shows the transmission of data link layer. First the *Sync-code* denoted as D_{sync} precedes the application data denoted as D_{app} to form the data sequence denoted as D. The data sequence D is represented in Eq. (1).

$$D = (D_{sync} \ll Len(D_{app}) \mid H_c(D_{app}). \tag{1}$$

Where the functions of $Len(D_{app})$ and $Hc(D_{app})$ represent the length of D_{app} and the D_{app} with 1-bit error correction hamming code, respectively.

The carrier audio (background sound) in Fig. 5 denoted as A_{sound}, is divided into frames denoted as x_i which represents the i'th frame. Each frame have s samples which must be the 2 power for FFT operations. In this implementation the s is 512.

The data sequence D must be embedded into carrier audio A_{sound}. Each frame of A_{sound} is embedded one symbol. The embedded processes is represented in Eq. (2).

$$F(SoundWave) = \begin{cases} F(x_i) + F(GainSymbol), & if\ i = 0, \\ F(x_i) + F(GuardSymbol), & if\ i = 1, \\ F(x_i) + F(Bit0Symbol), & if\ D[i-2] = 0, \\ F(x_i) + F(Bit1Symbol), & if\ D[i-2] = 1, \end{cases} \tag{2}$$

Where the function $F(x)$ mean the FFT operations of x. Finally, the frequency domain embedded sound frame $F(SoundWave)$ is inverted to the time domain sound wave via inverse FFT and playout to the speaker.

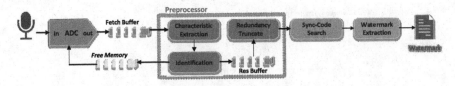

Fig. 6. The receiver of data link layer

The receiving process of the acoustics Transmission System is shown in Fig. 6. The sound wave signal is sensing by the microphone and digitalizing by ADC. The time domain sound wave data is converted to the frequency domain by FFT. In the pre-processor phase, we only find the basic frequency to identify whether the sound wave has embedded the digital data. If we found the basic frequency in preprocessor phase, we further do the sync-code search for delimitating the starting point of the digital data and extract the digital data.

3 Performance Evaluation

To evaluate the performance of sound-wave transmission system, an experimental model is proposed as Fig. 7 illustrates. The device noise of microphone and A/D converter is measured and built these noise model in Fig. 7. A de-noise model is applied to cancel the noise effect of microphone and A/D converter. The DB_{env} records four type environment background sounds which include road, peaceful, restaurant, and air condition. The spectrum of background sounds is shown in Fig. 8. We use HTC Bufferfly S as receiver and HTC Desire A818 as transmitter to measurement the performance. Table 1 shows the associated implementation parameters. Based on Table 1 parameter, the transmission rate of the system is 72.53 bps. The transmission accuracy is evaluated in the following.

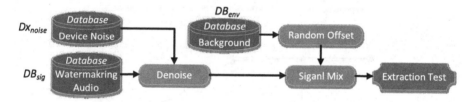

Fig. 7. The experimental model for performance evaluation

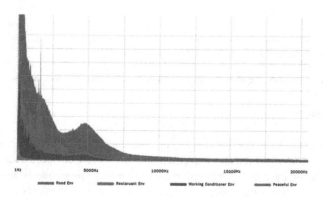

Fig. 8. The frequency spectrum of background sound

Table 1. The implementation parameters.

Parameters	Value
Element frequency	17 kHz
	18 kHz
	19 kHz
Sample/frame	512 samples
Sample rate	44100 Hz
Sync-code size	16 bits
Sync-code size	16 bits
D_{app}	96 bits

The comparison of average transmission accuracy under different distance and scheme is shown in Fig. 9. As Fig. 9 depicts, when the transmission distance increases, the scheme with hamming code and Gain symbol keep a better results than others. Under the transmission distance 100 cm, the scheme with hamming code and Gain symbol has 40% increasing than without any scheme.

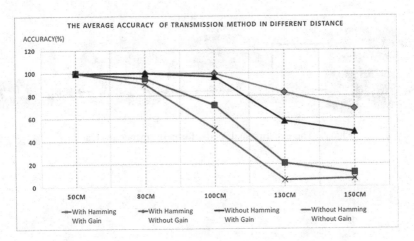

Fig. 9. Compare the average accuracy under difference distance and scheme

4   Conclusions

In this paper, based on the basic speaker and microphone, a analog sound-wave transmission system is design and implementation in mobile device. For increasing the transmission accuracy rate, a 1-bite error correction hamming code is applied in data link layer. To overcome the different frequency response of speaker/microphone, the physical layer adds Gain symbol to compensate sound wave attenuation of speaker/microphone. The performance measurement results reveal that the throughput of the system is about 72 bps. The average transmission accuracy in different environment can up to 90% under transmission distance 100 cm.

References

1. Lee, J., et al.: Behavioral hearing thresholds between 0.125 and 20 kHz using depth-compensated ear simulator calibration. Ear Hear. **33**, 315 (2012)
2. Xiang, S.: Audio watermarking robust against D/A and A/D conversions. EURASIP J. Adv. Signal Process. **2011**(1), 3 (2011)
3. Steinebach, M., Lang, A., Dittmann, J.: Audio watermarking quality evaluation: robustness to DA/AD processes. In: International Conference on Information Technology: Coding and Computing (ITCC 02), pp. 100–103 (2002)
4. Prasad, R.V., Sangwan, A., Jamadagni, H.S., Chiranth, M.C., Sah, R., Gaurav, V.: Comparison of voice activity detection algorithms for VoIP. In: Proceedings of Seventh International Symposium on Computers and Communications, ISCC 2002, pp 530–535 (2002)

UE-Group Based Multi-beams Subchannel Assignment for mmWave Cellular Networks (Invited Paper)

Zhongjiang Yan[1,2(✉)], Mao Yang[1], Bo Li[1], Yusheng Liang[1], and Xiaoya Zuo[1]

[1] Northwestern Polytechnical University, Xi'an 710072, China
{zhjyan,yangmao,libo.npu,zuoxy}@nwpu.edu.cn
[2] Science and Technology on Communication Networks Laboratory,
Shijiazhuang 053200, China

Abstract. In millimetre cellular wave (mmWave) networks, beamforming is an enabling technology. Although the beams in mmWave network are directional and in narrow shapes, there may also exist overlapped areas. To enable the multi-user simultaneous transmissions within the same time slot, the multi-beams subchannel assignment problem is formulated as a non-linear integer programming problem. To combat the complexity, a UE-group based subchannel assignment algorithm is proposed in this paper. According to the locations of the UEs' in the overlapped areas, or the non-overlapped areas, the subchannels are assigned to the UE/UEs, where the beam spatial reuse gain and subchannel multi-user diversity gain are both exploited. Simulation results evaluate the performance of the proposed algorithm, and reveal the relationships of the beam spatial reuse gain and subchannel multi-user diversity gain, with the UE numbers and the downlink traffic load of each UE, respectively.

Keywords: mmWave · Multiple beams · UE-group

1 Introduction

For the 5G applications, such as Internet of Things, Virtual Reality, etc., millimetre wave (mmWave) wireless communication technology is a promising proposal to meet the increasing mobile users demand on high data rate [1]. To combat the high path loss of mmWave, the large scale array is employed to form several directional and narrow shape beams to serve the multiple users. However, there may also exist overlapping area between multiple beams. How to design an efficient resource allocation algorithm for such a multiple beams communication system is a significant and challenging problem.

Due to the high transmission rate of each beam in the mmWave systems, multi-user transmission is desired in mmWave systems, and the mmWave channel can be modelled as a frequency selective steering channel [2]. Multicarrier

© ICST Institute for Computer Sciences, Social Informatics and Telecommunications Engineering 2018
Y.-B. Lin et al. (Eds.): IoTaaS 2017, LNICST 246, pp. 340–348, 2018.
https://doi.org/10.1007/978-3-030-00410-1_39

transmission technique, such as orthogonal frequency division multiple (OFDM), has been well established due to its advantages, mainly its robustness in multipath fading channels and the adaptivity in resource allocation. Particularly, when multi-user access is desired OFDMA can be applied. Thus the multiple beams resource allocation problem can be transformed as a multi-beams subchannel assignment problem.

In the literature, most of the related works on MIMO-OFDM resource allocation are on digital beamforming, such as [3–5] and the references therein. Ref. [3] considers to use joint spatial division and multiplexing method to mmWave channels, where clusters of multi-path components are used to serve several users. A conflict graph based method is proposed to select users and allocate the angular. Ref. [4] investigate the downlink massive MU-MIMO transmission with multiple antennas at each user, and a beam domain channel model is proposed. By selecting users with non-overlapping beams, the MU-MIMO channels are decomposed into multiple single user MIMO channel links. Ref. [5] considers to use coordinated/switched beamforming to serve the UEs' demand while avoiding interference across sectors, where the beam patterns among the base stations are scheduled. For the mmWave resource allocation problems, most of the related works study the problems in the wireless personal area networks or WLAN. For example, Ref. [6] considers the time spatial resource allocation problem to serve a mixed set of multimedia applications. A channel time allocation partial swarm optimization algorithm is proposed. We have studied how to concurrently schedule multiple links in one time slot in [7], and a heuristic clique based scheduling algorithm is proposed.

To the best knowledge of the authors, this paper is the first to study how to design a multiple beams subchannel assignment algorithm, to exploit both the beam spatial reuse gain[1] and the subchannel multiple user diversity gain[2]. The main contributions are three folds.

- The multiple beams subchannel assignment problem is formulated as a nonlinear integer programming problem.
- To combat the complexity of finding the optimal solution, a UE-group based multiple beams subchannel assignment algorithm is proposed, to exploit both the beam spatial reuse gain and the subchannel multi-user diversity gain.
- Simulation results evaluate the performance of the proposed algorithm, and reveal the relationships of the beam spatial reuse gain and subchannel multiuser diversity gain, with the UE numbers and the downlink traffic load of each UE, respectively.

---

[1] Suppose beam b_1 and b_2 share the same frequency, pointing to different directions. User n_1 and n_2 are covered by b_1 and b_2, respectively. Then user n_1 and n_2 can share the same subchannel of b_1 and b_2 at the same time. This is referred as the beam spatial reuse gain.

[2] For a given subchannel, different users may have different data rate on it, and when the user with highest data rate is selected then this selection bring a gain which is the subchannel diversity gain.

Section 2 present the system model, and formulate the subchannel-beam-UE assignment problem as a non-linear integer programming problem. Section 3 details the proposed UE-group based multiple subchannel assignment algorithm. The performance of the proposed algorithm is evaluated in Sect. 4. Section 5 concludes this paper.

2 System Models

Suppose there are B beams with fixed pointing directions fully covering a given sector of a mmWave small cell, where there are N UEs randomly distributed. Each UE associates with one beam according to its received SINR. All of the B beams are working on the same frequency channel in OFDMA mode, which is composed of K subchannels.

In the following, we use n, b, k to denote a specific UE, beam and subchannel, respectively. Let the binary matrix $\mathbb{A} = [a_{b,n}]_{B \times N}$ denote the association relationships between the UEs and the beams, where $a_{b,n} = 1$ meaning that the UE n is associated with beam b. In this paper, we assume each UE can only associate with only one beam, i.e., $\sum_{b=1}^{B} a_{b,n} \leq 1$. Furthermore, each beam can only assign its subchannels to the UEs associated with it. Let $\mathcal{B}_i^j$ denote the jth set of any i beams out of B, where $1 \leq j \leq C(B,i) = \frac{i!}{B!(B-i)!}$, and $1 \leq i \leq B$. And let $\mathcal{N}_{\mathcal{B}_i^j}$ denote the set of UEs covered by all of the beams in $\mathcal{B}_i^j$.

The path loss of mmWave is given as $PL[dB] = \alpha + 10\beta \log_{10}(d) + X_\sigma$, where d is the distance between transmitter and receiver, α is the intercept in dB, β is the slope, and X_σ is a zero mean Gaussian random variable with a standard deviation σ in dB. To decrease the large path loss impact, beamforming is employed by the antenna array, where the beams can point to different directions by changing the current of arrays. In this paper, the rectangular plane array is employed which are arranged in a rectangular grid unit in the XOY plane [8]. Beam b's transmitter antenna gain at UE n can be computed as $G_t(b,n) = [S_{norm}(b,n)]^2 G_{t_{max}}$, where $S_{norm}(b,n)$ is normalized array radiation factor received by UE n from beam b, and $G_{t_{max}}$ is the maximum transmitter antenna gain of beam b.

UE n's received power from beam b can be calculated as $P_r(b,n)[dBm] = P_t[dBm] + G_t(b,n)[dBi] + G_r[dBi] - PL[dB]$, where P_r and P_t are the received and transmitted power, respectively. At a given time slot, by taking the small-scale Rayleigh fading into account, the received signal power at subchannel k can be written as $P_r(b,n,k)[mw] = \frac{P_r(b,n)[mw]}{K} \times Y_\delta$, where Y_δ is a Rayleigh distributed random variable with parameter δ. Then, the received signal to interference plus noise ratio (SINR) from beam b for UE n in subchannel k can be calculated. And the data rate of UE n in subchannel k of beam b can be got from the SINR-CQI mapping table.

Since future wireless networks are expected to be designed for data applications with high and flexible data rates especially in the downlink, the investigations concentrate on downlink transmission. The BS holds the UEs' downlink traffic and want to transmit them to the UEs with the maximum network

throughput. Let $\mathcal{R} = \{R_n, 1 \leq n \leq N\}$ denote the downlink traffic rate requirement set of the UEs, where the unit of R_n is bits per second (bps). Then, the
proposed subchannel-beam-UE assignment problem can be formulated as follows

$$\max \sum_{n=1}^{N} \min \left(\left(\sum_{b=1}^{B} \sum_{k=1}^{K} a_{b,n} x_{b,k,n} r_{b,k,n} \right), R_n \right) \tag{1a}$$

$$s.t. \sum_{n=1}^{N} x_{b,k,n} \leq 1, \text{where } x_{b,k,n} = \{0,1\}, \tag{1b}$$

$$\sum_{b=1}^{B} \sum_{k=1}^{K} x_{b,k,n} r_{b,k,n} \geq R_n. \tag{1c}$$

In (1a), the objective of the formulated problem is to maximize the sum of the
total users' assigned data rate, which is the minimum of each user's assigned data
rate and its required downlink data rate. To avoid the co-subchannel interference
between UEs, a given sub-channel of one beam can not assigned to more than
one UE, and thus we have (1b), where $x_{b,k,n}$ is a binary variable and $x_{b,k,n} = 1$
indicating that the subchannel k of beam b is assigned to UE n. The assigned
subchannels to UE n can not be smaller than its traffic load R_n as shown in
(1c).

We note that the formulated problem (1a–1c) is a non-linear integer programming problem, which is always an NP-hard problem. Due to space limitation,
the proof is omitted. Next, we focus on designing a heuristic algorithm to solve
the proposed problem in the following section.

3 A UE-Group Based Multiple Beams Subchannel Assignment Algorithm

In this paper, a UE-group based multiple beams subchannel assignment algorithm is proposed. The basic idea is to divide the UEs into groups firstly according to the beams' overlapped coverage areas or non-overlapped coverage areas.
Then, the subchannels are assigned to the UEs to exploit the beam spatial reuse
gain and the subchannel multi-user diversity gain.

3.1 Dividing the UEs into Groups

The terms of *non-overlapped areas of beams* and *overlapped areas of beams* are
illustrated in an example, as shown in Fig. 1. UE 2 and UE 3 are located in
the overlapped area of Beam 1 and Beam 2, and UE 1 is located in the non-
overlapped area of Beam 1, and UE 4 and UE 5 are located in the non-overlapped
area of Beam 2. Therefore, when there are 2 beams the total UEs can be divided
into 3 UE-groups.

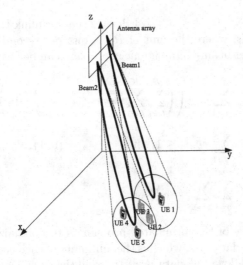

Fig. 1. Example of overlapped areas of beams

In the practical mmWave cellular networks, the measured SINR in each sub-channel of beams, or the mapped data rate, i.e., $r_{b,n,k}$, can be used to divide the UEs into groups. In this paper, if $\max_{1 \leq k \leq K} r_{b,n,k} \geq \gamma$, then UE n is covered by beam b, where γ is the lowest data rate corresponding to the minimum CQI. The physical meaning is that if the data rate of beam b's highest data rate of the subchannels is larger than γ, then at least one of the subchannels of beam b can be assigned to UE n.

3.2   The Proposed Algorithm

We note that the beam spatial reuse gain can be achieved by assigning the subchannel to the UE/UEs located in the non-overlapped areas. While the sub-channel multi-user diversity gain is achieved by assigning the subchannel to the UE which has the highest data rate. To jointly exploit the both gains, the UE-group based multi-beams subchannel assignment algorithm is proposed, and the pseudo-code of the proposed algorithm is given in Algorithm 1.

To avoid deep shadowing effect of the subchannels, the subchannel assignment sequence is randomly selected in each time when the proposed algorithm is run. Each subchannel is assigned sequentially. The inputs include the association relationship matrix of the UEs and the beams, i.e., $\mathbb{A}$, the data rate matrix of the UEs at each subchannel of each beam, i.e., $\mathbb{R}$, the set of downlink traffic requirements of the UEs, i.e., $\mathcal{R}$, and the non-overlapped UE-groups and the overlapped UE-groups $\{\mathcal{N}_{\mathcal{B}'}|\forall \mathcal{B}' \subseteq \mathcal{B}\}$. The output is the assignment binary variable matrix $\mathbb{X}$.

To exploit both the beam spatial reuse gain and the subchannel multi-user diversity gain, each subchannel k's two data rates is computed firstly, which is given by both that of the non-overlapped UE-groups, r_{ng}, and that of the overlapped UE-groups r_{og}. For the non-overlapped UE-groups, subchannel k's data rate is the sum of the maximum data rate of each non-overlapped UE-group, exploiting the beam spatial reuse gain. From line 4 to line 11, the data rate of the non-overlapped UE-groups at subchannel k is calculated as r_{ng}, and the set of UEs which can bring the data rate are presented as $\mathcal{N}_{ng}$. While for the overlapped UE-groups, subchannel k's data rate is the maximum of each overlapped UE-group's maximum data rate, without beam spatial reuse gain. From line 12 to 19, the data rate of the overlapped UE-groups is calculated as r_{og}, and the UE which can bring the data rate is presented as n_{og}. Next, the subchannel k is assigned to the UE/UEs which can bring the maximum data rate,

---

Algorithm 1. UE-Group based Multiple Beams Subchannel Assignments Algorithm

---

Require: $\mathbb{A} = [a_{b,n}]_{B \times N}, \mathbb{R} = [r_{b,k,n}]_{B \times K \times N}, \mathcal{R} = \{R_n | 1 \leq n \leq N\}, \{\mathcal{N}_{\mathcal{B}'} | \forall \mathcal{B}' \subseteq \mathcal{B}\},$
    where $\mathcal{B} = \{b_i | 1 \leq i \leq B, b_i \text{ is a beam}\}$
Ensure: $\mathbb{X} = [x_{b,k,n}]_{B \times K \times N}$
  1: $\mathcal{K} = \{1, 2, \cdots, K\}, \mathcal{N} = \{1, 2, \cdots, N\}, \mathbb{X} = [x_{b,k,n}]_{B \times K \times N} = zeros(B, K, N);$
  2: **while** $\mathcal{K} = \emptyset$ or $\mathcal{N} = \emptyset$ **do**
  3:     randomly select a k from $\mathcal{K}, \mathcal{K} = \mathcal{K} - \{k\};$
  4:     $r_{ng} = 0, \mathcal{N}_{ng} = \emptyset;$
  5:     **for** b from 1 to B **do**
  6:         $r_{max} = 0, n_{max} = -1;$
  7:         **for** $\forall n \in (\mathcal{N}_{\{b\}} \cap \mathcal{N})$ **do**
  8:             **if** $r_{max} < (a_{b,n} r_{b,k,n})$ **then**
  9:                 $r_{max} = r_{b,k,n}, n_{max} = n;$
10:         **if** $n_{max} \neq -1$ **then**
11:             $r_{ng} = r_{ng} + r_{max}, \mathcal{N}_{ng} = \mathcal{N}_{ng} + \{n_{max}\};$
12:     $r_{og} = 0, n_{og} = -1;$
13:     **for** $\forall \mathcal{B}' \subseteq \mathcal{B}$, where $|\mathcal{B}'| \geq 2$ **do**
14:         $r_{max} = 0, n_{max} = -1;$
15:         **for** $\forall n \in (\mathcal{N}'_{\mathcal{B}} \cap \mathcal{N})$ **do**
16:             **if** $r_{max} < (a_{b,n} r_{b,k,n})$ **then**
17:                 $r_{max} = r_{b,k,n}, n_{max} = n;$
18:         **if** $n_{max} \neq -1$ and $r_{og} > r_{max}$ **then**
19:             $r_{og} = r_{max}, n_{og} = n_{max};$
20:     **if** $r_{ng} > r_{og}$ **then**
21:         **for** $\forall n \in \mathcal{N}_{ng}$ **do**
22:             $x_{b,k,n} = 1, R_n = R_n - r_{b,k,n};$
23:             **if** $R_n \leq 0$ **then**
24:                 $\mathcal{N} = \mathcal{N} - \{n\};$
25:     **else**
26:         **if** $r_{og} > 0$ **then**
27:             $x_{b,k,n_{og}} = 1, , R_n = R_n - r_{b,k,n_{og}};$
28:             **if** $R_n \leq 0$ **then**
29:                 $\mathcal{N} = \mathcal{N} - \{n_{og}\};$
30: **return** $\mathbb{X};$

---

exploiting the subchannel multi-user diversity gain. If $r_{ng} > r_{og}$, subchannel k is assigned to the UE set $\mathcal{N}_{ng}$ from line 21 to line 24, and the downlink traffic loads of the UEs in $\mathcal{N}_{ng}$ are updated. The satisfied UE/UEs will not run for more subchannels.

4   Performance Evaluation

To evaluate the performance of the proposed algorithm, we compare it with a heuristic method, which exploit the subchannel multi-user diversity gain first, and then exploit the beam spatial reuse gain. In the simulation, the number of the antennas is set as 16×16, where 4 beams are formed according to [8]. The channel bandwidth is set as 500 MHz, with the center frequency 28 GHz, which is divided into 32 subchannels in OFDM mode. In each subchannel the noise power can be calculated as $P_N = 6.425 \times 10^{-11}$ mW. The channel model parameters are set as $\alpha = 45.3, \beta = 2.9, \delta = 0.04$. The height of BS antenna arrays is 10 m, and the height of UE antenna is 1.5 m. The radius of a sector is 50 m with angle $60°$.

The simulation results are demonstrated in Figs. 2 and 3. In Fig. 2, the requirement of each UE, R_n, increases from 50 Mbps to 350 Mbps with a step of 50, and then increases from 350 Mbps to 950 Mbps with a step of 100. And for each setting of R_n, the scenarios of UE number with 30, 60 and 90 are simulated. For the proposed method, the network throughput increases as R_n increases. While for the heuristic method, the networks throughput first increases and then decreases as R_n increases. Furthermore, it can be seen that there is a peak rate achieved by both the proposed method and the heuristic method. This can be explained as follows. When R_n is small, with the heuristic method the requirement of the UEs located in the overlapped area can be satisfied and a few of subchannels can be left, which can be used by the UEs located in the non-overlapped area. However with the increase of R_n, the number of the left subchannel goes to zero, which made the network throughput decreases. It can be seen that the lowest network throughput of the heuristic method is near 2.7 Gbps, which is almost equivalent to $(32 \times 86.79$ Mbps$)$, where 86.79 Mbps is the highest data rate achieved by one subchannel. In other words, the subchannel multi-user diversity gain is high when R_n is small, while when it is large the gain is low. This is also the reason that why there is a pulse with the proposed method when R is small. In Fig. 3, the number of UEs increases from 10 to 90 with a step of 10, under different download requirements of each UE. It can be found that the cures are similar with Fig. 2. And it can be concluded that when the UE number is small the multi-user diversity gain is high, while when as the increase of the UE number the multi-user diversity gain decrease.

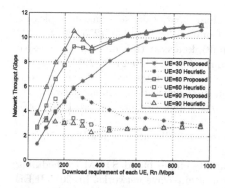

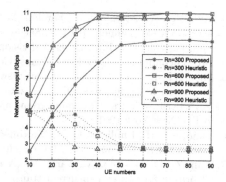

Fig. 2. Network throughput with various R_n

Fig. 3. Network throughput with various UE numbers

5 Conclusion

Beamforming is a promising technology to enable the mmWave network. How to assign the subchannels of multi-beams to multi users is studied in this paper, which is formulated as an integer programming problem. To combat the complexity, a UE-group based subchannel algorithm is proposed, to explore both the beam spatial reuse gain and the subchannel multi-user diversity gain. Simulation results evaluate the performance of the proposed algorithm. And it shows that the beam spatial reuse gain will increase with the increase of the download requirement of each UE and the UE numbers. However, the subchannel multi-user diversity gain will increase with the increase of the download requirement of each UE and the UE number, when they are small. However, it will decrease with the increase of the download requirement of each UE and the UE number, when they are large. Further characterizations of the beam spatial gain and the subchannel multi-user diversity gain will be studied in the future.

Acknowledgment. This work was supported in part by the Science and Technology on Communication Networks Laboratory Open Projects (Grant No. KX162600031, KX172600027), the National Natural Science Foundations of CHINA (Grant No. 61271279, and No. 61501373), the National Science and Technology Major Project (Grant No. 2016ZX03001018-004), and the Fundamental Research Funds for the Central Universities (Grant No. 3102017ZY018).

References

1. Roh, W., Seol, J.-Y., Park, J.: Millimeter-wave beamforming as an enabling technology for 5G cellular communications: theoretical feasibility and prototype results. IEEE Commun. Mag. **55**(2), 106–113 (2014)
2. Xiao, Z., Xia, X.-G., Jin, D., Ge, N.: Iterative eigenvalue decomposition and multipath-grouping Tx/Rx joint beamformings for millimeter-wave communications. IEEE Trans. Wirel. Commun. **14**(3), 1595–1607 (2015)

3. Adhikary, A., Al Safadi, E., Samimi, M.K.: Joint spatial division and multiplexing for mm-Wave channels. IEEE J. Sel. Areas Commn. **32**(6), 1239–1255 (2014)
4. Sun, C., Gao, X., Jin, S.: Beam division multiple access transmission for massive MIMO communications. IEEE Trans. Commun. **63**(6), 2170–2184 (2015)
5. Huang, Z.-E., Pan, J.-Y.: Coordinative switch beamforming scheduler for guaranteed service with service area subsectorization in next generation cellular network. In: 2015 IEEE Wireless Communications and Networking Conference, pp. 1000–1005. IEEE, New York (2015)
6. Sandra, S.-H., Emiliano, G.-P.: Multimedia resource allocation in mmWave 5G networks. IEEE Commun. Mag. **54**(1), 240–247 (2015)
7. Yan, Z., Li, B., Zuo, X., Yang, M.: A heuristic clique based STDMA scheduling algorithm for spatial concurrent transmission in mmWave networks. In: 2015 IEEE Wireless Communications and Networking Conference, pp. 1036–1041. IEEE, New York (2015)
8. Xue, Q., Li, B., Zuo, X., Yan, Z., Yang, M.: Cell capacity for 5G cellular network with inter-beam interference. In: 2016 IEEE International Conference on Signal Processing, Communications and Computing, pp. 1–5. IEEE, New York (2016)

SVC Based Multiple Access Protocol with QoS Guarantee for Next Generation WLAN (Invited Paper)

Run Zhou, Bo Li, Mao Yang$^{(\boxtimes)}$, and Zhongjiang Yan

School of Electronics and Information,
Northwestern Polytechnical University, Xi'an, China
zhourun_xsy@163.com, {libo.npu,yangmao,zhjyan}@nwpu.edu.cn

Abstract. With the increasing in demand for video traffic, video service has been becoming more and more diversified. Scaled video coding (SVC) has become one of the most common video code technology to meet the requirements of different video service types. Therefore, SVC based video users quality of service (QoS) guarantee is one of the most basic problems of the network, but there are few studies focusing on the SVC based video users QoS guarantee protocol for the next generation wireless location access network (WLAN). This paper proposes SVC based media access control (MAC) protocol with QoS guarantee for next generation WLAN, referred to as QoS-SVC. If there are some residual sub-channels resource after the first channel contention, the protocol offers another opportunity, named second random contention, for the video users both collided and successful in the first random contention phase and enables them to transmit their data in the residual sub-channels. The simulation results show that the throughput adopting QoS-SVC is improved by 154%, compared with non-second random contention access (Non-SRCA) protocol.

Keywords: SVC · WLAN · QoS · MAC

1 Introduction

With the increasing development of mobile Internet service and the growing prosperity of intelligent terminals, the ability of terminal continues to increase. The people's demand for mobile data shows a trend of explosive growth, especially the increasing in demand for video streaming traffic. From a global perspective, the video traffic in 2014 has accounted for 80% of the wireless network [1].

The wide popularization of video applications makes the video traffic diversified, such as video-on-demand, video conferencing, and video surveillance, coupled with the diversity of the network and the terminal, so the diversity of video traffic is the most basic feature. In order to deal with this feature to meet the needs of different video services, scaled video coding (SVC) has been generated.

© ICST Institute for Computer Sciences, Social Informatics and Telecommunications Engineering 2018
Y.-B. Lin et al. (Eds.): IoTaaS 2017, LNICST 246, pp. 349–356, 2018.
https://doi.org/10.1007/978-3-030-00410-1_40

It is a video stream that can be divided into a number of layers by the code technology such as in resolution, quality and the frame rate domain, and then the video traffic can be encoded into a basic layer and multiple enhancement layers. SVC as an extension of the H.264 standard is an approved standard, known as H.264-SVC [2].

In recent years, The widespread use of wireless network has promoted the rapid development of Internet of things(IoT), more and more of IoT and WLAN combination of applications in our real life, and now the emergence of Internet of Things is seen as the third wave of information technology. The development of WLAN and the popularity of mobile smart terminals has made the trend that the way watching the network video gradually moves to the mobile side. So both industry and academic dedicated to researching the key technologies of next generation WLAN. As early as March 2014, the IEEE standards committee formally approved the project authorization request (PAR) and established the IEEE 802.11ax working group. This working group clearly proposed to guarantee the video traffic QoS is one of the important goals of the next generation WLAN in PAR [3].

In order to be able to guarantee the QoS of the video traffic and improve the efficiency of multiple access control (MAC), IEEE 802.11ax standard draft has accepted OFDMA as a key technology currently in the next generation WLAN. That is the introduction of concurrent access and concurrent transmission. In recent years, OFDMA based MAC in next generation WLAN has been a number of researches. Our laboratory the MAC protocol based on OFDMA for the next generation WLAN has been proposed, referred to OMAX [4]. This protocol dramatically improves throughput and MAC efficiency. The other MAC protocol based on OFMDA for QoS guarantee has been recently proposed by our laboratory, referred to redundant accession (RA) OFDMA [5]. This protocol introduces the difference of service type in the access phase, and the video traffic adopts the redundant access mechanism (randomly selects multiple subchannels to transmit request to frames (RTS)), so that increases video traffic access success probability. However, redundant access to video traffic increases the collision probability of system and is unfair to the background traffic.

For the existing research, the two problems of the QoS guarantee of the video streaming traffic are non-SVC based coding and poor fairness. This paper proposes the QoS-SVC MAC protocol. After all the traffic nodes have finished first random content access, the access point (AP) allocates channel resource for access successful nodes according to their bandwidth requirements. If there are residual sub-channels after allocation, allowing video traffic nodes, including video nodes of collision and successful access in first random content access, make second random content access for transmitting their data in the residual sub-channels after allocation. The simulation results show that the QoS-SVC proposed in this paper can guarantee the fairness and improve the video traffic throughput by 154% compared with the Non-SRCA protocol.

The main contributions of this paper are given as follows:

(1) This paper proposes the QoS-SVC MAC protocol. It guarantees the video users QoS while taking into account the fairness of the low priority user. As far as we know, the MAC protocol proposed QoS-SVC is the first SVC based QoS guarantee for the next generation WLAN, which guarantees the fairness of low priority user and video user's QoS.
(2) Through establishing ns-2 simulation platform, the simulation results show that the video users throughput is improved by 154% compared with Non-SRCA protocol.

2   System Model

This protocol's scenario is based on the basic service set (BSS) of the next generation WLAN to study the QoS guarantee of uplink video streaming traffic. As shown in Fig. 1, in the BSS, there are m uplink video nodes and k uplink background users. Based on the OFDMA mechanism, the dividing sub-channel method is maintained on the AP side. The 20 MHz full channel of the traditional WLAN adopts the fixed division method and divides the whole channel bandwidth into N sub-channels. As the video service will occupy a large part of data in the future wireless network, so we divide the users into two categories: video streaming traffic and background traffic. The video stream traffic corresponds to the real-time constant bit rate (CBR) service which has strict transmission delay. Background traffic corresponds to non-real-time service which generates from the Poisson distribution and requires low QoS that tolerates a certain transmission delay. Of course, the basic idea in this paper can be easily extended to more traffic types. As the uplink access and transmission to the MAC design of next generation WLAN is more challenging, so this protocol is mainly concerned with uplink access and transmission.

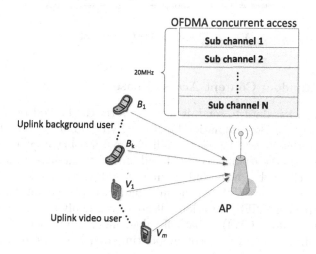

Fig. 1. Network scenario

3   SVC-QoS Protocol Design

This protocol idea isn't introducing additional overhead. It can not only guarantee the video user's QoS requirements, but also make low priority user to have fair transmission opportunities. The basic idea of the protocol design is to guarantee the video user's QoS requirements by introducing the second random contention, allowing both the access successful video users and the collision video users in the first random contention to independently randomly select subchannels from residual sub-channels after allocation to send their data. As the first random content access phase does not distinguish traffic type, low-priority users and video users have equal access opportunities, to guarantee the fairness.

As shown in Fig. 2, the protocol is divided into three phases, i.e., the first random content access phase, the resource allocation phase and the second random content access and data transmission phase.

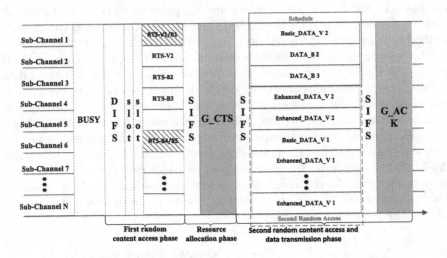

Fig. 2. SVC-QoS MAC protocol

3.1   First Random Content Access Phase

When the node has data to send, it must perform the backoff process same as traditional distributed coordination function (DCF). In order to ensure forward compatibility, this protocol uses the full channel sensing mechanism. That is the user considers the channel is idle if and only if all sub-channels are idle. As long as a sub-channel is busy, full channel would busy, so all users are pending in the backoff process. When the full channel is idle lasting for distributed inter-frame spacing (DIFS) duration, all nodes randomly select a number from (0 contention window (CW)) as backoff value, and begin to backoff. To improve the backoff efficiency, this protocol adopts time-frequency two-dimensional fast backoff mechanism. When the backoff has finished, user randomly selects a sub-channel to send the RTS frame for access. From the access process, it can be seen that the first content access doesn't distinguish traffic type, so all users have the same access opportunities in this stage and thus guarantee the fairness.

The first random content access phase as show in Fig. 2, V1, V2 and B1–B5 have finished backoff, each node independently randomly selects a sub-channel to transmit the RTS frame for channel access.

3.2 Resource Allocation Phase

As the video users using the SVC, so the video users bandwidth requirement is divided into the bandwidth requirement of basic layer data, expressed as m and the bandwidth requirement of enhancement layer data, expressed as Δm. The background users bandwidth requirement is fixed, expressed k. In order to serve more video users and guarantee more video users QoS, AP allocates m sub-channels for the access successful video users to only meet their basic bandwidth requirement. After the channel allocation is finished, the AP generates the group clear to send (G-CTS) piggybacking the sub-channel allocation result. The follow-up protocol process for this phase is the same as the OMAX protocol [4] and RA-OFDMA [5] proposed by this laboratory.

In order to describe the convenience, it is assumed that the video users basic bandwidth requirement $m = 1$, enhanced bandwidth requirement $\Delta m = 2$, and the background user's fixed bandwidth requirement $k = 1$. Other channel allocation algorithms are also suitable for the protocol framework proposed in this paper. Figure 2 reveals AP correctly received the RTS frames of V2, B2, B3, these nodes access the channel successfully. The AP allocates sub-channel 1 to V2 to meet its basic bandwidth requirement, and allocates sub-channel 2 and sub-channel 3 to B2 and B3 respectively, and piggybacks the sub-channel allocation result to the G-CTS frame. However, V1 and B1 select the same sub-channel 1 to send RTS frame, so collision occurs. B4 and B5 also collide as the same reason. So the AP can not receive their RTS frames, i.e., V1, B1, B4 and B5 fail in accessing the channel.

In order to guarantee the video user's QoS, the video users, include successful accession and collision in the first random content access, are allowed to make the second random content access in the residual sub-channel after allocation.

3.3 Second Random Content Access and Data Transmission Phase

The background node of successful access transmites data using allocated sub-channels according to the indication in the G-CTS frame. For the video users of the first random content access successful, the AP only allocates the bandwidth requirements for transmitting the basic layer data. So these video users use allocated channel by the indication in the G-CTS frame to send the basic layer data after the short inter frame space (SIFS) duration, and makes second random content access by randomly selecting Δm sub-channels from residual after allocation to send the enhancement layer data at the same time. The failed video users of the first random content access makes second random content access by randomly selecting $m + \Delta m$ sub-channels from residual after allocation to send the basic layer and enhancement layer data.

As show in Fig. 2, B2 and B3 send data using sub-channel 2 and sub-channel 3 respectively according to the indication in the G-CTS frame. V2 of access successful send basic layer data using sub-channel 1 according to the indication of G-CTS, and makes the second random content access. V2 randomly selects sub-channel 1 and the sub-channel 5 from residual sub-channels after allocation to transmit the enhancement layer data. The failed video user V1 of the first random content access, makes the second random access by randomly selecting sub-channel 6, sub-channel 7 and sub-channel N from residual sub-channels after allocation to transmit the basic layer data and enhancement layer data.

4   Performance Evaluation

4.1   Simulation Configuration

This paper uses the network simulation software NS2 to establish the simulation platform. The simulation scenario is as follows: nodes are randomly distributed in 10 m ∗ 10 m network, AP is located in the geometric center of the network. The single simulation time is 50 s, and the final result is the average of 5 simulation results. In the simulation, since the 20 MHz full channel is divided into nine sub-channels in the draft 802.11ax protocol, the number of sub-channels is also set to nine. The number of video node is fixedly set to 5, and the number of background nodes starts from 5 to 50. The other network parameters are set as shown in Table 1.

Table 1. Parameters

Parameters	Value
$CW_{\min}$	15
$CW_{\max}$	127
$DIFS$	34 μs
$SIFS$	16 μs
$Slot$	9 μs
Whole channel bandwidth	20 MHz
Basic bandwidth	$1 subchannel$
Enhanced bandwidth	$2 subchannes$
Packet size	$1500 Bytes$
Control packet PHY rate	6 Mbps
DATA packet PHY rate	54 Mbps

4.2   Simulation Results

Define the total amount of load that is sent by the video node in the network per unit time for the video traffic throughput. As shown in Fig. 3, because video traffic nodes are allowed to make second random content access to randomly select some sub-channels from residual sub-channels after allocation for transmitting packet data, the throughput of video traffic is higher than the Non-SRCA protocol.

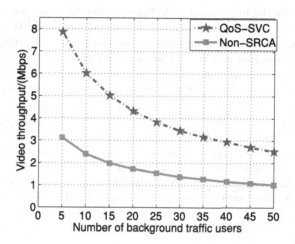

Fig. 3. Video traffic throughput versus the number of background traffic users.

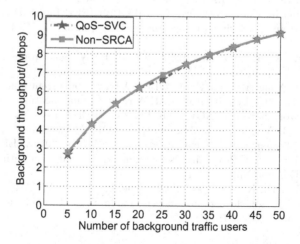

Fig. 4. Background traffic throughput versus the number of background traffic users.

Define the total amount of load that is sent by the background node in the network per unit time for the background traffic throughput. As shown in Fig. 4, the background throughput increases as the number of background nodes increase. We can see that the two curves coincide, so the QoS-SVC protocol proposed in this paper can provide the same fairness as the Non-SRCA protocol.

5   Conclusion

Aiming at solving the problem of SVC based guarantee video users' QoS in the next generation WLAN, this paper proposes the QoS-SVC MAC protocol. The protocol allows video users which access the channel successfully and unsuccessfully in first random content access phase to make second random content access for transmitting their data in residual sub-channels after allocation. The simulation results show that QoS-SVC video users' throughput is improved by 154% compared with Non-SRCA protocol. Follow-up research will be in the multi-channels scenario to further guarantee the video traffic users QoS.

Acknowledgment. This work was supported in part by the National Natural Science Foundations of CHINA (Grant No. 61271279, and No. 61501373), the National Science and Technology Major Project (Grant No. 2016ZX03001018-004), and the Fundamental Research Funds for the Central Universities (Grant No. 3102017ZY018).

References

1. Zhao, H., Zhang, S., Wei, J., Li, Y.: Channel width adaptation and access in high-density WiFi networks. In: 2014 URSI General Assembly and Scientific Symposium (URSI GASS), pp. 1–4. IEEE Press, Beijing (2014)
2. Lemarchand, L., Mensah, I.A., Babau, J.P.: Dynamic server configuration for multiple streaming in a home network. In: 2014 12th IEEE International Conference on Embedded and Ubiquitous Computing (EUC), pp. 39–45. IEEE Press, Beijing (2014)
3. IEEE Technical Presentations: IEEE 802.11 HEW SG Proposed PAR. Doc: IEEE802.11-14/0165r1
4. Qu, Q., Li, B., Yang, M., Yan, Z.: An OFDMA based concurrent multiuser MAC for upcoming IEEE 802.11 ax. In: 2015 IEEE Wireless Communications and Networking Conference Workshops (WCNCW), pp. 136–141. IEEE Press, New Orleans (2015)
5. Zhou, H., Li, B., Yan, Z., Yang, M., Qu, Q.: An OFDMA basedmultiple access protocol with QoS guarantee for next generation WLAN. In: 2015 IEEE International Conference on Signal Processing, Communications and Computing (ICSPCC), pp.1–6. IEEE Press, Ningbo (2015)
6. Kwon, H., Seo, H., Kim, S., Lee, B.G.: Generalized CSMA/CA for OFDMA systems: protocol design, throughput analysis, and implementation issues. IEEE Trans. Wirel. Commun. 8(8), 4176–4187 (2009)

Light-Weight Global Feature for Mobile Clothing Search

Guangshan Wen[1], Jing Wu[1(✉)], Chengnian Long[1(✉)], and Yi-Bing Lin[2]

[1] Department of Automation, School of Electronic Infomation and Eletrical Engineering, Shanghai Jiao Tong University, Shanghai, China
{jingwu,longcn}@sjtu.edu.cn
[2] Department of Computer Science, National Chiao Tung University, Hsinchu, Taiwan, R.O.C.
liny@cs.nctu.edu.tw

Abstract. Mobile clothing search on smartphones is extraordinary challenging on both embedded computer vision and networking search system design due to the flexible object, constrained computing, networking resource, and quick response requirement. In this paper, we propose a light-weight global feature LGF – threshold-LBP and color histogram, for mobile clothing search, which is effective for feature extracting and networking communication on smartphone. In addition, an incremental feature is proposed in rerank module to promote the rerank computation and achieve the quick response requirement. Our approach is evaluated through extensive experiments on the smartphones. It reveals that mobile clothing search based on our global feature is more effective than other clothing retrieval system using prevalent local descriptors, such as SIFT, RGB-SIFT.

Keywords: Smartphone · Computer vision · Flexible object
Global feature · Threshold-LBP · Color histogram · Incremental feature

1 Background

With the rapid development of e-commerce, many commodities are displayed by the way of image on Internet. Besides, as the mobile Internet industry becomes prevalent in these years, an efficient mobile clothing search system is expected for people to retrieve similar clothes from massive amounts of on-line commodities with the image they captured by mobile camera.

Comparing with traditional Content-Based-image-retrieval systems, clothing-item retrieval system is extremely challenging. As a kind of flexible object, it is impossible to extract shape feature from cloth item. In addition, the texture feature caused by clothing folds is hardly distinguished from real clothing

This work was supported by National Nature Science Foundation under Grant 61673275 and 61473184.

© ICST Institute for Computer Sciences, Social Informatics and Telecommunications Engineering 2018
Y.-B. Lin et al. (Eds.): IoTaaS 2017, LNICST 246, pp. 357–364, 2018.
https://doi.org/10.1007/978-3-030-00410-1_41

texture. Thus, the prevalent local feature such as SIFT, SURF, is not appropriate for cloth item retrieval. Besides, in the view of limited computation ability on mobile device, the extraction of local feature, such as SIFT, SUFT, is quite expensive. In addition, the high-dimensional local feature will also aggravate network traffic overhead.

There has been a great deal of work on clothing image retrieval in the past few years [1–8,11], which mostly based on traditional local feature, such as SIFT, SURF, and the recently developed deep feature. Besides, kind of global feature is also proposed in [1], which is only focus on color information, and the computation of Color Moment in their work is quite expensive. The recently developed deep feature is a kind of high-level feature, which can descript clothing image with multiple levels of abstraction [10], and be robust to clothing variation. However, as we can see from [9], the CNN used in [7] for clothing feature representation has millions of parameters and 500,000 neurons, which causes expensive computation.

The main contributions of this paper can be summarized as follows: (1)we propose a kind of global texture feature – threshold-LBP to collaborate with color histogram, which is more effective than local feature (2)we design sorted color histogram feature to speed-up the computation in re-rank model.

The remainder of this paper is organized as follows. we will deep into the detail of the proposed light-weight global feature in Sect. 2, and the evaluation is in Sect. 3. Finally, we conclude in Sect. 4.

2   Feature Design

2.1   Color Histogram

Color is the most important feature in clothing images, which contains the most information consumers care about.

The normal display system with 8-bit color can display up to 2^{24} colors in RGB space, which means the color histogram extracting from rgb-image will have high dimension of ten million. Apparently, high dimension will lead to expensive computation in the post-processing. Besides, due to the consideration of each kind of color, the color histogram will be sensitive to color variation caused by illumination, reflection and other external enviroment.

We utilizes color quantization to archive dimensionality reduction for color histogram. Color quantization involves dividing the RGB color space cube into a number of small boxes, and then mapping colors fall within box at the center of the box. Our implementation based on uniform quantization, which quantizes each channel uniformly. In our experiment, we partition R, G and B channel into 8 bins separately, while the total number of colors in color histogram will be fixed to $8 \times 8 \times 8$. Suppose the RGB value of pixel x is (r_x, g_x, b_x), then the quantization color of x is $((\lceil (r_x/32) \rceil \times 16), (\lceil (g_x/32) \rceil \times 16), (\lceil (b_x/32) \rceil \times 16))$, where $\lceil (x) \rceil$ is the least integer greater than or equal to x.

2.2 Texture Feature

Besides color distribution, the pattern design on clothes is also an important information for clothing image. Texture is an essential feature to describe the clothing pattern, which can extract the spatial arrangement of intensities in an image. As a result, our work makes use of texture feature to implement more accurate retrieval. There is a large number of texture feature can be chosen, such as HOG, GLCM, HAARS. In consideration to the limited computation ability of smartphone, we apply LBP (Local binary patterns), which is a powerful feature for texture classification. In traditional LBP feature extracting, each pixel is compared to its 8 neighbors, and when the pixel's value is greater than the neighbor's value, then the corresponding bit of LBP feature is 1, otherwise is 0.

$$f(x, y) = \sum_{p=0}^{P-1} s(g_p - g_c)2^p, \tag{1}$$

where

$$s(x) = \begin{cases} 1 & x \geq threshold, \\ 0 & x < threshold. \end{cases}$$

However, in the practical scenarios, the high degree of flexibility of clothing object causes the fold and shadow, which raises a large amount of noise for texture detection. In order to reduce the sensitivity of texture feature, the threshold between the comparison of pixel and its neighbors is increased, As shown in Eq. 1, where g_c is centroid of threshold-LBP feature at pixel(x, y), and the radius of threshold-LBP P is set to 8, and $g_p(p = 0, 1, 2, \ldots, P-1)$ is the feature region with the center of g_c. In our experiment, only when the value of pixel is at least 16 greater than its neighbors, can the corresponding bit set 1, which will lead to better result, as shown in the evaluation.

2.3 Sorted Color Histogram

The re-rank module will rerank the candidate result to refine the final returned list.

Given two color histograms $ch_1 = (x_1, x_2, \ldots, x_n)$ and $ch_2 = (y_1, y_2, \ldots, y_n)$, the traditional algorithm to measure the similarity is Euler distance $d = \sqrt{\sum_{i=1}^{n}(x_i - y_i)^2}$, while the complexity of which is liner to the dimension of color histogram, $O(n)$. Based on the characteristics of clothing that the more percentage of the color account for in a clothing, the more important the color is for clothing image retrieval, we proposes an algorithm to compute the similarity between any two color histograms by summing up each color's distance, where the color is distinguished by their importance and the computation sequence is in descending order of color's importance. The detail procedure is shown in Algorithm 1.

Algorithm 1 utilizes two extra parameters to speed up the similarity computation: $dis_{threshold}$ and $per_{threshold}$. $dis_{threshold}$ can stop algorithm when the

---

Algorithm 1. Efficient algorithm to compute the similatities between two color histograms

---

    Input   : Color Histogram ch_1 and ch_2

               Threshold: $dis_{threshold}$, $per_{threshold}$

    Output: Distance $distance$

1   $pert_1, color_1 = sort(ch_1)$;

2   $pert_2, color_2 = sort(ch_2)$;

3   $distance = 0$;

4   $percentage = 0$;

5   **for** (p_{1i}, c_{1i}) *in* $(pert_1, color_1)$ *and* (p_{2i}, c_{2i}) *in* $(pert_2, color_2)$ **do**

6   **if** $dis_{threshold} < distance$ **then**

7           $distance = +\infty$;

8           $break$;

9   **end**

10   **if** $per_{threshold} < percentage$ **then**

11          $break$;

12   **end**

13      $s = (p_{1i} + p_{2i})/2$;

14   **if** $c_{1i} == c_{2i}$ **then**

15          $distance+ = s \times abs(p_{1i} - p_{2i})$;

16   **else**

17          $distance+ = max(p_{1i}, p_{2i})$;

18   **end**

19      $percentage+ = min(pert1, pert2)$;

20 **end**

21 **return** $distance/percentage$;

---

current distance is greater than pre-setted threshold, which means there is small probability that the two color histograms are simillar. Besides, the function of $per_{threshold}$ is to control the degree of colors that have been involved in the calculation. A sentinel $percentage$ is used to record the current percentage of colors have been involved. When $percentage > per_{threshold}$, it can be regarded as the dominant colors have been considered, and the remain computation will have little effect on final result. So the algorithm can be stop.

Algorithm 1 makes best use of the fact that most clothes contain several dominant colors, and the proportion of other colors can be ignored. As a result, the computation focus on the few kinds of dominant colors, which will have less side-effect on searching result and be more efficient in time.

3 Evaluation

In this section, we design extensive experiments to evaluate the proposed feature in mobile clothing search. Besides, the comparison with other works will also be presented. Our experiment is based on a publicly available dataset in [7]. The images in the dataset have a variety of variations, such as illumination, occlusion, pose, which can better evaluate the robustness and retrieval accuracy.

3.1   Feature Parameter Analysis

Our work uses threshold-LBP feature and kind of incremental image feature in rerank module to efficiently refine the retrieval candidate result, which is also called Sorted Color Histogram (SCH). In this section, we will analysis the parameters *threshold* of threshold-LBP feature and $per_{threshold}$ of SCH.

The result shown in Fig. 1 demonstrates the retrieval accuracy of different threshold for LBP feature. We evaluate the threshold with 0, 6, 10, 12, 16, 20, 24 respectively. As we can see from Fig. 1, threshold with 16 results in the best performance. And the increasing of threshold larger than 16 will significantly reduce the accuracy, which is a result of high threshold that causes texture fuzzy, and leads to detail loss.

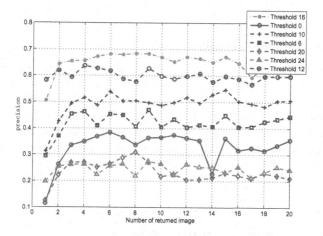

Fig. 1. Experiment of LBP with different threshold

In our experiment, high threshold even has worse perfomance than raw LBP feature. As clothing object is easily deformed, the folds on clothing surface may be misrecognized as texture, the evaluation result shows that appropriate threshold can rectify the fake texture. As shown in Fig. 1, the result with threshold from 6 to 16 surpass raw LBP. The following evaluation will based on threshold of 16.

For SCH, as shown in Fig. 2, for our testing image dataset, using 85% of colors can reach nearly the same result with 100%, which means the 85% colors contains almost all the color information in clothing image. In addition, we can see from Fig. 3 that the computing time used in similarity measurement for the most 85% important colors is less than half of the computing time for 100%, which is based on the fact that less than 50% of bins in color histogram includes more than 85% color information in clothing image. In the following evaluation, the $per_{threshold}$ of SCH is set to 85%.

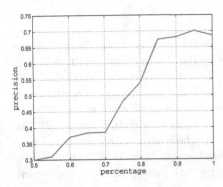

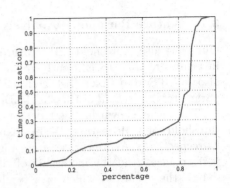

Fig. 2. Percentage vs precision   **Fig. 3.** Percentage vs time

3.2 Comparison and Result

We implement our light-weight global feature based clothing search system on a mobile phone to evaluate the practicability of our cloth retrieval system. The practical experiment is based a SONY Xperia with Android 5.1.1 OS and a remote server with the configuration of core i7. we estimate the retrieval speed by retrieval time. The feature packet for network communication is shown in Fig. 4. In *requestline*, the m indicates the number of returned images, n reveals the kind of feature for extraction, while the substance is in *requestbody*.

Request line	GET images\m Feature\n Version 1.0\
Request body	<feature name = color, length = size1, type = int>
	....
	</feature>
	\r\n
	<feature name = texture, length = size2, type = int>
	....
	</feature>
	\r\n
	\r\n\r\n

Fig. 4. Feature packet

To demonstrate the better performance on retrieval accuracy of our clothing image retrieval system, we compare with some other baseline Content-based Image retrieval methods using prevalent local descriptor, such as SIFT, RGB-SIFT, and Color Moment.

The result in Fig. 5 shows that our light-weight global feature – LGF based retrieval system has a gain of nearly 12.1% in average precision compared with SIFT, which is the result of that traditional SIFT descriptor has little attention in color information. Besides, a improvement about 5.6% and 6.1% respectively compared with Cascaded Color Moment and RGB-SIFT descriptor.

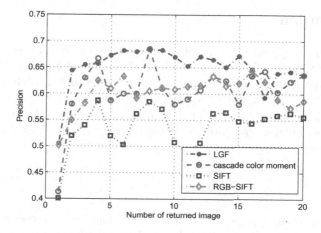

Fig. 5. Precision comparision

Table 1. Efficiency $-LGF/SIFT/RGB - SIFT/CascadeColorMoment$

Experiment case	Accuracy (10 images)	Retrieval time(s)
1	6/5/6/3	3.312/7.345/8.762/13.081
2	7/4/5/4	4.423/6.534/7.412/15.073
3	7/6/6/5	4.153/9.834/7.215/7.101
4	6/3/5/5	5.002/8.987/9.351/11.205
5	5/6/4/5	4.689/8.023/11.365/13.503
6	6/4/7/5	3.563/7.056/10.279/9.347
7	7/5/6/4	6.761/9.341/7.126/7.149
8	9/6/8/7	4.852/9.371/9.321/10.713
9	5/5/7/3	6.162/7.528/8.721/9.631
10	6/4/5/6	5.239/11.091/8.274/8.905
11	7/7/6/8	3.342/8.801/9.481/10.484
12	9/5/7/6	3.293/5.231/7.258/12.427
13	7/3/8/6	4.303/7.546/9.326/8.261
14	6/5/5/4	6.192/5.628/6.261/9.731
15	8/5/7/5	8.579/7.971/7.259/11.174
Average	6.733/4.867/6.133/5.067	4.924/8.02/8.49/10.52

The experiment result in Table 1 shows that our light-weight global feature based system has better performance on both retrieval accuracy and search efficiency. The light-weight global feature can speed searching up at least two times faster than complicated feature, such as SIFT/RGB-SIFT/Cascade Color Moment, without side-effect on retrieval accuracy.

4   Conclusion

In this paper, we presented a mobile clothing image retrieval system based on the proposed threshold-LBP feature and color histogram. Threshold-LBP feature can better overcome the noisy texture caused by high degree flexibility of clothing object. To refine the candidate result, Sorted Color Histogram is presented in re-rank module. The system evaluation demonstrates the effectiveness of the proposed global feature over other clothing retrieval systems based on prevalent local descriptors.

References

1. Weng, T., Yuan, Y., Shen, L., Zhao, Y.: Clothing image retrieval using color moment. In: Proceedings of the IEEE Conference on Computer Science and Network Technology, pp. 1016–1020 (2013)
2. Wang, X., Zhang, T., Tretter, D.R., Lin, Q.: Personal clothing retrieval on photo collections by color and attributes. IEEE Trans. Multimed. **15**(8), 2035–2045 (2013)
3. Liu, S., Song, Z., Liu, G., Xu, C., Lu, H., Yan, S.: Street-to-shop: cross-scenario clothing retrieval via parts alignment and auxiliary set. In: Proceedings of the IEEE Conference on Multimedia, pp. 1335–1336 (2012)
4. Di, W., Wah, C., Bhardwaj, A., Piramuthu, R., Sundaresan, N.: Style finder: fine-grained clothing style detection and retrieval. In: Proceedings of the IEEE Conference on Computer Vision and Pattern Recognition Workshops, pp. 8–13 (2013)
5. Cushen, G.A., Nixon, M.S.: Mobile visual clothing search. In: Proceedings of the IEEE Conference on Multimedia and Expo Workshops, pp. 1–6 (2013)
6. Yamaguchi, K., Kiapour, M.H., Ortiz, L.E., Berg, T.L.: Retrieving similar styles to parse clothing. IEEE Trans. Pattern Anal. Mach. Intell. **37**(5), 1028–1040 (2015)
7. Hadi Kiapour, M., Han, X., Lazebnik, S., Berg, A.C., Berg, T.L.: Where to buy it: matching street clothing photos in online shops. In: Proceedings of the IEEE Conference on Computer Vision, pp. 3343–3351 (2015)
8. Fu, J., Wang, J., Li, Z., Xu, M., Lu, H.: Efficient clothing retrieval with semantic-preserving visual phrases. In: Proceedings of the IEEE Asian Conference on Computer Vision, pp. 420–431 (2012)
9. Krizhevsky, A., Sutskever, I., Hinton, G.E.: Imagenet classification with deep convolutional neural networks. In: ACM International Conference on Neural Information Processing Systems, pp. 1097–1105 (2012)
10. LeCun, Y., Bengio, Y., Hinton, G.: Deep learning. Nature **521**(7553), 436–444 (2015)
11. Liu, Z., Luo, P., Qiu, S., et al.: DeepFashion: powering robust clothes recognition and retrieval with rich annotations. In: Proceedings of the IEEE conference on Computer Vision and Pattern Recognition, pp. 1096–1104 (2016)

Spatial Clustering Group Based OFDMA Multiple Access Scheme for the Next Generation WLAN (Invited Paper)

Yong Li, Bo Li, Mao Yang$^{(\boxtimes)}$, and Zhongjiang Yan

School of Electronics and Information, Northwestern Polytechnical University,
Xi'an, China
liyong6@mail.nwpu.edu.cn, {libo.npu,yangmao,zhjyan}@nwpu.edu.cn

Abstract. The next generation wireless local area network (WLAN) needs to significantly promote the area throughput in high dense scenario. OFDMA, considered as the key technology of next generation WLAN, has been adopted by IEEE 802.11ax. However, the existing studies on the OFDMA protocol have the interference extensions problem, i.e. multiple users are located in the dispersive area, and then the geographical interference area is expanded. In this paper, a spatial clustering group based OFDMA multiple access scheme (SCG-OFDMA) is proposed. SCG-OFDMA enables the users in close area to form spatial clustering groups dynamically, then the users in the spatial clustering group access channel and transmit data by OFDMA. It reduces the geographical interference area, and enhances the area throughput. Simulation results show that the area throughput of SCG-OFDMA is higher than OMAX and DCF by 20% and 36% respectively.

Keywords: Wireless local area network · High density scenario
Spatial clustering group · MAC · OFDMA

1 Introduction

In recent years, wireless local area network (WLAN) is one of the most important ways to carry wireless network services, through the 802.11 networks (Wi-Fi) or home micro-base station business has occupied 51% of the wireless network business [1]. Wi-Fi needs to support the Internet of Things (IoT) [2]. The next generation of WLAN high-density scenario requires about one user per square meter and the distance between adjacent access point (AP) 5 to 10 m [3]. In this densely crowded WLAN, inefficient channel utilization is a key factor that leads to its poor performance [4]. The next generation of WLAN based IEEE 802.11ax working group was established in 2014, which significantly enhances area throughput and medium access control (MAC) efficiency as one of the key technical goals [5].

In the distributed coordination function (DCF) protocol, only one user is allowed to access and transmit data at the same time, and MAC efficiency is low

© ICST Institute for Computer Sciences, Social Informatics and Telecommunications Engineering 2018
Y.-B. Lin et al. (Eds.): IoTaaS 2017, LNICST 246, pp. 365–372, 2018.
https://doi.org/10.1007/978-3-030-00410-1_42

in high-density scenarios [6]. Multi-user parallel access is one of the most important means to improve the efficiency of MAC, in which orthogonal frequency division multiple access (OFDMA) technology has been widely recognized by academia and industry [7–11]. OFDMA technology has been accepted by the IEEE 802.11ax draft [5]. The 802.11ax draft proposed OFDMA protocol based on the trigger frame, and access point by sending a trigger frame to schedule the station (STA) for uplink access and transmission [5]. When the STA received the trigger frame, it sends request to send (RTS) frame for access through the OFDMA way to randomly select a subchannel, and OFDMA is used for access and data transmission. An OFDMA based multiple access protocol OMAX [6] is proposed, and the backoff process of STA is consistent with that of traditional WLAN MAC. When the value of the backoff counter is decremented to zero, the STA randomly selects a subchannel and transmits RTS frame to access, while an OFDMA way is used for access and data transmission. However, there is a common problem of geographical interference area in the existing WLAN MAC protocols based on OFDMA. The STA at the different location initiates access and transmit at the same time, which enlarges the interference range of the transmitter, which affects the access efficiency and the improvement of the area throughput. While in the high density deployment of IoT, the impact of geographical interference becomes greater than its in the low deployment.

In this paper, a Spatial Clustering Group based OFDMA (SCG-OFDMA) scheme is proposed. This scheme could solve the interference diffusion problem with OFDMA access in existed research [6]. The main idea of SCG-OFDMA is that the STA with data transmission request has competed for the right to use, its surrounding stations with data transmission request are triggered by the access criteria to form a spatial aggregation group (SCG). The OFDMA accessing and transmission opportunities of SCG are shared with less overhead. Space utilization may be enhanced significantly by OFDMA access and transmission of SCG. SCG can be IEEE 802.11ax stations or IoT stations.

This paper has three contributions as follows:

- We design SCG-OFDMA scheme based MAC protocol.
- We design two new control frames, Request to Multiple Send (RTMS), Group Clear to Send (GCTS).
- Simulation results show that the area throughput of SCG-OFDMA is higher than OMAX and DCF protocols by 20% and 36%, respectively.

The rest of this paper includes three parts. SCG-OFDMA scheme based MAC protocol is illustrated in Sect. 2. The performance of MACs with SCG-OFDMA, OMAX, and DCF for WLAN are presented in Sect. 3. There is a conclusion of this paper in Sect. 4.

2   Spatial Clustering Group Based OFDMA (SCG-OFDMA) Scheme

The SCG-OFDMA scheme includes requesting SCG period, RTS of SCG collecting period and SCG DATA transmitting period, and works according to the three interdependence stages as described in Fig. 1. We suppose that the channel is divided into multiple subchannels and suppose all stations actively communicate to AP. We assume that the OFDMA technique used in the physical layer and its associated algorithm [10] can sufficiently restrict the frequency selective fading and interference, and the power control and related techniques can control the influence of near-field effects. We assume that OFDMA can be synchronized when the network range is small. The scheme proposed in this paper can calculate and test the received power threshold value according to the parameters of the network system before work, thus ensuring the optimal range of SCG.

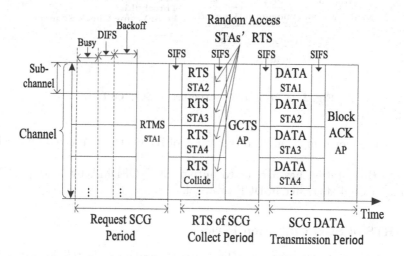

Fig. 1. Procedure of SCG-OFDMA.

2.1 Request SCG Period

The station with the uplink data transmission request senses the entire channel and uses the backoff mode specified in the IEEE 802.11 protocol when the channel is idle. When the value of the backoff counter reduced to zero, the station sends RTMS frame on the entire channel to identify SCG candidate stations and plays a role of timing signal for RTS transmission of SCG candidate stations.

RTMS and GCTS are two new control frames which are designed in detail shown in Fig. 2. Frame control, duration, transmitter address (TA) and frame check sequence (FCS) fields of RTMS are the same as IEEE 802.11 in addition to newly revised type and subtype for Frame Control field. We set type value 01 and set subtype value 0001 to RTMS as shown in Fig. 2a. We design a new field named BSS ID, described in Fig. 2a, which is Basic Set Service Identification (BSS ID) of station. We also design a new field named Rpt, described in Fig. 2a, which is receiver station's referring Received Power Threshold (RPT) value,

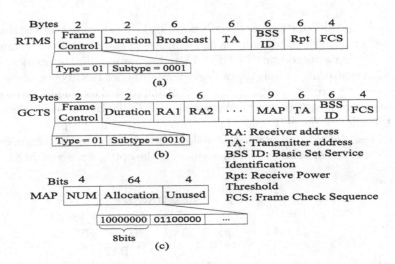

Fig. 2. Control frame structure of SCG-OFDMA.

which is used for comparing to power value of RTMS to be received by receiver station.

Note that station has a right to initiate SCG-OFDMA by sending RTMS through backoff stage like in DCF protocol.

2.2 RTS of SCG Collection Period

Other non-AP station receives RTMS frame, and records cell identification, received power threshold and other information. According to the information carried by the RTMS frame to determine whether access. Access rules are the station itself has uplink data to be sent, the RTMS frame is from the local cell, and the power value of RTMS frame to be received is greater than or equal to the received power threshold. If non-AP station meets the access rules, non-AP randomly selects one subchannel from a list of available subchannels to send Request to Multiple Send (RTS) frame after Short Inter Frame Space (SIFS). Otherwise the RTS frame is not allowed to send.

AP receives the RTMS frame and records carried MAC address, data length and cell identification and other information, and waits for PCF Inter Frame Space (PIFS) duration. In the PIFS duration, once AP receives RTS frame from one of subchannels, AP adopts round robin scheduling algorithm [6], and replies to group clear to send (GCTS) frame after SIFS. If no RTS frame is received, the AP replies to the GCTS frame after the PIFS duration. This means that AP has a right to allocate subchannels for SCG stations which successfully send RTS.

Frame Control, duration, transmitter address (TA) and frame check sequence (FCS) fields of GCTS are the same as IEEE 802.11 in addition to newly revised type and subtype for Frame Control field. We set type value 01 and set subtype value 0010 to GCTS as shown in Fig. 2b. We design a new field named MAP, described in Fig. 2c. MAP is corresponded with Receiver addresses of stations to be scheduled. MAP contains three subfields NUM, allocation and unused [4]. Num includes the number of stations to be scheduled, and allocation indicates subchannel or subchannels to be allocated to each RA of scheduled station in the front sequence. In allocation subfield, a binary string of 64 bits, every 8 bits in the sequence are corresponded with 8 subchannels for one scheduled station in RA subfield. For example, a binary string of subfield 10000000 are associated with subchannel 1 for one scheduled station in RA 1 subfield. However, subchannel 2, subchannel 3, subchannel 4, subchannel 5, subchannel 6, subchannel 7 and subchannel 8 are not allocated for one scheduled station in RA 1 subfield. Similarly, a binary string of subfield 01100000 are associated with subchannel 2 and subchannel 3 for one scheduled station in RA 2 subfield. Thus, subchannel 1, subchannel 4, subchannel 5, subchannel 6, subchannel 7 and subchannel 8 are not allocated for one scheduled station in RA 2 subfield, and so on.

2.3 SCG DATA Transmission Period

STA receives the GCTS frame and transmits the uplink data on the allocated subchannel or subchannels according to the channel allocation information carried into the GCTS frame. AP replies a block acknowledgment (BA) frame after receiving the uplink data using the entire channel.

3 Performance Evaluation

In order to evaluate the performance of MACs with SCG-OFDMA, OMAX, and DCF for WLAN by measuring the impacts of the number of stations which are randomly distributed in 20 m. * 20 m. WLAN, traffic load and data packet size. We adopts area throughput as an evaluation metric of space utilization which is the ratio of throughput to the geographical interference area. Some discrete event driven simulation programs are loaded in NS2 [11] to verify SCG-OFDMA, OMAX, and DCF, respectively. We make use of simulation parameters specified in OMAX [6] as given in Table 1.

Figure 3 depicts the throughput achieved through NS2 simulation versus number of stations changing from 1 to 100 with data packet size of 1500 bytes under the saturated traffic. At saturation traffic, the maximum throughput for SCG-OFDMA is achieved at 20 stations, and decreases slightly afterwards. SCG-OFDMA reflects the high efficiency of OFDMA access and transmission of SCG because SCG and OFDMA are worked when the station number greater than 1. A distributed access protocol DCF works better than OMAX with small number of stations from 1 to 10, but rapidly becomes bad when the number of stations increases as the access collision increases intolerably. In the number of one station, the throughput of DCF is slightly higher than that of SCG-OFDMA and OMAX because the gain caused by OFDMA of SCG-OFDMA and OMAX protocols is smaller than that of overhead for control frame transmission. Another

Table 1. Simulation parameters

Parameters	Value
Channel bandwidth	40 MHz
Number of subchannels	8
Basic rate	6 Mbps
Data rate	135 Mbps
CWmin	15
CWmax	1023
MAC header	32 bytes
PHY header	28 μs
DIFS	34 μs
SIFS	16 μs
PIFS	25 μs
Slot time	9 μs

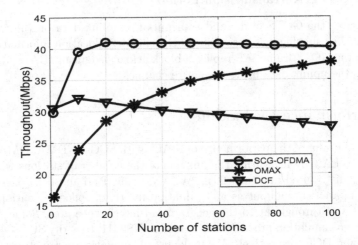

Fig. 3. Saturation throughput with the number of stations.

distributed access protocol OMAX works better than DCF with large number of stations from 30 to 100 because OFDMA is worked. Figure 3 shows that throughput of SCG-OFDMA outperforms the DCF and OMAX over various number of stations from 2 to 100 and that the SCG and OFDMA function as designed.

Figure 4 describes the area throughput achieved through NS2 simulation versus various number of stations from 1 to 100 with data packet length of 1500 bytes within the saturated traffic. At saturation traffic, the maximum area throughput for SCG-OFDMA is obtained at 60 stations, and decreases slightly afterwards. SCG-OFDMA reflects the space utilization high efficiency of OFDMA access and transmission of SCG because SCG and OFDMA is assumed and worked

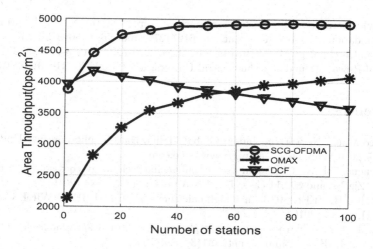

Fig. 4. Saturation area throughput with the number of stations.

when the station number greater than 1. A distributed access protocol DCF works well with small number of stations from 1 to 10, but rapidly becomes bad when the number of stations increases as the access collision increases intolerably. In the number of one station, the area throughput of DCF is slightly higher than that of SCG-OFDMA and OMAX because the gain caused by OFDMA of SCG-OFDMA and OMAX protocols is smaller than that of overhead for control frame transmission. Another distributed access protocol OMAX works better than DCF with the number of stations from 60 to 100 because OFDMA is worked. We observe that area throughput of SCG-OFDMA outperforms the DCF and OMAX over various number of stations from 2 to 100 and that the SCG and OFDMA function as designed. When the number of stations is 100, the area throughput of SCG-OFDMA is higher than OMAX 20% and DCF 36%, respectively. The main reason is that SCG-OFDMA reduces the geographical interference area compared with OMAX and DCF.

4   Conclusion

In this paper, an OFDMA protocol based on spatial aggregation group named SCG-OFDMA is proposed in densely crowded WLANs, which can effectively reduces the geographical interference area compared with the OMAX and DCF proposed in the existed literature, and uplink multiuser demands are taken care of. The simulation results show that the area throughput of SCG-OFDMA is higher than OMAX 20% and DCF 36%, respectively, when the number of stations is 100. For next generation WLAN, it is very important how efficiently area throughput is taken care of to obtain a good performance of MAC to be designed, while SCG-OFDMA works well as intended.

Acknowledgement. This work was supported in part by the National Natural Science Foundations of CHINA (Grant No. 61271279, and No. 61501373), the National Science and Technology Major Project (Grant No. 2016ZX03001018-004), and the Fundamental Research Funds for the Central Universities (Grant No. 3102017ZY018).

References

1. Cisco Visual Networking Index: Global Mobile Data Traffic Forecast Update for 2015–2020 Whitepaper. http://www.cisco.com
2. Ngangue, E.D.N., Cherkaoui, S.: On enhancing technology coexistence in the IoT Era: ZigBee and 802.11 case. J. IEEE Access **4**, 1835–1844 (2016)
3. Bellalta, B.: IEEE 802.11 ax: high-efficiency WLANs. J. IEEE Wirel. Commun. **23**(1), 38–46 (2016)
4. Lee, J., Kim, C.: An efficient multiple access coordination scheme for OFDMA WLAN. J. IEEE Commun. Lett. **21**(3), 596–599 (2017)
5. IEEE 802.11ax Proposed Draft Specification. https://mentor.ieee.org
6. Qu, Q., Li, B., Yang, M., et al.: An OFDMA based concurrent multiuser MAC for upcoming IEEE 802.11ax. In: Wireless Communications and Networking Conference Workshops (WCNCW), pp. 136–141. IEEE, New Orleans (2015)
7. Sun, W., Lee, O., Shin, Y.: Wi-Fi could be much more. J. IEEE Commun. Mag. **52**(11), 22–29 (2014)
8. Li, B., Qu, Q., Yan, Z., et al.: Survey on OFDMA based MAC protocols for the next generation WLAN. In: Wireless Communications and Networking Conference Workshops (WCNCW), pp. 131–135. IEEE, New Orleans (2015)
9. Deng, D.J., Lien, S.Y.: On quality-of-service provisioning in IEEE 802.11 ax WLANs. J. IEEE Access **4**, 6086–6104 (2016)
10. Jung, J., Lim, J.: Group contention-based OFDMA MAC protocol for multiple access interference-free in WLAN systems. J. IEEE Trans. Wirel. Commun. **11**(2), 648–658 (2012)
11. Lin, W., Li, B., Yang, M., et al.: Integrated link-system level simulation platform for the next generation WLAN-IEEE 802.11 ax. In: Global Communications Conference (GLOBECOM), pp. 1–7. IEEE, Washington (2016)

T-SCMA: Time Domain Sparse Code Multiple Access for Narrow Band Internet of Things (NB-IoT) (Invited Paper)

Zhenzhen Yan, Bo Li, Mao Yang[✉], Zhongjiang Yan, and Zhicheng Bai

School of Electronics and Information, Northwestern Polytechnical University,
Xi'an, China
{libo.npu,yangmao,zhjyan}@nwpu.edu.cn,
{yanzhenzhen,baizhicheng}@mail.nwpu.edu.cn

Abstract. Nowadays the development of internet of things (IoT) has become the next major growth point of wireless communication. And narrow band has become a new trend in the development of IoT. Achieving massive connectivity and ever-increasing network capacity has become an important subject of our research. We find that sparse code multiple access (SCMA), a type of non-orthogonal multiple access, is supposed to meet these needs, but it can hardly apply to NB-IoT because narrow band does not have the ability of spread spectrum. On this basis, we introduce SCMA into time domain, named T-SCMA, for NB-IoT. By multiplexing SCMA in the time domain and defining a MAC frame structure, we can significantly improve both connectivity and network capacity, ultimately obtain a much higher throughput property gain over time division multiple address (TDMA).

Keywords: Internet of Things · Sparse code multiple access
NB-IoT · Connectivity · Network capacity

1 Introduction

Internet of things (IoT) has become a vital technology in our life. Nowadays both the fifth generation wireless network (5G) and wireless local area networks (WLAN) have become important driving forces at the development of IoT [1, 2]. But we have to face challenges that IoT has massive connectivity demands especially in narrow band.

At present, narrow band has become a new trend in the development of IoT. Characteristics of wide coverage, massive connectivity, low energy consumption etc. make NB-IoT widely used. However, orthogonal multiple access methods are difficult to meet the requirements of both the massive connectivity and the increasing network capacity.

© ICST Institute for Computer Sciences, Social Informatics and Telecommunications Engineering 2018
Y.-B. Lin et al. (Eds.): IoTaaS 2017, LNICST 246, pp. 373–380, 2018.
https://doi.org/10.1007/978-3-030-00410-1_43

Sparse code multiple access (SCMA) is a non-orthogonal multiple access (NOMA) technology. Based on the characteristics of non-orthogonal multiplexing in the frequency domain, sparsity, overloading, SCMA aims to solve the massive connectivity and increasing network capacity problems of 5G [3]. But it can hardly apply to NB-IoT because narrow band does not have the ability of spread spectrum.

As a very promising application in the future, NB-IoT attracts keen interests of many scholars recently. A new NOMA strategy, named multi-user shared access (MUSA), applying to IoT, has proposed [4] which utilizes code domain non-orthogonality to implement massive connectivity in grant-free mode. Ding et al. [5] introduce a multiple-input multiple-output NOMA (MIMO-NOMA) technique for small packet transmission. It works co-efficiently, for that one user's quality of service (QoS) requirements are satisfied dynamically according to the channel condition and power allocation, while the demands of the other user are satisfied fully. In addition, the authors in [6] present a frequency-hopping based on SCMA (FH-SCMA) project to enhance the connectivity and interference alleviation. Summarizing current research about NOMA schemes apply to IoT, we can obtain that almost all of them do not consider using SCMA scheme in NB-IoT.

In order to make SCMA in motion in NB-IoT and satisfy the massive connectivity and increasing network capacity, this paper proposes an idea of time domain SCMA (T-SCMA) scheme, it introduces SCMA to time domain for the first time and then combines T-SCMA with NB-IoT together. By being multiplexed into time domain and making a MAC frame structure designed, T-SCMA can significantly improve both the connectivity and network capacity. Furthermore, masses of simulation results manifest that T-SCMA can effectively solve both the two challenges of NB-IoT.

The main contribution of this paper is summarized as following.

- This paper introduces SCMA into time domain for the first time and then combines T-SCMA with NB-IoT together to hoist capacity dramatically.
- Masses of simulation results prove that throughput performance of T-SCMA scheme is improved significantly in contrast to the traditional orthogonal way, for example, time division multiple address (TDMA) in our paper in the case that the packet error rate (PER) is almost the same.

The rest of this paper is organized as follows. The system model of this paper is described in Sect. 2. In Sect. 3, we introduce the principle of T-SCMA scheme and present a MAC frame structure. Then we record the simulation process in IV. Lastly, we summarize this paper in Sect. 5.

2   System Model

2.1   Network Scenario

As we all know, NB-IoT has many advantages such as massive connectivity, wide coverage, high reliability, low power consumption, low latency, etc. It is applicable to intelligent products, wisdom city and many other fields. And it is also expected to emerge a large number of innovative solutions or businesses.

However, it is a huge challenge of satisfying the massive connectivity and increasing network capacity of NB-IoT nowadays. It is precisely what our article wants to solve.

2.2 Resources Scenario

For uplink, NB-IoT defines two classes of physical channels. One is narrow band physics uplink sharing channel (NPUSCH) and the other is narrow band physics random access channel (NPRACH). In addition to NPRACH, all the data is transferred through NPUSCH.

NPUSCH is used for transferring uplink data and control information using single frequency or multiple frequencies. It defines two types of formats. For one type, NPRACH supports single frequency transmission when carrier space is 3.75 kHz, and supports single frequency or multiple frequency transmission when carrier space is 15 kHz. For the other, each resource block (RB) occupies only one frequency to transfer data.

Obviously, narrow band limits the connectivity and increasing network capacity to some degree. Increasing further those performances is exactly what to be solved in this paper.

3 T-SCMA Scheme

3.1 Basic Ideas

The basic ideas of T-SCMA system has the following characteristics as we can see in Fig. 1.

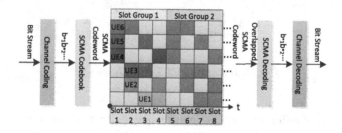

Fig. 1. Illustration of T-SCMA system

- Non-orthogonal multiplexing in the time domain. Codewords between different users are non-orthogonally overlapped on the same RBs, which are made up of several time slots. Compared with the traditional orthogonal method TDMA, T-SCMA can accommodate more users on the same number of RBs. Thus it can effectively improve connectivity and network capacity on narrow band.

– Overloading. Codewords of multiple users are overlapped in each RB. Obviously, overloading means the number of users exceeds the number of time slots on each RB. It is also the biggest characteristic of T-SCMA. Assuming that on each RB, J represents the number of users and K represents the number of time slots, then we can define the overloading factor as:

$$OF = \frac{J}{K} \tag{1}$$

– Sparsity. As given in Fig. 1, data is spread from single time slot to four time slots, every six users shares the four time slots on each RB. Every user's data occupies all the four time slots on each RB while only two time slots are allocated with non-zero elements. It is noteworthy that this feature helps to reduce the complexity of receiver.

3.2 Encoder

For the sender, the SCMA encoder directly maps the bit stream after channel coding to complex domain multi-dimensional SCMA codewords, which is defined by the SCMA codebook. Then the codewords are mapped to time domain and become T-SCMA codewords.

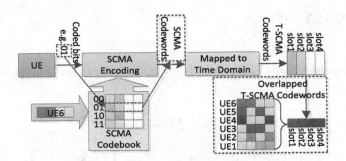

Fig. 2. Illustration of T-SCMA encoder

Codewords of different users are non-orthogonally overlapped on each RB by means of sparse spread spectrum. As shown in Fig. 2, per two bits after channel coding is corresponded to a four-dimension codeword, which occupies the whole four time slots on each RB, and we get the following formula:

$$Ts = 2^B \tag{2}$$

Here, Ts represents the number of time slots on each RB and B represents the number of dimensions corresponding to a codeword.

3.3 Decoder

SCMA decoder will carry out joint multi-user detection algorithm iteratively to decode overlapped SCMA codewords. This algorithm takes advantage of the low complexity of SCMA and increases the robustness of SCMA decoder. And it also supports higher overloading factor.

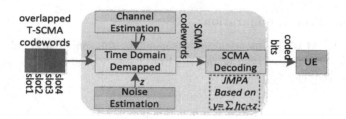

Fig. 3. Illustration of T-SCMA decoder

As shown in Fig. 3, y represents the received signal, h is the channel coefficient, c_i represents the SCMA codewords of each user and z represents the additive white gaussian noise (AWGN), then the received signal can be expressed as the following formula:

$$y = \sum h * c_i + z \qquad (3)$$

Thus we can obtain c_i from the above formula and complete restoring the bit stream by channel decoder.

3.4 MAC Frame Structure

In order to achieve the goal of this paper, we need to define a MAC frame structure as shown in Fig. 4.

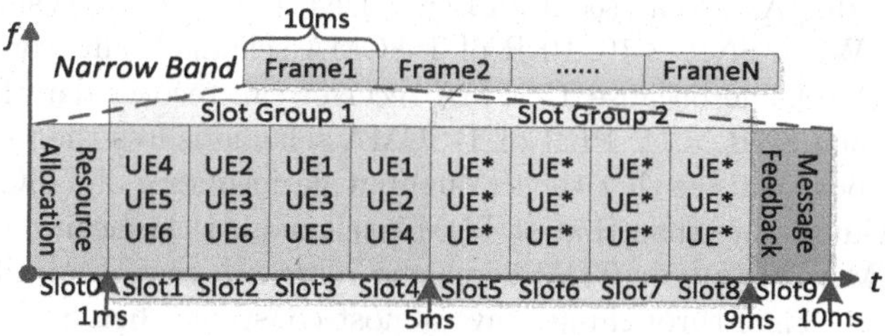

Fig. 4. Illustration of MAC frame structure

Under the background of NB-IoT, each MAC frame is divided into ten time slots, which can be divided into four parts, zeroth time slot, first slot group, second slot group and the last time slot respectively according to different functions.

The zeroth time slot works for resource allocation. Then follows two slot groups, each consists of four consecutive slots, as a T-SCMA RB. The two slot groups will access users and transfer data according to the T-SCMA transmission mode. The ninth time slot performs information feedback function.

4   Performance Evaluation

4.1   Simulation Configuration

Based on the MAC frame structure designed in this paper and other typical configurations in the standards and the literatures, we establish the simulation parameters as given in Table 1.

Table 1. Simulation parameters

Parameters	Value
Length of frame structure	10 Solts
Number of time slot group	2
Number of user group	2
Length of per time slot group	4 Solts
System bandwidth	1 MHz
Length of bit sequence on per slot	1000 Bits
Length of per time slot	1 ms
Channel model	AWGN channel without noise
Channel coding	LDPC with 1/2 coding rate
Transmission mode	Granted/Grant-free

4.2   Performance Comparison

Granted Mode. As we can see from Fig. 5, PER performance is similar for the two schemes. When SNR < 10, PER of T-SCMA scheme is slightly better than that of TDMA scheme because T-SCMA receiver can recover data from several time slots. When SNR > 11, PER of T-SCMA scheme is less than e^{-4}.

From Fig. 6 we can see that the throughput performance of T-SCMA scheme is about 1.5 times more than that of TDMA scheme. At the beginning, throughput of T-SCMA scheme or TDMA scheme increases monotonically with the growth of SNR. Then throughput stays almost constant when SNR > 9 as network capacity becomes gradually saturated.

Grant-Free Mode. By fixing signal noise ratio (SNR) to 11, we evaluate the throughput gain varying with the sending rate of users. Figure 7 shows the result. At first, throughput of both two schemes increases with the growth of sending probability. Then throughput based on TDMA scheme gradually comes to its

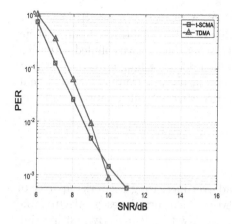

Fig. 5. PER versus SNR on granted mode

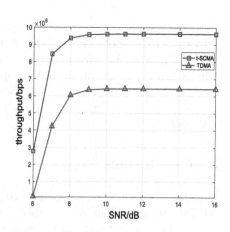

Fig. 6. Throughput versus SNR on granted mode

highest point as network capacity reaches saturation point and later drops off as signal collisions between users become seriously, causing unsuccessful data transmission. However, throughput of T-SCMA scheme sustains growth due to the superiority of overlapping.

As we can see from Fig. 8, PER of T-SCMA scheme is apparently higher than that of TDMA scheme because the poor performance of joint message passing algorithm (JMPA) than orthogonal decoding algorithms in this mode.

After fixing the sending probability to $\frac{2}{3}$, we evaluate the throughput gain varying with SNR. Figure 9 illustrates the result. At beginning, PER of T-SCMA scheme is much higher than that of TDMA scheme so throughput of

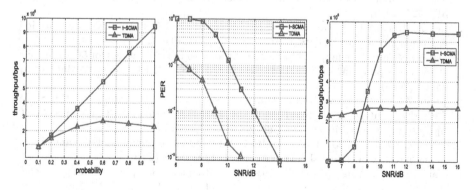

Fig. 7. Throughput versus probability on grant-free mode

Fig. 8. PER versus SNR on grant-free mode

Fig. 9. Throughput versus SNR on grant-free mode

T-SCMA scheme is far lower than that of TDMA scheme. When SNR increases, with the PER of both two schemes gradually decrease, the throughput of them increases as well. As different users of TDMA scheme may have collided with each other when accessing on the slot groups, which does not happen with T-SCMA scheme, throughput of T-SCMA scheme grows faster and gradually exceeds that of TDMA scheme. Then their throughput stay constant when network capacity is saturated.

5   Conclusions

In order to satisfy massive connectivity and ever-increasing network capacity of NB-IoT, we raise a method named T-SCMA which introduces SCMA to time domain for the first time and combine T-SCMA with NB-IoT. By multiplexing SCMA into time domain and defining a MAC frame structure, we can significantly improve connectivity and network capacity of NB-IoT. And masses of simulation results manifest that throughput performance of T-SCMA scheme increases very much in comparison to TDMA. So we can say that T-SCMA can effectively solve the above challenges of NB-IoT. In the future, other schemes of non-orthogonal multiple access applying to NB-IoT will be researched.

Acknowledgement. This work was supported in part by the National Natural Science Foundations of CHINA (Grant No. 61271279, and No. 61501373), the National Science and Technology Major Project (Grant No. 2016ZX03001018-004), and the Fundamental Research Funds for the Central Universities (Grant No. 3102017ZY018).

References

1. Palattella, M.R., Dohler, M., Grieco, A., et al.: Internet of things in the 5G era: enablers, architecture, and business models. IEEE J. Sel. Areas Commun. **34**(3), 510–527 (2016)
2. Lei, X., Rhee, S.H.: Performance improvement of sub 1 GHz WLANs for future IoT environments. J. Wirel. Pers. Commun. **93**(4), 933–947 (2017)
3. Dai, L., Wang, B., Yuan, Y., et al.: Non-orthogonal multiple access for 5G: solutions, challenges, opportunities, and future research trends. J. IEEE Commun. Mag. **53**(9), 74–81 (2015)
4. Yuan, Z., Yu, G., Li, W., et al.: Multi-user shared access for internet of things. In: 83th IEEE International Symposium on Vehicular Technology Conference (VTC Spring), pp. 1–5. Springer, Nanjing (2016)
5. Ding, Z., Dai, L., Poor, H.V.: MIMO-NOMA design for small packet transmission in the internet of things. J. IEEE Access **4**, 1393–1405 (2016)
6. Bai, Z., Li, B., Yang, M., et al.: FH-SCMA: frequency-hopping based sparse code multiple access for next generation internet of things. In: 18th IEEE International Symposium on Wireless Communications and Networking Conference (WCNC), pp. 1–6. IEEE Press, San Francisco (2017)

Semi-granted Sparse Code Multiple Access (SCMA) for 5G Networks (Invited Paper)

Mao Yang[✉], Bo Li, Zhicheng Bai, Xiaoya Zuo, Zhongjiang Yan, and Yusheng Liang

School of Electronics and Information, Northwestern Polytechnical University, Xian, China
{yangmao,libo.npu,zuoxy,zhjyan}@nwpu.edu.cn

Abstract. Sparse Code Multiple Access (SCMA) is a promising non-orthogonal multiple access technology for 5G radio access networks. It improves the connectivity and capacity. However, the two multiple access methods of SCMA: granted and grant-free cannot dynamically match the real-time demands since the resources allocated for the granted method and grant-free method are clearly separated with each other. This further deteriorates the system performance. This article proposes a semi-granted SCMA method, by enabling the granted demands and grant-free demands to share the same resources. Simulation results confirm that semi-granted SCMA matches the dynamically fluent demands and significantly improve the throughput of SCMA 5G system.

Keywords: Sparse code multiple access · SCMA
Non-orthogonal multiple access · Multiple access · Grant-free · 5G

1 Introduction

Since mobile Internet deeply penetrates most aspects of human life, the wireless connectivity and traffic are being proliferating in recent years [1]. The traditional wireless networks can hardly keep pace with these increasing demands. Therefore, the fifth generation (5G) mobile communication system is required to support massive connectivity, super-large capacity, and diverse services.

To improve the connectivity and capacity, sparse code multiple access (SCMA) [2], a promising non-orthogonal multiple access technology [3] for 5G, attracts increasingly attentions from both the academic and industrial communities in recent years. Directly mapping different coded bitstreams into multi-dimensional complex domain codewords generated by predefined codebooks, SCMA enables multiple users' information to be overload in the frequency domain but multiplexed in the code domain. The non-orthogonality achieves the overloading gain and diversity gain, while the sparsity guarantees the simplicity and feasibility of multi-user detection in receiver. Therefore, SCMA significantly improves the connectivity and capacity.

© ICST Institute for Computer Sciences, Social Informatics and Telecommunications Engineering 2018
Y.-B. Lin et al. (Eds.): IoTaaS 2017, LNICST 246, pp. 381–388, 2018.
https://doi.org/10.1007/978-3-030-00410-1_44

The increasingly diverse services pose a series of intractable challenges for wireless access network. For example, some Internet of things (IoT) services require ultra low access latency, while service with massive packets but small size aggravates the signalling storm problem, *and etc*. These diverse services ask for multiple access adaptation of wireless networks. Some existing studies introducing SCMA for the IoT system [4]. SCMA introduces two multiple access types: scheduling based multiple access (granted) and contention based multiple access (grant-free). Scheduling based multiple, all access opportunities are scheduled by the base station (BS), is the traditional access method of cellular network. In contrast, contention based multiple access method allows user equipments (UEs) to directly contend the spectrum resources without apply-and-grant [5,6], reducing both the access latency and signalling. Therefore, these two methods obtain the multiple access adaptation for SCMA.

However, the related studies assume that the time-frequency resources allocated for the granted method and that for the grant-free method are clearly separated with each other. This causes the mismatch between resources and real-time demands. The wireless demands continuously vary with time, thus it is quite difficult to "draw the borderline" of granted resources and grant-free resources dynamically. It means the resources allocated for granted and grant-free can hardly match the real-time demands. When the requirements of granted demands are less than the allocated resources and the grant-free demands sharply increase, there is no choice but waste the extra resources allocated for the granted method. Consequently, the collision grows and throughput decreases, and vice versa. Therefore, this mismatch actually leads to a stalemate: the system needs to know the real-time granted and grant-free demands in order to dynamically determine the appropriate resource allocation results, while the granted and grant-free demands are related to the resource allocation since different allocation results result different performance such as collision probability and throughput. Therefore, the clear division between granted resources and grant-free resources affects the system performance and decreases gain achieved by SCMA.

To break the stalemate and obtain further gain of SCMA, we propose semi-granted sparse code multiple access for 5G networks. Breaking the clear separation, semi-granted SCMA enables the granted demands and the grant-free demands share the same resources. In another word, each resource block (RB) can serve both the granted demands and the grant-free demand. In this case, like soft water filling in the hard stones, after scheduling proper resources to the granted demands, the BS indicates the grant-free demands contend all the remaining SCMA layers which are overloaded with the resources occupied by the granted demands. Thus, the resources can efficiently support the real-time demands. Simulation results confirm the flexibility and efficiency of our proposed semi-granted SCMA, and show that semi-granted SCMA significantly outperform the separation method in the system throughput.

The contributions of this article can be summarized as follows:

- To the best of our knowledge, this is the first work to introduce the semi-granted SCMA concept enabling the granted and grant-free sharing the same

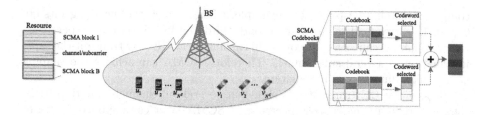

Fig. 1. System model.

resources. It guarantees the resource allocation to dynamically match the varying demands.
– A specific media access control (MAC) frame is proposed for the semi-granted SCMA.

2 System Model

2.1 Network Topology

As Fig. 1 shows, the BS is located at the center of the cell. UEs are distributed randomly in the coverage area surrounding the BS. For simplicity, we divide UEs into two group:

(1) The granted UEs, denoted as $\{u_1, u_2, \cdots, u_{N^S}\}$, where N^S indicates the number of granted UEs. The granted UEs are applicable to the granted access method.
(2) The grant-free UEs, denoted as $\{v_1, v_2, \cdots, v_{N^F}\}$, where N^F indicates the number of grant-free UEs. The grant-free UEs adopt grant-free multiple access method.

2.2 Resources

There are X sub-carriers/sub-channels in the frequency domain. Every K sub-channels are aggregated as a SCMA block. Thus, the total number of SCMA blocks is:

$$m = \lceil X/K \rceil, \tag{1}$$

where $\lceil * \rceil$ denotes the minimum integer that is greater than or equal to $*$.

2.3 SCMA Model

Assuming that the system possesses K subchannels. The codebook set as denoted as $\mathbf{C} = \{c_1, c_2, \cdots, c_J\}$, where J indicates the number of SCMA layers. The size of each SCMA codebook is $K * M$, denoted as $c_i^{K \times M}, i = 1, 2, \cdots, J$. The row in c_i indicates the subchannel i and the column indicates the information incoming bits. It means the SCMA encoder maps every $\log_2 M$ incoming bits into one complex constellation point. For example, when $M = 4$, the incoming bits 00, 01, 10, 11 correspond to the first, second, third and fourth column respectively. Every column is call as a codeword. This means every UE may transmit the same information in several subchannels. Therefore, SCMA can achieve the shaping gain of high dimensional modulation.

Since every UE transmits its signal in several subchannels, multiple UEs' signal overlaps in the shared spectrum. J SCMA layer can support J UEs to transmit concurrently. Thus, the overload factor is $J/K > 1$. These multiple UEs' signals multiplex in the wireless channels. And then the signal received in base station can be described as [4]:

$$\mathbf{y} = \sum_{j=1}^{J} diag(\mathbf{h}_j)\mathbf{x}_j + \mathbf{n}, \tag{2}$$

where $\mathbf{x}_j = (x_{1j}, \cdots, x_{Kj})^T$ is the codeword of layer j (UE j). $\mathbf{n}$ is the additive white gaussian noise vector. $\mathbf{y}$ represents the K-dimensional multiplexed receiving signal vector at the receiver. Diagonal matrix $diag(\mathbf{h}_j)$ represents the channel. $\mathbf{h}_j = (h_{1j}, \cdots, h_{Kj})^T$ is layer j's channel vector, and h_{1j} corresponds to the jth subchannel.

SCMA introduces the spares feature, which means every codeword has several, always more than a half, zero elements. Such sparse feature significantly simplifies the computational complex in receiver. Therefore, the receiver may use low complexity multi-user detection algorithms such as message passing algorithm (MPA).

3   Key Idea of Semi-granted SCMA

To easily and clearly introduce the key idea of semi-granted SCMA, an example is presents in Fig. 2. There are two SCMA blocks, each of which consists of four sub-channels. Each SCMA block possesses six layers, thus the overloading factor is $6/4 = 1.5$.

Figure 2(a) illustrates the multiple access method that the resources of granted and grant-free are clearly separated proposed by the existing studies. In this method, the granted UEs cannot use the grant-free resource even if the granted resources are not enough and the grant-free resources are quite vacant. The demands are continuously varying with time. In the time t_1, two granted UEs and eight grant-free UEs want to transmit uplink data. In this case, obviously, the granted resources are seriously wasted because only two granted UEs share the resources. The grant-free UEs collide with each other because in each sub-channel there are four UEs try to contend, which is larger than the max supportable UE number: three. Thus, the throughput in t_1 is low. Similarly, in the time t_2, eight granted UEs and two grant-free UEs want to transmit uplink data. Consequently, two granted UEs cannot be served because the granted resource can support six users at most. Although there are plenty of available grant-free

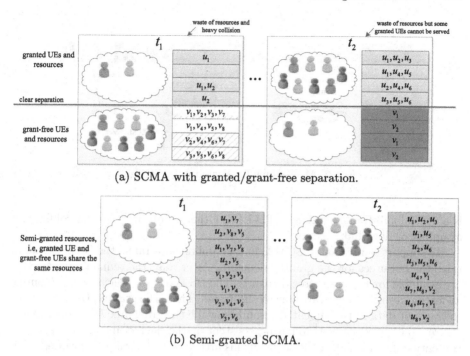

(a) SCMA with granted/grant-free separation.

(b) Semi-granted SCMA.

Fig. 2. Key idea of semi-granted SCMA.

resources, the two granted UEs have no choice but wait for the scheduling in the future. Thus, the throughput in t_2 is suppressed and the access latency of some UEs is increased.

Figure 2(a) shows the semi-granted SCMA method. In this method, we break the resource separation by enabling both the granted UEs and grant-free UEs share the same resources. Two SCMA blocks can support twelve UEs in total. In the time t_1 and t_2, there are ten UEs want to transmit uplink data. Thus, it is conspicuous that all the UEs can be serviced successfully. Therefore, we highlight that the proposed semi-granted SCMA method naturally matches the time-varying demands, and significantly improves the throughput and QoS.

4   MAC Frame for Semi-granted SCMA

Since every multiple access method needs a corresponding MAC protocol, we propose a MAC frame for the semi-granted SCMA, as Fig. 3 shown. For compatibility, we design the MAC frame based on TD-LTE. The wireless frame, 10 ms, is the basic unit of semi-granted SCMA. Each wireless frame is divided into ten sub-frame, and each sub-frame (SF) occupies 1 ms. Moreover, each sub-frame is composed of two time slot, then each time slot is 0.5 ms. Before each wireless frame, the BS configures the time slot allocation according to the uplink and downlink traffic. The sub-frame 0 (SF0) is configured as downlink, while the SF1

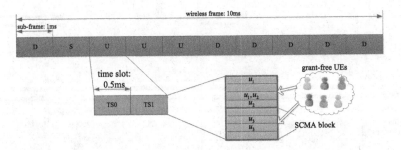

Fig. 3. MAC frame for semi-granted SCMA.

is a special sub-frame similar as TD-LTE. Other sub-frames can be configured as uplink or downlink flexibly.

To support semi-granted SCMA, in each uplink sub-frame, the BS firstly allocates the resources for the granted demands. After that, the remaining resources are available for the grant-free demands. The BS needs to indicates the resource allocation results in the start of each sub-frame. Then, the granted UEs just need to transmit data in the allocated resources, while the grant-free UEs contend for the remaining resources through p-persistent or the backoff mean. The specific contention mean is out of the scope of this article. If the number of granted UEs are large, the BS may reserve some resources for the grant-free UEs. Similarly, if the number of grant-free UEs are large, the BS may adjust the access probability or contention window (CW) for the grant-free UEs. Therefore, this MAC frame is a general frame. It supports not only the semi-granted SCMA, but the specific access means and scheduling algorithms.

5   Performance Evaluation

The system has 10 SCMA-block in total. During each timeslot, 0.5 ms, 1,000 bits are transmitted by each UE. LDPC is adopted for channel coding. Figure 4 shows the throughput verses the granted UE number. For the granted/grant-free separation scheme, 4 SCMA-blocks are fixed as the granted resources and 6 SCMA-blocks as the grant-free resources. When the granted UE number is unsaturated (less than 24), both two schemes achieve the same performance for granted UEs, but the proposed semi-granted scheme outperforms the separation scheme in throughput for grant-free UEs. Further, When the granted UE number is saturated (more than 24), both schemes almost share the same performance for grant-free UEs, but semi-granted outperforms the separation scheme in throughput for granted UEs.

In Fig. 5, the granted UE number is fixed as 24 and we change the ratio of granted SCMA-block. Obviously, 0 means no resources are allocated for the granted UEs, and 1 means all the resources are allocated for the granted UEs. We achieve the similar results from Fig. 5 that semi-granted scheme outperforms the separation scheme before and after saturation (ratio = 0.4).

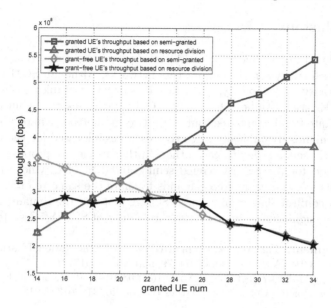

Fig. 4. Performance with granted UE number changing

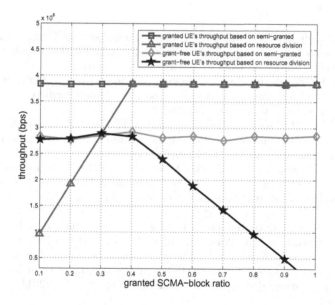

Fig. 5. Performance with granted SCMA block ratio changing.

Thus, we can obtain that semi-granted scheme matches the dynamically feature of user demands and achieve higher throughput and spectrum efficiency.

6   Conclusion

Sparse Code Multiple Access (SCMA) is a promising non-orthogonal multiple access technology for 5G radio access networks. Although SCMA improves the connectivity and capacity, there is still some intractable challenge to be addressed. Existing studies show that SCMA possesses two multiple access method: granted and grant-free, but these two methods can hardly match the real-time demands dynamically since the resources allocated for the two methods are clearly separated with each other. In this article, we propose a multiple access method for the SCMA named semi-granted SCMA, which enables the granted demands and grant-free demands to share the same resources. Simulation results confirm that semi-granted SCMA matches the dynamically fluent demands and significantly improve the throughput of SCMA 5G system.

Acknowledgment. This work was supported in part by the National Natural Science Foundations of CHINA (Grant No. 61271279, and No. 61501373), the National Science and Technology Major Project (Grant No. 2016ZX03001018-004), and the Fundamental Research Funds for the Central Universities (Grant No. 3102017ZY018).

References

1. Ericsson: Mobile report on the pulse of the networked society. In: Ericsson Mobility Report, November 2016. https://www.ericsson.com/assets/local/mobility-report/documents/2016/ericsson-mobility-report-november-2016.pdf
2. Nikopour, H., Baligh, H.: Sparse code multiple access. In: 2013 IEEE 24th Annual International Symposium on Personal, Indoor, and Mobile Radio Communications (PIMRC), London, UK, pp. 332–336 (2013)
3. Dai, L., Wang, B., Yuan, Y., Han, S., Chih-Lin, I., Wang, Z.: Non-orthogonal multiple access for 5G: solutions, challenges, opportunities, and future research trends. IEEE Commun. Mag. **53**(9), 74–81 (2015)
4. Bai, Z., Li, B., Yang, M., Yan, Z., Zuo, X., Zhang, Y.: FH-SCMA: frequency-hopping based sparse code multiple access for next generation Internet of Things. In: 2017 IEEE Wireless Communications and Networking Conference, Sanfrancisco, US, pp. 1–6 (2017)
5. Au, K., et al.: Uplink contention based SCMA for 5G radio access. In: 2014 IEEE Globecom Workshops (GC Wkshps), Austin, US, pp. 900–905 (2014)
6. Bayesteh, A., Yi, E., Nikopour, H., Baligh, H.: Blind detection of SCMA for uplink grant-free multiple-access. In: 2014 11th International Symposium on Wireless Communications Systems (ISWCS), Barcelona, Spain, pp. 853–857 (2014)

A Flow Network Based Backhaul Path Planning Algorithm for mmWave Small Cell Networks (Invited Paper)

Zhongyu Ma[1,2,3], Bo Li[1], Zhongjiang Yan[1(✉)], Mao Yang[1], Xiaoya Zuo[1], and Bo Yang[1]

[1] Northwestern Polytechnical University, Xi'an 710072, China
mazy@mail.nwpu.edu.cn, {libo.npu,zhjyan,yangmao,zuoxy}@nwpu.edu.cn
[2] LanZhou Institute of Technology, Lanzhou 730050, China
[3] Science and Technology on Communication Networks Laboratory, Shijiazhuang 053200, China

Abstract. In this paper, a flow network based backhaul path planning algorithm (FBPA) is proposed for mmWave small cell networks, to obtain the backhaul path with minimum energy consumption on the basis of maximum backhaul traffic. Firstly, the backhaul path planning problem is formulated as an integer programming (IP) problem, which is always an NP-hard problem. Then, to obtain the near-optimal solution of the proposed IP problem, a liner relaxation technique is used to make it be a liner problem. Finally, the FBPA algorithm is proposed to find the minimum energy consumption solution on the basis of maximum backhaul traffic based on the flow network theory for the IP. Extensive simulations are conducted and the simulation results show that the FBPA outperforms other traditional backhaul path planning algorithm in terms of energy efficiency and backhaul traffic.

Keywords: 5G · mmWave backhaul · Flow network

1 Introduction

With millimetre Wave (mmWave) small cells densely deployed in 5G for the applications, such as Internet of Things, Virtual Reality and so on, it is costly to connect the small cells with the core network, and to forward data to the gateway using fiber based backhaul [1]. Although mmWave wireless backhaul can be a competitive backhaul solution for the small cells in 5G networks, backhaul path planning is an important issue that needs to be addressed.

Recently, there is a few related works on designing wireless backhaul path. A joint routing and scheduling algorithm of backhaul link for ultra dense mmWave network is proposed in [2], and an maximum flow model based path planning method for the static mesh network with directional antenna is proposed in [3]. However, both of them do not consider the energy conservation issues. Ref.

© ICST Institute for Computer Sciences, Social Informatics and Telecommunications Engineering 2018
Y.-B. Lin et al. (Eds.): IoTaaS 2017, LNICST 246, pp. 389–397, 2018.
https://doi.org/10.1007/978-3-030-00410-1_45

[4] presents a cognitive green topology management mechanism in 5G network. However, each node in the algorithm is assumed to be with cognitive ability, and the algorithm is not suitable to the scenes with massive data transmissions for mmWave backhaul network. Ref. [5] proposes an energy saving method which dynamically change the operating states of the small cells. Although the energy consumption can be saved, the algorithm assumed that all of the mmWave small cells could be connected to macro base station in one hop, so the path planning problem of the multi hop backhaul is not considered.

To the best knowledge of ours, there has been few related works focusing on designing the backhaul path with minimum energy consumption based on the maximum traffic in given time period for mmWave small cells, which reasonably motivates our work. The main contributions of this paper can be summarized as follows. Firstly, the problem of path planning which is aiming at minimizing energy consumption on the basis of maximizing the backhaul traffic is formulated as an integer-programming (IP) problem for ultra dense mmWave small cells. Secondly, the IP problem is made more easier to resolve using liner relaxation. Thirdly, a flow network based backhaul path planning algorithm (FBPA) is proposed to solve the problem. Finally, simulation results show that the proposed algorithm outperforms the existing path planning algorithms, in terms of backhaul traffic and energy consumption.

2   System Modelling and Problem Formulation

The network scenario that considered in this paper is shown in Fig. 1. Suppose that the network is composed of N small cells (SCs) that connect with mmWave link, and M gateway nodes that connect the core network using fiber. Without loss of generality, the number of the mmWave links between adjacent nodes can be equal, which is denoted as K.

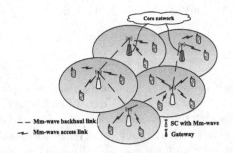

Fig. 1. Network scenario.

The network that shown in Fig. 1 can be modelled as an undirectional multigraph, i.e., $\mathcal{G} = (\mathcal{V}, \mathcal{E})$, $\mathcal{V} = \{\mathcal{V}_S, \mathcal{V}_G\}$, where $\mathcal{V}_S = \{s_i | 1 \leq i \leq N\}$ denotes the node set of SCs, $\mathcal{V}_G = \{g_j | 1 \leq j \leq M\}$ denotes the node set of gateways, and $\mathcal{E} = \{\mathcal{E}_{SS}, \mathcal{E}_{SG}\}$, where $\mathcal{E}_{SS} = \{e^k_{s_{i_1} \leftrightarrow s_{i_2}} | 1 \leq i_1, i_2 \leq N, i_1 \neq i_2, 1 \leq k \leq K\}$, while $\mathcal{E}_{SG} = \{e^k_{s_i \rightarrow g_j} | 1 \leq i \leq N, 1 \leq j \leq M, 1 \leq k \leq K\}$ denotes the set of wireless edges from SC to gateway. Besides, denote $T^k_{i_1 i_2}$ and $t^k_{i_1 i_2}$ as the total number of available time slots and active slots on the k-th mmWave link $e^k_{s_{i_1} \leftrightarrow s_{i_2}}$. Similarly, denote T^k_{ij} and t^k_{ij} as the total number of available time slots and active slots on the k-th mmWave link $e^k_{s_i \rightarrow g_j}$, where $0 \leq t^k_{i_1 i_2} \leq T^k_{i_1 i_2}$ and $0 \leq t^k_{ij} \leq T^k_{ij}$. Let $R^k_{i_1 i_2}, R^k_{ij}$ be the transmission rate within a slot on the k-th mmWave link $e^k_{s_{i_1} \leftrightarrow s_{i_2}}$, $e^k_{s_i \rightarrow g_j}$. L_i is the backhaul load of s_i generated by cell users. S_j is the total receiving capacity of g_j. $P^k_{i_1 i_2}$, P^k_{ij} is the consumed energy within a time slot on the k-th mmWave link $e^k_{s_{i_1} \leftrightarrow s_{i_2}}$, $e^k_{s_i \rightarrow g_j}$.

The goal of the proposed problem is to plan the backhaul paths between each mmWave SC and gateway node, which aims to minimize the total energy consumption with maximum backhaul traffic in given time period. The problem is formulated as follows.

$$\min\left(\sum_{i_1=1}^{N}\sum_{i_2=1}^{N}\sum_{k=1}^{K} t^k_{i_1 i_2} \times P^k_{i_1 i_2} + \sum_{i=1}^{N}\sum_{j=1}^{M}\sum_{k=1}^{K} t^k_{ij} \times P^k_{ij}\right) \tag{1}$$

$$s.t. \ \max \sum_{i=1}^{N}\sum_{k=1}^{K}\sum_{j=1}^{M} t^k_{ij} \times R^k_{ij}, \tag{2}$$

$$s.t. \ 0 \leq t^k_{i_1 i_2} \leq T^k_{i_1 i_2}, 1 \leq i_1, i_2 \leq N, 1 \leq k \leq K, \tag{3}$$

$$0 \leq t^k_{ij} \leq T^k_{ij}, 1 \leq i \leq N, 1 \leq j \leq M, 1 \leq k \leq K, \tag{4}$$

$$t^k_{i_1 i_2}, t^k_{ij} \in \mathcal{Z} \forall i, 1 \leq i \leq N, \tag{5}$$

$$L_i + \sum_{k=1}^{K}\sum_{i_1=1}^{N} t^k_{i_1 i} \times R^k_{i_1 i} \leq \sum_{k=1}^{K}\sum_{i_2=1}^{N} t^k_{ii_2} \times R^k_{ii_2}, \tag{6}$$

$$\sum_{k=1}^{K}\sum_{i=1}^{M} t^k_{ij} \times R^k_{ij} \leq S_j, \forall j, 1 \leq j \leq M, \tag{7}$$

The problem is denoted as *Problem-I*, where Eqs. (3) and (4) mean that number of actual active slots within the mmWave links do not exceed the maximum number of active slots. Equation (5) denotes that the number of actual active slots is an integer, where $\mathcal{Z}$ is the set of integers. Equation (6) denotes that for any one of mmWave SCs, the total amount of data being sent out is no less than total amount of data being received and the traffic loads that generated by itself. Equation (7) represents that the total amount of data that flows into the gateway node is no more than the maximum capacity of the fiber. Problem-I is an IP problem, which is always an NP-hard problem. A new variable $d^k_{i_1 i_2}$ is introduced, which denotes the amount of data on the k-th backhaul link from s_{i_1} to s_{i_2}, i.e., $e^k_{s_{i_1} \rightarrow s_{i_2}}$. Similarly, the other variable d^k_{ij} is also introduced, which denotes the amount of data on the k-th backhaul link from s_i to g_j, i.e., $e^k_{s_i \to g_j}$. The relationship between variables $d^k_{i_1 i_2}$, d^k_{ij} and $t^k_{i_1 i_2}$, t^k_{ij} can be obtained as

$$t^k_{i_1 i_2} = \left\lceil \frac{d^k_{i_1 i_2}}{R^k_{i_1 i_2}} \right\rceil, t^k_{ij} = \left\lceil \frac{d^k_{ij}}{R^k_{ij}} \right\rceil. \tag{8}$$

Then, the Eq. (2) can be rewritten as

$$\max \sum_{i=1}^{N} \sum_{j=1}^{M} \sum_{k=1}^{K} d^k_{ij}. \tag{9}$$

The Eqs. (3)–(4) can be rewritten as

$$0 \leq d^k_{i_1 i_2} \leq T^k_{i_1 i_2} \times R^k_{i_1 i_2}, 1 \leq i_1, i_2 \leq N, 1 \leq k \leq K, \tag{10}$$

$$0 \leq d^k_{ij} \leq T^k_{ij} \times R^k_{ij}, 0 \leq i \leq N, 1 \leq j \leq M, 1 \leq k \leq K, \tag{11}$$

respectively. For each s_i, Eq. (6) can be rewritten as

$$L_i + \sum_{k=1}^{K} \sum_{i_1=1}^{N} d^k_{i_1 i} = \sum_{k=1}^{K} \sum_{i_2=1}^{N} d^k_{i i_2}, \forall i, 1 \leq i \leq N, \tag{12}$$

and the constraint (7) can be rewritten as

$$\sum_{k=1}^{K} \sum_{i=1}^{M} d^k_{ij} \leq S_j, \forall j, 1 \leq j \leq M. \tag{13}$$

Finally, denote $\eta^k_{i_1 i_2}$ and η^k_{ij} as the energy efficiency[1] on the k-th transmission link between s_{i_1} and s_{i_2}, s_i and s_j, which are given as $\eta^k_{i_1 i_2} = \frac{P^k_{i_1 i_2}}{R^k_{i_1 i_2}}$, $\eta^k_{ij} = \frac{P^k_{ij}}{R^k_{ij}}$. Thus, the objective of *Problem-I* defined in formula (1), can be rewritten as

$$\sum_{i_1=1}^{N} \sum_{i_2=1}^{N} \sum_{k=1}^{K} d^k_{i_1 i_2} \times \eta^k_{i_1 i_2} + \sum_{i=1}^{N} \sum_{j=1}^{M} \sum_{k=1}^{K} d^k_{ij} \times \eta^k_{ij}. \tag{14}$$

Therefore, *Problem-I* can be transformed as a linear program (LP) problem. The LP problem above is denoted as *Problem-II*. Note that Eq. (12) satisfy the demands of flow conservation in the flow network model, Eqs. (10) and (11) satisfy the capacity constraints of the flow network model. Therefore, the method named minimum cost maximum flow in the flow network model is used to obtain the optimal solution of *Problem-II*, and this optimal solution is considered as an approximate solution of the *Problem-I*.

---

[1] Energy efficiency is the energy consumed by transmission one bit.

3   The Proposed FBPA Algorithm

Note that mmWave backhaul network $\mathcal{G} = (\mathcal{V}, \mathcal{E})$ is an undirected multi graph, where there exist multiple undirected edges between two adjacent nodes. Therefore, to solve *Problem-II*, the FBPA algorithm is proposed. Firstly, the undirected multigraph is transformed into a directed multi-graph. Secondly, the directed multi-graph is transformed into a directed simple graph. Thirdly, a flow network graph is constructed based on the transformed directed simple graph, the problem with minimum cost and maximum traffic of the flow network graph is solved using the Push-Relabel method.

- *Step 1:* As shown in Fig. 2, any two connected nodes s_{i_1} and s_{i_2} in the undirected multi-graph $\mathcal{G} = (\mathcal{V}, \mathcal{E})$ are transformed into two node sets $\{s_{i_1^{in}}, s_{i_1^{out}}\}$, $\{s_{i_2^{in}}, s_{i_2^{out}}\}$, where $s_{i_1^{in}}$ and $s_{i_2^{in}}$ are virtual entry nodes, which are belong to the set $\mathcal{V}_{s_{in}}$. In addition, $s_{i_1^{out}}$ and $s_{i_2^{out}}$ are virtual export nodes, which are belong to the set $\mathcal{V}_{s_{out}}$.
- *Step 2:* The edges $e_{s_{i_1^{in}} \to s_{i_1^{out}}}$ and $e_{s_{i_2^{in}} \to s_{i_2^{out}}}$ are added respectively, where $e_{s_{i_1^{in}} \to s_{i_1^{out}}}$ and $e_{s_{i_2^{in}} \to s_{i_2^{out}}}$ are belong to the set $\mathcal{E}_{s_{in}s_{out}}$. Then the undirected edges (denoted as $e^k_{s_{i_1} \leftrightarrow s_{i_2}}$) between s_{i_1} and s_{i_2} are transformed into a directed edges set $\{e^k_{s_{i_2^{out}} \to s_{i_1^{in}}}, e^k_{s_{i_2^{out}} \to s_{i_1^{in}}}\}$.

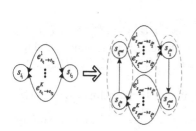

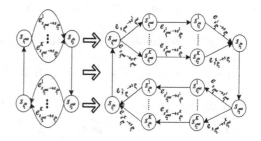

Fig. 2. Undirected multi-graph is transformed into directed multi-graph.

Fig. 3. Directed multi-graph is transformed into directed simple graph.

- *Step 3:* As shown in Fig. 3, k virtual entry nodes $s^k_{i_1^{in}}$ and $s^k_{i_2^{in}}$ that belong to the set $\mathcal{V}_{s^k_{in}}$, are added for $s_{i_1^{in}}$ and $s_{i_2^{in}}$ in the directed multi-graph. Similarly, k virtual export nodes $s^k_{i_1^{out}}$ and $s^k_{i_2^{out}}$ that belong to the set $\mathcal{V}_{s^k_{out}}$, are introduced for $s_{i_1^{out}}$ and $s_{i_2^{out}}$.
- *Step 4:* The k-th edge from $s_{i_1^{out}}$ to $s_{i_2^{in}}$ in the directed multi-graph, i.e., $e^k_{s_{i_1^{out}} \to s_{i_2^{in}}}$ is transformed into a set of edges $\{e_{s_{i_1^{out}} \to s^k_{i_1^{out}}}, e_{s^k_{i_1^{out}} \to s^k_{i_2^{in}}},$ $e_{s^k_{i_2^{in}} \to s_{i_2^{in}}}\}$, $e^k_{s_{i_2^{out}} \to s_{i_1^{in}}}$ is transformed into a set of edges $\{e_{s_{i_2^{out}} \to s^k_{i_2^{out}}}, e_{s^k_{i_2^{out}} \to s^k_{i_1^{in}}}, e_{s^k_{i_1^{in}} \to s_{i_1^{in}}}\}$. For clarity, the sets

are separately defined as $\mathcal{E}_{s_{out}s_{out}^k} = \{e_{s_{i_1out}\to s_{i_1out}^k}, e_{s_{i_2out}\to s_{i_2out}^k}\}$, $\mathcal{E}_{s_{out}^k s_{in}} = \{e_{s_{i_1out}^k\to s_{i_1in}^k}, e_{s_{i_2out}^k\to s_{i_1in}^k}\}$, $\mathcal{E}_{s_{in}s_{in}} = \{e_{s_{i_1in}^k\to s_{i_1in}}, e_{s_{i_2in}^k\to s_{i_1in}}\}$.

- *Step 5:* A virtual source node x and a virtual destination node y are introduced. Correspondingly, the edges from x to s_{i_1in} and s_{i_2in} are introduced, i.e., $e_{x\to s_{i_1in}}$ and $e_{x\to s_{i_2in}}$, and the set of which is denoted as $\mathcal{E}_{xs_{in}}$. Moreover, the edges from g_{jout} to y are introduced, i.e., $e_{g_{jout}\to y}$, and the set of which is denoted as $\mathcal{E}_{g_{out}y}$.

- *Step 6:* The attributes of each edge in the directed simple graph can be assigned as follows. In $\mathcal{E}_{xs_{in}}$, the capacity and cost of each edge are given as $a(e_{x\to s_{i_1in}}) = L_i, c(e_{x\to s_{i_1in}}) = 0$. In $\mathcal{E}_{s_{in}^k s_{in}}$, $\mathcal{E}_{s_{in}s_{out}}$, $\mathcal{E}_{s_{out}s_{out}^k}$, $\mathcal{E}_{g_{in}^k g_{in}}$ and $\mathcal{E}_{g_{in}g_{out}}$, the capacity and cost of each edge are given in Eq. (15). In $\mathcal{E}_{s_{out}^k s_{in}^k}$ and $\mathcal{E}_{s_{out}^k g_{in}^k}$, the capacity and cost of each edge are given in Eq. (16). Besides, in $\mathcal{E}_{g_{out}y}$, the capacity and cost of each edge are given as $a(e_{g_{jout}\to y}) = S_j$, $c(e_{g_{jout}\to y}) = 0$.

$$\begin{cases} a(e_{s_{i_1in}^k\to s_{i_1in}}) = a(e_{s_{i_1in}\to s_{i_1out}}) = a(e_{s_{i_1out}\to s_{i_1out}^k}) = a(e_{g_{jin}^k\to g_{jin}}) = a(e_{g_{jin}\to g_{jout}}) = Inf \\ c(e_{s_{i_1in}^k\to s_{i_1in}}) = c(e_{s_{i_1in}\to s_{i_1out}}) = c(e_{s_{i_1out}\to s_{i_1out}^k}) = c(e_{g_{jin}^k\to g_{jin}}) = c(e_{g_{jin}\to g_{jout}}) = 0 \end{cases}$$
$$(15)$$

$$\begin{cases} a(e_{s_{i_1out}^k\to s_{i_2in}^k}) = a(e_{s_{i_2out}^k\to s_{i_1in}^k}) = T_{i_1i_2}^k \times R_{i_1i_2}^k, \quad a(e_{s_i\to g_j}^k) = T_{ij}^k \times R_{ij}^k \\ c(e_{s_{i_1out}^k\to s_{i_2in}^k}) = c(e_{s_{i_2out}^k\to s_{i_1in}^k}) = \eta_{i_1i_2}^k, \quad c(e_{s_i\to g_j}^k) = \eta_{ij}^k \end{cases}$$
$$(16)$$

- *Step 7:* The minimum cost with maximum flow of $\mathcal{G}_m = (\mathcal{V}_m, \mathcal{E}_m)$ can be obtained, using the Push-Relabel algorithm. Therefore, the values of data flow on each edge of the *Problem-II* is obtained as $\mathcal{F}_m = \{f_{i_1out\,i_2in}^k, f_{i_1out\,jin}^k\}$.

According to the solution of the *Problem-II*, it can be transformed into the solution of the *Problem-I* as $t_{i_1i_2}^k = \left\lceil \dfrac{f_{i_1out\,i_2in}^k}{R_{i_1i_2}^k} \right\rceil, t_{ij}^k = \left\lceil \dfrac{f_{i_1out\,jin}^k}{R_{ij}^k} \right\rceil$. The maximum amount of data and the minimum energy consumption are given as

$$\begin{cases} d_{\max} = \sum_{i=1}^{N}\sum_{j=1}^{M}\sum_{k=1}^{K} t_{ij}^k \times R_{ij}^k \\ P_{\min} = \sum_{i_1=1}^{N}\sum_{i_2=1}^{N}\sum_{k=1}^{K} t_{i_1i_2}^k \times P_{i_1i_2}^k + \sum_{i=1}^{N}\sum_{j=1}^{M}\sum_{k=1}^{K} t_{ij}^k \times P_{ij}^k \end{cases}$$

4   Simulation Results

In the simulations, SCs are uniformly distributed within $500\,\text{m} * 500\,\text{m}$ square, and the maximum distance between two SCs or SC and gateway node is $120\,\text{m}$. There exist four gateway nodes respectively. Besides, it is assumed that line-of-sight (LOS) mmWave links are located at $60\,\text{GHz}$, the bandwidth of each is

2G MHz. Other simulation parameters are given [6]. We compare our proposed FBPA algorithm with the shortest path algorithm and exhaustive algorithm.

Figure 4 are the path selection results generated from FBPA algorithm. It can be seen that FBPA algorithm can establish multiple paths to multiple gateway nodes, e.g., SC that marked with rectangle in Fig. 4.

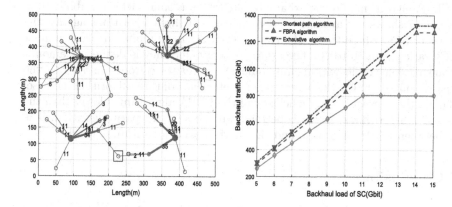

Fig. 4. FBPA path selection.   **Fig. 5.** Backhaul traffic vs load of SC.

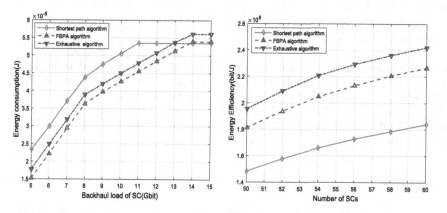

Fig. 6. EC vs load of SC.   **Fig. 7.** EE vs number of SCs.

Figures 5 and 6 show the backhaul traffic and energy consumption against backhaul load of each SC. As shown in Fig. 5, with the constantly increasing of the load, the proposed FBPA algorithm and the exhaustive algorithm outperform the shortest path algorithm, this is because the SCs in both algorithms can select multiple paths to different gateway nodes. When the backhaul load of each SC exceeds 14 Gbit, the backhaul traffic of the proposed FBPA algorithm outperforms the shortest path algorithm by nearly 62% and is close to the exhaustive algorithm, the difference of which is less than 5%. As shown in Fig. 6, the energy consumption for the three algorithms increase when the backhaul load is relatively small, and the network energy consumption using shortest path algorithm is almost highest until the backhaul load is about 11 Gbit, this is because the path selection in the shortest path algorithm is only based on the distance, the energy consumption is not considered. Moreover, the gap between the FBPA algorithm and the exhaustive algorithm is small, which is about 10%.

Figure 7 shows the average energy efficiency of three algorithms against the number of SCs, where the traffic load of each SC is 10 Gbits, and the number of SCs varies from 50 to 60. The average energy efficiency is defined as amount of transmission traffic within unit joule. As we can see from Fig. 7, with the increase number of SCs, the average energy efficiency of three algorithm increase. Although the average energy efficiency of the FBPA algorithm is lower than the exhaustive algorithm's, it much better than the shortest path algorithm. The gain between FBPA algorithm and the shortest path algorithm is nearly 18%.

5   Conclusions

We have studied the backhaul path planning problem in a mmWave small cell network. We aimed at exploring the path planning with minimum energy consumption based on maximum traffic in given time slot. The problem is formulated as an IP problem, then the IP problem is transformed into a easier LP using liner relaxation. FBPA is proposed to find the approximate solution of the IP problem. Extensive simulation are conducted and the efficiency of the proposed algorithm are demonstrated.

Acknowledgment. This work was supported in part by the Science and Technology on Communication Networks Laboratory Open Projects (Grant No. KX162600031, KX172600027), the National Natural Science Foundations of CHINA (Grant No. 61271279, and No. 61501373), the National Science and Technology Major Project (Grant No. 2016ZX03001018-004), and the Fundamental Research Funds for the Central Universities (Grant No. 3102017ZY018).

References

1. Niu, Y., Li, Y., Jin, D., et al.: A survey of millimeter wave communications (mmWave) for 5G: opportunities and challenges. J. Wirel. Netw. **21**(8), 2657–2676 (2015)
2. Pateromichelakis, E., Shariat, M., Quddus, A.U., et al.: Joint routing and scheduling in dense small cell networks using 60 GHz backhaul. In: 16th IEEE International Conference on Communication Workshop (ICCW), London, pp. 2732–2737. IEEE Press (2015)
3. Zhang, G., Quek, T.Q.S., Kountouris, M., et al.: Fundamentals of heterogeneous backhaul design-analysis and optimization. J. IEEE Trans. Commun. **64**(2), 876–889 (2016)

4. Lun, J., Grace, D.: Cognitive green backhaul deployments for future 5G networks. In: 1st International Workshop on Cognitive Cellular Systems (CCS), Germany, pp. 1–5. IEEE Press (2014)
5. Cai, S., Che, Y., Duan, L., et al.: Green 5G heterogeneous networks through dynamic small-cell operation. IEEE J. Sel. Areas Commun. **34**(5), 1103–1115 (2016)
6. Auer, G., Giannini, V., Desset, C., et al.: How much energy is needed to run a wireless network? J. IEEE Wirel. Commun. **18**(5), 40–49 (2011)

Author Index

Printed in the United States
By Bookmasters